W9-DGL-822

This is the first comprehensive study of the evolving role of socialist countries, in particular the Soviet Union and the countries of Eastern Europe, within the existing international economic order. Jozef Van Brabant explores how feasible and desirable it is for the major countries in the world economy to foster closer integration of the Centrally Planned Economies within the global economic, trading, and financial frameworks.

In the first two chapters Van Brabant overviews the emergence of the postwar economic order and examines the key features of three kinds of Centrally Planned Economies (CPEs). These are the orthodox centrally planned system; the partially decentralized economic system that emerged in the 1960s and resurfaced in the 1970s; and the currently envisaged decentralized economic system tailored to the needs of a socialist society. Jozef Van Brabant then analyzes the role of the International Monetary Fund, the World Bank, and other financial institutions in ensuring smooth economic relations among market-type economies and he details the problems of linking typical CPEs to this international monetary framework. He continues by looking at the international trade system. He discusses the ambitions of the International Trade Organization, the constitution of the General Agreement on Tariffs and Trade (GATT) and the experiences of the CPEs within it. Finally, Van Brabant explores the possibility of reconstituting a multilateral economic order that can provide greater security, predictability, stability, and reliability in international economic relations.

The planned economies and international economic organizations is written at a time when the Soviet Union and other CPEs are seeking closer links with the mainstream world economy. It will therefore be of interest to governments and institutional economists in international banking, trade, and finance, as well as to students and specialists of Soviet and East European studies, international relations, and comparative economics.

THE PLANNED ECONOMIES AND INTERNATIONAL ECONOMIC ORGANIZATIONS

Soviet and East European Studies, under the auspices of Cambridge University Press and the British Association for Soviet, Slavonic and East European Studies (BASSEES), promotes the publication of works presenting substantial and original research on the economics, politics, sociology, and modern history of the Soviet Union and Eastern Europe.

Soviet and East European Studies

77 JOZEF M. VAN BRABANT
The planned economies and international economic organizations

76 WILLIAM MOSKOFF
The bread of affliction: the food supply in the USSR during World War II

75 YAACOV RO'I
The struggle for Soviet Jewish emigration 1948–1967

74 GRAEME GILL
The origins of the Stalinist political system

73 SANTOSH K. MEHROTRA
India and the Soviet Union: trade and technology transfer

72 ILYA PRIZEL
Latin America through Soviet eyes
The evolution of Soviet perceptions during the Brezhnev era 1964–1982

71 ROBERT G. PATMAN
The Soviet Union in the Horn of Africa
The diplomacy of intervention and disengagement

70 IVAN T. BEREND
The Hungarian economic reforms 1953–1988

69 CHRIS WARD
Russia's cotton workers and the New Economic Policy
Shop-floor culture and state policy 1921–1929

68 LÁSZLÓ CSABA
Eastern Europe in the world economy

67 MICHAEL E. URBAN
An algebra of Soviet power
Elite circulation in the Belorussian Republic 1966–1986

66 JANE L. CURRY
Poland's journalists: professionalism and politics

65 MARTIN MYANT
The Czechoslovak economy 1948–1988
The battle for economic reform

64 XAVIER RICHET
The Hungarian model; markets and planning in a socialist economy

63 PAUL G. LEWIS
Political authority and party secretaries in Poland 1975–1986

62 BENJAMIN PINKUS
The Jews of the Soviet Union
The history of a national minority

Series list continues on page 315.

THE PLANNED ECONOMIES AND INTERNATIONAL ECONOMIC ORGANIZATIONS

JOZEF M. VAN BRABANT

CAMBRIDGE UNIVERSITY PRESS

Cambridge
New York Port Chester
Melbourne Sydney

Published by the Press Syndicate of the University of Cambridge
The Pitt Building, Trumpington Street, Cambridge CB2 1RP
40 West 20th Street, New York, NY 10011, USA
10 Stamford Road, Oakleigh, Melbourne 3166, Australia

First published 1991

Printed in Great Britain at the University Press, Cambridge

British Library cataloguing in publication data

Brabant, Jozef M. van
The planned economies and international economic organizations. – (Soviet and East European studies; 77)
1. Eastern Europe and Soviet Union. Economic conditions
I. Title II. Series
330.947

Library of Congress cataloguing in publication data
Brabant, Jozef M. van
The planned economies and international economic organisations – Jozef M. van Brabant.
p. cm.–(Soviet and East European studies: 77)
Includes bibliographical references.
ISBN 0 521 38350 1
1. Europe. Eastern–Economic policy. 2. Central planning–Europe. Eastern. 3. International finance. 4. International economic relations. I. Title. II. Series.
HC244.B7274
338.947–dc20 90-1470 CIP

ISBN 0 521 38350 1 hardback

UP

To Anja, Katja, and Miyuki
with gratitude

Contents

Tables

Preface

This monograph grew out of my first hesitant explorations of the potential problems of bringing the Soviet Union into the global trade system. Surprised by the sharp rebuff evoked by the Soviet request to play some role in the Punta del Este negotiations, I drafted a note for discussion in June 1987 at Mario Nuti's seminar at the Istituto Universitario Europeo, San Domenico di Fiesole (Firenze) in Italy, which I subsequently reworked and expanded into a full-length paper (Brabant 1987d). Little did I then realize that this would build a momentum that would keep me going for over two years. The present monograph is the result of these reflections and discussions in international fora on how best to associate the centrally planned economies with international economic organizations.

I am most grateful for the support by the Istituto and other organizations as well as the constructive comments of many individuals on my work in progress over the years. The major portions of this book were written in my spare time, while being officially a staff member of the Department of International Economic and Social Affairs of the United Nations Secretariat in New York. The opinions expressed here are my own and do not necessarily reflect those of the United Nations Secretariat. Of course, I alone remain responsible for the shortcomings of this product.

As with most of my earlier research efforts, I owe a great deal to the women in my family, and I therefore also dedicate this book to them.

Note on transliteration, referencing, and units

Cyrillic language publications or names of persons from Cyrillic-script countries or regions are transliterated according to the so-called scientific transliteration system advocated by the USSR Academy of Sciences. A distinction is made between the three Russian *e*s and, in the case of Bulgarian sources, the Russian *šč* is replaced by *št*. Whenever possible, names of personalities, writers, or places are spelled according to the convention of the home country, possibly followed by transliteration as indicated. However, in the reader's interest, familiar names, such as Mikhail S. Gorbachev, have been left in the generally accepted 'western' form, albeit inconsistent with the transliteration system.

For brevity's sake, bibliographical references in the text are identified by author and date of publication. In the absence of a name, the reference consists of a simple acronym of the organization sponsoring the publication, an abbreviation of the sponsoring organization, or one key word from the title. Because they are meant to be codes to the bibliography, where full details are listed, name prefixes are deleted from the text references.

Throughout the volume, a billion is understood to equal a thousand million, and all dollar magnitudes are expressed as US dollar values. References to the currency denominations of the Slavic countries, other than the ruble, follow the standards of the countries in question. That is to say, the inflection of the currency denomination depends on the magnitude of the preceding number. All dates are specified according to European custom: 1.4.70 means 1 April 1970.

Abbreviations

BIS	Bank for International Settlements
BLEU	Belgian–Luxemburg Economic Union
BTPA	bilateral trade and payments agreement
BWS	Bretton Woods system
CMEA	Council for Mutual Economic Assistance
CPE	centrally planned economy
CTC	Centre on Transnational Corporations
DE	developing economy
DME	developed market economy
EC	European Communities
ECE	Economic Commission for Europe
EcoSoc	Economic and Social Council
ECU	European currency unit
EMS	European monetary system
EPU	European Payments Union
FAO	Food and Agriculture Organization
FTO	foreign trade organization
GATT	General Agreement on Tariffs and Trade
GDR	German Democratic Republic
GSP	general system of preferences
IBEC	International Bank for Economic Cooperation
IBRD	International Bank for Reconstruction and Development
ICITO	Interim Commission of the International Trade Organization
IDA	International Development Association
IEO	international economic organization
IFC	International Finance Corporation
IFS	international financial system
IIB	International Investment Bank
ILO	International Labor Organization

IMF	International Monetary Fund
IMS	international monetary system
IPC	Integrated Programme of Commodities
IPS	independent price system
ITO	International Trade Organization
ITS	international trading system
JSC	joint-stock company
ME	market economy
MFA	Multifibre Arrangement
MFN	most-favored nation
MFT	state monopoly of foreign trade and payments
MTN	multilateral trade negotiation
MTPA	multilateral trade and payments agreement
NEM	new economic mechanism
NIC	newly industrializing developing country
NIEO	new international economic order
NTB	nontariff barriers
ODA	official development assistance
OECD	Organization for Economic Cooperation and Development
OEEC	Organization for European Economic Cooperation
OTC	Organization for Trade Cooperation
QR	quantitative restriction
RITO	Reconceived International Trade Organization
RTAA	Reciprocal Trade Agreements Act
SDR	special drawing right
SEI	socialist economic integration
STC	state-trading country
TR	transferable ruble
TRP	transferable ruble price
UNICTRAL	United Nations Commission for International Trade Law
UNCTAD	United Nations Conference on Trade and Development
UNIDO	United Nations Industrial Development Organization
WMP	world market price
WTO	Warsaw Treaty Organization

Introduction

This volume offers a modest inquiry into the desirability and feasibility of finding common ground among major participants in the world economy that would enable the centrally planned economies (CPEs), Asian as well as European, to become more closely associated with the global economic, trading, monetary, and financial frameworks. Though I focus my lens at an exceedingly vast panorama of a rugged landscape, my ambition is deliberately limited. This objective requires some explanation, which I do in section 1 by briefly painting the backdrop to what motivated me to embark on writing this monograph.

The rather unusual background to this study on the role of the CPEs in organized international economic relations may help the reader to assess the purposes, accomplishments, and remaining lacunae. It certainly clarifies precisely what I hope to accomplish. Because this is a personal statement, I have written it chiefly in the first person singular. In view of the specific objectives of the study, this is meant to be the *singularis modestis*, certainly not *majestatis*, in Myrdal's (1963, vii) sense. This personalized mode emphasizes that the account reflects my understanding of how the international economic framework came about, the current state of affairs, and what could be achieved prospectively by integrating the CPEs more fully into the international economic organizations (IEOs) and the regimes they purport to serve.

1 Backdrop to the study

On 15 August 1986, the Soviet Union unexpectedly requested some form of observer status in the Punta del Este deliberations about the launching of a new round of multilateral trade negotiations (MTNs) slated to commence in September that year. This mild overture to the General Agreement on Tariffs and Trade (GATT)[1] should not have been all that startling. For one thing, the sociopolitical framework of the USSR had been undergoing measurable changes since mid-1985, including seeking more active participation in global economic and financial affairs. Especially important were the then just announced intentions to introduce more or less far-reaching domestic economic and trade reforms. Possibly more surprising were a sequence of rumors launched and unofficial feelers emitted by highly placed Soviet officials in private discussions and in pronouncements at international meetings in the first half of 1986. These in effect led to some expectation that the Soviet Union would soon seek some association with, perhaps even full membership in, other multilateral institutions, chiefly the International Monetary Fund (IMF or Fund) and the International Bank for Reconstruction and Development (IBRD, Bank, or World Bank).[2] These statements have since been confirmed and denied with various degrees of alacrity, depending upon the particular Soviet spokesperson and the circumstances of the "rumor."

Whatever the intrinsic merit of this stance, the announcement to petition for some form of association with the international trading system (ITS) in place by itself signaled a major modification, if perhaps not yet a full reversal, of the USSR's traditional position regarding global economic cooperation through the institutions and their underlying regimes created after World War II. It could thus have quite important ideological, political, economic, and institutional ramifications, certainly when placed in the context of other changes that had by then been transpiring in the USSR's economy and society.

There was doubtlessly a good deal of political posturing in both the request for accession to the MTN round and in the ill-conceived western rebuff. But there was also good economic logic underlying these developments. Two important concurrent events may be adduced in evidence. First, in connection with the reform of the foreign trading system, which was officially endorsed on 19 August 1986 but had been mooted earlier, it was perfectly logical to explore ways of "normalizing" relations with other countries and some of their institutions. This would have been particularly relevant to widen the maneuvering room for the enterprises, associations, and ministries that henceforth would be entitled to engage autonomously in external commerce. But the eventual impact could have been much more profound if only because there is some, arguably circumstantial, evidence to buttress the conjecture that "participation in the GATT and economic reform feed on each other" (Patterson 1986, 203). In other words, if leaders are keen on the then envisioned – since elaborated – reforms in the Soviet Union succeeding, efforts should be made to facilitate participation in the GATT and perhaps in international economic affairs more generally.

Secondly, the external economic environment in early 1986 was unusually adverse, partly on account of the sharp drop in oil prices and weak global oil demand. This threatened to scuttle the domestic modernization drive envisioned in the five-year plan for 1986–90 before it could get properly under way. In February 1986, Mikhail S. Gorbachev and his team had placed great emphasis on the high priority of the endeavor at the 27th Congress of the Communist Party of the USSR. All-around modernization in engineering sectors was selected as the linchpin of the new five-year plan and the broader-based economic reconstruction envisaged by the current Soviet Administration. The marked shortfall in investment activity and modernization during the first full year of *perestrojka* on account of unanticipated foreign events may have made it imperative to broaden the scope, and perhaps even the depth, of the moves originally envisaged, or at any rate to accelerate their pace of implementation. At the least, the precipitous events of early 1986 compounded the already severe constraints on pursuing comprehensive economic reform with the vigor that had been called for, most notably at that Party Congress.

Negotiations about joining the GATT would realistically have taken several years because of the stylized accession procedure (see chapter 4). The direct advantages accruing from membership could therefore have alleviated the short-run problems of the Soviet economy in only a minor way, if that. The interpretation that following up on the USSR's request to become associated with the ITS would have helped to "bail [it] out now that it has economic problems" (Dirksen 1987, 229) is without merit. Even if the initiative had in the end been aborted, it could have yielded immediate indirect effects in terms of "good will" and related intangibles whose value should not be underestimated.

Against this backdrop, seeking closer cooperation with the near-global IEOs, such as the GATT, should certainly not have come as a complete surprise. It definitely should not have triggered bewildering alarm signals in western media and government circles, and also in some IEOs. The considerable confusion that beset the formulation of a proper response to the request was even less understandable. As it transpired, western governments, chiefly on the instigation of the United States, whose rebuff squarely reflected a "lack of candor" (Kennedy 1987, 24), summarily dismissed the GATT approach. This was one possible response to the Soviet overture. At least three others could have been taken, namely unconditional accession, conditional admittance, or fact finding and reciprocal exploration of policy positions. The latter could usefully have been undertaken.

This negative response became the official GATT position when the Ministerial Meeting that launched the Uruguay Round, unlike the framework set for the preceding major MTN (Tokyo) round (1973–9), invited only Contracting Parties[3] (that is, countries that are full "members" of the GATT as explained in chapter 4) and developing economies (DEs) that had expressed a serious interest in becoming a Contracting Party to participate (Haus 1989). Others could avail themselves of a new, informal channel by which high-level GATT officials would brief them privately. Both the German Democratic Republic (GDR) and the USSR have been utilizing this communication channel intermittently. Because of the highly placed GATT interlocutors, this is an important, if informal, channel for exchanging views between participants and others.

Even so, the response to the Soviet request was most unfortunate. The premature short-circuiting of the overture may have inadvertently curbed Soviet confidence in the potential support to be garnered for restructuring the domestic economy from properly streamlined international economic relations. If western leaders are genuinely interested in the metamorphosis of Soviet society into what Gorbachev appears to be coveting, the response to the GATT feelers was most regrettable. The warm reaction by, among others, the US Administration (*New York Times*, 28 August 1987, D1, D3) to the more recent Soviet request to join the Multifibre Arrangement (MFA) can be regarded as an implicit admission of the *faux pas* committed in August 1986 (Richter 1988). Finally, the understanding reached between the US and USSR in early December 1989 to admit the Soviet Union as an observer into the GATT, after the conclusion of the Uruguay Round, can be regarded as the definitive admission of an erroneous policy pursued since mid-1986. There are several reasons for this interpretation.

First, it is generally not good diplomatic practice simply to dismiss out of hand an overture in international relations without at least assessing what precisely may be at stake. This holds especially when these relations have been strained for so many years by conditions that do not lend themselves readily to compromise without losing political face.

Secondly, from a strictly economic viewpoint, it has always been problematic to associate CPEs on an equal basis with the postwar IEOs and to implement these deviant approaches to reciprocity. This applies particularly to the GATT because the trade framework of the CPEs rests quintessentially on foundations that are at considerable variance with those that form the backbone of the more general approach to multilateral trading and financial regimes. Given the absence of market-type price signals and supporting institutions in the USSR as basic props for decentralized decision making, and the then still unclear intentions behind the economic reforms it had just announced, it would have been useful to clarify what precisely was at stake, even if only in its strictly technical context.

Thirdly, when such an unusual announcement is issued by a major "outsider" to the postwar global economic framework, it should be worth some effort to assess with dispassion and intelligence to what extent the Soviet Union would have been prepared eventually to revise key aspects of its economic policies and domestic economic mechanisms, including its mutating trade model, so as to make a plausible case for accession. This need not necessarily have been brought up immediately in terms of GATT "entrance fees," that is, the concessions the USSR would have to grant Contracting Parties in exchange for most-favored nation (MFN) treatment under GATT rules, an issue that could have been broached at a more appropriate future time. Even a cogent argumentation of why the USSR desired to request accession and thought this was a viable gambit might have been highly illuminating. The argument in favor of exploration rather than defiance from the start is even more compelling because the Soviet step of August 1986 was not preceded by the usual diplomatic sounding out of major partners about the chances of a favorable response. Diplomatic channels were not even activated in an informal way. This was particularly unusual for two reasons. The well-known opposition for decades of US interest groups to freeing east–west trade from the straitjacket imposed on the basis of political, strategic, and security ingredients, most of which have little to do with "national security" proper (see Hanson 1988), would in any event have complicated matters. Also, ever since the USSR first approached the GATT, reportedly in late 1982 (based on interview material and Pankin 1986), the GATT secretariat has instructed Soviet emissaries first to sound out the key Contracting Parties. This *démarche* reportedly made in the past, which would have provided a perfect excuse for dealing with the Soviet gambit on an informal basis before providing an indirect response at Punta del Este, was not repeated in 1986.

Fourthly, it would at the same time have provided useful pointers to the extent to which key members of the international community are presently prepared to modify important pillars of the international economic environment, including the ITS. As is well known, its multilateral features in particular have been rapidly crumbling in recent years. In fact, the ITS has been disintegrating into multiple systems that are only poorly interlinked. Major and minor shifts in trade policy stances may be required not only to accommodate countries that have traditionally absented themselves from the GATT approach, but also to make the "global" trade system sufficiently flexible to come to grips with realistic preconditions for such wider participation, as argued in section 2. At the same time, it could also have revealed the potential for hammering out solutions for issues that have arisen since the institutions were first created but that have not so far been tackled in a rounded way. In particular, it would have provided some indication[4] of the degree to which the "world" community, in contrast to the inactivity of the past two decades, may now be prepared to address the so-called new protectionism and revert to multilateralism from the "minilateral" stance (Gilpin 1987, 372) on international economic relations gradually adopted since the late 1960s.

Finally, the curt refusal even to entertain the Soviet request may undermine the GATT's severely tainted aspirations to universality (Kennedy 1987, 25). Although this argument may appear to conflict with the second one above, the two provide a paradox that derives only from the point of departure one may wish to take in seeking to regulate world trade. If as some contend "there is more to be gained by full and universal participation in the international discussions of economic affairs than there is by the exclusion of certain states" (Jackson 1969, 777), then the stance adopted in 1986 was regrettably shortsighted.

2 Motivations for the investigation

It was against this backdrop that I felt compelled to outline a radically different, hopefully more productive, way in which the western community could have reacted.[5] My view centers not on whether the USSR should be permitted to accede or be kept out altogether. Instead, I firmly believe in the benefits of fact finding and exploration rather than defiance from the start. Such an approach seems imperative if there is any justification for making the global economic framework universally accessible; for seeking easement of the traditional east–west conflictive relationship, in economic matters as elsewhere; in devising remedies for the rather awkward way in which CPEs fit into the existing IEOs; and in exploring means of coming to grips with the contemporary economic problems whose nature is quite different from the criteria upon which the pillars of organized international economic relations were erected largely for the benefit of developed market economies (DMEs).

This book is a personal assessment of the answers that might have been forthcoming to some of the aforementioned questions regarding the relationship between the USSR and the GATT had they been ventilated in response to the Soviet overture. Because I do not intend to second-guess what may have been on the mind of policy makers in mid-1986, my answers are phrased largely within a broader framework of economic analysis. This owes much to my abiding intellectual and professional curiosity in examining ways and means of enhancing international economic security in the postwar period. Stalin is said to have declared during the Yalta conference (quoted in Byrnes 1947, 44) that:

> It is not so difficult to keep unity in time of war since there is a joint aim to defeat the common enemy, which is clear to everyone. The difficult task will come after the war when diverse interests tend to divide the Allies. It is our duty to see that our relations in peacetime are as strong as they have been in war.

I shall therefore discuss the stance during and after World War II on the international economic order, including the position of the Soviet Union in these postwar negotiations; the traditional standoffish attitude of key CPEs toward these organized multilateral economic relations; the evolution of the association of the CPEs with the basic pillars of that order, including their involvement in international trade and finance; and the potential for mutually reinforcing economic reform in the CPEs and coming to grips with the chronic need for revamping the international economic order, given the ongoing changes in the environment for global economic cooperation.

It is difficult to specify precisely where the topics treated here belong. This volume touches upon macroeconomics, comparative economics, economic reform in CPEs, economic history, international economic relations, commercial and financial diplomacy, political science, and even international law. But its subject is in fact none of the latter. Its hybrid form can perhaps best be described as a study in international economic diplomacy, as Richard N. Gardner (1969, ciii) labeled his seminal study of Anglo-American relations in the 1940s. But I have no ambition to compete with his monumental investigation, if only because east–west economic relations by themselves offer sufficient complexity. For one thing, my focus is the CPEs and the future, rather than what happened in the past. Also, I am more concerned with what could be contemplated in terms of coordinating the economic policies of various groups of countries than with the motives and objectives of policy makers in key countries at any one moment.

The second major concern that brought me to this study is the erosion of the liberal international economic order established after World War II. There has been a significant transformation in the key determinants of the global economy, resulting in a reversal of the trend toward liberalization of trade and multilateralization of finance through official institutions. The principles of multilateralism, unconditional MFN treatment, and casting national priorities, at least in part, with a view to their global implications, as heralded in the Bretton Woods system (BWS) of international economic relations, are being displaced by bilateralism and discrimination. For these and other reasons, the liberal international economic order has been rapidly receding under the impact of profound structural changes in the international distribution of power, in supply conditions, and in the effectiveness of demand management. In its wake, a mixed system of "nationalism, regionalism, and sectoral protectionism is replacing the [BWS] of multilateral liberalization" (Gilpin 1987, 395). These developments have been reflected in the ascendancy of the nation state and of national economic power in international economic relations, the growing struggle for world markets, and the benign or malevolent mercantilist successes of Japan and the newly industrializing developing countries (NICs). For example, with the collapse of the fixed exchange rate system and the management of fluctuating exchange rates largely in line with national objectives and constraints, conflicting interests have given rise to intense clashes over exchange values and other monetary issues, particularly among the larger, most advanced DMEs. As some argue (Gilpin 1987, 394), these developments may be attributed to the decline in the hegemonic role of the United States and the emergence of divergent national interests among the advanced countries, which have so far found only partial reflection in modifications of the organizations established to regulate international relations. There is hence a need to reevaluate the international economic order, especially now that the CPEs appear to be willing to play a more constructive role therein. To clarify this, some preliminary remarks on east–west relations and participation in IEOs may be appropriate.

Before doing so, however, recall that the international economic environment, especially as regards the European CPEs, has been changing dramatically since mid-1989. This has had its drawbacks for meeting the goals set for this volume, particularly the outlook for the participation of reforming CPEs in the IEOs. It may therefore be useful to be aware of the fact that this manuscript was completed in August 1989. I was afforded the opportunity to add only minor changes in early December 1989, upon verifying the copy editing. The ongoing extraordinary mutations in Eastern Europe may soon relegate the "hard-core" features of CPEs, as discussed mainly in chapter 2, to the dustbins of economic history. The adoption of more market-oriented policies, institutions, and policy instruments would facilitate the speedy and fuller integration of Eastern Europe into the global economic framework. Nevertheless, one should not lose sight of the fact that most of the technical economic opportunities and problems of associating the CPEs more fully with the international regimes in place remain to be addressed head-on, regardless of the political events in Eastern Europe or the prospect of associating the area more closely with one of the Western European integration schemes.

3 East–west economic relations

Anyone surveying the broad field of east–west economic relations from, say, the Russian revolution to the present will be struck by the number of times that western politicians and businessmen, and sometimes also eastern statesmen and political leaders, have announced that now east–west trade is poised for a major take-off. If anything, such assurances have persistently failed to materialize. Whenever a spurt occurs, it tends to be highly unstable, unpredictable as to its strength and duration, and thus unreliable as a gauge for firm commercial and investment decisions. East–west trade cannot blossom predictably for a number of reasons (Hanson 1986, 407–9). There are many that could be cited. I shall touch only upon the most important ones, which I divide into two groups.

Basic institutional, systemic, and economic obstacles

There would appear to be five critical issues here. First, the CPEs are all at a substantially lower level of development than the advanced market economies (MEs) and much less exposed to external competition than the most dynamic DEs. The backbone of the dynamism in postwar trade in the case of the former group has been provided overwhelmingly by within-group intrasectoral commerce. Some members of the latter group have displayed a great deal of poise in capturing market shares in DMEs. They have done so largely with products that would not "make" it in CPEs for policy reasons, but also because of the rather modest income levels and confined consumption patterns in these economies.

Secondly, east–west relations are strongly influenced by political hostility and suspicion, which, although not precluding trade, certainly compress the arena within which fruitful commercial relations across the systemic divide can be solidified. This is perhaps most pronounced in interactions between the two superpowers, given the xenophobia in the USSR and the self-righteousness that at times dominates US foreign economic policy (Lavigne 1979, 65ff.). Various western strategic trade controls, trade denial for reasons that have little to do with security or economic fair play or other rational considerations, and Soviet reluctance to provide economic information or to sign away part of its sovereignty, whether in a humiliating manner[6] or in a more businesslike fashion, are the sort of phenomena that impart east–west trade its peculiar character.

Thirdly, MEs and CPEs have different economic systems that create fundamental hindrances to trade expansion (Wilczynski 1969, 21–4). Here one needs only to reflect upon the limited information value of prices in

CPEs for identifying trade opportunities. Currency inconvertibility, although not absolutely forbidding, is certainly a core obstacle to smooth commercial relations between market and planned economies. Also, trade in CPEs has traditionally been conducted by state enterprises guided by the state monopoly of foreign trade and payments (MFT), on which more in chapter 2, whereas trade on the western side has been conducted largely by private firms.

Fourthly, systemic obstacles constitute one factor that has thus far limited the movement of capital and labor between east and west, even though from a rational economic point of view there are considerable opportunities in allowing especially risk capital to move eastward and labor the other way. The CPEs have traditionally shielded themselves against such flows, even when a demonstrable positive contribution to their growth effort and maturation process could be documented.

Finally, the east–west divide is much more fundamental. Insulation not only is against movements of traditional production factors, but also extends, perhaps in an even more pronounced way, to all foreign influences – especially ideas, at any particular time, almost regardless of their nature – that might undermine some cherished aspect of the socialist society that policy makers feel ought to be attained by all means.

Statecraft, military threats, and east–west relations

Perhaps of even greater concern than the above systemic and philosophical obstacles to buoyant east–west trade is the fact that east and west have been opposing blocs – economically, politically, strategically, and philosophically – at least since the Cold War erupted in the second half of the 1940s. For that reason, east–west relations involve more than the simple calculation of economic benefits. Rather than being capable of reduction to the pure economics of external trade and finance, east–west economic relations belong to "economic statecraft," as David A. Baldwin (1985) termed it and Philip Hanson (1988) recently elaborated upon so illuminatingly.

Economic statecraft is defined by Baldwin as "all of the economic means by which foreign policy actors might try to influence other international actors." But Hanson (1988, 6–7) has made a plausible case for restricting its meaning to "a policy instrument used by governments." Although this narrowing of the purview of economic statecraft is useful, if only to preclude getting bogged down in picayune, citizen-inspired protests (such as the refusal of longshoremen to unload Soviet ships at a time of east–west tensions), it inadvertently omits some of the essence of economics. In what follows, economic statecraft is understood as the complex of economic measures by which governments try to influence other national and international leaders in order to buttress a desirable level of economic security, to exert influence through foreign policy on other actors, and to pursue a long-term strategy concerning the outreach of national values.

When duly factoring into the equation that the "Western alliance has a capacity for chaotic mismanagement of East–West trade policy which is hard to underestimate" (Hanson 1988, 3), it is still true that east–west economic relations are something special. Western economic policy consists of a bundle of measures that amounts to imposing conditions on trade with the east that do not apply elsewhere. These coexist with deliberate decisions not to deviate from business as usual in dealing with the east. As such it consists of economic sanctions, economic warfare, and strategic embargoes.[7]

Given this state of affairs, one may well question whether there is a sustainable and desirable – normal if you wish – state of economic relations between east and west. Hanson (1988, 40) defines "normal conditions" as those obtaining when political relations are stable but both eastern and western countries continue to find it necessary to prepare for possible east–west military confrontation. Unfortunately, there is no clear-cut consensus in east or west on what constitutes "normal east–west economic relations." Such an agreement would be useful not only in order to wield various weapons of economic statecraft in the most effective way, but also in order to separate the arena for normal economic interaction from areas where special considerations might be applied.

4 On international economic regimes

I consider the existence of international organizations in which many countries participate and air their own interests, as well as their perceptions of more global issues, to be an essential ingredient of a "normal" state of affairs, in east–west as in other relations. This point is argued at length in chapter 5. It may be useful at this juncture, however, to state more generally what is meant by an international regime or system[8] and why countries may wish to partake in organized international relations.

In designating the various rules and regulations that form the conventions within which trading, monetary, and financial relations are settled, I have encountered serious terminological problems. At one time academic and political discussions referred to "international systems." Thus, for example, the use of the term "international monetary system" (IMS) is quite common. Like Voltaire's Holy Roman Empire which "was neither holy, nor Roman, nor an empire," the IMS is not truly international (if only because CPEs have been absent from it for most of the postwar period), it is by no means wholly confined to monetary affairs (Solomon 1982, 5), and it was certainly, from its inception, less coherent or systematic than it might have been. For example, the existing IMS has never had generally accepted rules or criteria to govern changes in par values, yet such changes were necessary as economic policies and conditions diverged among nations, even at the very inception of the IMS (Solomon 1982, 363). Further, there was no systematic means for increasing countries' reserves in a growing world economy, though the need for steering such steady expansion was obvious. Similar observations apply *pari passu* to the international financial system (IFS) and, even more, to the ITS.

If by system we mean an "organized whole," as the *Oxford English Dictionary* defines the term, the English language has to be stretched considerably to justify the designation "system" for any postwar set of rules and regulations. Likewise for the use of "order." Inasmuch as trading, financial, and monetary arrangements since World War II have been rather disorderly, even when viewed from within the preconceived arrangements, the term "order" would not seem to be *le mot juste*. International relations specialists have increasingly resorted to the use of the term "regime" to describe the kinds of rules and regulations that set boundaries for some classes of international economic transactions. But I am aware of the controversy that they are engaged in.

Regime is probably the most satisfactory of the three terms. In what follows, however, I shall intermingle the three if only to avoid deviating too far from what is common usage. Thus the acronyms for the three sets of rules and regulations use the old term "system." When referring to the general streamlining of international economic relations, I identify it as an attempt to promote "order." Finally, when I refer to a particular set of rules and regulations, I utilize the term "regime." These choices are admittedly not wholly satisfactory. But it might be useful nonetheless to amplify a little on what is meant more concretely by a regime.

There is certainly no shortage of competing views in the literature about international regimes and the role of hegemony in ensuring the stability of such arrangements. For our purposes, it suffices to define an international economic regime within the context of a global economic order. The latter itself can be thought of as a set of gradually accepted rules and conventions regarding how countries are expected to conduct those of their economic policies that have significant external repercussions. Without endowing this order with full-fledged organizations or state arrangements (such as colonialism) through which these rules and conventions can be enforced, an international economic order is likely eventually to dissolve into a state characterized by, at best, "weak rules and light-hearted breaches" (Williamson 1983a, 37) thereof, resulting in countries adopting entirely at their own discretion policies that have pronounced international repercussions.

Being part of an international economic order, a regime can be thought of as a subset of the gamut of rules and regulations affecting the behavior of nations with respect to their international repercussions. As such, an international economic regime consists of "explicit or implicit principles, norms, rules, and decision-making procedures around which actors' expectations converge" (Krasner 1982, 186) in a given component of the international economic order and which may help to coordinate their behavior (Finlayson and Zacher 1981, 563). Principles are essentially beliefs of fact, causation, and propriety or rectitude. In contrast, norms are standards of behavior set in terms of general rights and obligations. These two terms constitute the fundamental traits of a regime and are consistent with a variety of rules and decision-making procedures. Rules are specific prescriptions or proscriptions regarding behavior for action. Finally, decision-making procedures are prevailing or existing practices for making and implementing collective choices. Because changes in rules or decision-making procedures do not fundamentally alter the regime as such, they are usually treated as within-regime transformations. In any case, a regime is by its nature distinct from a temporary arrangement that can mutate or is altered with every shift in power or interest. It should not be based purely on short-term or even unilateral calculation of interest of one or a few actors. These will be further detailed with respect to the IFS, IMS, and ITS in chapters 3 to 5, respectively.

A regime's usefulness derives from the fact that it improves the intermeshing of the behavior of individual states or élite groups within individual states, as composed with what can be achieved when the latter all base their actions on uncoordinated individual calculations of self-interest. Because it may satisfy the realization of a common purpose beyond what individual actors can attain by themselves, a regime is essentially a vehicle to maximize the benefit derived from a public good according to some acceptable understanding on the sharing of benefits and costs. The importance of the externalities that affect the welfare of individual actors or well-defined élite groups is likely to grow when the degree of interdependence in the world is inexorably rising. Put another way, if relations among states (or their élites) approximate a zero-sum outcome in a game-theoretic setting, the usefulness of an international regime is in doubt.

Membership in IEOs entails a number of costs normally to be defrayed in convertible currency. Because all CPEs are notoriously short of such reserves and their ability to generate convertible currency revenues from exports is hampered by various systemic problems, one may well ask why these countries should be bent on joining IEOs. The costs consist of a variety of direct and indirect outlays (Cooper 1988b). A member must typically make a contribution to the organization's regular budget. Secondly, it is obligated to participate in meetings, and so must prepare them and dispatch diplomats and technical experts. In addition to preempting skilled human and financial resources, membership in most cases requires that the country maintain a permanent representative office attached to individual IEOs. This entails staffing and maintenance costs. There are other outlays as well, usually in the form of explicit or implicit constraints on the behavior of the state in international relations. These may take the form of substantive commitments and obligations that restrain the country's freedom of action.

To justify such costs, the leadership of a country seeking to join an IEO must perceive palpable advantages and, depending on the political structure of the country, may have to justify them. Benefits can take the form of an enhanced status in global affairs or offering opportunities for policy makers and civil servants to travel abroad and establish "contacts" that they deem useful for themselves, their interest group, or their perception of national needs. Secondly, a country's view on some set of problems at times cannot attain the desired visibility without an affirmative presence in the "proper" international forum. Thirdly, being an insider may yield valuable intelligence and other information that supplements and, from an individual country's perception, complements the information available in the public and not-so-public domains. Often it is faster than waiting for it to be aired in the usual media, and thus permits timely reaction if necessary. This includes advance information on what actions nations and international secretariats are proposing; forming judgments on the merits and strengths of such proposed actions well before they can be implemented and assessing the likelihood that they will be carried out and when, on the basis of "adequate" information; and gaining access to a plethora of political, economic, administrative, scientific, or technological background papers and documents prepared to facilitate deliberations about the proposal in question. Fourthly, membership may confer tangible economic, strategic, and other gains. Finally, some desirable actions cannot be undertaken by any one country in isolation. Examples include combatting acid rain or eradicating smallpox. On both counts, individual countries can accomplish substantive work through their own initiative. But it will fall well short of the objective without some loose or more regimented international cooperation and organization.

5 The main geographical focus of the inquiry

To clarify unambiguously what I hope to accomplish, the particular geographical focus of the monograph and the specific topics addressed in the five chapters of the study need to be detailed. The latter will be taken up in the next two sections. Here I shall look at the group of countries that forms the core of concern in this inquiry.

This account is chiefly about the actual and potential role of the traditional members of the so-called socialist world economic system in organized international economic relations. A brief clarification at this stage of the members of that group of CPEs is in order. This is useful if only to specify the rather arbitrary exclusion of many countries that profess to be socialist (including a number of Arab countries, such as Algeria, Iraq, and Syria) and of others (including Afghanistan, Angola, Ethiopia, and the People's Democratic Republic of Yemen) that in fact manage their economies in a very similar way to that in which the traditional CPE steered its economy in its early stages.

Since 1979, the socialist world economic system has comprised fifteen countries, namely Albania, China, the other Asian CPEs (Laos, Mongolia, North Korea, and Vietnam), Cuba, Eastern Europe (Bulgaria, Czechoslovakia, the GDR, Hungary, Poland, Rumania, and the Soviet Union; when there is no room for confusion, the term Eastern Europe will on occasion be limited to the group without the Soviet Union), and Yugoslavia. From 1962 until the coopting of Laos into this select group in the late 1970s, the socialist world economy comprised the other fourteen countries. Prior to that, Cuba was not, of course, a member of the socialist fraternity and hence there were only thirteen countries so classified. The main focus of the present account will be on the experiences and aspirations of the European CPEs.

Much less attention will be devoted to the remaining CPEs, which are all DEs proper. Their closer integration with the international economic framework poses particular questions, some of which belong to the *problématique* of DEs proper.[9] The wide array of issues that pertain to the problems of the DEs in the international monetary, financial, and economic frameworks will be touched upon only parenthetically. To deal with them adequately within my frame of analysis, I would have to undertake a separate investigation. This I eschew, if only because the role of the DEs in organized international economic relations has been the subject of a number of lengthy studies (for example, Dell *et al.* 1987; Tussie 1987) by authorities in matters concerning the DEs. Certainly, the latter's economic system shares several features with that of the CPEs. Those elements are, of course, covered here but without specific reference to the DEs proper.

Even when the compass of the analysis is geographically and otherwise bounded as explained, the group as such has rarely issued common statements or taken explicit positions on the issues pertinent to this inquiry. Policy positions on economic matters are rarely adopted explicitly by the entire group of CPEs. In fact, there is no recent uniform, formal policy stance on the past, present, or future global economic order or parts thereof that could be unambiguously classified as a common statement on behalf of all CPEs. This is due in part to the absence of some CPEs from institutions and groupings that normally issue pertinent policy statements, on which more below. But it also reflects the considerable variation in levels of development and the diversity in other respects among the CPEs themselves – hence their substantially differing interests on these issues. Inasmuch as one of the purposes of the volume is to ascertain the position of the CPEs on the present IFS, IMS, and ITS and how the latter could be rendered more effective and thus amenable to greater participation by CPEs, it is useful to bear in mind the major fora where declarations of evaluations and intentions with regard to international regimes are usually aired.

Policy positions have been formulated on occasion in declarations issued by members of the Council for Mutual Economic Assistance (CMEA), which was founded in 1949. Among the CPEs, ten are active full members (all European CPEs [except Albania], Cuba, Mongolia, and Vietnam), one (Yugoslavia) is an associate member, and one (Albania) an inactive full member.[10] Similarly, the Warsaw Treaty Organization (WTO) comprises all active European CMEA members. In four of the United Nations Conference on Trade and Development (UNCTAD), the CPEs are usually placed in a category called Group D. This includes the active European members of the CMEA, Albania, and the two special Soviet republics (Byelorussia and Ukraine) in the United Nations. But Group D's positions are rarely endorsed by Albania and Rumania. As a rule, they are shared explicitly by Cuba and Mongolia. Thus reconfigured, I shall refer to this as Modified Group D. Of course, at least six CPEs (Cuba, North Korea, Laos, Rumania, Vietnam, and Yugoslavia) are members of the so-called Group of Seventy-Seven, which speaks on behalf of the DEs in UN fora, and usually join with that Group on policy matters of direct concern to them. I shall therefore also have to refer here to some of the statements of the Group of Seventy-Seven.

Because few instances can be identified when the CPEs as a group endorsed a common platform on the international economy and related matters, except perhaps in abstruse ideological or political exhortations, it is instructive to clarify briefly the evolution of the policy stances and attitudes of the CPEs *vis-à-vis* the "first-world economic system." Some crucial incompatibilities between the CPEs and the global economic framework at its inception arose largely from disagreements among the major powers over the postwar international economic and political order. But there are also genuine systemic obstacles to closer cooperation between the two, as I shall demonstrate in the following chapters. Other problems associated with key features of the global economy that clash either with the economic characteristics of the CPEs or, more likely, with their political postures or ideological precepts are investigated also, but in much less detail. The official position of the CPEs on an eventual transformation of the economic, trading, monetary, and financial systems in the context of international policy topics of relevance to a new international economic order (NIEO) – not necessarily the one adopted in 1974 in the UN context – is discussed mainly in chapter 5.

6 The main topics of the study

It is perhaps only a curious footnote to the international economic order established after World War II that it envisaged universalism without providing explicitly for the participation of the CPEs therein. Neither did the makers of that order have the foresight to set up the necessary machinery to come to grips with the special features of the DEs, which would soon constitute the majority among the sovereign countries of that "universe." The paradox in the latter case stems from the fact that the major founders conceived the new order in part as a way to forestall the voluntary or forced dissolution of the colonial systems. Yet moral indignation and indigenous demands for independence would fundamentally transform the character and alter the scope of international economic relations less than two decades later. The seeming contradiction in the first case is perhaps easier to explain but also more convoluted.

At the end of World War II, there was only one genuine CPE in the world, namely the Soviet Union.[11] The latter's role in global affairs had not been very rewarding from the revolution in 1917 to the implementation of plan Barbarossa in June 1941. For all practical purposes, the Soviet Union had remained at the fringes of global diplomacy and had involved itself with world trade only peripherally, largely to acquire imports necessary for rapid domestic industrialization even in the wake of the calamitous collapse in its terms of trade and the abrupt evaporation of agricultural surpluses in the 1930s. By virtue of the leadership's commitment to fomenting world revolution, in fact, little was done to alleviate this situation through diplomatic channels.

Matters changed measurably with the formation of the grand wartime alliance among the three big Us – the USSR, the United Kingdom, and the United States. Certainly, the primacy of the Anglo-American relationship was never left in doubt. Winston S. Churchill and Franklyn D. Roosevelt managed to forge a unique symbiosis between the "English-speaking peoples" which at least Churchill anticipated becoming the bulwark of global economic and political organization in the postwar period. The Soviet Union was fused into this alliance only by necessity. Among the multiple concerns, overriding were efforts to press the war against the Axis powers with determination, while Britain and the United States prepared the second front, and to water down as much as possible continental Europe's claim to big-power status after the war.

Even though this *trojka* constituted a far from homogeneous relationship, there was little doubt that some power sharing between the Anglo-American alliance and the Soviet Union would be required. For that, it was thought useful to formulate plans for postwar reconstruction and managing the world economy that could accommodate the USSR and its peculiar economic and financial systems. For a while, Soviet leaders actually encouraged the refinement of this scenario. Until early 1946, there was still considerable hope that the three pillars of the new economic order would be constructed around the three big powers. By March–April 1946, however, the erosion in the relationship among the three allies had taken such an ominous turn toward disharmony that Soviet participation in the postwar international economic order was unlikely to materialize, coopting the USSR was not really desired by policy makers, and the peculiarities of CPEs were no longer given major consideration in the constitution of the basic IEOs. To the extent that the original intentions behind global economic regimes survived the political precepts of the negotiations, the global economic order developed essentially as a means to smooth monetary, commercial, financial, and more general economic relations among the DMEs. Little remained of the considerations that were at one time formulated regarding how to set up the institutions to enable them to come to grips with the needs of either CPEs or DEs.

The Soviet Union and its newly won allies in Eastern Europe, all of which soon thereafter transformed themselves into CPEs proper, decided not to seek participation in IEOs at that early stage or – those that had initially joined – chose to withdraw on one pretext or another. As a result, the environment within which the IEOs had to mature began to crumble into a *de facto* bipolar world. One was organized around the Fund and the Bank, which transformed itself into the World Bank or the World Bank Group.[12] The third pillar of postwar multilateral organization, namely the

International Trade Organization (ITO), never materialized and so trade matters remained confined to the framework set up under the umbrella of the General Agreement, a legal instrument negotiated in 1947 as detailed in chapter 1. The other emerged around the CMEA, or the "second-world economic system" in Stalin's view of postwar relations.

As a result of the rupture in the dialogue, the original objective to make the postwar IEOs nearly universal became untenable. At any rate, efforts to strive for such universalism were strongly compromised. Yet, by virtue of the creation of these institutions, the considerable isolation of the CPEs from global economic affairs, and the only gradual emergence of the DEs as a "third" world, next to the capitalist and socialist paths to socioeconomic development, this *de facto* truncation of the dedicated task of the three institutions did not matter too much. They functioned fairly well for the purposes for which they were conceived for as long as the membership of the organizations did not hanker after enlargement, and outsiders did not covet accession and hence voluntarily eschewed exploring ways and means of associating themselves with them. The international economic order functioned fairly well, though not as smoothly as had been forecast by the champions of the organizations. But that time stretch was relatively short.

The *caesura* between the socialist and capitalist world weakened and active interaction between the two world economic systems moved to some priority on the policy agenda fairly quickly after abrogation of the founding debate. The chasm began to be bridged under force of economic necessity, political expediency, or simply the desire of some countries, most notably the Soviet Union and later China, to be represented in world affairs on a par with their economic might and, failing that, their political aspirations to world status commensurate with their position as superpowers, at least in terms of military might and geographical and demographic size. As a result, the questions that had been at the roots of the postwar economic system during the deliberations roughly from 1941 to 1947 resurfaced fairly quickly less than a decade later. Not only did these reemerge under fundamentally different circumstances than those within which the discussions during and after the war had evolved; they were also being examined at a time when experimentation with alternative forms of global economic order would require adaptations of systems in operation rather than adjustments of the future international behavior of countries at war or emerging from it in considerable disarray.

This monograph is not meant as an economic history of relations of the CPEs with the IEOs. Although it inevitably touches upon the antecedents of the present regimes, it addresses in the first place the myriad questions of whether there is room at all for CPEs at the end of the 1980s to become more fully integrated within organized international relations. The latter will be narrowed chiefly to the arena circumscribed by the postwar economic order as it has evolved or in ways in which it could be reconstituted. I derive a positive, if qualified, answer from an examination of the key motivations of the architects of postwar global economic organization, the constitution and evolution of the IEOs, the experience of CPEs in these organs, the obstacles of associating CPEs with the IEOs without their first enacting ambitious economic reforms, and the need for organized international relations at the present juncture.

Perhaps even more important is that key CPEs have been implementing substantial economic reforms that could be solidified through firmer anchoring in the global context. Consider only the foreign trade reforms. As clarified in chapter 2, the Soviet Union aims at economic decentralization of decision making, the linking of trade results with domestic commercial conditions, disengaging government from overly interfering in market relations, and accelerated modernization through a variety of external relations. The other reforming CPEs have revised their foreign trade participation mechanisms and institutions for at least a decade in the case of China and no less than a quarter century, albeit with protracted lapses, in the case of Eastern Europe. If only for that reason, it would be perfectly logical for China and the Soviet Union to explore ways of "normalizing" relations with other countries and for the USSR to encourage its CMEA partners to do the same. In this way the maneuvering room for enterprises and organizations henceforth entitled to engage autonomously in trade could be widened. But the eventual impact could be much more far-reaching if only because suitable participation in IEOs can encourage and strengthen market-oriented reforms.

Seen against the backdrop to domestic and regional reforms, seeking closer cooperation with the IEOs should certainly not be surprising or have given rise to bewildering alarm signals in western media and government circles, and also in some IEOs. In this volume, I seek to clarify the ways in which the CPEs have been able to participate in principle and in fact in IEOs, the reforms that would solidify these regimes as anchors of a more secure global economy, and how the CPEs could be more fully accommodated as equal partners in such revamped regimes. In this context, recall that the hard-core features of the traditional trade and payments regimes associated with the CMEA have been rapidly disintegrating under the impact of the still ongoing political and economic changes in Eastern Europe. The evident need of these countries to carve out for themselves a viable competitive position in world markets makes it all the more urgent at the present juncture to reassess comprehensively how these countries can be merged more fully into the global economic framework.

The fuller participation of CPEs in the global economy has multiple benefits for all participants. Some advantages are direct, though perhaps not immediately accruing. Others are largely indirect and, in some cases, purely qualitative benefits that accrue from such wider participation for both the present membership and for the CPEs and DEs that have thus far remained on the periphery of the IEOs or have distanced themselves from them altogether. Among the benefits that hardly lend themselves to cause-and-effect quantification are the need to ensure stability and progress in the global economy and normalcy in international relations more generally. Of course, the perceived balance of the costs and benefits of belonging to IEOs discussed in section 3 has shifted too in favor of *rapprochement*. My advocacy of exploring global association rests primarily upon the benefits that such further globalization might yield for minor and major participants in the world economy.

7 Summary of the volume

The monograph is divided into five chapters, followed by a conclusion with a recommendation regarding the desirability of fostering closer integration of the CPEs into the world economy. Chapter 1 summarizes the wartime negotiations, hopes, and objectives and how these became stymied or frustrated soon after the end of hostilities. It essentially examines the period 1941–7. The opening date is suggested by the first plans for postwar economic relations elaborated independently by both the British and American civil services. None of these appeared to have been inspired by any grand design. Instead, in the case of the United States it was probably the lessons of Versailles, the aborted attempt at global government through the League of Nations, and the trauma of the Great Depression and its ramifications for weakened economic security and stability more generally that called for "preparedness" on the part of US negotiators.

The initial British stance also emerged from the failures of Versailles and the calamitous turn of events on the continent in the 1930s. Perhaps more important were the concerns of the British government about its ability to service its wartime debt, to ensure a return to steady growth and prosperity, and indeed to resume its role in international finance and trade, both within the Commonwealth and in the world at large.

Though Stalin's interests in postwar organization have not so far been divulged as fully as those of Roosevelt and Churchill, he does not appear to have had a grand plan either. This lack of a comprehensive blueprint applies to what precisely the USSR wanted to accomplish with the heavily contested areas of Eastern Europe. The main motives originally derived from a desire to weather the appalling devastation wrought by the war and to ensure greater economic, political, and strategic security for the Soviet Union. In other words, in the absence of mutually conflicting positions, common ground for postwar global order, in the economic sphere as elsewhere, might have been found. A weak search for such a solution did emerge, but it quickly petered out under the impact of recriminations, misunderstandings, apprehensions, fears, and lack of candor.

Chapter 2 summarizes key features of economic organization and management in CPEs. I deal here with four types of CPEs, namely the orthodox centralized planning system, the partially decentralized economic system that emerged chiefly in the 1960s, the partially recentralized, heavily constrained economic format in the 1970s, and the current policy sentiment for so-called *radikal'naja reforma* or the constitution of a decentralized socialist economic system. The primary goal is to clarify the context within which economic organization and policy making of the CPEs need to be ascertained if one is bent on exploring global participation. I also assess in particular the implications of each variant for the participation of the CPEs in global trading, financial, and monetary arrangements. Their own regional accommodation within the context of the CMEA is briefly summarized for it introduces its own peculiarities into the more specialized discussion of the next three chapters.

Chapter 3 focuses on key features of the IMS, particularly the Fund but also the Bank's IFS and other financial relations. It analyzes the main roles of these institutions in ensuring smooth economic relations among MEs, with increasing attention being devoted to the needs and special requirements of DEs. The attitudes of the CPEs toward key components of the IMS are examined in some detail. The problems of associating typical CPEs within this monetary regime will be detailed as well.

The parallel as far as the ITS is concerned is provided in chapter 4. I first look at the main tasks of the stillborn ITO, the constitution of the GATT and its evolution over time, and the present preoccupations of that organization. With respect to the latter, I devote some attention to liberalizing trade in agriculture and services; the reduction of nontariff barriers (NTBs); the restitution of the multilateral trade order that existed until the early 1970s, before the new protectionism wreaked havoc in the world economy; and the particular problems of the DEs. The peculiar difficulties of associating typical CPEs within this global economic framework will be discussed here at some length as well. The CPEs' experiences in the GATT are summarized with a view to identifying the actual advantages and drawbacks of their participation.

The last chapter is concerned with the broader questions of reconstituting international economic relations, particularly with reforming the trading, monetary, economic, and financial frameworks to obtain three broad results. One encompasses international economic reform to update the order put in place after World War II in line with the present conditions and requirements of the global economy. A related issue is how much to adjust these frameworks to enshrine acceptable obligations of the international community *vis-à-vis* the various layers of the DEs, which fit only partly – or just awkwardly – into the international frameworks in place. Finally, some adjustments may be undertaken jointly in conjunction with the ongoing and envisioned reforms in the CPEs. Such accommodation that MEs could provide to reduce the problems inherent in merging market- and plan-based systems with a view to fostering greater integration in the global economy depends critically on perceptions of world leaders with respect to the desirability of associating CPEs with these reconstituted frameworks.

A summary of the major points made, especially with respect to reforms of the trading, monetary, and financial systems in the context of the ongoing transformations in pivotal CPEs, concludes the volume.

1 Wartime planning for a new economic order

Because this book is not meant to be a history of postwar international economic cooperation, I shall not delve at length into the various concepts of postwar collaboration hatched during World War II. What I intend to accomplish is vastly more modest: to draw attention in chapter 5 to the opportunities for enhancing international economic cooperation that emanate from the external implications of ongoing economic reforms in the CPEs. The benefits are, of course, a function of the environment, and for that I need to isolate the key objectives entertained during the germination of the postwar economic order. For, by harking back to the motives that prevailed prior to the caesura brought about by the Cold War, solid arguments in favor of universalism may be identified. However, to clarify more comprehensively what reform may mean for the participation of CPEs in the global economy, some backdrop is required to the envisaged postwar economic organization, its crystallization in the late 1940s, and its evolution.

I shall not argue the case of universal participation. Its appropriateness will be discussed in chapter 5. For now I take the usefulness of a universal economic order for granted, without detracting from the platitudinous maxim that the pursuit of universalism at any cost may be more harmful than beneficial (Gardner 1969, 383). In a complex world where one party doggedly pursues a singular objective, however worthwhile in and of itself, striving for universalism would by definition be inadvisable. To the extent that there is a desire to fuse the interests of as many countries as possible within the realm of IEOs and that it can be satisfied without debilitating the economic order into unreality, a recapitulation of the principal motives that prevailed during and immediately after World War II may be highly instructive. My major objective, however, is not to inquire in depth into the *pax Americana* and how it diverged from the *pax Britannica*. Neither do I intend to delve into the degree to which this emerging order resulted from premeditation, planning of foreign policy, or crystallization as an accidental outcome of rather unusual conditions. Instead, I reexamine the wartime and postwar deliberations insofar as they are still relevant for the present participation of the CPEs in IEOs and pertinent to speculating about the potential for improving international cooperation.

Section 1 details the background to the protracted discussions about global economic organization initiated during World War II and carried forward to a certain stage of fruition shortly thereafter. The next section sketches the course of negotiations among the major partners. Section 3 picks up the story with respect to the attitude of the CPEs regarding the BWS and its institutions. The same is pursued with respect to the CPEs and the ITS in the next section. The salient features of the ITO are briefly recalled in section 5. Next I examine the Soviet rationales for absenting itself from these IEOs, even though it had participated in their gestation, for shunning altogether the trade deliberations, and for remaining standoffish in subsequent years. How all of this might have jelled into a coherent framework for international economic collaboration under the UN's umbrella will be briefly clarified in the last section. My particular interest there will be the bearing of this collaboration on the enhancement of what would now be called global economic security.

1 Backdrop to wartime negotiations

After a brief exploration of two important paradoxes in the objectives embraced by wartime planners, this section details the key elements of the Anglo-American positions regarding the envisaged postwar economic order.

Two paradoxes of wartime planning

The emergence of the postwar economic order is associated with at least two paradoxes. One revolves around the interest shown by key negotiators for establishing a free liberal economic order, in spite of the adverse experiences during the interwar period; the appalling disarray caused by the war, especially in Europe; and the adjustment problems that, without firm government guidance, were expected to emerge upon launching efforts to restore buoyant economic activity once hostilities ceased. Perhaps even more paradoxical was that the first inducement to the Anglo-American plans for postwar economic organization was inspired by a project devised by Nazi Germany. This is explained in the next subsection. But a word here is needed to reconcile the ambition to reestablish a free trading world with the recognition of the inevitability of an ascending role of the state in national and international economic management.

In particular, the US planners of the postwar economic order never presumed that the individual parts of the total solution of the world's economic problems should be dealt with in isolation. It was realized that relief, reconstruction, and development lending; balance-of-payments adjustments; monetary and trading matters; countercyclical income policies; and national and international economic policies were all highly interrelated. Consequently, fully independent IEOs were never envisaged. The major objective was to provide for a world within which competitive market forces could operate with minimal state interference. This core US philosophy was propagated in the belief that, in the longer run, market forces yield optimum results for all.

Yet the eventual role of the state in domestic and international economic management figured prominently in the deliberations about the specific tasks of trading, financial, and monetary institutions to be created. Certainly, there were large differences of opinion, chiefly between the UK and US negotiators, but by and large "both sides accepted the Keynesian argument that the state had an important role to play in managing financial, commodity and labour markets" (Ansari 1986, 54). That is to say, the US commitments to multilateralism and free trade, among other things, were part of a broader concern among policy makers about how best to ensure steady growth and full employment through national and international state regulation. A major source of inspiration was provided by the depreciation of currencies after World War I and the cycle of devaluations in the 1930s. The first was believed to have interfered with economic recovery and contributed to internal inflation. The latter and its associated deflationary policies distorted international trade in a number of respects (Mikesell 1947b, 60). Moreover, though concern about the international trading, monetary, and financial regimes was widespread, the prime motivation for regulating them was to maintain a high level of domestic economic activity and indeed to restore economic equilibrium in the war-torn countries. At the time, countries other than Sweden, Switzerland, and the United States had little disposition to get rid of exchange and licensing controls all at once or even in the medium term. There was even doubt that such an aim would be a useful and desirable policy objective.

The Funk plan and the western allies

Soon after Hitler had begun to swallow one country after another, on 25 July 1940 his then Minister of Economic Affairs and President of the Reichsbank, Dr. Walther Funk, announced the first practical plan for a postwar monetary and economic order conceived under the Nazi aegis (Dormael 1978, 5–7). As a sign of the times, this was not surprisingly referred to as a "New Order."

The economic organization for the conquered territories, once hostilities ceased, was to be buttressed through the transformation of the existing methods of bilateral economic relations, which Germany had begun to perfect soon after the ascent to power of the Nazi regime, particularly in relations with many Eastern European countries, into a multilateral trade system. According to this project, bilateral imbalances were to be settled not through convertible currency flows among sovereign countries but through a system of exchange clearing. This was to provide the transition mechanism toward another order. Each government of the associated members would be responsible for managing its own balance of payments so that the problem of debits and credits would gradually disappear, evidently after some practical transition phase. This would require fixed parities and stable exchange rates, however. Funk expected that the prevailing pervasive currency restrictions would gradually be removed, except for capital transactions.

Although this system would be built around Germany and its voluntary or forced allies, Funk left no doubt that the region would – and could – not be completely segregated from the rest of the world. Yet it would seek, and enforce by its own means, a considerable degree of intragroup economic security. Funk was well aware that Europe's prosperity could only be ensured if raw materials, foodstuffs, and other goods could be imported from elsewhere in exchange for high-grade manufactures, and that the pursuit of autarky as a policy goal in and of itself would therefore have been self-destructive. The cooperating region would operate under a good deal of surveillance, however. One overriding concern was that Europe must be able to counter emergencies, if necessary by compressing its level of effective absorption and making itself almost economically self-sufficient.

In other words, the Funk plan envisaged a measure of economic security, a separation of current from capital account transactions, the gradual transition from bilateralism to multilateralism based on fixed and stable exchange rates, and considerable government guidance to ensure stable growth. The underlying assumption of the plan was that, after a short transition period to overcome unavoidable imbalances, the participating countries would return to equilibrium at a high level of economic activity, possibly full employment. This coveted state of affairs would have to be protected, through government policies, against various kinds of outside interference. In case of serious disturbances, domestic deflation was to be the chief means to rectify the external imbalance.

Whether it was this pronouncement on Nazi objectives with respect to the "New Order" or other concerns that had similar motives of stability, reliability, predictability, and mutual assistance that inspired the western allies to formulate their own postwar ambitions will never be known. It is unavoidable that, with hindsight, we know what came about before we consider the beginning of it all. Such is the fate of history, which is inevitably "lived forward but written in retrospect," as Richard Gardner (1969, cvi) put it so pointedly.

Nonetheless, in recapturing the various motives that may have been at play at the time, it would not be quite accurate to stress only the master plan. There were also short-term practical concerns that led several of the participants, including Keynes, to hope for a coherent postwar economic order. In addition, policy thinkers on both sides of the Atlantic had been devoting substantial attention to the ways and means of avoiding repeating the mistakes made after World War I. At the time, neither policy makers nor economic leaders – nor the general public for that matter – were prepared for the fundamental changes brought about by the war and its ramifications. Whereas a return to "normalcy" had ranked highly among the concerns of policy makers after World War I, in the 1940s it was realized by many that returning to "normal" would be meaningless at this inauspicious juncture.

Ambitions of allied planning for the postwar economic order

Rationalizations of the debates during and after World War II tend to suggest that the major participants were bent on working out a master plan for postwar international economic collaboration. This would form one cornerstone of foreign policy. In some instances, this is seen essentially as a hegemonic goal explicitly pursued by the only country then in a position to do so, hence the *pax Americana*. Others contend that the US hegemonic position emerged essentially as an afterthought or by default: that is, the main structural components of the economic order through the 1960s materialized because of the weakness of partner countries with respect to what was initially by and large a set of very practical policy objectives. Accordingly, as Condliffe (1950, 644) conceived of it, the program for postwar collaboration was intended to permit as substantial a degree of free multilateral trade as possible without stripping countries with strained balances of payments of their safeguards against cyclical pressures on those balances. The greatest obstacles to freer trade were exchange controls and import quotas – the main safeguards to which countries with a weak balance of payments had resorted in the 1930s and to which they were bound to adhere in the postwar period, if only on account of the inflationary pressures built up during the war.

Aside from efforts to prepare for the postwar economic order as a matter of overall foreign policy, the chief participants in the UK–US debates had more limited, practical, and pragmatic objectives. Resource mobilization in support of the war effort had distorted the production and price structures of every country. Because modern war cannot be waged after the taxes to finance its machinery are collected, the affected countries had issued more currency than would be available for purchases, and so inflationary pressures were bound to erupt and create havoc as soon as price and exchange controls were lifted. Such negative factors could be curtailed through severe deflationary policies, but recent memory of the protracted and painful stabilization efforts after World War I made this option none too attractive. There was therefore eagerness to devise plans that would permit countries to foster full employment if necessary by availing themselves of exchange controls for balance-of-payments purposes. In this, wariness about the US business cycle and the anticipated deflation in the postwar period there played an important role, particularly in the thinking of key UK advisers to postwar planners (Bernstein 1984, 15).

Whatever may have been lingering in the minds of those who participated in laying the foundations of the postwar economic order, it is a fact that for several months Nazi Germany had a monopoly on propaganda of this kind. By November 1940, John M. Keynes, as quoted by Dormael (1978, 7), announced that the United Kingdom would propose "the same as what Dr Funk has to offer except that we shall do it better and more honestly." Soon thereafter Keynes started to elaborate systematically upon his views concerning the so-called European Reconstruction Fund, from which countries would be able to draw loans to purchase foodstuffs and raw materials from abroad. The principal objective would be to prop up a high level of domestic economic activity and thus to avoid repeating the mistakes of Versailles. The key force in these deliberations was the need to be prepared for postwar economic reconstruction and development as integral components of the inevitable debates about political frontiers and safeguards, and other concomitants of a peace settlement. By April 1941, Keynes declared (Dormael 1978, 10): "We intend to develop a system of international exchange in which the trading of goods and services will be the central feature. Financial and capital transactions will play their proper auxiliary role of facilitating trade." This leaves little room for anything but commercial policy being at the heart of the postwar economic system. In this, financial arrangements undertaken as a means to buttress profitable commerce – that is, the current account through proper exchange rate policies and trade liberalization – were to serve in support of the overriding macroeconomic goal of reaching and maintaining high employment.

At about the same time on the other side of the Atlantic, in a letter to Cordell Hull dated 16 May 1941, President Roosevelt prompted the State Department to initiate negotiations with Britain on postwar economic policy. The specific concern underlying this step was the need to contain the adverse impact of wartime financing on British short-term economic performance. Hull's instinct, a fundamental belief of long standing, was that the postwar trading world and commercial relations should be based on nondiscrimination as the central credo of the US government and on making the trading world as multilaterally free as possible, with only *ad valorem* tariffs mediating between domestic and foreign markets. This would find its expression in the MFN clause and convertibility. Since becoming Secretary of State in 1932, Hull had fought for over a decade for the official sanctioning of his trade principles, including moving US trade policies away from the high Hawley–Smoot tariff. Dean Acheson (1970, 31) described Hull's stance: "The Secretary – slow, circuitous, cautious – concentrated on a central political purpose, the freeing of international trade from tariffs and other restrictions as the prerequisite to peace and economic development." In this, in essence Jeffersonian, view of the global economy, Hull thought that such principles ought to be made equally applicable to all nations.

Independently of the official steps initiated through the State Department, Harry D. White at the US Treasury had started in the middle of 1941 to draft his "Suggested plan for a United and Associated Nations Stabilization Fund and a Bank for Reconstruction and Development of the United and Associated Nations" (the first complete draft of which is reproduced in Oliver 1975, 279–322). Its first conception was not officially sanctioned or mandated. Just the same, it became of critical importance in subsequent deliberations. White believed that the first international monetary problem to be tackled should be how to secure stable, though not rigid, foreign exchange rates and freely convertible currencies. For that reason, he proposed his stabilization fund. At the same time, he stressed that other US objectives could be served best by having an international investment bank to stimulate long-term lending at low interest rates for the reconstruction of Europe and the development of low-income countries. It might also finance an international development corporation, a stabilization program for commodity prices, and loans to combat international business fluctuations. This initial germ of what later became the IBRD has unfortunately not received as much emphasis in the literature as it deserves (but see Oliver 1957, 1975).

Regarding the basic US objectives on trade, MFN and convertibility were well removed from the state of affairs envisioned by Keynes and UK negotiators more generally. Keynes regarded nondiscrimination and MFN clauses as "old lumber... which was a notorious failure and made such a hash of the old world" (as quoted in Dormael 1978, 28). His preference was for buoyant domestic economic activity, whose guarantee should be among the prime tasks for government policy. For that purpose, he stressed that any means would be justified, including discrimination and bilateral trading arrangements, to protect the balance of payments and thus ensure the level of employment desired by policy makers.

Trade and payments issues were in Keynes's view of the global economy intimately intertwined. Long-term capital flows, however, remained outside his purview for two reasons. One was that capital flows would have to be undertaken by the surplus countries, chiefly the United States. For capital mobility to resume some buoyancy, it was up to the United States to stimulate demand, for imports from Europe among other things. Also, Keynes felt that long-term capital flows might injure the lending country by placing pressure on the value of its currency, something that Britain could not possibly envision in addition to the array of other payments problems (Oliver 1957, 273–4). In this connection, Keynes believed that once the balance-of-payments disequilibria were removed through concerted action on the foreign exchange and trade fronts, the issue of long-term capital flows in support of economic development would resolve itself. If not, concerted action on this too could be considered later.

Headstrong as Keynes was, he felt that the subjects of trade and foreign exchange measures had to be thought through in a comprehensive manner. But one had to commence from some angle. He chose the foreign exchange one, probably in view of Britain's precarious international financial position during the war and the import pressures that would erupt after the war. He himself declared that "it was perhaps an accident that the monetary proposals got started first... but I am not sure that it was not a fortunate accident" (quoted in Dormael 1978, 31). This may have been proper at the time, particularly in view of the UK's predicament. However, had Keynes first zeroed in on the commercial rather than the financial aspects of international relations, a different policy stance might have emerged with respect to the ill-fated ITO. I realize that it is intrinsically hard to dissociate tariffs from currency depreciation, and thus commercial from financial considerations. Yet, twin aspects of trade *per se* would have been the subject of negotiations with quite a different outcome than what eventually came to the fore. At the very least, the timing for laying the trade infrastructure would have been more propitious.

Within the Anglo-American alliance, a division of labor emerged by default. Though British contributions to the initial exchanges of views were important (Culbert 1987b), the emphasis of UK negotiators was more pronounced on international finance. Their primary motivation was to ensure balance-of-payments stability and provide assistance in economic rehabilitation, reconstruction, and development. As a result, their views weighed more heavily in the shaping of the Bretton Woods institutions than in creative thinking about either the trade organization or the organ to guide capital investments. Regarding monetary affairs, perhaps John M. Keynes, although not in the British civil service for he was coopted as a member of the Consultative Council of the Chancellor of the Exchequer, towered over the UK's policy on money and finance.

By contrast, the ITO was the keystone of US thinking about the postwar global economic framework. The US State Department was indeed foremost among the participants endeavoring to turn this plan into reality (Bidwell and Diebold 1949, 187–91). Yet key components of the postwar trading world, in fact, originated in Britain. James Meade, then at the Economic Section of the War Cabinet Secretariat, already in late 1942 formulated his "Proposal for an International Commercial Union" (Culbert 1987b), which was to complement Keynes's plan for an International Clearing Union (Culbert 1987a, 388). However, on the other side of the Atlantic, Harry D. White had started to draft his views on postwar financial organization while at the State Department Cordell Hull kept pursuing alternatives for postwar trade organization.

Though the alternative views on postwar economic organizations were known, as various drafts were exchanged, it was not until September 1943 that Anglo-American negotiations on postwar economic policy began in earnest in Washington, DC. These deliberations were conceived within the spirit of article VII of the Mutual Aid Agreement, which set out reciprocal obligations of the United States and the United Kingdom for the harmonious conduct of postwar economic relations. Among other things, the Agreement contained the obligation to promote mutually advantageous economic relations on the basis of agreed actions, including "the elimination of all forms of discriminatory treatment in international commerce" and "the reduction of tariffs and other trade barriers" (Oliver 1957, 269). But it was then and there resolved to move ahead first with the financial issues, as both Keynes and White had worked out parallel programs for the postwar international financial order that they felt could usefully be harmonized. The State Department, and perhaps other agencies, objected to giving primacy to financial matters as it felt that the postwar problems would fundamentally revolve around trade relations; monetary arrangements would be of no avail unless the problems on the trade side were solved (Dormael 1978, 63).

Attaching primacy to financial over commercial considerations was also odd because the vast bulk of postwar economic interaction among countries could not but center around merchandise trade, rather than services or capital transactions. Moreover, this trade would have to be cleared for a considerable period of time, perhaps as much as a decade, in the presence of palpable domestic and external imbalances in all major participants in that commerce, excepting the United States. Certainly, having a smooth financial mechanism available to permit settlement of accounts without necessarily immediately revoking all foreign exchange controls was critical. Finally, the importance that the United States had attached to trade liberalization and the lifeblood of merchandise trade for the United Kingdom would have pleaded for commencing discussions first with commercial policy. The United States had committed itself to freer trade with its Reciprocal Trade Agreements Act (RTAA) of 1934 and its successors as well as other measures to move away from the high-tariff protection provided by the Hawley–Smoot Act of 1930. It had found a staunch and convinced advocate of that shift in Cordell Hull (Condliffe 1950, 659). Likewise, keeping the Commonwealth together around the Ottawa Agreement ranked very highly among the UK's policy priorities. It was perhaps the latter's intransigence and the commitment of the US Administration to dismantle preferential trade provisions such as imperial preference that made the two major advocates of the postwar economic order choose to defer commercial matters until a satisfactory solution could be found first for financial matters.

This is not to say that financial issues got absolute priority during the earliest phase of the postwar deliberations. But they tended to dominate the transatlantic debate and were the subject of tugs of war within the respective Administrations. In the United States, the financial issues were within the bailiwick of the Treasury Department, whereas the trade issues fell within the competence of the State Department, although the latter had earlier been given overall responsibility for drafting alternatives to be considered in pondering the postwar economic order in general. Likewise in Britain, the financial issues fell under the Chancellor of the Exchequer whereas trading issues were dealt with in the Board of Trade and the Cabinet. Policy coordination may have been less difficult in Britain than in the United States, not only in view of war priorities but also owing to the different nature of the democratic process of governing there (Gardner 1969, xixff.). However this may be, it was the intellectual towering of Keynes over his co-thinkers in matters concerning postwar IEOs as well as the UK's precarious financial treasury that contributed immeasurably to granting primacy to financial matters.

2 The early history of negotiations about postwar organization

When the allies started to draw up plans during the early 1940s for a postwar global economic system, they sought to design interlinked organizations capable of preventing the reemergence of the factors that contributed to and aggravated the global economic crises of the 1930s (Knorr 1947), which set the stage for World War II. The key architects of such a blueprint for global economic security envisaged an institution to deal with balance-of-payments needs; another one to assist in the formation and distribution of assets for economic rehabilitation, reconstruction, and development; and a third to ensure a multilateral trading world (Gadbaw 1984, 33–4). Moreover, the paramount actors in these global negotiations (Culbert 1987a) hoped that these institutions would attract most, if perhaps not all, actors in the world economy. Near-universal membership was in itself sought as a guarantee for reversing the sharp rise in state intervention in economic affairs, particularly in its nationalist form (Knorr 1947, 542), that had come to the fore in the 1930s. It was certainly hoped from the earliest discussions (Culbert 1987b, 401) that the Soviet Union as the major nonmarket economy could be persuaded to join, even though it would not stand to benefit greatly from managed exchange rates, short-term balance-of-payments financing, and the elimination of tariffs and other barriers to international trade for as long as it sought to shield its domestic planning processes against perturbations from abroad.[1] Clearly, the USSR would be far more interested in relief, rehabilitation, and reconstruction – and for this reason had been agitating for a substantial US loan and for reparation payments from the former enemy countries. These concerns loomed large in Soviet approaches to the Bretton Woods negotiations. However, the various supports of the international order were to be mutually reinforcing, and global participation was hence strongly coveted. It was particularly the US participants in the deliberations who felt that the stability of the international economic order depended upon Soviet support for that order and were thus willing to go out of their way to facilitate Soviet participation.[2]

It is difficult to reexamine these negotiations of over forty years ago with an unencumbered mind. For one thing, it is "impossible to capture the mood of this bygone era" (Oliver 1957, 274). Also, so much of what actually materialized got lost in the usual diplomatic record keeping. Other issues were twisted out of shape, or indeed remolded altogether, by the political expediency of the Cold War. Nevertheless, regarding trade there is no confusion possible about the fact that the negotiators envisaged the creation of an institution affiliated to the United Nations, hence with global participation. The financial institutions then conceived as UN specialized agencies would have their gravitational point of reference also in the framework adopted by the United and Associated Nations. But, by their very nature as technical institutions, only the broad guidelines for their functioning would be referred to the United Nations. However, these specialized agencies took on a largely autonomous existence in connection with the emerging Cold War and its frustrations. In spite of objections, mainly by the USSR and its allies (Assetto 1988, 65–6), the UN's Economic and Social Council (EcoSoc) in 1947 voted to abdicate its right to review and comment upon Fund and Bank lending procedures and budgets. At their conceptualization and inception, however, there was never any serious doubt about building such organizations explicitly with Soviet participation.

The International Monetary Fund

Because initial Anglo-American economic relations[3] revolved around financial matters, I sketch first the backdrop to the Bretton Woods institutions. It may seem odd that so much of the attention of the major actors in the wartime debates was taken up by the determination of the postwar monetary regime. First of all, economic disequilibrium was so pervasive that a protracted transition phase would have to be factored into the process before one could even start laying the foundations for a balanced order. The road to convertibility would be long and arduous. In the end it would take more than a decade (Tew 1967, 100ff.), the need for which was not quite realized at the time. Certainly no less important was the pervasive destruction wrought by the war, which would require fundamental streamlining of postwar investment.

It was perhaps with this concern in mind, and challenged by the Funk plan, that Keynes first set his mind to the formulation of suggestions for the reconstruction of Europe. His contemplated European Reconstruction Fund was undoubtedly inspired by his first-hand experience with the negative effects of the Versailles settlement (Dormael 1978, 8). This fund would allow each participant to be supplied with the amount of credit required to purchase foodstuffs and raw materials from outside. The organization would actually exclude the United States as it was judged to be too preoccupied with exports and not sufficiently amenable to increasing its imports from Europe.

But the subsequent Anglo-American agreement and the Atlantic Charter separated short-term transactions for balance-of-payments purposes from the structural disequilibria caused by wartime financing. Keynes set his mind to that and formulated his "Proposals for an International Currency Union." At the same time, Harry D. White and his assistants at the US Treasury had formulated a plan called "Inter-Allied Stabilization Fund." Although the plans drafted by Keynes and White differed in a number of fundamental ways, they covered the same ground, had the same purposes, and presented striking similarities in approach to international financial matters. The Keynes plan aimed at overcoming trade bilateralism and the deflationary bias of the gold standard by providing for the unrestricted clearing of each member's credit and debit balances, and for automatic credit financing through a clearing union (Triffin 1957, 93ff.). The White plan embraced similar goals but without the creation of a powerful international monetary authority.

The heart of the Keynes plan was the clearing of current-account transactions through a supranational policing body that would not use any national currency or gold as backing. Instead, it would conduct its business in an "ideal" unit called "bancor." The major drive of the proposed scheme was to apply among countries the essential principles of domestic bank clearing in the United Kingdom. Because it was intended simply to facilitate the restoration of unfettered, thus automatic, multilateral clearing among the members, this clearing union would not have its own capital fund. Corrective action would be required only when a country was out of balance with the system as a whole. Transitional imbalances would be covered through the union. More fundamental adjustments in fixed exchange rates would have to be covered through agreed-upon changes in par values. Adjustment would, however, have to be made symmetric by subjecting to surveillance and penalties both debtors and creditors to the clearing union. Keynes initially devoted himself to what he referred to as an International Clearing Union, which was conceived in a similar fashion to his earlier plan for a supernational bank with a global monetary authority. His initial approach was to establish a system of overdrafts enabling members to finance balance-of-payments deficits. This project proved unacceptable to the United States, which felt that deficit nations would be allowed to finance more than temporary imbalances, total overdraft provisions would exceed temporary deficits, and nations would accumulate bancor balances indefinitely, thus leading to a "possible gigantic dollar-give-away program over which [the United States] would have no control" (Oliver 1957, 375–6).

The White plan originally envisaged that the stabilization fund would be used during the war to give monetary aid to actual and potential allies, to hamper the enemy, to provide the basis for postwar international monetary stabilization, and to emit sufficient international liquidity. The lend–lease agreement essentially took care of the first parts of this plan. Harry White therefore redrafted his proposals into the "United Nations Stabilization Fund and Bank for Reconstruction of the United and Associated Nations," which dealt equally with monetary stabilization and postwar recovery and reconstruction. But as time went on the latter problem came to be overshadowed by the preoccupation with the former.

Unlike Keynes, White envisaged a much more passive institution with its own capital fund from which members would be able to draw, subject to certain limitations set by the clearing institution. But there were great asymmetries in creditor–debtor adjustment in the sense that it was chiefly the debtor applying for funds from the union that would come under surveillance. The second difference with the Keynes plan was the amount of liquidity to be provided. Keynes saw this as being very substantial whereas White opted for a much more modestly funded capital. Finally, the conditions for the availability of these funds differed markedly between Keynes and White. Neither had made provisions for the transition problem, that is, the return to postwar normalcy, which could occur only through imbalances on current accounts.

The two plans were the subject of frequent meetings of experts beginning in early 1943, when Keynes and White met for the first time. Although there were considerable differences between the two plans, talks had progressed sufficiently to invite other countries to participate and indeed to finalize the charter of the organization. Thus the United Nations Monetary and Financial Conference was convened. It met from 1 to 21 July 1944 in Bretton Woods, NH in the United States and drafted the final versions of the documents that soon afterwards gave rise to the Fund and the Bank – hence the origin of the BWS and its associated institutions. This meeting had been preceded by a long preliminary meeting at Atlantic City, NJ in June 1944 as well as earlier, preparatory discussions in Washington, DC.

Backdrop to the World Bank

The story of the origin of the World Bank has received scant attention in the literature and has at times been misrepresented as having come about as "almost an afterthought which began to emerge as an important issue only after substantial agreement on the payments union concept (IMF) was reached" (Assetto 1988, 10). This and similar erroneous views stem in part from the fact that most histories of the BWS have concentrated on the Fund and usually begin with the publication in 1943 of Keynes's proposal for a clearing union. Further, the two plans were never considered together in international discussions about the separate issues of capital formation for reconstruction and development on the one hand, and the financial problems associated with the transition and post-transition periods on the other (Oliver 1975, 134). White's original contribution to postwar thinking has also in good measure been relegated to footnotes in consequence of the rather tragic fate of the originator of the idea for the World Bank.[4] Finally, perhaps most important was the fact that Keynes never devised his own plan for an international investment institution and was actually quite opposed to such an organ because he felt that long-term capital exports might injure the lending country (Oliver 1957, 273) and was otherwise antagonistic toward international investment (Oliver 1957, 283). He took this position throughout the preparatory stages of what later became known as the Bretton Woods negotiations. Ironically perhaps, at the conference he was asked to chair the meetings ("Commission II") that led to the creation of the Bank and negotiators did not broach the relevant issues till well into the conference (Mason and Asher 1973, 21). But by then the outlook for the Bank had become very different from what White had originally envisaged. Unlike the Fund, over which discussions lasted for nearly two years, basic agreement on the Bank was reached in little more than two weeks (Oliver 1975, 182). Admittedly, during the transatlantic voyage aboard the *Queen Mary*, Keynes and his advisers had discussed the forthcoming negotiations in Washington and Bretton Woods, and had prepared what was called the "Boat Draft" of the Articles of Agreement. This greatly facilitated discussions in Commission II (Mason and Asher 1973, 13).

White's draft had been inspired by the proposed Inter-American Bank in which were combined the functions of an intergovernmental bank, an international stabilization fund, and an ordinary commercial bank (Mason and Asher 1973, 16). White felt that private investors could not be relied upon to provide the capital required for postwar reconstruction and that the flow of long-term capital from rich to poor countries could not be left at the discretion of private investors. The interwar period had made it abundantly clear that long-term private capital movements as a rule reinforced, rather than mitigated, the international spread of business fluctuations. Furthermore, high interest rates and relatively short maturities of private portfolio investments tended to undermine the solidity of otherwise productive ventures. The depression of the 1930s had amply underlined that unilateral national action could not bring about a revival of international trade and investment along the liberal lines that had existed during the greater part of the nineteenth century.

In its original conception. White's plan also envisaged the Bank as supplying short-term capital to finance foreign trade, strengthen the monetary and credit structures of the member countries, combat international business cycles, stabilize the prices of essential raw materials, or promote equitable access to scarce, essential raw materials (Oliver 1975, 156).[5] This was, then, an extremely ambitious international bank. Its departure from conventional wisdom was particularly pronounced in the initial suggestion that the Bank should be entitled to issue noninterest-bearing notes, christened "unitas," which, like gold, would serve as an international reserve and a medium of exchange. This was similar in nature to the bancor but, unlike the latter, it would not have been issued at the discretion of borrowing nations as readily as the envisaged bancor overdrafts, nor would it have financed general balance-of-payments deficits. Unitas would have been issued only to finance reconstruction or development projects approved by the Bank.

White proposed to pool capital from member countries to be used, in addition to borrowed funds, to supplement rehabilitation and long-term capital investments for productive purposes. Financing requirements because of lax or careless budgetary profligacy, short-term balance-of-payments problems, or repayment of maturing loans would not qualify for the envisaged IEO. The Bank would stimulate private investment flows in the postwar transition period by guaranteeing private loans. It would make loans directly, for reconstruction as well as in support of economic development, only when it approved of a worthwhile project that could not be financed privately at a reasonable rate of interest. It might also finance an international development corporation and an international basic commodity price stabilization program, and arrange its lending policies so as to combat international business fluctuations (Oliver 1957, 377). All these projects were based on the notion that reconstruction and surplus funds channeled to DEs could not be left solely to the initiative of private investment markets. Long-term capital flows in the 1920s had reinforced rather than attenuated business fluctuations and high interest rates combined with relatively short maturities, all of which tended to render unproductive what might otherwise have been productive private portfolio investments. In other words, one of the primary purposes of the Bank was ultimately to "blaze the trail for private international investment" by breaking "the logjam of investment" (Condliffe 1950, 656–7), smoothing a return to private portfolio investment, in the less developed parts of the world as elsewhere.

The originally ambitious nature of the proposal was sharply truncated as a result of several rounds of negotiations before the draft was published in November 1943. It was further modified by subsequent intergovernmental negotiations. The European, mainly British, input focused on replacing a substantial own capital by borrowed funds and pushing the Bank in the direction of being more a guarantor of private investment than a provider of funds. The British evidently felt that for a good part of the postwar period international lending would have to be provided by the United States, not from the already scarce funds of war-torn countries short of capital for civilian investment.

The twin part of the "Proposals for an International Currency Union" would be an IEO to provide postwar relief and reconstruction. The main purpose was to avoid all risk of any one country having to assume a burdensome commitment for relief and reconstruction elsewhere in the world economy. This was originally seen as accruing from countries having credit balances on their clearing accounts of a chronic character for which they had no immediate use and were voluntarily leaving idle. However, Keynes soon thereafter reassessed his priorities and felt that it was necessary to dissociate relief and reconstruction from providing mutual assistance to relieve temporary current-account constraints.

As a result, the pillars of the IFS and IMS as they emerged after World War II have been the Fund to take care of transitory payments difficulties and the Bank to provide structural finance. An agreed-upon exchange regime and a shared system for balance-of-payments financing administered under the guidance of the IMF were the paramount philosophical precepts of the BWS. The latter's key objectives hence concerned regaining convertibility, multilateralism, and equilibrium exchange rates that functioned as real prices. For countries in need of reconstruction or development finance, the Bank was designed to redeploy funds from various origins. There are, of course, other important ingredients of the BWS as conventionally understood, but the above features suffice for now.

Commercial organization and the ITO

The first UK–US preparatory talks about an international trade organization were held as early as 1941. In fact, as noted, they found their origin in earlier US trade policy stances (Bidwell and Diebold 1949; Culbert 1987a; Gardner 1969; Wilcox 1947). Very critical in this was the decision of the Roosevelt Administration as part of the New Deal in 1934 to reduce substantially the highest tariffs in US history imposed in 1930 by the Hawley–Smoot Tariff Act (Tussie 1987, 10–11). Hull was the major mover for reducing tariffs on a reciprocal basis in combination with adherence to the existing policy to seek to avoid discrimination among sources of supply. These considerations provided the "basic technique of tariffs negotiations for the next thirty years" (Evans 1971, 6).

Talks about commercial organization were broached in 1943 with the publication of the US's *Proposal for consideration by an International Conference on Trade and Employment*, which dealt separately with employment and the establishment of an ITO. The Anglo-American exploratory talks in the autumn of 1943 revealed a broad measure of consensus on basic principles of commercial collaboration. This near unanimity was displayed in recognizing, for example, the fundamental interdependence of trade and employment policies, the need to curtail and eventually to eliminate quantitative restrictions (QRs), and the desirability of finding an automatic tariff-reducing formula to facilitate a substantial cutback in tariffs and elimination of discriminatory treatment, including QRs and other nontariff measures. There was also a broad agreement on the need to establish some IEO that could interpret a code of multilateral principles and settle disputes between members.

For reasons detailed in section 1, deliberations about commercial organization did not resume until November 1945, when the United States published its *Proposals for the expansion of world trade and employment* (henceforth *Proposals*) and soon thereafter invited fifteen countries to negotiate for the reduction of tariffs and other trade barriers (Diebold 1988, 2). This was instrumental in bringing about the various international negotiations that led to the Havana Charter, examined in the last subsection here.

Before entering into a discussion of what the ITO was all about, a few historical markers need to be recalled. As suggested, the negotiations about the ITO got under way with the publication of the *Proposals*, which the United States and the United Kingdom accepted as a basis for negotiations after they had signed their financial agreement of December 1945. This had also found initial support and approval on the part of other countries, including Czechoslovakia, France, Poland, and the USSR (Condliffe 1950, 613). Through discussions and quiet diplomacy, this first draft was modified into the basic document of the negotiations about the ITO with the publication of *Suggested charter for an International Trade Organization* (henceforth *Suggested charter*). The latter was acted upon in response to an EcoSoc resolution of 18 February 1946 (Condliffe 1950, 663),[6] whose original draft had been tabled by the United States. By design, then, the United States sought to infuse greater coherence into the international trading world through negotiations that took place in sequence in London, New York, Geneva, and Havana.

The original resolution called for the convening of an International Conference on Trade and Employment, which later (21 November 1947–24 March 1948) materialized as the Havana Conference; the setting up of a Preparatory Committee entrusted with drafting the ITO's charter, which first met in late 1946 (15 October–26 November) in London and subsequently (10 April–22 August 1947) in Geneva, Switzerland, after a meeting of the Drafting Committee of five participants in Lake Success, NY from 20 January 1947 through 25 February 1947 (see Restoration 1947); and the preparation, circulation, and publication of *Suggested charter* (Wilcox 1947, 529). The London meeting of the Preparatory Committee was attended by eighteen nations; EcoSoc's resolution had called for nineteen participants, but the Soviet Union did not respond to the invitation.[7]

Suggested charter was the major document discussed in London, where it was modified into *Preliminary draft charter for the International Trade Organization of the United Nations* (henceforth *Preliminary charter*). This was entrusted to a Drafting Committee, which met in Lake Success, NY in early 1947 to redraft the document for consideration at the second meeting of the Preparatory Committee, which sat in Geneva from 10 April through 22 August 1947. That meeting finalized the deliberations of the preceding two–three years by further modifying the document into *Draft charter for the International Trade Organization of the United Nations* (henceforth *Draft charter*). The Geneva deliberations were instrumental in setting the stage for the plenary conference on the Havana Charter for the creation of the ITO in Havana, Cuba (Dam 1970, 10–11).

Note that the Geneva meeting of the Preparatory Committee was held in parallel with negotiations about commercial policy. Not only were the latter negotiations attended by twenty-three nations that had shown keen interest in reciprocal and multilateral tariff bargaining, but they continued until October 1947, when the General Agreement was signed. These provisions were not, however, seen as separate from those coming under the commercial policy part of the Havana Charter. This preoccupation with commercial policy in parallel with the other concerns embedded in the various drafts of the Havana Charter had arisen as a result of the US efforts during the London Conference to convene as a stopgap measure, in parallel with the second meeting of the Preparatory Committee, a number of interested countries for more technical negotiations with a view to finalizing the commercial policy provisions of the *Draft charter* on a tentative basis in a General Agreement. This was to provide the means of recording, and underpinning, the results of the first round of tariff negotiations (then scheduled for the spring of 1947, but which in fact lasted from 10 April through 30 October 1947) to ensure that the benefits of multilateral cooperation in trade matters would not be frustrated by governments resorting in the meantime to nontariff methods of protection (Culbert 1987a, 396). This was, however, slated to be an interim measure, and the GATT was for a long time referred to as the "Interim Commission of the ITO" (ICITO); its official status is still that, though hardly anyone refers to the GATT by this peculiar name (see chapter 4).

The General Agreement reached in October 1947 was originally conceived as a trade agreement recording the results of a tariff conference. At the time, it was envisaged as being the first of a number of such conferences soon to be convened under the auspices of the ITO. To ensure that the tariff concessions listed in the General Agreement would not be undercut by other aspects of trade policy measures coming within the purview of the ITO, the General Agreement incorporated many of the stipulations pertaining to commercial policy embodied in the pertinent chapter of the ITO's draft charter, which the United States considered to be the cornerstone and substance of the Havana Charter. Unfortunately, when the United States decided not to seek ratification of the Havana Charter, for reasons to be touched upon below, the General Agreement became by default the founding document for an unusual IEO known as "the GATT."

As noted in more detail in chapter 4, the General Agreement does not incorporate some aspects of commercial policy or any of the other major topics addressed in the Havana Charter. Nor does it include any of the latter's organizational or procedural provisions. It was, however, endorsed as a temporary measure and thus was not likely to stand by itself; hence the GATT's status as the Interim Commission of the ITO (Krappel 1975, 22). It is a tribute to the old adage that *c'est le provisoire qui dure,* for that preliminary agreement is still the major regulator of world trade.

3 The socialist countries and Bretton Woods

Whereas the Soviet Union elected not to participate in the discussions about the ITS, it played an active role in the Bretton Woods and related discussions about the future global economic, financial, and trading frameworks. It continued to participate until the first Board of Governors' meeting of the IMF in Savannah, GA in March 1946 (Brabant 1987a, 237–40). Thus the Soviet Union attended the final Bretton Woods conference and signed the Articles of Agreement in 1944. But in the end it failed to ratify them. Furthermore, the USSR chose not to join the Preparatory Committee first convened in London in 1946. It did not attend the Havana Conference, although it had been invited. It was not asked to participate in the tariff conference and the deliberations about the General Agreement in Geneva in 1947. As a result, it stayed outside the multilateral economic institutions. This evolution of policy stances and of the negative attitude eventually embraced requires some explanation.[8] But other countries that later became CPEs did fully partake in the deliberations on the Havana Charter. These included China, Cuba, Czechoslovakia, Poland (although it refused to sign the Havana Charter), and Yugoslavia. Neither Poland nor Yugoslavia became founder members of the GATT.

The CPEs have traditionally also been important missing actors in the BWS. But some members of that grouping actively participated in the debates about the Fund's creation – indeed Czechoslovakia and Poland were founder members. Other countries that existed at the time and became founder members – although they were not then quite "socialist" – included China, Cuba, Vietnam, and Yugoslavia. The People's Republic of China, of course, could not have been a founder as it came into being only in October 1949. In the early 1950s, Czechoslovakia agitated on its behalf for the expulsion of the Republic of China, a move that failed. But China did not actively covet the chair held by the Republic of China until the early 1970s. The Socialist Republic of Vietnam assumed the membership obligations of the Republic of Vietnam after reunification. However, by the time the key institutional and policy features of the typical CPE (as examined in chapter 2) were fully in place, for all practical purposes the socialist countries ignored the BWS, and Czechoslovakia and Poland formally withdrew. Cuba also withdrew in 1960 from the Bank and in 1964 from the Fund, ostensibly because it could not meet its financial obligations. The real reason for the severing of relations stemmed, however, from Cuba's revolution and societal changes of the early 1960s.

For many years the CPEs shunned the Washington organizations and in fact were most critical of their institutional and behavioral features. The latter were felt to have been put in place chiefly for the benefit of a select few DMEs, which were allegedly seeking dominance through currency hegemony or through the insistence upon a unilaterally favorable distribution of voting power in the management of these organizations that ran counter to the respect for greater equity in international life, on which most CPEs insist as a matter of principle. Of course, this lofty socialist principle has not always been a guiding beacon of the CPEs' behavior in global affairs!

The CPEs derive their view of international economic relations in particular from a set of fundamental principles that are anchored to a clear commitment to and an interest in enhancing international interdependence when such relations are mutually advantageous and conducted on the basis of an equitable division of labor. With reference to the basic issues under review, the CPEs consider "it obviously impossible to limit the process of transformation to specific fields of international economic relations" (Spröte 1983, 23). A reform of the IMS will therefore have to be conceived holistically within the context of "a radical restructuring of the entire system of international economic relations." This assertion refers in particular to the "international organizations whose charters and practices remain profoundly undemocratic and deprive the developing [MEs] of the opportunity of taking an equitable part in their work" (UNCTAD 1979, 181). The position held on subsidiary issues, when explicitly spelled out in detail, can be inferred from the above general assessments.

The postwar history of the involvement of the CPEs with the world's monetary system can be divided essentially into four periods: (1) the early stages that eventually led to the creation of the Fund and the Bank, (2) the severing of most international relations outside the CMEA framework, (3) the exploration of ways of joining the monetary institutions, and (4) the experiences of the countries that did participate or continue to participate actively in the multilateral institutions. All of these will be considered in more detail in chapter 3. Here I focus on the first two stages.

The negotiations about the BWS

Several present socialist countries were important participants in the preparation, or even in the early activities, of the Bretton Woods institutions. The USSR, as the only CPE of the time, was active in the deliberations about the fundamental aims and prerogatives of the global institutions. In the debates that led up to the creation of the Fund, the USSR tended to favor the White plan over the Keynes plan. But it did not always make it clear which of the two plans it favored from the point of view of its own financial needs and its views on postwar economic organization. It did lean toward the White plan, perhaps because it contained explicit recommendations with respect to lending for rehabilitation and reconstruction and moreover did not entail the kind of strict institution of global monetary control that Keynes had earlier advocated. A modified version of the former was in the end adopted.

During the initial negotiations, the USSR gave the distinct impression that it would definitely be one of the founders. Moreover, key negotiators went out of their way to assuage Soviet concerns in order to improve the chances of attaining a more universal organization and hence full participation of the USSR in the postwar international economic order.[9] Several of the Fund's articles were therefore drafted with a view to assuaging specific Soviet concerns, including the following. First, the quota proposed by the United States was held to be too small. The USSR wanted sufficient voting power to be able to veto a uniform change in par values; because the latter were expressed in terms of the gold content at a fixed dollar exchange rate, Soviet concern thus focused on the world price of gold.[10] Secondly, it contended that the gold share of the quota should be reduced from 25 to 15 percent of quotas for all, and to 7.5 percent of quotas for the then "occupied" countries, including the USSR and France, which seconded the Soviet position. Thirdly, the USSR argued that the ruble's exchange rate should not be controlled by the Fund because, given its MFT, and thus the separation of domestic from foreign prices and the wide autonomy of economic decision making thereby afforded (see chapter 2), any change in the par value of the ruble would be without effect on the competitive position of other countries. Fourthly, it insisted that rubles made available for drawings be used only for purchases from the USSR. It also contended in this connection that newly mined gold should not be used for repurchases of the members' own currencies from the Fund. Fifthly, the USSR objected to depositing its gold tranche for storage in the United States. Finally, it advocated that it should not provide any more economic information than it agreed with the Fund. It further proposed that members more generally should not be obliged to heed the Fund's views on any existing or proposed monetary or economic policy.

This formidable catalog of requests for amendments of the Fund's draft Articles of Agreement in and of itself could have deterred the USSR from joining. Nevertheless, it continued to partake actively in the shaping of the new institution and thus kept its options for membership unencumbered.

During the negotiations of 1943–4, it remained unclear whether the USSR was basically negotiating about a settlements institution. At the time the USSR did not distinguish between stabilization, which was to become the focus of the Fund, and development assistance, which was to be the center of attention of the World Bank. But a central motivation of Soviet involvement with this particular aspect of collaboration between the Atlantic partners was economic and financial aid for reconstructing its war-devastated economy. In fact, there are several pointers to the effect that the Soviet Union may have visualized the proposed Fund more as a development institution than as an organ preoccupied with balance-of-payments and stabilization measures.[11] This was perhaps also the prime obstacle in the negotiations about the eventual conclusion of a peace agreement and the exacerbation of the Cold War.

At the Atlantic City conference of June 1944, several of the USSR's key reservations were tabled and satisfactorily resolved. For instance, the USSR's quota was expanded to 14 percent; though France supported the Soviet view on gold subscriptions, the USSR failed to persuade the chief negotiators; a compromise was reached on the question of information to be submitted and on the monitoring of exchange rates for members whose currency does not affect their international transactions; and a satisfactory resolution of the deposit of gold was found.

The USSR's reservations about the Bank in particular had either been convincingly clarified away or had been taken into account in preparing the Articles of Agreement by Commission II. It failed to obtain satisfaction on the request for preferential treatment on account of war damages for which it had sought more favorable interest rates, maturities, and priority in the distribution of loans; in the reduction of the gold contribution; or in forestalling the endorsement with respect to the obligation of the Bank to investigate thoroughly any loan request and its merits and to follow up once the project was approved, possibly through on-site inspections. But it was agreed that only up to half of the paid-in capital subscriptions in gold and convertible currency would be held in the United States—at least 40 percent would be distributed over the other four largest subscribers with at least the own gold subscription in any of those four (Oliver 1957, 458, 564–5). Also, as regards voting rights, though the suggestion to allocate at least 10 percent to the four largest contributors (China, United Kingdom, United States, and USSR) regardless of subscription was rejected, the USSR was persuaded in the end to agree to a substantial subscription – much more than it had earlier been willing to accept, possibly because Bank loans would not be in proportion to paid-in shares as in the Fund – which yielded more than 10 percent of the votes for the USSR and also made some allowances to ease the process of paying in the subscription (Oliver 1975, 165–6).

These compromises were incorporated into the draft Articles of Agreement, which were signed, by the Soviet delegation as by the others, at Bretton Woods without any oral or written reservations at all on some of the thorniest issues (Horsefield 1969, 105, 117). But the Soviet delegation, in a little noted statement after signing the Articles of Agreement, asserted that it was "reserving the full right of the USSR Government to make a free and independent study of the Draft"; it having signed the draft did not constitute "approval of the Draft in whole or in any of its parts on behalf of the USSR Government" (Proceedings 1948, 1087, 1091). With hindsight, this declaration must necessarily be interpreted as a reservation, though it certainly was not generally perceived as such at the time.

Whatever the precise nature of this declaration, in subsequent statements, beginning with the UN debate in 1947, Soviet observers argued that the basic principles embodied in the Articles of Agreement "combined a number of articles which were totally unacceptable to them" (Fomin 1978, 106). These allegedly included the allocation of votes, the reporting on gold and exchange reserves, the transfer of gold to US territory, convertibility for current account purposes, and the conditionality provisions associated with drawings.

Although the USSR never formally refused to join the Fund and the Bank, it decided to partake no longer in the institution's affairs after the first governors' meeting in Savannah, GA (March 1946), where it held the status of observer, for reasons detailed in chapter 3. Formally, its delegation argued that membership was pending, though more time was required to study the matter. Never since has the USSR formally contacted the Fund or the Bank, largely for noneconomic reasons. But diplomatic, exploratory, and noncommittal feelers have been extended to these institutions, particularly since the mid-1980s.

The early experiences with and withdrawal from the BWS

In contrast to the USSR's tacit decision not to accede to the BWS, Czechoslovakia and Poland (as well as China, Cuba, and Yugoslavia) wee among the founders of the BWS – but not for long. Poland resigned in March 1950, alleging that the Fund had failed in its original purpose and that it had become subservient to US interests.[12] Czechoslovakia remained in the Bank and the Fund until the end of 1954, when it was formally expelled; but, in May 1955, it opted voluntarily to resign from both institutions before the Fund's Board of Governors could implement the expulsion, an action that would soon thereafter have been followed by a similar decision on the part of the Board of Governors of the Bank – hence the two different interpretations that are upheld by the Washington institutions and Czechoslovakia. Formally, the bone of contention revolved around the fact that the latter had not consulted the Fund and refused all information and cooperation about the June 1953 koruna devaluation and the monetary reform associated with it. Cuba seceded from the Washington institutions in 1960 in the case of the Bank and in early 1964 in the case of the Fund when it became known that it was bound to be issued a similar censure by the respective Boards of Governors because of repeated infractions of the Articles of Agreement.

The other socialist countries have been ambivalent toward the Washington institutions. Albania and Bulgaria's tentative inquiries in 1948 remained without further consequence. China's seat at these institutions was taken by the Republic of China until the Beijing Administration decided to play a more active role in world affairs, beginning in 1978; it was seated in both institutions in 1980. Poland apparently first approached the Fund in October 1956 (Kranz 1984, 32). But the Fund made it then politically impossible to contemplate membership seriously (Blusztajn

1982, 109). At the first session of UNCTAD in 1964, both Hungary and Rumania held exploratory talks with IMF representatives, but there was no follow-up (Kranz 1984, 32). Vietnam became a member because, after the Democratic Republic of Vietnam won the civil war, Hanoi simply took Saigon's place under its new name of Socialist Republic of Vietnam, in spite of strenuous objections on the part of the United States. So only Yugoslavia is an original socialist member of the Fund and the Bank.

4 Toward an international trading system and the CPEs

The Soviet Union elected not to attend the formal conferences and working sessions convened after the Bretton Woods deliberations, though it had been invited to do so. Nonetheless, successive drafts of the Havana Charter contained provisions for state trading as a result of the Soviet Union's wartime and later involvement in plans for a global economic, financial, and trading framework (Brabant, 1987a, 237–40). Its particular place in the ITO, to which the General Agreement was meant as a component prelude, was to be regulated later if and when the Soviet Union chose to participate.

The basic objectives of the ITO

The various participants in the debates leading up to the Havana Conference were keen on advancing one cause or another in the process. By virtue of the fact that the US State Department did more than anyone else to translate thought into reality (Bidwell and Diebold 1949, 187–91), its precepts on the postwar trading world mattered most and should therefore be highlighted somewhat more explicitly than the positions held by other countries.

It is important to recall that the elaboration of the foundations for a world with free, that is, nondiscriminatory, trade was a critical cornerstone of US thinking about the postwar global economic framework. This position was anchored to two fundamental principles: (1) the complete and immediate abolition of NTBs, including QRs; and (2) the gradual reduction of all tariffs through negotiations. Both goals were to be fostered within the framework of a comprehensive code governing world trade, which itself would be based on reciprocity and MFN. It was envisaged that such codification of emerging international law would ultimately severely restrict the right of individual governments to interfere with the free flow of private trade. Governments were expected to be strictly law-abiding.

Against this backdrop, the main tasks of the international body would be to interpret the convention, investigate complaints, settle differences among members, and if need be enforce the code (Gardner 1969, 104). That is to say, the ITO was to function very much like an international trade court. The institution's role in persuading governments to resort to more responsible trade policies, in providing a framework for accommodating divergent viewpoints, and in setting up the machinery for mediating disputes would be strictly secondary. Nonetheless, as initially conceived,[13] the ITO was to be entrusted with the surveillance of commercial policy; ensuring full employment and balanced economic activity; and assisting with economic development, reconstruction, the abolition of restrictive business practices, the regulation of capital flows, and the monitoring and facilitation of intergovernmental commodity agreements.[14] But, as far as mainstream US thinking went, commercial policy was the ITO's alpha and omega. Other countries, including the United Kingdom, attached more importance to measures to ensure full employment, economic reconstruction, and buttressing the development process than to free trade policies.

Clearly, the assumption that governments can reasonably be expected to abide voluntarily by strict laws, particularly in commercial policy, was too simple, if not naïve altogether. Those most affected by the war, beset by unemployment, and hemmed in by ingrained protectionist policies were loath to dismantle these features, at least until the transition to a civilian economy could be completed. This was certainly the case for those that sought to foster import substitution or to bolster economic development within a system of planning that could hardly withstand international competition. Similarly, the United States faced domestic lobbying and had to honor its commitments to protectionism, particularly in agriculture.[15] Further, the insistence of British interests in retaining the imperial preference and the right to protect a fragile pound sterling with QRs had to be reckoned with. Finally, views on the role of the state in economic affairs held by a great many countries were too diverse to be quickly reconciled.

To allay this wide range of concerns, increasingly more restrictive compromises were incorporated during successive negotiation rounds, thus rendering the rather simple document suggested by the United States increasingly more voluminous, cumbersome, and ponderous. The document thus tended to become "grotesquely complicated" (Dam 1970, 14). But Clair Wilcox, perhaps the main architect of the Havana Charter in the US State Department, saw the exceptions to the prohibition of QRs as "dictated not by political expediency, but by economic necessity" on the ground that "it would have been unwise to have proposed a rule so rigid that it could not be enforced" (Wilcox 1947, 534). Similar sentiments prevailed in the foreign relations establishment, which felt that a rigid legal code "would soon fracture, unless the rules were so general that they had no concrete meaning" (Bidwell and Diebold 1949, 208). but business interests in particular objected (see Bidwell and Diebold 1949, 208ff.; Committee 1949). Even US economists were markedly divided over whether it was still worthwhile to seek implementation of the Havana Charter (see Committee 1949; Knorr 1947; Mikesell 1947a; and Wilcox 1947).

The United States seized upon the overloading of the document and the watering down of the simple principles on free trade to secure general acceptance (Diebold 1972, 346) as an excuse to abort the ratification of the Havana Charter. In reality, while the charter was being debated and refined in 1946–7, a sharp reversal in the internationalist perception of US policy makers and in their commitment to globalism occurred for reasons to be touched upon shortly. US authorities were initially bent on obtaining Congressional ratification. When Congress did not act upon the issue in 1949 and criticism about the organization had been mounting, in part under impact of the hysteria about communist infiltration, the Administration continually postponed its submission to the Congress and finally publicly admitted defeat when, at the fifth session of the GATT in December 1950, it declared that the Contracting Parties should not count on US ratification of the Havana Charter. Under the circumstances, it was feared that Congressional approval, which US policy makers had earlier announced as a precondition for ratification of the Havana Charter, although in the view of some observers there had initially not been a legal obligation to do so, would not be forthcoming, and so the ITO was dead (Gardner 1969, 348–80). Without US participation, the chances of ratifying the Havana Charter would have been very slim; in fact, only Haiti and Liberia ratified it; Australia did so conditional upon US and UK ratification, and Sweden subject to US ratification (Diebold 1952, 24; Tussie 1987, 12).

The envisaged organization of the ITO

Organizationally the ITO would have comprised four layers (Krappel 1975, 25). As the highest organ, the Conference would seat all members with equal voting rights. It would normally be convened once a year, but extraordinary sessions could be called to order. It would be entitled to recommend certain policies upon a two-thirds majority. Members were not obligated to take action, however, but they would have to justify why they chose not to heed recommendations issued by the Conference.

The steering of the ITO at the behest of the Conference was to be entrusted to the Executive Board, consisting of eighteen members, of whom the eight most important industrial countries (Benelux, Canada, China, France, India, the United Kingdom, and the United States, in addition to the reserved seat for the USSR) would be permanent. As an arm of the Conference, the Executive Board would execute assignments issued by the supreme organ. It was also called upon to supervise the Commissions and to ensure follow-up to recommendations of the Conference, including those directed at other interstate organs.

The final two organs would have been Commissions and the Secretariat. Upon recommendation by the Conference, the ITO would create Commissions to take care of special tasks of the organization. The highest administrative office, the Director General, would be in charge of the Secretariat, liaise with the Commissions, and represent the organization on the Executive Board (Bidwell and Diebold 1949, 229–35).

The ITO and the Soviet Union

Because the ITO was stillborn, it is difficult to evaluate how it might have accommodated the special trade requirements of the Soviet Union, which, as noted, was expected to become one of the key founders. The USSR initially openly supported the Anglo-American endeavor to entrust an IEO with the regulation of trade matters (Kostecki 1979a, 2), as it did with respect to the other components of the envisioned postwar international economic order. Although one cannot know how the USSR would have behaved, it is nonetheless useful to detail how the institution was meant to integrate so-called state-trading countries (STCs), a designation employed throughout the 1930s and a term that lives on in the General Agreement as well as in other IEOs, including the European Communities (EC). This designation was probably chosen to avoid political labels such as socialist or communist countries and to differentiate between socialist countries and CPEs proper.

Although initially invited to become a member of the Preparatory Committee, the USSR decided not to respond to the invitation. At the London Conference, key participants of a number of delegations, including those from the United Kingdom and the United States, hoped that the Soviet Union could yet be persuaded to join in time for the finalization of the document. But these efforts did not bear fruit. As a result, successive revisions of the various drafts deleted one after another the tentative provisions designed to integrate economies guided by nonmarket mechanisms into the global concert.

Suggested charter, as well as earlier and subsequent drafts, included provisions of direct relevance to countries with "a complete state monopoly of imports." It bears stressing that several other countries that later became STCs in the sense of the General Agreement did then actively participate in the negotiations. These include China, Cuba, Czechoslovakia, Poland, and Yugoslavia. But none was at the time an STC in the sense in which this systemic feature prevailed in the Soviet Union.

Given the then rapidly deteriorating political environment for postwar cooperation among the allies (Brabant 1987a, 22–30, 237–42), the Soviet Union absented itself from the trade deliberations and provided not an inkling of the sort of conditions it would find acceptable in order to partake in a global trading body. In the face of these realities, the paragraphs of *Suggested charter* dealing with STCs (see Gerschenkron 1947) were not actively negotiated after the London Conference. But some "bracketed" articles, meaning that parts of tabled provisions were discussed and not rejected out of hand, were still in the Geneva draft (see Restoration 1947, 582–6). Until the Havana Conference, key members of the negotiating teams had been prepared to deliberate over state-trading principles and practices, provided the Soviet Union joined in the deliberations (Kock 1969, 51).

The Havana Charter as it later emerged contained some stipulations on state trading that were embodied in part in the General Agreement (see p. 49). It was hoped, though, that the charter would otherwise prove to be sufficiently elastic to accommodate other economic systems and indeed that it would be flexible enough to facilitate eventual Soviet participation in the ITO. The charter was to form the framework and the ITO the forum to promote the codification of the common law of state trading. This would gradually reconcile the interests and purposes of STCs with those of countries that conduct their commerce through market-type instruments and institutions (Bidwell and Diebold 1949, 227). It was also implicit in the decision to reserve the eighth permanent seat of the Executive Board for the USSR.

As compared with the American hopes placed on elaborating a liberal trading world, the draft provisions for countries with an MFT were exceedingly tolerant of Soviet economic centralism. They took the MFT for granted and offered technical arrangements to align it with the principles of the ITO to ensure trade expansion and equal treatment. The key stipulation stated that the relevant STC:

> shall promote the expansion of its foreign trade with the other members in consonance with the purposes of this charter. To this end such member shall negotiate with the other members an arrangement under which, in conjunction with the granting of tariff concessions ... and other benefits ... it shall undertake to import in the aggregate over a period

> products of the other members valued at not less than an amount to be agreed upon. This purchase arrangement shall be subject to periodic adjustment.

These provisions specifically pertaining to the integration of economies guided by nonmarket mechanisms were carried over into the final draft of the Havana Charter, though the Soviet Union had not participated in the formal conferences and drafting sessions that preceded the adoption of the charter.

Anyway, because of Soviet reluctance to participate in any of the three postwar IEOs, whatever may have been the motive force behind the efforts to accommodate STCs tended to get blurred, or fully glossed over, in the General Agreement. This does deal with state trading (mainly article XVII). But these provisions are hardly germane to the practical, rather technical problems and policy concerns relevant to countries whose economy is organized chiefly along other than market criteria (see chapter 4). Before proceeding, it is useful to widen the perspective on the ITO in several respects.

5 Salient features of the ITO

A better understanding of the attempt to organize within the context of the ITO and the Havana Charter can be gained only if the purview of inquiry is not restricted to trade issues in the conventional sense. This wider scope will be particularly important to clarify the rationale behind the proposals advanced in chapter 5. As Margaret S. Gordon (1949, 242) noted in the late 1940s: "If we are to arrive at a fair evaluation of the ITO Charter, we must avoid the temptation to compare it with an ideal blueprint for world trade or to appraise its contents in one or two sweeping generalizations. Only a sober analysis of all the important provisions will yield any conclusive judgement on its value." This section summarizes the central objectives envisaged in the late 1940s, the salient features of the charter, and the major reasons for the ITO's early stillbirth – hence the rather tenuous foundations of the postwar ITS.

Envisaged objectives

As examined in section 1, the postwar deliberations around the ITS aimed at diverse goals. In the first place, US negotiators especially were bent on restoring their concept of a multilateral free trading environment with domestic markets globally interlinked mainly through *ad valorem* tariffs. The political concerns raised in this connection found their justification in part in the prevailing economic rationale on free commerce, although the very foundations of that country were laid through other means and the United States had earlier levied a prohibitively high tariff with the Hawley–Smoot Act of 1930. This stance argued that trade based on comparative advantage considerations that do not get blunted by interferences, such as tariffs and other instruments of commercial and foreign policy, contributes maximally to global welfare and in the process benefits each country, though not necessarily to an equal degree.

Secondly, participants in the debate were keenly interested in fostering such a multilateral trading world for a variety of reasons. Some were chiefly motivated by concerns about simply promoting efficient trade. Others were bent on managing the global economy. Their purview ranged over a wide spectrum of measures, including the national and international requirements to ensure full employment, rapid reconversion of the war economy and recovery to full employment in the civilian sector, the reanimation of international capital flows, support for global economic development, for example through private capital flows, and similar objectives.

Thirdly, an important feature of the coveted economic order was certainly universalism. Some sharing of responsibility for the management of the world economy would be entrusted to the community of nations as a whole, but particularly to the large economic and political forces. At least some of the participants in this part of the debate showed more than casual interest in coming to grips with distributive aspects of the economic development process, although equity considerations were not high on the policy agenda.

Finally, the debates were fueled to no small extent by the sentiment that an orderly trading system governed by widely accepted rules lessens the risks of trade wars and thus constitutes an essential ingredient of broader efforts to maintain durable peace, stability, predictability, and reliability in world affairs – international economic security, in short. As such, the tasks entrusted to the ITO would provide the capstone on earlier agreements, mainly those addressing balance-of-payments adjustment with the Fund, facilitating and complementing private capital investments with the Bank, and regulating commercial policy in the General Agreement.

Salient features of the Havana Charter

The ITO Charter deals with many aspects of "trade and employment." The charter contains 106 articles that range over practically every conceivable aspect of international economic relations not previously circumscribed by other agreements. In addition to elaborating provisions on commercial policy, which amplified the General Agreement, the charter dealt with employment, international investment, restrictive business practices, international commodity agreements, and the institutional infrastructure and management of the ITO.

No doubt, the central chapter of the Havana Charter focused on commercial policy. Its provisions included the basic commitment to the MFN principle and reciprocity anchored to tariff bargaining and the elimination of preferences. They extended to the rules governing the invocation of trade policy measures, such as national tax treatment, the valuation of goods for customs purposes, QRs, subsidies, antidumping and countervailing duties, and state trading. Of these, the commitment to tariff bargaining and the eradication of discrimination were central, in part because of the messianic nature of Hullian trade policies.

Against this backdrop, the elimination of the QRs that had become so pervasive in the 1930s ranked very highly among the priorities of the policy makers. In fact, this commitment paralleled the elimination of foreign exchange controls under the guidance of the Fund. It was also the item over which much bad blood was shed as countries fenced for exceptions to the elimination of QRs. In the end, the charter allowed them for balance-of-payments difficulties (similar to exchange controls in the context of the Fund), agricultural management schemes, intergovernmental commodity agreements, and programs of economic development. As a result, the only firm commitment of the charter was to the elimination of import quotas in lieu of tariffs purely for the protection of established industries. This was not a very powerful positive statement at the time. Nonetheless, in the long run this general prohibition could have become the cornerstone of much more liberal international trade arrangements.

It is worth pausing for a minute over the issue of economic development. This amounted in fact to the recognition that nations have a legitimate ambition to develop new industries, which, under certain circumstances, justifies resorting to restrictive measures to nurse such industries through their infancy; but such measures should not intolerably prejudice the established trading interests of other nations. The recognition that particular preferential arrangements might be required to assist industrialization and economic development more generally was a question on which it proved most difficult to reach consensus, particularly as it related to commercial policy (Condliffe 1950, 665). The item was adamantly defended by DEs and strongly contested by other negotiators. In fact, the DEs negotiated for months on having economic development and joint responsibility of developed and developing countries for fostering it proclaimed to be the ITO's primary objective (Gardner 1969, 365). But this failed.

Two further features of commercial policy need to be stressed. These were the commitment to the elimination of subsidies to foster exports *per se* and nondiscriminatory treatment, that is, the application of MFN. The first would be eliminated after a two-year transition period but with some exceptions for primary commodities. Exceptions to nondiscrimination were enshrined in order to accommodate certain existing preferential arrangements, including the UK's imperial preference and the limited types of new preferential arrangements permitted under the charter. Finally, the charter contained a number of other commercial policy provisions, including those on antidumping, customs valuation procedures, internal taxation of foreign products, and the like.

Taken together as a code, these provisions represented a comprehensive and fairly satisfactory international arrangement for preventing arbitrary, burdensome, and discriminatory restrictions on external commerce. Even though restricting governmental trade intervention, whose provisions on merchandise trade had earlier been further negotiated by a subset of countries into the General Agreement (see chapter 4), international trade could still have been influenced by operations emanating from private business agreements and international cartels. The charter sought to counter such undercutting of the coveted trade order by outlawing certain practices, similar to what was then in place in the United States under the Sherman Antitrust Act. As such, members were entitled to submit complaints to the ITO for investigation, recommendation for remedial action, and follow-up policy measures. Members were committed to legislating away certain practices, including price fixing, allocation of markets, restriction of production, and the like. There certainly was a high degree of optimism on the part of some observers, whose ambitions reached well into the realm of the impracticable. Thus, M. Gordon (1949, 247) argued for including a provision that would compel every member to have its nationals register "the terms of all international business agreements to which they are party."

The third substantive part of the charter was an attempt to come to grips with intergovernmental commodity arrangements. It aimed at stabilizing prices through the regulation of production, trade, and inventory policies. These at first sight would appear to conflict with the free trade spirit embodied in the prescriptions discussed earlier. However, it was recognized that under certain circumstances (for example, as a transitory mechanism, for some types of situations and without being unduly harmful to consumer interests) intergovernmental commodity agreements may be necessary.

The ITO was to explore all possible avenues of coping with particular maladjustments, including convening formal international commodity conferences.

Whereas, as noted, the major motivation on the part of the United States had been free multilateral trade, that on the part of UK negotiators was ensuring full employment. The fourth substantive part of the charter, therefore, deals with the relationship between employment and economic activity. In it, each member obligates itself to "take action designed to achieve and maintain full and productive employment and large and steadily growing demand within its own territory through measures appropriate to its political, economic and social conditions" (Havana Charter 1948). But there was considerable disagreement on the role of and the scope for macroeconomic policies in ensuring high employment levels and indeed in achieving coordinated international action to enhance employment and economic stability. Although the ITO's activities would help to attain this goal too, the trade organization itself would not seek to lay down rules and regulations regarding coordinated international actions. That activity would be delegated to EcoSoc, one of the UN's three subsidiary parliamentary organs (in addition to the Trusteeship and Security Councils).[16]

The charter also incorporated some stipulations on international capital movements, preferences for DEs, and fair labor standards. Regarding the latter, "unfair labor conditions," especially in production for export, create trading obstacles. Members therefore agreed to take action to eliminate such conditions and to cooperate in this regard with the International Labor Organization (ILO); trading disputes on account of alleged unfair labor conditions would have been dealt with by the ITO. Though the charter recognized the contribution of capital mobility to reconstruction and development, it also reserved to members the right to restrict the inflow of foreign capital and to set conditions for foreign investors. Members obligated themselves to consult and negotiate with a view to concluding bi- and multilateral agreements on foreign investment.[17] Finally, the charter would have permitted reciprocal trading preferences for DEs that are contiguous or located in the same geographical area. Other preferential arrangements, such as customs unions and free trade areas, including among noncontiguous DEs, could be envisaged but needed the ITO's approval.

Regarding preferential arrangements, the usefulness of customs unions and free trade areas was recognized. For that reason, the charter sought to minimize their adverse impacts, for example by requiring that such arrangements should not raise the general level of duties for third parties.

Moreover, the schemes instituted must be legitimate ones and the members thus inclined were obligated to submit interim agreements embodying a plan and schedule for transition to full customs-union status to the ITO. The latter would have the power to examine these intentions and evaluate their bona fides. If necessary, the ITO could require reformulation or even abrogation of the schemes.

The last substantive part of the charter is devoted to the relationship between trade and reconstruction and between trade and economic development more generally. The latter provisions had been included in the course of the negotiations to satisfy the demands of DEs, as related. The former entitled the war-devastated countries to exceptions from the ITO code during the transition toward economic normalcy. The ITO was to provide suitable technical and financial assistance to members to ensure that exceptions would not unduly harm other members and to arrange consultations directed at bi- and multilateral agreements regarding investment opportunities and security.

Finally, the charter dealt with the ITO's institutional setup, including its powers of decision making, which were limited to collecting information, carrying out studies or investigations, convening conferences, and making recommendations on matters within the ITO's competence. Complaints would be dealt with too, but the organization itself, strictly speaking, would have no power of enforcement. It could, however, release injured members from their obligations or concessions equivalent to the assessed harm inflicted by the culprit.

All in all, the charter had several strengths as well as major weaknesses. The first derived from the basic aims of instituting multilateral agreements. The second emanated essentially from the recognition of prevailing realities, politics in some member countries, and indeed shortcomings in trying to design a comprehensive legal code for a "new order" *ab ovo*. Nonetheless, the charter could have constituted a first, if somewhat experimental, step toward the development of a more satisfactory arrangement to govern international economic relations. Perhaps too much attention was then paid to the weaknesses of the Havana Charter, although it was recognized explicitly in the document that it was not to be a final, definitive document. The charter required that a general review be held after five years of experience and information gathering. On this basis, constructive amendments and possibly the elimination of some of the more onerous escape clauses could have been carefully considered.

Reasons for the ITO's failure

One may divide appraisals of the Havana Charter that greatly influenced the failure to ratify it into three groups. One centered around the clash of views between those who advocated "free enterprise idealism," as opposed to "socialist collectivism," and others who were essentially concerned with coming to grips with "realism" in economic and especially in trading conditions of a highly diverse set of countries. The first group of critics directed their objections chiefly to the many escape clauses and exceptions from the free trading system. These would have involved some degree of governmental interference and accommodation. The latter ranged from involvement in measures to maintain near-full employment levels, to stabilization of international commodity prices, abolition of cartels and restrictive business practices, and other measures (Diebold 1952, 17) that were unacceptable to US tastes for the market mechanisms and hence at times portrayed as "radical collectivism."[18]

The admonishment on behalf of US industrialists regarding the benefits of multilaterally free trade was an odd stance to take, for, if anything, these interest groups were "late converts to the principle of removal of trade barriers and controls" (Hoover 1949, 277). As is frequently the case with newly won converts, US entrepreneurial leadership tended to be exceedingly impatient with the new credo enshrined in the Havana Charter: they were unwilling to go along with anything other than the pure and simple removal of barriers and controls, but did not offer any plausible alternative to the ITO (Diebold 1952, 14, 22). The realists recognized an intermediate philosophy between the latter and "radical individualism." Their stance was to accept the centrality of market-determined price formation and entrepreneurial decision making as the foundation of the ITS. In addition, they were prepared to admit government interference as an exceptional method to maximize national income and ensure a more equitable distribution of income than would have been possible otherwise (Furth 1949). There was furthermore a group of skeptics about the wisdom of trying to move the world back to multilaterally free trade at any cost (Henderson 1949). Clearly, the short-lived experience with sterling convertibility from 15 July through 20 August 1947 (Mikesell 1947b, 73) foreshadowed the grave difficulties to be faced in restoring domestic and external equilibrium. These commentators found that the charter, as Henderson (1949, 605) put it, had been "wrapped up and swaddled in thick layers of exceptions and saving clauses, through which it may be hard to penetrate." He deemed this scheme clearly inferior to nationally oriented policies, in some cases tied in with bilateral trading arrangements (Ellsworth

1949, 1271). Of course, with British interests in mind, Henderson (1949, 611–12) felt that no "useful purpose can be served by a reduction of Imperial Preference in the altered circumstances of the present day" and recommended that the United States facilitate the reequilibration of the balance of payments by raising imports much faster than its exports. In this view, exchange-rate depreciation would not solve the problem of structural redirection of imports as the very adverse price experiences of the 1930s had clearly underscored.

Secondly, the political situation in the United States had taken a decisive turn for the worse. Foremost was the emergence of the Cold War and its repercussions on the internationalist outlook of US political leaders. As a result of the difficulties encountered in securing Soviet cooperation, for example, in the United Nations, in the Foreign Ministers' Conference, in the negotiations about peace agreements with former enemy countries, and in the postwar settlement of Eastern Europe, particularly Poland, the United States experienced a rapid decline in interest for multilateral solutions that it could not fully control. As an alternative, it resorted to economic cooperation within the provisions of the Marshall Plan and its outgrowth – the Organisation for European Economic Co-operation (OEEC), later rechristened Organisation for Economic Co-operation and Development (OECD). In addition to the Cold War, the new Administration under President Truman had to legitimize itself *vis-à-vis* Congress. Also the fear that the Soviet Union would simply mobilize its resources to aggrandize its imperial dreams of old loomed large.

Finally, the charter ran into trouble because of changes in the global setting. Had it been submitted in 1945–6, say in conjunction with the Articles of Agreement of the Bank and the Fund, it would have had a much better chance of being ratified. As Gardner (1969, xxxix) noted with respect to the Bretton Woods conference, "it would have been difficult, perhaps impossible, to have held [it] after the war. Not only would the wartime spirit of idealism and solidarity have been dissipated," but one would also have had to negotiate agreements that affected actually functioning markets.

In a world revolving around nation states, it would have been unwise in any case to anticipate governments remaining committed to a purely internationalist legal code. The ITO would in practice not have been able to force members to change their domestic policies. But it could have questioned such policies, clarified their positive and negative impacts for all members, and suggested remedial actions that could have led to consultations and discussions at the policy-making level and thus "contribute[d] substantially to the restoration of sanity in international economic relations" (Furth 1949, 255). Unfortunately, this "most ambitious attempt ever made to reach agreement on a comprehensive code of rules of international trade quietly ended in failure" (Diebold 1952, 2). It did so, in Diebold's words (1952, 37):

> because not enough people had confidence in the way it tried to bridge gaps between different concepts of the nature of the economic process, between the supposed interest of the United States and most of the rest of the world, and between faith and practice. The gaps are still there; they may narrow or widen; but a multilateral trading arrangement, covering most of the free world, cannot be successful – it can bridge them.

Admittedly, much was wrong with the ITO. For one thing, it did not distinguish sufficiently between the short- and the long-term ambitions of the organization and the policies to be pursued in its midst. The debate was also confounded by the mixture of so-called facts and opinions on international commercial policy and related efforts to buttress fast economic growth and full employment (Condliffe 1950, 614). By not sharply distinguishing between the feasible and the ideal and what could be obtained over time, postwar commercial and monetary policy deliberations proceeded in a sense at cross-purposes.

6 Toward a rationale for nonparticipation

As seen from the western side, the emphasis on trying to woo the Soviet Union into the international fold was partly genuine, partly naïve. As George Kennan (1969, 308), then at the US embassy in Moscow, observed in connection with the apparent unwillingness of the Soviet Union to adhere to the Bretton Woods institutions:

> It should be remembered that nowhere in Washington had the hopes entertained for postwar collaboration with Russia been more elaborate, more naïve, or more tenaciously (one might almost say ferociously) pursued than in the Treasury Department. Now, at long last, with the incomprehensive unwillingness of Moscow to adhere to the Bank and the Fund, the dream seemed to be shattered, and the Department of State passed on to the embassy, in tones of bland innocence, the anguished cry of bewilderment that had floated over the roof of the White House from the Treasury Department on the other side. How did one explain such behavior on the part of the Soviet government? What lay behind it?

This question has remained puzzling. The Soviet Union has never given an official explanation of why it ceased to participate in these and related negotiations. But it is relatively straightforward to conjecture about the most likely reasons that explain the decline of Soviet enthusiasm for international monetary cooperation and its subsequent extremely negative attitude toward the Fund. They can be grouped into political, organizational, and economic ones.

The most outstanding of the political difficulties was undoubtedly the emerging Cold War with its adverse climate for international relations. One should recall here Churchill's Fulton, MO address of 5 March 1946 – just three days prior to the Savannah, GA meeting of the Board of Governors of the Fund – and subsequent rhetoric, none of which was apt to reassure the Soviet Union at the time that the wartime spirit of cooperation was not quickly evaporating. By 1946, the "Diplomatic Battle for Europe," as Oliver (1975, 229) so aptly refers to the Cold War, was in full swing. This in itself had a number of political, strategic, and economic overtones that I shall not examine in detail.

The Soviet attitude transpired in part because of the USSR's failure to obtain a substantial recovery loan from the United States or the reparation payments it felt it had been promised by its wartime allies. These developments aggravated Soviet fears that by promoting freer trade and better investment opportunities the United States would solidify its *pax Americana* – the culmination of its aspiration to global political and economic hegemony (Mee 1984). Also, it had to insulate itself against a marked economic depression that it felt was bound to follow upon the war's end. Full adherence to the Havana Charter might also have jeopardized the increasingly tightening network of bilateral trade and payments agreements (BTPAs) with Eastern Europe and indeed the emergence of an economically integrated region in that part of Europe (Baran 1947). For example, the ITO's draft provision restricting the activities of state monopolies, on which more in chapter 4, would have conflicted with the operation of the joint-stock companies (JSCs) that the USSR had set up right after the war, mainly in the Eastern European countries that had sided with the Axis powers (Gerschenkron 1947, 630). These had been formed with local capital and assets captured or confiscated from the Axis powers or their collaborators during the war and were utilized as a crucial vehicle to steer economic policy in the former enemy countries. As such, the JSCs provided a key mechanism for the transfer of reparation payments to the Soviet Union. They also afforded the latter considerable latitude in directing economic policy in Eastern Europe. The notorious Trojan horse role of these JSCs is well known, though many details have never come to light. Finally, the Soviet Union may have felt that in a world with haves and have-nots, particularly after the devastation wrought by the war, nondiscrimination and reciprocity in trade were inappropriate principles.

The USSR probably also felt it had ample justification for refusing membership in the IEOs for organizational reasons. First, the proposed quotas in the Fund and the World Bank, and the corresponding votes, afforded veto power only to the United States. Gaining such a status had been an important objective of Soviet negotiations, for example over the United Nations. A second factor revolved around the required provision of economic information, particularly with respect to gold reserves and production. Even if the prospects of loans had been brighter, the need to divulge sensitive information could have been construed as unwelcome "interference" in Soviet domestic affairs. As the Polish delegate at Havana declared, his country did not sign the Havana Charter because the "main point of departure should have been what the Charter treated as exceptions" (quoted in Kock 1969, 55). He advocated, no doubt echoing the Soviet point of view, that the ITO should balance more equally the economic and political conditions of various countries. Of course, the fact that accession to the Fund was a precondition for entrance into the Bank – hence access to loans in which the Soviet Union was keenly interested – did not help matters. Finally, the entire aura of the organizations, wrapped as their debates and policies were in free market competition, proved to be repugnant to CPEs.

Perhaps a much more crucial reason for the lack of interest in participating in the BWS was economic, namely that in Soviet calculations the cost of Fund and Bank membership outweighed the benefit (Assetto 1988, 65). To understand the initial reaction of the CPEs it is useful to look at the objectives of the Fund and the Bank, and the possible interests of the CPEs in the technical aspects of the BWS. Some of these issues are clarified in the next two chapters. Suffice it here to put matters bluntly in a nutshell: the Fund then had little to offer to economies that had adopted comprehensive physical planning, adhered to strict commodity and currency inconvertibility, and practiced rigid bilateralism, and whose exchange rates were not real prices and served no substantive function.

No less important was the frustration incurred over obtaining reconstruction loans, which had been the primary motivation for Soviet participation at Bretton Woods, as World Bank resources were woefully inadequate to meet the challenge. The Soviet Union was keenly interested in securing substantial funds, including reparation payments and loans from the United States. When that threatened to founder, some interest was shown in the Bretton Woods institutions, but even that quickly dissipated. This stemmed in part from Soviet fears that lending by these institutions would be influenced by political considerations, particularly those that would blend with US precepts.

The Fund's principal purpose initially was to mobilize its resources for the stabilization of agreed-upon exchange rates with the objective of gradually eliminating foreign exchange controls for current-account transactions, promoting multilateralism, liberalizing capital flows, and similar developments that hinge on the existence of real markets. The comparatively small volume of trade of the CPEs and the fact that the bulk of it was conducted under reciprocal BTPAs left little room indeed for stabilization. This feature became very much stronger as traditional central planning was implanted throughout Eastern Europe by the end of the 1940s and commercial relations with MEs were being forcibly curtailed. Secondly, given the rapidly deteriorating east–west environment, the CPEs decided that it was not in their best interest to provide extensive economic intelligence to the Fund that would inevitably be disseminated on a more than trivial scale. Thirdly, they had no reason to subject their exchange regime and broader macroeconomic policies to Fund surveillance. Finally, though it was attractive to gain access to finance, this was obtainable only through Fund membership, for which the price to pay was probably deemed to be excessive.

Not to be forgotten was the circumstance that had led UK negotiators to explore various ways of fostering transatlantic cooperation: the prospect of a deep economic recession in the United States would work its way through the global economy, possibly entailing a repetition of the disastrous competitive devaluations and financial crises of the 1930s. Although Soviet observers did not quite see it the same way, they clearly expected the US economy at the war's end to be thrown into a deep recession for lack of effective civilian demand and to utilize the opportunities offered by its economic strength to conquer markets abroad, if necessary through a particular kind of hegemonic control (Varga 1947a, 1947b, 1947c). Although loaded by a degree of hyperbole, these Soviet attitudes, as reflected in Varga's work for example, also contained an underlying element of truth. The Soviet Union saw this deep recession in the United States largely as a confirmation of the impending crisis of world capitalism, from which it desired to distance itself (Varga 1947a, 1947b, 1947c; Voznesenskij 1948, 147–50).

7 The evolution of the CPEs in the international economy

With hindsight, World War II and its aftermath proved to have been an important watershed in profiling Eastern Europe internationally. Soon after the outbreak of the Cold War the CPEs severed nearly all contacts with international organizations in which MEs also participated. In the case of the most important operational organizations, this took the form of a formal withdrawal. In others, especially those with a more intergovernmental character (such as the GATT or the United Nations and its affiliated specialized agencies), membership was not relinquished altogether, though active participation in the deliberations of these organs or in the execution of their mandate ceased for a number of years. As a result, a constructive dialogue on east–west relations could not get off the ground. The CPEs chose this behavior and policy stance for a variety of reasons. In some cases, these organizations were not really suited to the political or economic purposes of the CPEs. In others, though they could have participated in a fruitful manner, the CPEs chose not to largely for political reasons.

A gradual *rapprochement* between DMEs and CPEs began in some cases as early as the mid-1950s. In others, the whittling down of what stood in the way of a more active involvement in the institutionalized forms of international economic affairs started later. By the mid-1970s, however, the majority of CPEs had jettisoned most of their earlier inhibitions on the principle of participation in IEOs, even those previously characterized as quintessentially capitalistic in nature. In the process, some became full members of these organs while others continued actively to reassess their positions; some even started to agitate for a reform of these organizations from without.

The degree of interest shown in particular for the multilateral financial organizations took a quantum leap with the recent world economic disturbances. Though well aware that more active intermeshing with such interdependent trading and financial regimes would not provide a panacea for their economic and other ills, some CPEs were hoping nonetheless, to derive important gains from membership. Of special interest in this evolving process of east–west economic relations are questions such as how the CPEs fit into, or could participate in, the international monetary, financial, and trading systems and how they have viewed the chief instruments associated with them. These systemic, behavioral, and institutional aspects will be explored in the next chapter.

2 Basic features of CPEs

An international economic order is about the organization of relations among sovereign states. To assess in principle the compatibility of various economic models in a given order, in addition to economics *per se* one must come to grips with historical, organizational, political, ideological, and other features of interstate relations. These metaeconomic factors may, and usually do, influence in a more than trivial way the key conditions that ensure smooth economic intercourse among nations, with their goals of enhancing ulterior policy ambitions. Such factors revolve around full employment, external payments equilibrium, and price and exchange rate stability; but they usually comprise other matters also.

I focus in this chapter on the organizational and economic aspects that determine compatibility of the CPEs within the global economic order, with a dual purpose. One is to underline the purely institutional and technical obstacles to fusing the CPEs into the established world economic order. These formed one of the central concerns in the decision of the Soviet Union and its allies to spurn the IEOs for a long time. I also clarify why slight modifications in the underlying philosophy of the monetary and trading systems could have measurably eased tensions in the postwar period. These issues remain pertinent even today, as explained in chapter 5. Carving an accommodative path could significantly enhance global economic security and thus further more predictable, stable growth policies throughout the world. The details of these elaborations are clarified in subsequent chapters. But they can be cogently introduced only if founded on a rounded picture of the institutional structures, economic policies, policy instruments, and behavioral features typical of the CPEs.

There is no such thing as *the* CPE system, although the traditional one developed in the Soviet Union and transplanted after World War II into Asian and Eastern European CPEs was initially quite homogeneous. Section 1 discusses the backdrop to the multiplicity of CPE "systems" and what this entails for their interaction with the global economy. Then I examine the key features of the traditional, highly regimented, and centrally managed CPE. The evolution thereof is sketched in section 3. The next section clarifies the trading and monetary regimes of the CPEs. Section 5 outlines key features of economic reconstruction or *perestrojka* currently targeted by the majority of CPEs. The tangents for the CMEA and hence the transforming trading and financial regimes are discussed in the final section.

1 The multiplicity of CPE systems

Since about the middle of this decade, most CPEs have announced intentions to introduce minor and major changes in their macroeconomic management policies, policy instruments, and associated institutions. In some, policy makers are already cementing in the first vestiges of far-reaching modifications, including those to socioeconomic policy broadly defined. Others are still not only in the process of conceptualizing the purposes to be served by these as yet incompletely defined changes, but are also designing the architectural nuts and bolts of the transition phase. Note, however, that countries such as Albania, Cuba, the GDR, North Korea, and Rumania do not intend to join this bandwagon. Actually, they have expressed more than once their antagonism to Soviet *perestrojka*, although recent events, for example in the GDR and Rumania, have been radically modifying this stand. Irrespective of the firmness of this policy commitment, however, some mutations are bound to emerge in time even in the most reform-averse country because modifications of decision making in key trading partners by necessity affect their external sector. In addition, the weight of the reforming countries is bound to exert pressure for adjustments within the CMEA framework, and hence on how nonreforming CPEs can interact in their primary markets. These matters are amplified in sections 4 and 6.

Though ongoing reforms call for a reassessment of the role of the CPEs in organized international relations, which I do in chapter 5, for a long time there has in fact not been a single planned environment whose compatibility with the core of IEOs could be tested. Social organs are by definition in flux. The CPEs form no exception to that rule if only because of the rapid sociopolitical and economic transformations expressly sought by their "vanguard" leadership. This applies notably to the diversity of reform concepts. It will therefore be useful first to define key notions, including economic reform, model, and mechanism.

Because of the CPE's organization and the prevailing socioeconomic precepts, which are deeply rooted in Marxist–Leninist ideology and outlook, a CPE reform is a complex phenomenon that tends to affect virtually all dimensions of society. Even its principal features are rarely restricted to economics, if only because modifications sought in economic behavior, for example through price and wage stimuli, cannot but spill over into social attitudes and actions more generally. In fact, virtually every single reform of the traditional CPE has been in response to acute social concerns and has altered social precepts. The two need therefore to be addressed holistically, although few CPEs are prepared to look at society as an organic whole and tailor reform programs accordingly. As a result, blueprints dealing with all of these aspects in a single, coherent framework are yet to be formulated. Although these systemwide ramifications of reforms are very important in the dynamics of the socialist society, I shall nonetheless chiefly address here the economic tangents of the evolving CPE.

In its most general connotation, an economic reform is a process aimed at enhancing the way in which resources are allocated with the goal of satisfying present and future, private as well as social, needs better than heretofore. As such, its features may range from the philosophy of development policies to economic institutions and technical guidelines for economic behavior. In this respect, it may be useful, even if only for heuristic purposes, to separate the envisaged development strategy from the economic model. Both ultimately derive from the metaeconomics of Marxist–Leninist precepts on the historical path to development, which has spawned a special doctrine on economic laws (see Brabant 1980, 63–9) that is critical in clarifying past CPE policies and interpretations.

Following the doctrinaire precepts emanating from the ideology of the economic laws of the socialist transition to communism, the initial development strategy adopted by socialist policy makers aims, among other things, at full employment, a rapid pace of socioeconomic growth, extensive industrialization as the foundation for steady economic development, and a substantial degree of domestic policy autonomy. The latter two, in particular, differentiate socialist growth policies from the development process in DEs. But there are, of course, many other differences between alternative roads to industrialization. The CPEs accord a pronounced priority role to selected industrial branches and policy makers mobilize material and human resources chiefly for rapid industrialization in breadth. Such objectives can be pursued with alternative policy instruments and institutions. For the traditional CPE, however, this process involves the creation of large-scale enterprises capable of capturing economies of scale and utilizing modern production technologies for "new" products. It deliberately disregards all but the crudest static scarcity indicators in reaching policy decisions about accumulation and investment; at any rate, such allocation criteria are at best accorded a secondary place in the formulation and implementation of policy. Furthermore, these decisions are carried out through the central planning process and its associated institutions and instruments rather than on the basis of real scarcity indicators and their associated policy instruments and institutions. The rationalization of this policy choice, in good measure, harks back to the doctrine on the labor theory of value and its ramifications in the socialist economy (Brabant 1987b, 13–33).

In consequence, a particular economic model was embraced in furtherance of rapid growth in breadth. When first introduced, this model consisted of the following: (1) central planning of nearly all economic decisions and strict central regulation of the decision-making role of economic agents; (2) nearly full nationalization of virtually all production factors, certainly capital, natural resources, and, in most cases, land (but with variations among the countries); (3) strict regulation of labor allocation; (4) collectivization of agriculture in combination with state agricultural enterprises; (5) a deliberate and pronounced disregard of indirect coordination instruments and associated policies and institutions in favor of directive planning in physical detail as the overwhelming form of steering resource allocation; (6) managerial autonomy highly circumscribed by central planning and by the controls exerted by local Party and, in most countries, also trade union interest groups; (7) the channeling of most economic decisions through a complex administrative hierarchy, which tends to handle matters rather bureaucratically; (8) in spite of central regulation and administration, a minimum of personal initiative is tacitly condoned to implement plan instructions at all levels of production and consumption, but this cannot be properly coordinated with overall plan intentions; and (9) rather rigid separation of the domestic economy from foreign economic influences.

Economic reform includes measures that modify one or more aspects of this economic model. It may be pursued also in conjunction with, or in response to, a shift in emphasis on development priorities, possibly involving a rounded reappraisal of the socialist development strategy. Such transformations usually entail some modifications in the bearings of economic rationality in the CPE context and how it is enforced. Obviously, it would be well beyond the confines of this chapter to clarify in detail the various shifts from the highly centralized to the market-oriented approach. The latter appears to be the current format envisaged by several CPEs. It is in this connection that the concept of economic mechanism *per se* has come into its own.

The economic mechanism is similar to what used to be referred to in the mainstream specialized literature on CPEs as "economic model." But it reaches well beyond that because it calls for the creation of new institutions and policy instruments either to replace or to complement the existing environment. Also, an economic mechanism as a rule incorporates more active monetary, financial, fiscal, trade, price, and income policies. Virtually all of these areas are allotted at best a neutral role under central planning in physical detail as a system-immanent feature. As such, an economic mechanism may be defined as an economic model that helps to allocate resources through indirect economic coordination instruments and institutions under the guidance of macroeconomic policies. The latter in turn depend on medium- to long-term structural transformations planned by central policy makers. Such macroeconomic planning usually accords much greater importance to foreign economic cooperation than prevails under the traditional economic environment. Although at that level trade policies attempt to foster decentralized decision making by foreign trade organizations (FTOs), economic reform does not usually envisage the wholesale introduction of foreign competition.

Because changes in the economic model must necessarily start from the policy instruments and institutions in place, an economic reform is an evolving process, even if it is introduced all at once as a comprehensive blueprint. Gradual maturation is required to formulate and anchor the necessary laws and regulations, and to elicit at least a minimum of attitudinal change in economic agents, partly in response to appropriate material and other incentives, so that their behavior can suitably be coordinated at the macroeconomic level. Thus, a transition from a situation characterized by pervasive central physical planning to one based on microeconomic accounting requires incisive adjustments in monetary policies, in the financial infrastructure (including the role of the central budget and the banking sector), and in the behavior of firms. All these shifts are to be enacted through formal laws that hopefully promote new managerial styles, shifts in worker attitudes, and changes in household and managerial behavior that cannot materialize overnight. To appreciate how this can be ushered into the existing CPE, it is necessary to examine in some detail the key features of the original CPE economic system.

Before doing so, it may be useful to digress briefly and explain what I mean here by "rationality" in alternative social settings. This is particularly important as the alleged degree of "price rationality" – a shorthand for all indirect policy instruments that coordinate economic decisions – accounts for perhaps the most conspicuous substantive difference between a CPE and an ME, and indeed the evolving CPE types. Many of the divergences in the role of rationality in alternative economic systems arise for systemic, institutional, and policy reasons. Barring unintentional errors on the part of planners, prices in the CPE certainly have not been administered arbitrarily in the sense that they have been selected randomly, for instance. Quite the contrary: fiat prices have performed functions that form an integral part of the logic of the development objectives adopted by socialist planners and their political and bureaucratic mentors. As such, centrally administered prices in a CPE have had a rationality of their own that differs palpably from the ME stereotype.

Price rationality in a CPE must therefore be appraised against the background of the economic aims, development conditions, social priorities, economic mechanisms, or other features that set apart a typical CPE from a standard ME. Of course, this cannot possibly mean that all prevailing price relations in a CPE should automatically be declared rational. It does suggest, however, that it could be utterly irrational to transplant the price structures and mechanisms of any economic system whose policy aims and development conditions are at marked variance with the ambitions of a socialist economy. It also suggests that the "environment" should be fully heeded when evaluating how good price systems are or in what ways they could be suitably modified with a view to foster *prevailing* development goals.

2 Basic features of the traditional CPE

Key characteristics of the prototype economic model and development strategy were specified above, but some need to be amplified for future reference.

The first-generation strategy of socialist economic development

A growth strategy is a complex of measures to ensure resource allocation with a view to attaining one or more long-term development objectives. Excepting the immediate postwar period, when most energy and time were devoted to economic reconstruction and the consolidation of the supremacy of Communist Party rule, the quintessential socialist development strategy has as its central aim the industrialization in breadth of mostly backward, agrarian economies. This objective was to be implemented by manipulating key policy instruments, by transforming the economic institutions in place, and by prescribing some behavioral rules that together make up the model as defined. Eastern European development processes until the early 1960s were overwhelmingly anchored to an economic policy in pursuit of forced industrialization. This played a crucial role, even to such an extent that decision making about the overall allocation of resources was almost exclusively geared to the priority role of industry.

Socialist economic development has as its prime objective the elaboration of a more or less autarkic economic complex. Autarky here is not synonymous with complete severance of all foreign contacts, although at one time a narrowly defined self-sufficiency was certainly immanent in the socialist concept of how best to allocate scarce resources. The pivotal focus of economic policy is the creation of a well-balanced, diversified industrial economy that can function relatively independently of business fluctuations and other disturbances propagated from abroad. Such an ambitious development goal is predicted on the establishment of the prototype economic complex borrowed from the Soviet Union. Using the "laws of socialist development" as inspiration or rationalization after the fact, the key goals of this strategy are centrally steered, balanced growth, primarily in extending industrialization in breadth, to complete in record time the material–technical foundations of socialist society.

A central place in the socialist growth strategy is reserved for amassing production factors in priority sectors and appropriating most of the current "surplus value" not for present consumption but for the financing of the expansion of selected production sectors, at the expense of agriculture and services in particular. This strategy also implies that consumption levels should not be raised by as much as productivity gains could warrant, which is reinforced through the model. As evinced during the early stages of the industrialization drive in virtually all CPEs, levels of living of the population could even decline for a few years.

The traditional economic model

A growth strategy must be buttressed by an economic model. In the case at hand, the model consists of a combination of institutions, policy instruments, and micro- and macroeconomic behavioral rules that help to implement planned, if not outright forced, industrialization. The behavioral prescriptions are by definition normative and sanctioned as such. As noted, the traditional economic model is dominated by a hierarchical planning and management system. Decision-making authority is essentially vested in the center of national power to ensure a close interrelationship between political and economic functions.

The key features of the traditional socialist model were introduced in section 1. To understand the potential incompatibilities between the CPE and the international economic order erected after World War II, however, some of these characteristics need to be clarified briefly.

Comprehensive central planning This is perhaps the most critical element of the traditional economic model. Planning means selecting development targets and allocating resources to fulfill those aims as well as possible. In the traditional CPE, the planning instruments and objectives are determined by a select circle of Party members, especially the Politbureau, on behalf of the Communist Party as society's vanguard. Resources are essentially allocated by central fiat. However, not all plans are drawn up by one central administration. This would have been impossible in such a vast country as the USSR. It would also have been organizational nonsense to plan local produce, for example, solely from the center. Nonetheless, the fiat system does indicate that all *Gosplan* offices at lower rungs of the planning hierarchy depend on the central office and cannot in principle autonomously resolve allocative matters.

Production and distribution of critical goods and services are planned in physical detail and thus circumscribe other economic transactions. The plan endeavors to formulate instructions so that they leave no alternative to their execution. The objective is to ensure a close association and a particular interrelationship between political and economic functions. For that reason, the plan assigns producing units mandatory targets pertaining to inputs, outputs, prices, wages, capital allocation, and other aspects of what would normally be within the compass of entrepreneurial behavior. In other words, questions concerning what is to be produced, how production is to be organized, what inputs are to be used, and so on are, in principle, settled by plan norms and not by the foresight, risk taking, and creative innovation of an entrepreneurial élite. Moreover, the latter's initiative and leadership, if present, are not to impinge on the priority of physical yardsticks.

Needless to say, the real world of production and consumption differs substantially from this ideal paradigm. For one thing, conscious human activities cannot be reduced to the simple act of pulling a lever. Some scope for decision making needs to be reserved for economic agents because the planning center cannot possibly steer the economy in all its details. Even if this omniscience is not already fictitious at the outset of socialist planning, the appropriate functioning of an increasingly complex economy on the basis of coordinated directives and regulators demands that modifications be introduced. In fact, its compelling logic as a rule emerges very soon after the creation of the traditional CPE, if only to come to grips with uncertainty in economic decisions.

Apart from the uncertainty associated with the existing or rapidly growing complexity of steering an economy, planning is by definition a stochastic process if only because of the difficulties inherent in forecasting accurately all the complex interrelationships of an economy. Some sectors, including international trade and agriculture, are by their nature unpredictable. The specification of their activity parameters depends on events that are largely beyond the scope of the information at the disposal of central planners and, moreover, beyond their control. Such uncertainty has to be mitigated in time either by introducing a flexible type of planning (such as continuous planning) or, more likely, by *ad hoc* solutions formulated by microeconomic agents.

Because the lower tiers of the planning hierarchy, including the final producer and consumer, may harbor other preferences (such as private income considerations or the promotion of local activities) than those of central policy makers, their decision-making sphere coincides with the center's only by fluke. As a rule, therefore, the plan eventually has to be supplemented with proper criteria for guiding the decisions of economic agents.

Efficiency indicators in resource allocation The second crucial feature of the model is that technical rules on static economic efficiency are rather primitive and, moreover, passive. The theory of planning generally crystallized around quantity calculations, as distinct from value planning. Ideological and historical precepts as well as economic backwardness, exiguous entrepreneurial talent, and the strong preference for extensive industrialization all contributed to this choice. In consequence, the dynamic results of economic expansion were considered far more important than static efficiency indicators.

From the beginning of socialist economic organization, it has been accepted as axiomatic that socialism implies: (1) the effective control of the economy, in particular of productive resources, by society in pursuit of its objectives by appropriate policy instruments and associated institutions; and (2) the planned steering by the state of the course of economic life. Without this being necessarily well articulated, the accepted premise of traditional planning has been that tools of indirect regulation are not dependable. Resource allocation in a CPE therefore proceeds largely through other signals, some of which may be concealed as a result of the discretionary authority of the political leadership in the selection of priority targets, the allocation of cheap but rationed credit and critical primary inputs, and the regional allocation of resources.

Indirect coordination instruments and institutions The traditional CPE operates with primitive and passive market-type instruments and institutions. Many features typical of MEs are simply usurped by central planning. Price policies provide a case in point of the subordination of value criteria to physical targets. Prices are traditionally calculated by the center on the basis of average sectoral cost without making due allowance for capital and land scarcities. They are generally held unchanged for long periods of time, not necessarily because price theory calls for such stability (Brabant 1987b, 34–62). Inadequate information at the disposal of the center to set correct product-specific prices for all goods and services, the price stability cherished by planners to facilitate plan implementation and guide consumer behavior, sociopolitical considerations in determining prices that are often conflictual and resolved *ad hoc*, and lack of feedback from either the production or the consumption side all lead to the ossification of prices at their "historical" level.

The deliberate choice to underplay value planning through the price mechanism was carried over to nearly all familiar market-type instruments and institutions. In fact, the organization of the economy and economic policy were simply to enhance the realization of priority goals expressed mostly in physical terms. Other policy instruments were not to interfere with the plan's execution, although they did to some extent. Because of the critical importance of pricing in resource allocation, further details are considered in the last subsection.

The CPE's fiscal policy is almost exclusively concerned with indirect taxation (that is, turnover taxes) to ensure some equilibrium between demand and supply of consumer goods. Incomes in sectors other than agriculture, handicrafts, and some services are essentially limited to wages and bonuses, with little variation among workers or correlation with effective productivity levels. Wage rates are not, of course, identical throughout the economy. But the differentiation is rather narrow, particularly within given sectors. In cooperative agriculture, incomes depend on nominal profits derived from assigned output and sales at administratively set procurement prices. Additional revenues are obtained through sales on free peasant markets and the initially highly confined second economy. Both are regulated indirectly by the center.

Based overwhelmingly on the "real bills" doctrine, which posits that credit should reflect real flows, in which sense it becomes "productive" and hence conducive to monetary equilibrium, monetary policy in the traditional CPE is, at best, passive. Accordingly, loans are extended for well-specified purposes, granted for fixed periods of time, secured by real assets, repayable, and centrally regulated or even administered on a planned basis. At the macro level, this model operates with a monobanking system. Money plays a passive role, particularly in the production sphere. Funds are simply made available to facilitate the allocation of resources previously earmarked in physical terms in the plan. Financial assets for households are generally limited to cash, lottery tickets, savings deposits, and occasionally government or enterprise bonds. Government bonds, especially, are often disposed of with only minimal regard for consumer sovereignty. Financial assets of firms are as a rule limited to bank deposits. Fiscal policies are subordinated to the general aims of the plan and social precepts on income differentiation, profits, and price regulation. Most enterprise profits and losses are ventilated through the central budget. Managerial and worker incentives seek to enhance the fulfillment and overfulfillment of quantitative production targets.

Credit policy is geared toward facilitating the implementation of investment targets chosen by the center, regardless of how these decisions are formulated. Capital investments, usually financed through the budget, which collects for this purpose virtually all enterprise profits, are undertaken with minimal regard for macroeconomic efficiency and no scarcity levies are applied. A more active monetary policy to equate consumer revenues plus net changes in private savings with the value of the amount of consumer goods earmarked for distribution during the plan period is at times instituted to counter severe inflationary pressures.

Foreign trade and payments regime Arguably the outstanding feature of the CPE economic model, at least for the purpose of this study, is its foreign trade and payments regime. Foreign trade does not play an important role either in the determination of the development strategy or in its implementation. An integral element of the CPE model is the more or less complete disjunction of the domestic economy from external influences, especially in the microeconomic sphere, by means of special instruments and institutions. This choice might have been variously inspired by the fact that an ambitious growth path must be trodden without taking into account all relevant internal and external market conditions; policy makers do not make use of sophisticated plan techniques and instruments to guide and control plan execution by indirect means; and growth targets are not selected on the basis of real opportunities. Interaction with other economies is compressed to the minimum still compatible with the overall development goals centered on rapid industrialization. However, for economies that cannot be autarkic because of size or resource endowment, severing domestic decision making from world market criteria has important drawbacks.

The particular configuration of the institutions and mechanisms selected for conducting trade was a direct consequence of the failure to adopt a regional economic policy in the late 1940s (see Brabant 1989a, 29–42). Instead of anchoring economic development to an internally consistent, comprehensive CMEA-wide program, each CPE sought to isolate its national economy from the rest of the world, thereby protecting itself against foreign events and reducing the interaction with other economies – including other CPEs – to the minimum still compatible with rapid industrialization. An MFT was expressly instituted to neutralize all influences from abroad, whether positive or disruptive, and thus to further domestic policy autonomy.

External economic relations do not form a coherent component of the CPE. Organizationally, there is virtually complete disjunction between the domestic economy and economic activities abroad. This is accomplished by the "nationalization" of the foreign trade and exchange systems (Grote 1981; Konstantinov 1984). The former resides under the Ministry of Foreign Trade, which is in principle in charge of the MFT. Though the latter is entrusted with all foreign economic transactions, it usually delegates the authority to trade to FTOs. As a rule, these are organized by broad economic sectors separately for exports or imports; they may even be assigned by trade-partner grouping, such as socialist and others. These organizations purchase domestic products destined for export and sell earmarked imports at domestically prevailing prices. Differences between domestic and trade prices in domestic currency are offset through what is called the price-equalization account, a component of the central government budget.

Trade decisions in the CPE depend on economic and other factors. Trade serves chiefly as a means to fulfill the overall development goals. The planning of the level and composition of trade, as of other economic activities, is largely intermeshed with the overall system of material balances. Whether to import or to produce domestically is usually resolved by considering domestic availability and the need to pay for imports. In any case, the central planner exhibits only a marginal interest in reaping the potential benefits of export-led growth or in minimizing the real economic cost of the preferred import substitution. The technique of material balances might be highly useful in ensuring that physical demand and supply in the economy even out. But it is hardly conducive to the exploitation of trade opportunities. Planning the geographical distribution of earmarked trade is largely a function of the home economy's need for noncompeting imports and their availability in alternative markets, export pressures, and BTPA commitments embedded in material balances. Comparisons of prevailing prices as basic inputs into trade decision making are rarely undertaken, as the price-equalization mechanism siphons off (covers) apparent trade profits (losses). Such differences are inconsequential for subsequent allocation policies. This near irrelevance of prices applies, of course, also to the official exchange rate.

Trade is by definition a sector that eludes the complete control of one planning center and can hardly be managed in quantitative terms only. To gain greater stability in the domestic economy, the CPEs nevertheless try to forecast trade flows as accurately as possible. But not all activities abroad are predictable. Born out of necessity in the immediate postwar setting, detailed *ex ante* BTPAs at relatively stable, if artificial, prices suited the administrative planning system fairly well. It also facilitated the implementation of one or another CPE's political aspirations, whose realization would have been much more chancy with multilateral trade and payments agreements (MTPAs) or multilateralism more generally.

To the extent that trade cannot be forgone, the CPEs insulate domestic processes from direct interaction with agents abroad. In the real sphere, this is accomplished by keeping producers and consumers away from their counterparts abroad, with the FTOs acting as buffers. Indirect influences are minimized as well. Actual trade events can impact on the domestic economy, but usually not through price pressures because domestic prices are set autonomously. The nominal gains and losses from trade are simply absorbed by fiscal means. But there are possibly macroeconomic impacts of trade developments. A deviation from planned import cost and export return, if accommodated, affects the disposable budget, and ultimately consumer incomes, as well as the foreign exchange situation (see Brabant 1987a, 110ff.; Lawson 1988; Wolf 1988). Planners attempt to neutralize the impact of this perturbation by sterilizing trade results that deviate from planned magnitudes. Alternatively, they offset trade gains or losses by varying other budgetary expenditures or they postpone adjustment until the next plan permits policy makers to replenish foreign exchange reserves or service the foreign debt incurred in the process of weathering the disturbance. This potential indirect influence does not play an overriding role in decision making, however, because the bulk of trade is in any case regulated through comprehensive BTPAs and rather autonomous prices.

A crucial implication of this trade model has been that macroeconomic decision makers have been unaware – at any rate, far less than fully in the picture – of the real economic cost of their import-substitution policies. From the planner's point of view, this does not matter much so long as autarky reigns supreme and domestic price autonomy is adhered to. However, if external processes supplement domestic availabilities, it is not quite clear how best to dovetail trade opportunities with the rigidly centralized domestic economic relations. Once a more active trade policy is to be explored, this formidable drawback of the existing trade model receives top priority on the policy agenda.

There is, of course, a microeconomic equivalent to the lack of interest in trade results *per se* by central decision makers: economic agents remain ignorant of the true scarcity cost of availabilities and requirements abroad. This assumes particular importance once the potential for extracting the surplus from the traditional sector nears exhaustion and policy options in the CPEs come to parallel those typical of DMEs. In particular, the CPEs stand to benefit, politically as well as economically, from improved allocatory efficiency and from reduced imbalances, which would make it possible to relax the coercive redistribution imposed by the state.

Pricing policies in the traditional CPE It is against the above backdrop on the aims of central planning and the overriding policy priority of rapid, forced industrialization in breadth that several features of price policies in CPEs need to be rationalized. First, a relatively autonomous three-tier system of producer (or wholesale), agricultural procurement, and consumer (or retail) prices emerges as the familiar trireme of socialist price policies. There are, of course, other prices, such as for handicraft products and in free peasant markets, as well as related scarcity indicators, such as interest and exchange rates. I lump all of these elements together under the price label because none has ever adequately reflected prevailing scarcities. Secondly, each price regime is steered separately through institutional and policy choices. Finally, as noted, domestic price processes are insulated from external trade. The disparity between prices paid by the state to the producer and prices paid by the consumer is very considerable. It derives not only from commercial margins and the government's fiscal needs. One price system is in fact largely independent of the other. This divorce is maintained because the price regimes are modified according to criteria deemed suitable to reach specific objectives either in the social sphere or in the sphere of plan formulation, implementation, and control.

Prices of producer goods are based on some average cost figures of the past that are usually justified by reference to socially necessary labor expenditures.[1] In the CPE environment, this structural adjustment process is controlled by plan iterations that in principle are designed to yield an efficient solution. The wholesale price of consumer goods is normally set after the imposition of the turnover tax or the deduction of the subsidy from the producer price. The latter is the aggregate of the average branch cost of labor and capital as well as a profit markup. The industry price is derived from the sum of the producer price and any applicable tax or subsidy. The wholesale price is the industry price augmented with the wholesale margin, including a wholesale profit markup. Finally, the retail price equals the wholesale price plus a retail margin, which also includes a profit markup. Note that prices of agricultural products and foodstuffs more generally may be set differently, depending on the organization of agriculture, the specific goals the government intends to pursue through its agricultural procurement, and the planning center's influence over free peasant markets.

Because average branch production costs constitute the core of all price computations, how these are assessed is crucial for how "informative" these administered prices can be. The basic approach is to distribute overall branch costs of live and embodied labor plus some standard markups over total branch output. As pure Marxian value prices, the latter should generate overall surplus value sufficient to fund the reproduction process in the aggregate. But this is not necessarily the sole preoccupation of planners.

A defect of traditional pricing in CPEs in that respect has been the relative disregarding of an appropriate scarcity cost of land, capital, and nonreproducible natural resources – initially largely for doctrinaire reasons. Similarly, the true domestic cost of imported intermediate goods is rarely fully assessed in the computation of domestic prices. This misconception of the economic composition of costs leads in particular to a significant downward bias in the wholesale price of commodities with very little transformation relative to that for processed goods, manufactures in particular. The chronic undervaluation of goods with a large natural-resource content is characteristic for a whole range of scarce, hence valuable, industrial primary products, fuels, and agricultural products (Petrakov 1986, 1987).

Because average production costs are inferior to marginal costs with an upward-sloping supply curve for the branch as a whole, the pricing rule in a CPE suggests that there are always firms that lose money and others that gain. This occurs not simply as a transitional phenomenon but as a process immanent in the logic of the traditional CPE. As a result, there is a continual redistribution of value added in each production sector, which may be perfectly rational in the CPE context. Yet price equalization is not a convincing justification for the widespread redistribution of value added among sectors so typical in the traditional CPE. Neither can it explain the need to manipulate price levels and relative prices with a view to generating adequate means to finance accumulation.

As a matter of socialist policy, prices of consumer goods are normally fixed in such a way that a reasonable balance is struck between supply and demand; feedback from prices has, therefore, invariably been left to the discretion and ingenuity of production managers. Once set, price overhauls occur at long intervals – at least the medium-term plan period – and even then they do not normally encompass all individual prices. Even on the free market, particularly in peasant outlets, prices can only marginally influence production. As a result, such prices may exhibit considerable fluctuations due to seasonal variations and governmental supply policies.

Wholesale and retail prices are normally separated by turnover taxes, budget subsidies, and trade markups or discounts (including normal insurance, handling, and transportation charges). Of course, each country leaves room for negotiating the actual price effect of product quality and modernity, which further compounds the precarious relationship between retail and wholesale prices. In the worst case, there is no longer any readily discernible parametric relationship between the two price levels and their dynamics over time.

Consumer-price stability has been a solid constant of the credo of socialist policy makers and their ideological exhortations, at least until fairly recently. In fact, Marxist economic theory as interpreted by Soviet policy makers during the early phases of revolutionary industrialization posited that prices should exhibit a steadily declining trend because the socially necessary labor inputs shrink as a result of technical progress, the growth of labor productivity, and rising efficiency in the exploitation of the other means of production (see Miastkowski 1980, 896–7). In the initial euphoria of socialist construction, it was even argued that this tendency should also surface in pricing the reciprocal relations of the CPEs (see Kohlmey 1955, 267–8). For decades, the population in most of these countries has been coached to believe that price stability holds under socialism. Furthermore, low prices for essentials and high prices for all but a few key manufactured goods have been upheld only because of the government subsidy-cum-retail tax policies. As a result, consumers in recent years have been very reluctant to tolerate any retail price change.

As experience has demonstrated, the centralized economic model was useful for carrying out a consistent, rapid, and radical transformation of a relatively backward economy into an industrial society. It allowed the CPE to accelerate economic growth, to transform major segments of the structure of its economy, and to improve levels of living by overcoming various obstacles to steady growth. These included an unstable regional or global economic environment, initially domestic strife over sociopolitical organization, inexperienced management, a labor force unaccustomed to the industrial production mode, a burdensome agrarian overpopulation, and other impediments. But the centralized model is less suited to ensure steady growth in a moderately to highly diversified industrial economy that can no longer extract the desired output increments chiefly from the addition of primary factors to the production process.

3 Reforming the traditional CPE

Any discussion of economic reform has to heed the circumstances in which the CPE arose and the particular ideology embraced in the process. Given that the current cycle of broad-based economic restructuring is by no means without precedent, a brief review of economic reform, particularly its external features, is in order. Because I cannot here discuss individual reforms, it is useful to have some time perspective. The core of the traditional CPE, as summarized, applied to virtually all countries under consideration from the late 1940s at least through the early 1960s. Since the convulsions of the mid-1950s, however, there have been nearly continuous modifications in the traditional economic model. These may take on major or minor dimensions. Minor modifications are usually introduced to fine-tune certain production, distribution, consumption, income, or trade regulators without substantively changing the basic features of the model in place. Major changes in the economic model signal economic reform.

But there is no neat distinction in practice between the two. In fact, they may occur simultaneously. Even when reform can be unambiguously identified, it is a considerable simplification to speak of the first or second wave of economic reforms or to associate a reform with any particular date without making it crystal clear what precisely is meant. Three generic types may suffice to set the stage for a discussion of the changes in the CPEs since the weakening of the highly centralized model: (1) the selectively decentralized model that was aimed at in the 1960s, though there were striking differences among the reform blueprints; (2) the modified centralized model that came about after the reform attempts of the 1960s were reversed or interrupted, chiefly in the early 1970s; and (3) the decentralized model currently envisaged in several CMEA members.

Selectively decentralized economic model

Most policy makers as a rule realize relatively quickly that the extensive growth strategy eventually needs to be replaced by one that stimulates factor productivity. Designing the proper model not only for the intensive growth phase, but especially to facilitate the smooth transition to that new model, has been a much more arduous assignment, however. Various attempts were launched in the late 1950s and throughout the earlier part of the 1960s. Though these national attempts were anything but uniform, for expository purposes the experiences can be summarized under the second form of the CPE economic model.

Various circumstances induced the traditional CPE, starting with the second half of the 1950s, to seek broad changes in its managerial and incentive systems. One key motivation was the growing complexity of detailed physical planning for a fast-maturing economy and considerable shifts in the external environment. Some policy makers also found themselves in agreement with the proposition that strictly centralized physical planning is not really indispensable to support the development strategy. The selectively decentralized economic model exhibits in some respects fundamental transformations in the organization, the infrastructure for decision making, the habitual policy instruments, and some of the supporting institutions of the highly centralized economic model.

Reforms in this context therefore focused almost exclusively on a more pragmatic division of administrative and economic duties between the center and local planning tiers. Changes were sought to activate an enterprise policy that could facilitate local decision making on the basis of cost–benefit analyses and in recognition of market preferences, especially with regard to foreign economic interaction. But the basic philosophical precepts on the regulation of economic development to which the centralized model was originally anchored, including the broad goals of extensive growth and the domestic core of the traditional economic model, are kept intact. In that sense, the selectively decentralized model aims largely at administrative streamlining.

As a rule, central planning and its administrative machinery are retained. Some decision-making responsibilities are delegated to associations of firms in a given branch or to regional planning bodies; the devolution may even extend to individual enterprises. In any case, the latter can now influence the formulation or the implementation of the central plan. The number of directive plan indicators is generally significantly reduced. Gross output measures are replaced by other control levers such as sales, net output, profits, net export revenues, and so on. Material incentives are attached to other plan targets and, in some cases, formally to actual values of the aforementioned success indicators through a variety of norms that specify the permitted level of incentives associated with a particular magnitude of the chosen success indicators. The latter are in principle set annually for each economic agent through a complex administrative decision process, basically for lack of a flexible price system. Without it, the actual accounting indicators of economic performance cannot reliably reflect the appropriate scarcity magnitudes.

Almost without exception, in the course of the 1960s, firms were absorbed in or brought under the authority of much larger economic associations. Devolution emerged in the sense that ministries or central administrators no longer vied to determine enterprise policy unilaterally. The associations were invested with the responsibility of guarding the "social interest" of the firm. But the separate units obtained greater latitude in the formulation of an appropriate enterprise policy. The tasks of the associations consisted not only in promulgating measures to facilitate attainment of the centrally prescribed targets, but also in working out at the lower planning levels some of the norms previously dictated by fiat from above.

The logical outcome of the most determined reform, had it been carried to fruition, would have enabled central planning to guide and control microeconomic decision making by indirect means. Also, by disengaging itself from some of the detailed chores of instructing production units, the central planning board was henceforth expected to formulate a better selection of strategic decisions on the CPE's future. Enterprise activity would proceed chiefly on the basis of selective indirect coordination instruments within the framework of medium- to long-term socioeconomic development goals. Detailed prescriptions for how much of what the individual firm should produce with given resources were to be replaced by genuine enterprise decisions. These were to be guided by qualitative and quantitative macroeconomic policies so that the center could ensure that the gap between the precepts underlying the central plan and the motivation of agents entrusted with day-to-day local planning and decision making would not become an abyss. There might have been some continuing need for the associations but their role in formulating enterprise policy and appraising their performance would by necessity shrink ultimately to the purely administrative intermediation between the center and autonomous economic agents.

When economic decisions are no longer the exclusive prerogative of central planners, the task of coordination becomes more urgent and complicated in comparison with simply dovetailing physical yardsticks. One of the key elements here is the improvement of relative prices (including, as noted, interest rates, exchange rates, rents, capital levies, and so on) which began to be envisaged in the mid-1960s. The ultimate goal has been to establish linkages among the various domestic price tiers and also between trade and domestic wholesale prices, as discussed. But a price overhaul is by no means the exclusive focus of the coordination instruments to be adjusted. Extensive use of selective income, fiscal, and credit policies that aim at inducing firms and households to act in accordance with overall plan objectives was to be fostered too, although in this model authorities cling to direct control over key economic processes.

This is not really surprising, owing to the situation upon which indirect instruments and their underlying institutions are grafted. As a result, even in the most market-minded CPE, the envisaged selectively decentralized model typically entails significant, if perhaps concealed, elements of nonprice resource allocation. These may be intended as transitory elements, but subsequent events tend to inhibit the removal of the nonprice allocation criteria as originally envisaged. Furthermore, even after completion of the transition period, the social preferences of the ruling political and administrative élites continue to be accorded a disproportionate weight.

For example, credit and interest-rate policies in the selectively decentralized model are intended to guide the allocation of capital funds. Instead of gratis budgetary appropriations, a greater role is reserved for banks, where individual firms can procure loans to finance improvements in their production capacity and where consumers can obtain temporarily the means to purchase durable goods. Bank financing remains closely supervised by central authorities, however. The interest-rate policy associated with this devolution of financial policies was to guarantee greater economic rationality in the allocation of investment funds. Key investment decisions, such as the establishment of new factories and their financing, were to remain the exclusive prerogative of the central authorities, however. None of the reforms envisioned the creation of autonomous financial markets in which local or foreign agents could mobilize voluntary savings.

Firms obtain more authority, though by no means the exclusive right, to determine premiums, basic salary scales, the hiring and firing of personnel, and so on, to foster productivity. Exclusive authority cannot be delegated to them because the objective of full employment and the social aims of socialism remain vital elements of overall policies. Instead of many detailed prescriptions with regard to employment and wages, there is a tendency to confine controls to a few norms and indirect regulators. But this is not a linear, unidirectional process for it is interfered with and, after some experimentation, abrogated altogether.

In the traditional CPE, the firm controls profit only by reducing nominal production costs below the planned level, provided entrepreneurs behave as postulated by the center. With the advent of the reforms, however, firms begin to be entitled to influence costs directly through a more careful selection of inputs and suppliers, by producing according to market demand, and, in some cases, by using their authority over price formation. Profit is slated to become a more meaningful category, especially to determine premiums and social benefits to workers, to provide for self-financing, and to guide entrepreneurial behavior.

Perhaps the most pivotal of the instruments to be enhanced when planners decide to devolve decision making to the lower planning tiers is price determination. Establishing wholesale and retail prices that are indicative of relative scarcities prevailing in the economy, relative to both domestic and worldwide indicators, may act as the fulcrum for reforming the entire economic mechanism. Three components of such a transition placed in its proper institutional context need to be stressed for liberalization should not be equated with freely fluctuating prices: loosening the stickiness of the price regime, the information content of fiat prices, and the linkup between domestic and trade prices. In fact, prices in such a partially decentralized CPE can assume one or more of the following three functions: (1) an accounting tool for aggregating physical targets or for controlling the performance of economic agents by synthetic criteria, rather than the physical success yardsticks typical of the classical CPE; (2) a means of transmitting information between the planning center and the periphery of decision making; and (3) a key parameter on real scarcities as one basic foundation for genuine microeconomic autonomy.

Liberalization of the price regime means that prices are reset approximately in line with relative production costs, if only to reduce subsidies and attain the desired level of profitability for different branches of the economy. However, comprehensive price revision by itself is not likely to move prices closer to underlying costs unless a more appropriate computation of average production costs is first specified. Even if properly recomputed, planners need to maintain prices in line with real or perceived scarcities on a timely basis, at least intermittently. By proceeding in this way, shifts either in domestic production conditions or in world markets will be reflected in price adaptations, although this cannot materialize instantaneously. But the lag should be comparatively brief for otherwise the information value of prices for proper resource allocation will soon dissipate again.

Regardless of the chief aim of the price reform, actual calculations can be executed in many different ways. Even in the most conservative CPE the spirit of reform brought about the periodic revision of administratively set prices to take into account fluctuations in domestic and foreign demand and supply. Greater flexibility in administrative price formation is aimed at so that prices continue to convey meaningful information to the plan executors. This has assumed the form either of more frequent recalibrations of centrally set prices or the greater delegation of authority over price formation to the lower planning tiers, but with considerable ideological and political shackles.

With respect to the information content of prices, all CPEs have gradually made room for a more active role of prices in regulating production and distribution processes, even if these parameters are set by central fiat. Although prices never fully reflect objective economic relations, they undoubtedly are moved closer to actual production costs. In some cases they even react to changes in supply and demand. Elsewhere, however, most prices continue primarily to be parameters that transmit orders from the center to the lower planning units as well as units for accounting and control. This, of course, begs the question of the degree to which prices can act as guidelines for the decision making of firms. It may well be the case that the latter have no direct control over price formation, although they are expected to react to the parameters issued by the central pricing authority. These may or may not reflect somewhat better the true scarcities of capital, land, natural resources, and foreign currency at the time of their introduction. In a few countries, prices provide feedback on the state of product markets to central policy makers, and firms or their associations dispose of some authority to revise prices from time to time in response to changes in costs. Even in CPEs in which price adjustments are now a quasi-continuous process, price movements are permitted only within preset narrow margins, if they are not altogether rigidly controlled by the pricing center through administrative channels.

In some countries, fiat prices for some products can fluctuate depending on demand and supply, possibly within preset boundaries. There are three generic price types that come to the fore: administratively set prices as in the classical CPE, market-determined prices (but subject to a vast array of informal controls), and prices whose flexibility is bounded from below or above, or both. The countries that allow such partial flexibility normally commit themselves gradually to broaden the scope for periodic price adjustments. The category of centrally controlled prices should shrink in favor of the "from–to" group and, to a lesser extent, freely fluctuating prices. But this planned evolution is only rarely adhered to for practical reasons. Retail prices are also modified, but they continue to be adjusted by the pricing authorities, in principle to ensure equilibrium in consumer markets and to hold down inflationary pressures. The process is not entirely devoid of administrative arbitrariness, however, as resource allocation does not generally proceed according to true scarcity values.

Though prices in most partially decentralized CPEs continue to play much the same role as under the traditional model, for economies that depend on foreign trade for a substantial part of their aggregate product the linkup in some fashion between the domestic economy and the trade sector is crucial for reaching proper decisions. Some of the key issues at stake concern the degree to which real foreign trade costs are reflected in domestic prices and the speed at which this transmission takes place. The majority of CPEs set pseudo exchange rates and gradually impart a more important role to real foreign-trade opportunities when prices are centrally recomputed. Very few, however, allow trade results to influence domestic prices directly, even if economic agents in the process obtain latitude in generating individual product prices.[2]

A sharp distinction should be drawn between using trade results in domestic resource allocation and using them in profit calculations. The former is introduced in an attempt to motivate producers or traders to promote selected export and import contracts with segregated trade partners. But enterprises are not necessarily entitled to pass on real costs. So their decisions on matters not covered by the plan are perforce reached on the basis of what appears to be profitable from the microeconomic point of view. Although foreign trade prices undeniably exert a growing influence on domestic prices, the price system in most CPEs has, on the whole, remained relatively inflexible, more so for consumer than for producer prices. For the former, various systematic and *ad hoc* subsidies and taxes buffer against socially undesirable changes in the cost of living. Though ensuring a high degree of stability, the rigidity inherent in setting administrative prices comes into sharp conflict with the desire of planners to utilize prices as one of the key allocation levers at all levels of decision making.

To buttress greater enterprise autonomy and decision-making responsibility, this selectively decentralized model generally seeks to assign a greater role to money and finance. Budget financing of investments in existing firms, except for major expansion, is as a rule replaced by retained profits and bank loans. Centralized investment decisions continue to foster the development strategy, but enterprises that obtain such assets must pay capital levies. In some countries, more flexible use of interest rates, credit, and fiscal levers is enforced through greater differentiation. Furthermore, retail and wholesale trade networks are improved to service consumers and to facilitate the transmission of their preferences to producers. But retail price flexibility and enterprise autonomy fall well short of the minimum required to ensure smooth adjustments between demand and supply in individual markets.

Partial decentralization aims at elevating foreign trade to a crucial activity in propping up domestic growth, which itself is guided by and harmonized with domestic decision making. To face up to the multiple opportunities in both the domestic and foreign trade sectors, the selectively decentralized CPE begins to explore various ways to stimulate more efficient trade relations without, however, completely abandoning its autonomous economic policies. This involves both the decision making and the organization of trade (see section 4).

Modified centralized economic model

Movement toward decentralization initiated in most CPEs in the first half of the 1960s came to an abrupt halt at the latest in the early 1970s in all but Hungary. Even the reform pace under what was called the new economic mechanism (NEM) slowed down markedly or was reversed for a while; in any case, key components of the NEM formulated in 1968 remained on the drawing board until the mid-1980s (see section 5). Some of these derailments were due to sociopolitical concerns. Other reforms faltered because the hoped-for stimulus to factor productivity failed to materialize. To rectify the situation, most CPEs reverted to central resource allocation, reduced the autonomy of firms, curbed the flexibility of decision-making instruments, and enacted other retreats from partial reforms.

The label "modified centralized model" refers in particular to the fact that essential aspects of the MFT's transformation in the 1960s are retained and, in a number of respects, strengthened. The gradual change in enterprise organization and in the methods of planning and control is continued in the foreign trade sector, although some setbacks are encountered here as well, in marked contrast to the abrogation of other reform components. This is the logical consequence of the need to face up to multiple opportunities in foreign trade when autarky and industrialization as overriding policy objectives recede into the background.

Though recentralization is embraced in part because of disappointment with the earlier partial decentralization, there is no return to strictly centralized planning. This stems from the simple fact that the original motives for the organizational streamlining do not evaporate with the abandonment, downsizing, or curbing of the reforms. Particularly important in this regard are the needs to boost factor productivity, to provide sufficient resources for consumption, and to finance accumulation to modernize the economy. The modified centralized economy explores other means than indirect economic coordination to attain these goals. Two are important. Many CPE policy makers view the crystallization of political east–west *détente* as a signal to import technology, if necessary through capital borrowed in DMEs. The second path taken by some CPEs harks back to the question of how to reconcile output maximization with certain rules and regulations on input minimization when the coordination mechanism is exceedingly incomplete. This applies to experiments in virtually all CPEs that earlier had made intermediate economic units responsible for their own decisions. The all-embracing control hierarchy of the centralized model, though reshaped, is essentially kept in place. The shift from sectoral planning to the creation of large units with economic accounting responsibilities in the 1960s and 1970s (in Czechoslovakia, the GDR, and Poland) or the fusion of economic agents engaged in related activities in the 1980s (in Czechoslovakia and the GDR) did not affect the principle that all economic agents are administratively subordinated to the center and form integral parts of one comprehensive "planning" hierarchy. The only exceptions occurred in Czechoslovakia in 1967–8 and in Hungary when it started to implement its NEM in 1968.

Modified centralization involves abolishing or transforming medium-level control agencies into the central management of nationwide enterprises. The remaining firms are formally released from their administrative subordination to the state administration. Strict plan targets and physical norms are replaced by general requirements to satisfy domestic demand, to meet obligations contracted abroad by the state or firms, and to achieve satisfactory export performance in MEs. Centralized resource allocation is in some respects complemented, but not generally replaced, by market-type transactions in the means of production. But the latter remain highly monopolized and strongly controlled by the state. Though still under political control, frequent price revisions and changes in enterprise profit-tax rates are enacted to reflect modifications in macroeconomic policy and the gradual movement toward genuine microeconomic decentralization. Excepting the GDR, where the experiment between 1978 and 1989 was carried farthest, the partially recentralized model is replete with hedges because the experimental stage has not so far been abandoned or because policy makers have resumed the on–off partial reform cycle of the late 1950s.

As already indicated, this modified centralized economic model tends to be unstable. Major and minor aspects of the model are revised rather frequently, chiefly under the impact of transformations in the domestic and external economic environment. Emerging imbalances in domestic service sectors, in raw materials and fuels procured within the CMEA, and in the external payments situation of a number of CPEs, particularly in their relations with MEs, play an important role in launching a search for an appropriate positive adjustment strategy.

The decentralized economic mechanism

The pivot of this mode of organization is effective decentralization and coordination of decisions through indirect policy instruments and their supporting institutions, in contrast to the simple devolution of administrative authority typical of earlier reforms. As noted, the emergence of such a mechanism is, as a rule, associated with other societal mutations of a more or less radical character, but these will not be considered here.

Economic decentralization aims at curbing administrative guidance in determining output, resource allocation, and the distribution of incomes; eventually it should be abolished. Entrepreneurial activity is coordinated through market-type economic links rather than through vertical chains of administrative command. Supply and demand can influence more flexible domestic prices that are related to world market prices (WMPs). They can thus guide input–output decisions. Profits are to become the appropriate measure of an enterprise's contribution to the economy as a whole and the basis for rewarding staff. The state's control extends to three spheres. The nonmaterial sectors and infrastructure by necessity remain the responsibility of central authorities. Central planning of the material sphere gets focused more and more on structural decisions and on economic strategies in the medium to long run. But a coherent macroeconomic policy needs to emerge to regulate income distribution, saving and investment behavior, monetary policy and the financial sphere, fiscal policy, wage and price behavior, and so on.

Among the instruments of the decentralized economic mechanism, the following are the most critical. First, rather than losing in importance, the role of planning for structural decisions is reinforced, as discussed. Secondly, the material–technical supply system is decentralized with economic agents obtaining the responsibility to decide by themselves on the disposition of outputs and some inputs. Thirdly, economic agents are expected to react to changes in indirect economic parameters. These include prices, exchange and interest rates, and larger differentials in wage schedules. Fourthly, enterprise behavior is evaluated largely on the basis of net performance indicators with profit acting as the paramount criterion of success. Subsidies for wholesale and retail prices or for ailing enterprises are to be compressed and gradually abolished. Firms that cannot be turned around need to be discontinued, and this requires a government policy on bankruptcy.

Finally, the decentralized mechanism necessitates changes in and additions to the traditional economic institutions of the CPE. The transformation in the planning sphere is, of course, associated with the downsizing of the role of ministries and associations in the day-to-day affairs of economic agents under their jurisdiction. Secondly, a credible monetary policy requires that the monobank becomes a bank of issue and lender of last resort in charge of monetary policy. At the same time, its former tasks are to be entrusted to a network of financial institutions that cater on a competitive basis to the financing requirements of economic agents, possibly including consumers.

In the foreign trade sphere, FTOs are transformed into effective self-accounting trading enterprises or their tasks are assigned to individual producing enterprises. The decentralized economic mechanism may change the character of cooperative organizations, including agricultural co-operatives. It invariably imparts some important role to small-scale private or cooperative enterprises, particularly in service sectors. Finally, the emerging economic mechanism may seek to promote new forms of ownership not only within the domestic sphere, such as through the encouragement of small-scale private enterprises, but also by attracting capital from abroad through joint ventures or the establishment of special economic zones.

4 The trade and payments regimes of the CPEs

From the many features of the traditional CPE it is important to recall three. First and foremost is the role of comprehensive central planning, chiefly by way of physical yardsticks with little regard for static efficiency indicators. Secondly, the CPE leadership harbors a very strong desire for a substantial degree of domestic policy autonomy, including autonomy in prices and in the decision making of economic agents. Finally, the leadership has a pronounced ambition to foster its own dynamic pattern of development under exclusive state guidance, almost regardless of comparative advantage considerations. This initial setting explains in part why the CPEs at that early stage chose to adhere to strict bilateralism in foreign trade and payments. Particularly constraining was the maintenance of commodity and currency inconvertibility in preference to pursuing policies to facilitate greater integration in the world economy.

A separate pricing regime and the labor theory of value

The goals, instruments, and institutions of the traditional CPE explicitly deemphasized or neglected value indicators and most indirect instruments of economic management, as noted. The role of money, in particular, was minimized. The traditional CPE also curtailed its interaction with other countries beyond the already substantial contraction engineered on account of political disagreements. Yet such features typical of CPEs as multiple exchange rates, which reflect the multitier price systems; inconvertibility, which derives from the planned allocation of resources; bilateralism, which was embraced to facilitate the planned conduct of foreign trade; and exchange controls to insulate domestic from foreign markets, and thus to enhance the effective realization of centrally planned decisions, are all logical and legitimate ingredients of the economic setup of CPEs. But they complicate intermeshing the CPE within the global economy and its key institutional pillars.

A state may successfully cripple the allocatory function of the price mechanism on a national scale. If trade is needed or allowed, it is not quite clear how outside opportunities, which are inherently difficult to control, can be dovetailed with the traditional economic model. This is not a trivial matter because, particularly in Eastern Europe, fairly extensive use of foreign trade imposed itself on an otherwise autarkic domestic economic policy, even though few instruments were available to justify "rational" choice between domestic and external sourcing or sales. Because of the high degree of domestic autonomy desired by the CPE planner, the proper simulation of the relationship between domestic and external prices in the preparation of economic decisions is crucial. In accordance with the precepts of autonomous planning and administration, for more than two decades the link between trade and domestic prices was severed through the MFT and its price-equalization mechanism. This divorce is not apt to foster a rational allocation of resources in the sense defined in this chapter.

When the focus of policy formulation is shifted from the domestic economy to the conditions governing international relations, matters become quite different. Particularly in the sphere of their intragroup relations, CPEs claim that the objective necessity of the law of value ensues from the existence of socialist property and the autonomous material interests of commodity producers. These derive from the precept that each CPE is keen on minimizing the part of national income "expended" as an input for the procurement of imports as "output" from the foreign trade process (Bautina 1968a, 70; Bautina 1968b, 41ff.).

The basic determinant of international value is not the level of socially necessary labor expenditures in the individual producing country, just as labor actually expended in the exchange economy may differ from what is socially necessary. Instead, international value is the magnitude of labor necessary at the international level to generate equilibrium between two or more countries, for any well-determined product (Gräbig, Brendel, and Dubrowsky 1975, 30–1). The main function of trade prices, including those for reciprocal exchanges among CPEs, should be the "accounting of internationally socially necessary labor expenditures for the production of goods" (Popov 1968, 69). This should apply in world markets, but conditions there are often influenced by monopolistic pressures, business cycles, exploitation, and other factors that make prices deviate from their underlying value, even in equilibrium. In their intragroup trade, however, "competitive world prices" need to be simulated to preserve equivalent exchange. Instead of using domestic prices and proper exchange rates as in orthodox MEs, intragroup trade of the CPEs is based on a set of artificial, so-called socialist WMPs. Because of the importance of the transferable ruble (TR) in these intragroup transactions, I call this the "transferable ruble price" (TRP) regime. But TRPs have a number of other tasks aside from ensuring equivalence of labor values in intragroup exchanges.

Because of the extensive domestic policy autonomy desired by central policy makers, one might surmise that the traditional CPE by its very nature is rather protective. Does this feature change in the course of mutating toward a more liberal environment? Before answering this question it is legitimate to ask whether one can properly speak of protection in the case of the CPEs and the CMEA as a regional grouping. This is not a trivial issue if only because in international fora the CPEs are frequently accused of being "overly protective," a terminology that often results from rather careless transposition of the term protectionism from the ME to the CPE context (see Caffet and Lavigne 1985, 288ff.). Recall that, in the ME environment, the link between domestic and foreign trade prices is often taken to be the single most important parameter for measuring the degree of protection. The systemic, structural isolation of the CPEs individually and as a group relative to third-country markets enables these economies to do without explicit commercial policies. As a result, it is difficult to speak of CPE protectionism without clarifying what is mean by it.[3]

As reforms are introduced, the modified CPE strongly feels the need also to decentralize trade decision making. It must, therefore, adopt other coordination policies, institutions, and instruments. Among this arsenal, instruments of typical commercial policies, including customs duties, active exchange rate policies, and QRs, are eventually addressed. This does not necessarily mean that the modified CPE is less protective than the traditional one. Given the paramount role of trade considerations in the panoply of reform measures, however, raising trade dependence and rationalizing trade by partners and commodity groups are usually high on the policy agenda. One may therefore surmise that the modifying CPE becomes less protective, certainly after some initial transition period. But it is hard to verify this conjecture by simply depending on differences between domestic and trade prices, in comparisons either over time or across economies.

In what follows I shall nonetheless adhere to the convention that describes the CPE as having chosen a substantial proclivity for a "protective environment." I mean by this especially a trade regime that proscribes spontaneous access to domestic markets. This was certainly the sense in which Lenin (1964) envisaged the operation of the MFT (Hough 1986, 495). If the CPE implements reforms so that prices are invoked to discriminate between domestic and external markets, the concept "protective environment" should suggest a trade regime that does not permit spontaneous access to markets in response to price differentials. Note that this particular meaning of protectionism in the case of CPEs is not the mainstream view, which transposes the concept from the market environment to the CPE (see Hough 1986). But I do not find this a particularly useful approach.

The trading regime of the CPEs and the CMEA

Because after World War II several CPEs emerged with rather similar institutions and policy objectives, they launched attempts to cooperate. Given their common concern about fostering industrialization, income redistribution, and social equality, the CPEs all had a common interest in adhering to an international regime that would support their domestic aspirations (Brada 1988, 654ff.). This reinforcement of within-group relations stemmed also from sanction and embargo policies pursued by key DMEs, especially the United States. These needs were further cemented by the exclusion of the CPEs, for political and economic reasons, from the trading, financial, and monetary regimes established after World War II. These institutions did not really meet the needs of the CPEs. Thus the stress on currency convertibility in the BWS was inconsistent with central planning. The GATT's overriding concern with reducing all barriers between domestic and international markets to tariffs and to suppress them gradually was simply irrelevant for nations that chose to conduct their foreign trade within the context of a sweeping MFT. Not only that, the GATT's principle of nondiscriminatory treatment of Contracting Parties, apart from being widely flaunted in one guise or another by the Contracting Parties themselves, was at odds with the notion of socialist solidarity for development. But they also decided to collaborate for political, strategic, and ideological reasons. These are just a few of the many convoluted considerations that may have led the CPEs to create the CMEA in January 1949 and to gradually erect within that context trading and monetary regimes that differed palpably from those eventually attained in MEs. Within that context, the CPEs chose to promote their own integration format, with rules for trading and payments at marked variance with those prevailing among MEs. But these rules proved to be more suitable to the promotion of the national objectives sought by the CPEs themselves. As such, in Brada's (1988, 658) rationalization, "CMEA is a regime wherein members are able to promote both their own individual and the collective welfare, in part by voluntarily adhering to a regime whose benefits outweigh the costs of membership."

The CMEA trading and payments regimes emerged largely from the expressed needs of the participants to foster rapid domestic industrialization through central planning within a sheltered environment, rather than from a comprehensive approach to identifying the preconditions for catering in the most effective way to the collective requirements of regional economic integration. CMEA economic cooperation has been regulated mainly through detailed BTPAs that are rarely negotiated within the framework of an agreed CMEA-wide policy. Even so, the absence of a central planning agency at the CMEA level, at the same time that component economies cling to centralized forms of domestic and trade management, is responsible for major weaknesses of the CMEA cooperation mechanisms.

The CMEA trade and payments system consists of: formal multilateral settlements of bilateral payments imbalances through the TR as accounting unit, but keeping intact bilateral accounting of real trade flows; the creation of the TR, the establishment of nominally multilateral settlements procedures, and the management of short-term credit at the International Bank for Economic Cooperation (IBEC), but maintaining the caesura between money and commodity transactions; coordination of investment intentions and the promotion of joint investment financing through the International Investment Bank (IIB); the introduction in CMEA trade of TRPs that are relatively autonomous and stable through the plan period, but are in fact set bilaterally, almost on an *ad hoc* basis; the elaboration of a multiple exchange rate regime for various types of transactions that are, at best, poorly interlinked; the establishment of regional economic organizations, chiefly to facilitate the coordination of decisions in production, science, and technological progress; and other fields. The CMEA mechanism as it has matured until today does not, however, embody a clear-cut set of macroeconomic policies for the region as a whole – or regional central planning for that matter.

To understand the CMEA trading regime, it is essential to realize that none of the aforementioned links of the CMEA economic mechanism ever operated automatically. Because of the centrality of BTPAs, not just for ordinary commerce but even for implementing MTPAs, integration endeavors can only be fostered within the frameworks afforded by concrete bilateral intergovernmental arrangements. That is not to deny that in some cases individual firms cooperate directly without the intermediation of the MFT. But these activities develop only when the MFT explicitly arranges for such links to emerge and flourish. In other words, the linkup between the CMEA as a regional organization and the institutions of the member economies has been exceedingly indirect. The CMEA organizations simply aided the member economies, if the latter so wished, in the formulation and realization of various types of BTPAs.

The monetary regime of the CMEA

If the CPEs had established a regional planning organ similar in makeup to the domestic central planning agencies, there would never have been any need to institute mechanisms and institutions to ease balance-of-payments adjustments or even to foster currency convertibility. In fact, all intra-CMEA transactions would have become truly regional transactions in a single currency, perhaps the TR. Perfect double-entry bookkeeping with accounting similar to that typical of domestic economic relations would have sufficed. Furthermore, the regional planning center would have been in a position to manage trade and payments relations with third markets in much the same way as the individual CPE. That is, full control is in principle within the compass of central planning.

However, there never has been a central planning agency at the CMEA level, the member countries have jealously guarded their economic sovereignty, and national planning, including that of trade, has been less than perfect. As a result, payments imbalances do occur and need to be redressed through positive policy measures. Unlike the IMS, where temporary imbalances are automatically accommodated through quasi-automatic credit facilities and structural imbalances need to be corrected through fiscal and monetary policies, including a revaluation of the currency, the CMEA has sought to correct imbalances through short- and medium-term plan coordination.

It is worth recalling here for later reference that the CMEA's own regional monetary unit and settlements bank, both established in late 1963, embody important ingredients molded along the fundamental formal lines of the bancor and the clearing union as advocated by Keynes. But essential elements thereof, including global management of liquidity, purely "ideal" money creation, and symmetric penalization of debtors and creditors, have not been emulated in the CMEA. Whereas the bancor was conceived as a pure credit currency unit, the CPEs decided to set up a bank with its own capital fund.[4]

The above proposition can be illustrated by the ineffectiveness of the IBEC in multilateralizing trade and payments. Because in the CMEA commodity streams drive monetary flows and the IBEC has never been assured of a partnership role in negotiating BTPAs, the bank has remained a highly passive institution. It essentially takes care of the accounting operations associated with various kinds of regional economic transactions. But it plays no role whatsoever in actual trade, payments, or cooperation negotiations. Precisely to avoid this, at its inception the bank was to take part in trade negotiations at two levels. In the *ex ante* negotiations, it was to help clear intended flows that the CPEs could not cope with in their BTPAs. It would also get involved *ex post* to help offset bilateral imbalances incurred either because of partial noncompliance with the provisions of the BTPA or possibly because one member voluntarily expanded its deliveries over and above contracted volumes in the balanced BTPA. These ambitions have not been realized, however (see Brabant 1989a, 204–5).

The CMEA and economic reform in CPEs

Inasmuch as the movement toward partial decentralization took place in part in reaction to the failed attempt to set in train a socialist-type division of labor as advocated in the first policy document of the CMEA,[5] domestic reforms were pursued largely independently of debates at the regional level. This was facilitated in part by the measurable increase in the room for east–west trade and cooperation, beginning in the mid-1960s particularly among the smaller countries of Europe.

Almost the reverse relationship prevailed with the movement toward partial recentralization. The reason is simple: the first reform wave was essentially abrogated through political intervention (the invasion of Czechoslovakia by WTO members and the ensuing Brezhnev doctrine) and led to resentment as well as a search for laying a firmer foundation for genuine socialist economic integration (SEI). (This ferment led to the endorsement of the second policy blueprint of the CMEA, which is known as *Integration program.*[6]) Regional economic cooperation is to be strengthened also because, though the role of trade in micro- and macroeconomic decision making about development undergoes some changes with the move toward partial recentralization, its contribution to the growth effort becomes even more essential than before. This concern is further heightened by the gradual commitment to pursue full decentralization as a firm policy aim (see sections 5 and 6). In an environment more receptive to indirect economic coordination, foreign trade decentralization can proceed farthest.

Foreign trade reform as a rule affects four areas: (1) price formation, price levels, and relative prices, possibly including a more effective link between domestic and external markets through the intermediary of surrogate exchange rates; (2) the central regulation of trade, largely on a macroeconomic basis; (3) the specific operation of the MFT, which is being strengthened and weakened at the same time; and (4) the promulgation of direct links with foreign enterprises, including joint ventures of some kind. Although the various measures residing under these four headings are loosely connected in partial reforms, innovations in the trade sector are harmonized with each other and with internal changes in the comprehensive reforms, as detailed in section 6.

At the level of CMEA cooperation, the period of the modified centralized economic model is directly related to the difficulties encountered with the effective interlinking of the member economies on the basis of *Integration program* as a loose policy blueprint and SEI as the ill-defined strategy for forging ahead. Also at that level, various experiments were tried, including concerted plans and target programs (Brabant 1989a, 253–63). Ultimately, however, what could materialize at the CMEA level, at least until about 1985, very much reflected the rather conservative attitude of Soviet policy makers toward economic reform, on the one hand, and the growing concern in virtually all CPEs about coming to grips with a variety of unanticipated domestic and external constraints on short-term policy flexibility.

5 National economic reforms and the economic mechanism

Many arguments (see Brabant 1989a, 395–7) support the proposition that most CPEs presently have little scope for accelerating the pace of growth from probable increments in factor supplies or redistribution.

Instead, they increasingly need to base their growth efforts on stimulating factor productivity through modifications in policies, institutions, and policy instruments. In other words, they are in need of an economic mechanism capable of blending the interests of economic agents with those of the state more coherently than central planning has been able to achieve to date. This priority becomes especially pronounced once the opportunities for the voluntaristic expansion of industry in breadth have been exhausted because of either physical supply constraints or ill-affordable costs. Modifications in policy instruments and their supporting institutions can render the environment within which expansive economic policies can be envisaged more sensitive to the preconditions for factor productivity growth. As detailed elsewhere (see Brabant 1987a, 403–7; Brabant 1989e), this requires measures that focus primarily on indirect coordination instruments and supporting institutions, including the CMEA. But other institutions might be required to formulate proper monetary, fiscal, and income policies.

In recognition of prevailing growth obstacles, since the mid-1980s the CPEs have been seriously concerned about economic reforms. I cannot examine here in detail the reform ambitions, the measures already enacted, or the steps about to be implemented in some countries. Instead, I point out the salient features of the prevailing reform drift in China, most of Eastern Europe, Mongolia, and Vietnam. This provides the basic backdrop to the identification in chapter 5 of new conditions for these countries to play a more constructive, coherent, and supportive role in IEOs.

Autonomy and accountability of enterprise decision making

One critical reform lever is the devolution of decision-making authority and responsibility from the higher levels (planning offices, branch ministries, and possibly associations) to the ultimate economic units. There is substantial consensus in principle about the degree to which microeconomic decision making should be devolved to the firm, subject to more or less broad macroeconomic guidance rules. Firms need greater latitude in setting input and output mixes and prices, in determining individual wages and bonuses in proportion to actual profits and related performance yardsticks, in borrowing from banks at realistic interest rates, and in taking greater risks in the expectation of gaining rewards, in particular from technological progress. To what degree this movement is currently being realized in the various reforms under way is a different matter.

One basic objective of any economic reform anchored to administrative decentralization is to link enterprise autonomy with economic accountability, that is, self-financing and profitability. But the two need not coincide. In past reforms, they became decoupled shortly after the reform's start because the Party leadership, government authorities, and managers reacted with traditional peremptory actions to imbalances that the reforms were intended to address as well as to those unleashed by the reform. Microeconomic autonomy and responsibility can be combined effectively only if the proper signals are provided to economic agents and if the latter are able to mold the level and composition of inputs and outputs in accordance with what they perceive to be in their best interest. Because of the distortions in the evaluation criteria typical of the CPE bent on reform, enterprise accountability is as a rule fully attainable only after a protracted, often socially and politically bruising, transition. With distorted wholesale prices, it is counterproductive to expect economic agents to formulate decisions on the basis of wrong signals, from society's point of view, and to hold them accountable for disappointing results that are, however, quite "rational" within the prevailing microeconomic context. Because prevailing institutions, rules, regulations, and behavioral patterns cannot be altered overnight, enforcement of "wrong" behavior is almost inevitable. Bankruptcy provisions in conjunction with greater flexibility in staffing policies should come to grips with the transition toward rationality in economic behavior. Otherwise, bankruptcy can only demote the leadership of the firm and wipe out bookkeeping losses on state capital assets.

Even though interest and wage rates are far from market clearing, firms can be held accountable for managing capital and labor resources more responsibly than under strict central planning. In the same vein, they can be asked to shoulder the burden for excessive inventories – at any rate, for hoarding material and capital resources that could be productively employed elsewhere. Firms can also be expected to show greater concern for proper pricing, inventory control, catering to user or final demand, and so on. These partial ways of entrusting economic agents with greater responsibility than under traditional planning fall well short of full-scale economic decentralization. But they can provide a useful first step in launching a meaningful transition toward that stage.

Role of the banking sector

The monobanking system has been slated for decentralization in all CPEs except Albania, North Korea, and Rumania. The farthest advanced in this respect is Hungary, where the central bank has been transformed mostly into a bank of issue and domestic lender of last resort that seeks to control the money supply and to manage the financial and monetary systems more generally. The more practical day-to-day aspects have been left increasingly to specialized banks, where economic agents obtain loans that are in principle rationed by economic means. Most of these institutions have been set up to serve particular purposes, including regular banking business, investment, foreign trade, and construction. In some of these branches, multiple banks compete for business. It is important to note that these specialized institutions have been called upon to provide commercial banking services within macroeconomic guidelines, particularly the monetary policy of the central bank. Similar objectives lie behind the Bulgarian, Chinese, and Vietnamese reforms and are currently being considered in Mongolia, Poland, and the Soviet Union.

Financial reforms have not so far come to grips with two critical issues. One is the stock of assets and liabilities of the banks to be decentralized. Invariably the portfolio of the monobank has been disaggregated into sector-specific assets and liabilities. Because in the past loans were made chiefly to enable implementation of centrally prescribed enterprise plans rather than on their economic merit, not only do the various banks start from very unequal initial conditions, but the portfolio is of unequal quality and needs to be restructured. This cannot but entail losses to be absorbed by the new institutions, which will not fail to petition for some form of easement from the central budget. It would have been much more useful for the monobank to preserve its loan portfolio, endow the new institutions with a startup capital, let them compete for assets from economic agents, and thus enable them to reach decisions for which they can be held responsible. The latter would include competitive bidding on loans held in the monobank's portfolio.

The second critical issue is how best to allocate funds among borrowers and whether the center will allow positive real interest rates to ration loans even if that would lead to bankruptcies and a temporary slowdown in the sustainable pace of economic activity. Proper interest-rate policies to enforce capital scarcity and motivate agents to save for productive purposes are a *sine qua non* for banks to be viable autonomous entities. In the most stalwart CPEs, ideological inhibitions have kept overall interest rates at modest levels and their differentiation and variability within narrow bounds. Rarely has there been serious effort to control the money supply by technical–economic means, as distinct from rather crude *obiter dicta*.

The role of prices

Price reform is one of the most complex and politically sensitive tasks for reforming economies, not just CPEs. It is one that has undone reforms and reformers on more than one occasion. Because of its practical obstacles, the complexity of introducing acceptable and meaningful changes in price levels and pricing policies has certainly slowed down the pace of reform in all CPEs, even those with the greatest proclivity for substantial modifications in the economic mechanism. It is also likely to be strongly resisted by the population, firms, and entrenched Party and trade union interests (see section 2).

Policy makers have found it increasingly counterproductive, as well as financially taxing, to maintain prevailing distortions through large consumer-price subsidies; to avoid passing on basic changes in trade prices, in CMEA relations and especially those incurred in relations with MEs; and to command production and consumption decisions mainly through physical appropriations. In other words, circumstances have compelled nearly all CPEs to reevaluate their pronounced preference for stable prices. As a result, instead of the erstwhile predictable landscape of constant retail and inflexible wholesale prices with changes introduced only after long intervals, the situation since the late 1970s has become increasingly differentiated. Greater price adaptability to levels that ensure harmony between demand and supply over the plan period has been a feature of policies even in stalwart CPEs.

Nonetheless, a palpable multiplicity of approaches to pricing remains, including approaches to the price level and the structure of prices, as well as the relationship between the various domestic and trade price tiers. In addition, intricate questions arise regarding the desired speed of price adjustment because core sociopolitical facets of a CPE may be affected by the particular choices made. Finally, the comprehensiveness of the reform and at what levels it should be carried out need to be determined. But policy makers are wary of its implications, especially as the redistribution of incomes is usually in favor of the better-off layers of society.[7] Yet, price reforms are essential not only to correctly assess economic scarcities, but also to provide economic agents with the necessary guidelines for decision making. This indicates that there continues to be ample scope for improvement.

It is particularly important to distinguish between two broad types of price reform. Reforms may aim at the administrative restructuring of prices, basically with a view to resetting fiat prices in line with perceived domestic and import costs at a given time. In some cases, however, the adaptability of the price structure over time is a major concern. In most countries, the former has at best been envisaged and attained rather incompletely. Only Hungary and Vietnam are committed to realizing the latter form. Other countries (Bulgaria, China, Poland, and the USSR) may have the same ambition, but they are as yet far removed from anything like real implementation.

Price reform cannot be undertaken at once without major socioeconomic shocks and disturbances that are as a rule intolerable in a socialist system. The reform is hence a process spread out over time, and the architecture of its intertemporal modifications is critical. In the most ambitious price reform, various categories are usually envisaged (including fixed prices as in the traditional CPE; prices that can move up to, from, or between certain limits; and free prices). Because of the dichotomy between producer and consumer prices in the CPE, these categories usually apply variously in these two spheres. Of course, a proper link between trade and domestic prices needs to be set. To anchor such a link, it is critical to establish a realistic exchange rate or a surrogate (Brabant 1987a, 198–207). In fact, price reform should be intimately intermeshed with the reform of the "monetary–financial" sphere in its entirety (Petrakov 1987, 55). In most countries, such links are calculated on the basis of average ratios of some domestic prices and prices of exported goods, usually manufactures, in the given trade structure or subsets thereof and by differentiated trading partners at discrete intervals. Rarely have countries let the exchange rate find its equilibrium, with price adjustments undertaken in line with the government's pricing policy.

Interfirm cooperation

This is much more difficult to organize than is generally taken for granted, principally because there are so few parameters at the disposal of economic agents to devise effective wholesale trade contacts. But there are certainly areas of convergence. Economic agents are undoubtedly interested in endeavors for which it is in any case difficult to set a true scarcity cost without allowing for uncertainty. The larger the maneuvering room and the more exploratory the venture, the greater scope there is for interfirm cooperation.

Matters are of yet another order of complexity when it comes to organizing contacts in production and marketing. But some areas of cooperation are at hand. For example, it may be quite beneficial either to allow the trading of excess resources in one firm intertemporally or to let them swap excess resources at a mutually satisfactory price. This is not likely to mop up all imbalances because there is a price imputable to the uncertainty of acquiring the resources when they become urgently needed. But it is likely to contribute to greater economic balance. Even with absolutely fixed fiat prices well removed from true scarcities, direct enterprise contacts may help to boost efficiency. But the room for socially counterproductive microeconomic decisions is likely to be larger than otherwise or than needed.

Where precisely the drive toward interfirm negotiations may lead to is anybody's guess. In spite of frequent calls to establish genuine wholesale trade, the road to its realization is bound to be protracted and arduous. I have the impression that they are still largely slogans or reflect a rather poor understanding of the requirements and behavioral conditions of true markets. If genuine wholesale trade is to be at the core of a new development strategy, it must be given greater scope and purpose in the evolving reform than is the case so far. The ultimate shape of the wholesale trading environment is less important than the formulation of a transition mechanism that the leadership will fashion in accordance with the fundamental reform strategy.

These skeptical observations about what is presently meant apply to both east–west and CMEA joint ventures or direct enterprise contacts. Regarding east–west ventures, opportunities are at the same time poorer and more promising. They are poorer because the CPE is primarily bent on attracting capital, managerial expertise, and technology from the west and on acquiring convertible currency through exports of the products thus being generated. In contrast, the western partner is likely to be motivated primarily by the relatively cheap, rather skilled labor resources of CPEs and the trading opportunities of socialist markets. The need to gain a CMEA-wide entry is particularly acute for joint ventures with Eastern European countries because their local market size is generally too confined. Moreover, these small markets depend for part of their input on CMEA supplies. To offset any adverse impact on the TR current accounts, these ventures need to generate TR revenues. But in this respect the CMEA mechanism faces formidable obstacles from the habitual CMEA rules and regulations.

The role of planning and macroeconomic policy

Just as important as the effective introduction of indirect coordination instruments and their associated institutions are appropriate macroeconomic policies. The latter must prop up and fine-tune the policy instruments, and indeed guide economic units in raising factor productivity. Another task of macroeconomic policy, and here lies the central role of statewide planning, is structural change and revamping growth strategies, through, for example, large-scale investment projects. Finally, central planning and macroeconomic policy need to maintain control over the so-called nonmaterial sphere, that is all activities that are quintessentially socialistic in nature, including education, medical care, the arts, basic infrastructure, and other public services.

It is regrettable that, owing to ideological precepts and the primacy of quantitative planning, key macroeconomic policies on monetary, fiscal, and income issues are primitive in the classical CPE. The traditional management of credit in line with the "real bills" doctrine needs to be revised so that decentralized banks can grant loans to economic agents that command access to resources. Monetary policy needs to be activated and extended to many new economic activities to ensure stability at the macroeconomic level, to let the central bank act as the effective lender of last resort for decentralized financial institutions, to regulate absorption in line with available domestic and borrowed resources, and to provide greater diversity of assets to households. The latter can be created without necessarily encroaching on the socialist ideology regarding property (see Nuti 1987).

Looking at the individual CPE, if meaningful devolution of economic decisions is to be introduced with a view to capitalizing on "information" of economic agents and present and foreseeable resources, the leadership needs to realize that the reform will be a protracted process rather than a once-and-for-all switch based on a single coherent blueprint. Steady progress during the transition needs to be ensured in a number of respects. The most important levers to be activated are wholesale prices anchored to trade prices, effective exchange and interest rates, wage compensation according to performance, much more active consumer prices, greater coordination of the economy as a whole according to clearly identified parameters set in line with social profitability criteria, and more active credit policies. Perhaps of the utmost importance is rule certainty for all economic agents. This presupposes that the room for lower-level decisions needs to be unambiguously delineated and that the interests of economic agents be reflected in the criteria by which these decisions can be reached. Such modifications in the "economic mechanism" of the CPEs are entirely plausible if a determined effort is made to separate the basic premises of the socialist economy from its more incidental features and if policy makers wed themselves to the overriding priority to foster flexibility in resource allocation, including personnel policies and the exit and entry of firms.

It would be unwise to advocate a greater parametrization of the CPE's economic environment without addressing the need to transform domestic and regional institutions. Medium- to long-term structural policy issues, including issues such as income distribution, aggregate savings and investment, the nonmaterial sphere, productive infrastructure, and especially the evolving situation of the economy, should become the primary concern of each planning center. Most other decisions can be reached under macroeconomic guidance. It is also crucial to foster greater competition among CMEA members and, where possible, also with enterprises of third markets. Trade guidance can be provided indirectly, for example, through an effective tariff policy, the abolition of nonparametric subsidies and taxes that buffer domestic from foreign prices, and an active exchange rate policy.

Foreign trade and payments regimes

Instead of maintaining the foreign trade and payments regime as a key pillar in support of substantial autonomy in domestic policy, most reforms seek to entrust greater responsibility in trade, including self-financing, to individual firms or to FTOs. In terms of requirements for the behavior of firms, this is a quite different environment from the one in which FTOs are kept afloat through price equalization to compensate for enforced (through BTPAs in the case of clearing trade or central prescriptions for trade with convertible currency partners) or unplanned divergences between domestic and foreign prices. Reforms rarely address these two spheres in a coherent fashion.

Regarding convertible currency trade with MEs, producing or trading firms are as a rule permitted to engage autonomously in trade to the extent that foreign exchange can be earned from exports and made available for imports. Initially, these operations tend to be subject to export or import licenses, which are a prerequisite to obtaining the necessary foreign exchange. But this is as a rule eventually transformed into foreign exchange licensing or auctioning (as in Bulgaria, China, Czechoslovakia, Poland, and now also the Soviet Union). Most countries make an effort to take into account the real price of trade with MEs either in the periodic resetting of domestic prices or through actual transaction prices. This is especially the case when a large share of trade in a particular product is transacted with MEs. Real export revenues and import returns are of necessity taken into account in guiding autonomous trading agents. Convertible currency trade within the CMEA and with some other CPEs (China and Yugoslavia in particular) is usually dealt with separately.

Trade with clearing-currency partners, particularly within the CMEA, is generally a very different story. For the reforming CPE in isolation, such as Hungary for many years, there was little choice beyond buffering domestic pricing and decision making against CMEA currency and trade operations that could not be reconciled with the objectives of the NEM. Now that the USSR is in the van of the reform thinking, there is a better than even chance not only that TRPs will become more realistic and linked to domestic pricing policies, but also that there will be much greater scope for direct interfirm relations so that the envisioned devolution can be carried out.

Regarding foreign exchange policy, most reformers realize that the exchange rate is a price that needs to be treated as such. That is to say, it should be nearly uniform and flexible, depending upon demand and supply. Most reforming CPEs aim at replacing the multiplicity of prevailing exchange rates by narrowing the differentiation of each group of commercial and noncommercial coefficients in the two or three major clearing zones (TR, convertible currency, and clearing), in order to harmonize these commercial and noncommercial rates per currency zone and eventually to reach a uniform exchange rate subject to overall foreign exchange policy. In some cases, the ultimate aim may even be to transit to currency convertibility, at least for current-account transactions.

6 Economic reform and the CMEA

Inasmuch as the CMEA is the key market for nearly all CPEs undergoing reform, what a country in isolation can achieve depends importantly on the degree to which CMEA conditions differ from those of world markets. Regarding CMEA organization, policies, policy instruments, and opportunities for individual actors to influence events through their own behavior, it is essentially up to the CPEs in their groupwide concert to enact desirable modifications. Improved economic performance through shifts in the methods and goals of economic policies in the CMEA context is critical in this regard. The CMEA's system-specific policies, institutions, and instruments are not well geared toward propping up reform measures spontaneously. It is also against that backdrop that the obstacles arising from the dichotomy between TRPs and WMPs should be dealt with.

Given the importance of the CMEA, what role could be assigned to the CMEA as a regional economic institution, a forum for guidance with experimentation, and a regional "market" in support of as yet unsynchronized reform attempts? Should this assistance be minimal or maximal; that is, should the CMEA be envisaged as a buttress to the CPEs embarking on the most ambitious reform, while protecting the other members of the group that choose to move more slowly? Alternatively, should the changes in the CMEA as a regional organization be targeted at supporting chiefly the greatest common denominator of the economic mechanisms of the various members at any one time, in which case they should accommodate at the regional level some features of the most conservative reform? Secondly, given present policy stances on economic restructuring, to what extent can one logically search for feasible and desirable adjustments in the CMEA to accommodate national reforms? These include especially the mechanisms, institutions, and policies that condition the foreign trade, exchange, and settlements regimes within the CMEA context. This by necessity impacts on the conduct of economic relations with outside partners.

These central concerns have been on the CMEA debating table now at least since 1984 without the members having thus far arrived at a consensus on the desirable relationship between national and SEI reforms. In spite of the many political, ideological, legal, organizational, and economic obstacles to CMEA reform, measurable modification in model and strategy is likely to crystallize in the years to come not only as a policy goal in itself but also in support of *perestrojka* in key member countries. The process of reforming SEI, with all its attendant institutional and behavioral repercussions, is likely to center around direct enterprise relations, the implementation of the strategy on science and technology as enshrined in the third policy document of the CMEA, here referred to as *Scientific–technological progress*,[8] and the policy statement presently being finalized for endorsement later in 1989, here referred to as *Collective concept*.[9] These concerns may take on dimensions that were not even considered three years ago or so, when these issues were first mooted. This applies in particular to *Scientific–technological progress*.

It is unfortunate that we know only the rough contours of the proposed, although still unofficial, changes that were gaining support and approval by the key members prior to the ongoing political upheavals in Eastern Europe. Instead of seeking broad-based reforms of the CMEA as the regional economic organization of the majority of CPEs, there is presently serious talk of the CMEA's demise and shifting foreign economic relations much more toward Western Europe. This prevailing political sentiment may well render the CMEA *de facto* superfluous. It will not, however, remedy overnight the hard-core problems associated with bilateralism in relations among the CPEs. Nor will it revamp quickly the dependence of the CPEs on each other for critical raw materials and fuels without introducing untold socioeconomic hardships on already strained societies. In other words, for the foreseeable future bilateral ties among the CMEA members are likely to remain strong, although they may undergo further modifications themselves if only to buttress the ongoing economic reforms.

Given the importance of intragroup ties among the CMEA members, we should remind ourselves that the CMEA as it has evolved since 1949 is not well suited to support, let alone to enhance, the shifts in economic policies and mechanisms currently envisioned in most CPEs. It may therefore be useful to study the desirable modifications of cooperation modes, the extent to which prevailing conditions are sufficiently mature to facilitate the swift realization of these intentions, and what conditions need to be met for these envisioned transformations to materialize. In this process, I assume that key CMEA members will continue with reforms and that there is no ready alternative to emphasizing SEI as a prime source of domestic economic growth and of the well-being of the CMEA community. This implicit primacy of developing CMEA relations will hold at least until the members succeed in restoring domestic and external balances at a level and structure of economic activity that enhance their global competitiveness.

The 44th Council Session[10] of the CMEA (Prague, 5–7 July 1988) resolved that the members would henceforth aim their cooperation at establishing as soon as possible a common or unified market in Eastern Europe. Whether this decision signals new horizons for SEI depends very much on what the near future may hold. Nonetheless, the key determinants of the decision to move toward a common market derive from the sequence of unsettling economic developments in the region during the 1980s, as briefly touched upon earlier. These have been pressing the political leaderships to formulate positive actions in support of economic reform. Efforts to change institutions, policy objectives, behavioral patterns, and economic instruments depend to a large extent, particularly in the smaller CPEs, on bolstering export capacities and importing advanced technologies. Export-led growth, at this stage of lingering internal and external imbalances and the overall bleak outlook for conquering third markets, depends critically on making a quantum leap with SEI.

Such a measurable step forward requires unorthodox, imaginative initiatives that motivate economic agents by bolstering their material and other interest in integration matters. Hence the emphasis on eventually opening up capital, labor, and goods markets to regain a faster, export-led growth path. Concrete details on how the unified market may shape up are as yet unknown. If only for that reason, the still ongoing debate provides an opportunity to examine shifts that may facilitate in a number of respects the ways the CPEs can cooperate with IEOs and the global economy as a whole (see chapter 5).

At least since the preparations for the first economic summit[11] of the 1980s, which eventually was held in June 1984, there has been considerable agitation for reversing the passivity of the CMEA as a regional economic institution and enacting profound changes in the SEI mechanisms and policy objectives. A broad-based debate has been waged primarily around revamping the CMEA's institutional setup with a view to rationalizing the bureaucracy, streamlining the mechanisms through which issues get tabled, and rendering the deliberative organs more effective. Also, the ultimate purposes of SEI, the supporting institutions, and the instruments at the disposal of agents to coordinate structural macroeconomic policies were to be reexamined from the bottom up. Finally, the institutions and instruments to enhance day-to-day integration matters – the integration mechanism in the strict sense – were to be refocused to provide, among other things, effective support for emerging reforms.

These three problem bundles have been at the center of numerous investigations conducted at various hierarchical levels and from a number of different angles. They have been the preoccupation of debates in the CMEA's highest policy-making organs, including successive Council Sessions, several economic summits, and frequent meetings of the Central Committee Secretaries in charge of economic affairs. Consensus has at best been only slowly emerging since mid-1987 and the important 43rd CMEA Session (Moscow, 13–14 October 1987), which revealed *ex post* the pivotal contribution of the November 1986 summit in polarizing the movement toward SEI reform (Brabant 1988b; Brabant 1989a, 121–5; Brabant 1989h). Nonetheless, important decisions have in the meantime been taken; a few have already been implemented or are in the process of being carried out. There are, however, many critical issues that continue to form part and parcel of the ongoing policy agenda for deliberation. Five groups of issues can be identified.

At the 43rd Session the members agreed to streamline the CMEA organization. This involves abolishing organs that have not performed well over the years, consolidating units that duplicate each other, enacting a sizable retrenchment of the civil service, and generally gearing the tasks entrusted to the CMEA less to the day-to-day planning of resource allocation than to charting medium- to long-term strategic directions for structural change. All these objectives are in fact quite similar to the intentions of *perestrojka*, with the Soviet version providing the major impetus to change.

Some organizational modifications were carried out in early 1988 but not all details are available. From a variety of sources, I gather that the statutory official CMEA organs, which in late 1987 numbered forty (the Session, the Executive Committee and its four Committees, the Secretariat, twenty-three Standing Commissions, seven Conferences, and three Institutes), were reduced very sharply in early 1988 and again in mid-year, following the 44th Session. The changes have affected the Committees, Conferences, Institutes, and Standing Commissions (Ikonnikov 1988). Four new Committees of the Executive Committee were created and one (on material–technical supply) was abolished. The number of Standing Commissions was severely cut back. Of the twenty-three extant at the end of 1987, there are only a few left. By adding new macroeconomic and secretarial Commissions in Moscow, as distinct from the sectoral ones located throughout the CMEA, their number presently stands at eleven. The Management Institute was apparently also abolished. Finally, one of the Conferences (legal affairs) was transformed into a Standing Commission and five others were abolished altogether, leaving only the Conference of

Water Administration and Shipping. Moreover, it was decided to slash about one-third (roughly 600 to 700 individuals) of the civil service that primarily forms the CMEA Secretariat. But there is no hard evidence on how this decision has been implemented, if at all. There evidently remains considerable room for further retrenchment and coaxing the CMEA civil service into greater efficiency (Širjaev 1988). All this forms part and parcel of a much more sweeping reform of the CMEA organization and personnel, including the dozens of autonomous and other regional organizations affiliated with the CMEA that are entrusted with particular integration tasks. But details are lacking.[12]

Secondly, there was widespread agreement in Moscow and Prague to rechart assistance policies to the non-European CMEA members (Cuba, Mongolia, and Vietnam), although the assent in some cases was rather reluctant. Past economic development assistance to these countries was deemed to have been less effective than desired by both donors and recipients. The former agreed to elaborate a coherent multilateral approach in a medium- to long-term dovetailed assistance program so as to improve measurably the benefits accruing from these efforts.

Separate drafts of comprehensive economic cooperation with each of the non-European members were presented in Prague. Once harmonized into a firm stance on technical and economic assistance, it will become part and parcel of the emerging new integration strategy (see below). The basic objective is to involve these countries more fully in CMEA efforts on an equal, commercial basis. The programs also envisage that specific projects will be commissioned.[13]

Thirdly, the Moscow Session agreed virtually unanimously to work out *Collective concept* as a new SEI strategy to be presented in an advanced draft form to the Prague Council Session. This program would jell around efforts to move beyond previous plans and programs for integrating the region by taking a fresh look at the objectives, policies, instruments, and basic institutional supports of regional cooperation which have been on the debating table since the earliest calls for holding a top-level CMEA economic summit earlier in the decade. Its major objective would be to lay the foundations for a unified market and thus to ensure the "transition to a qualitatively new level of cooperation" (Syčëv 1988, 3) in the years ahead. The new concept focuses on accelerating technological progress, intensifying production, broadening production specialization, and integrating more fully the non-European CMEA members. It also singles out the main branches, chiefly engineering and electronics, for accelerated integration efforts and pays attention to the use of raw materials, social issues, and cooperation in environmental protection.[14] In addition to reiterating well-tested integration forms and strengthening the role of central planning in streamlining structures according to medium- to long-term development aims, the new program should foster economic efficiency and place centerstage the economics of commodity and financial relations of all agents involved in regional economic interaction. All this is to be seen in connection with the aim, first expressed in Moscow in October 1987, to move with determination toward a unified CMEA market.

Fourthly, directly related to the program are major decisions revolving around the precise nature of the integration mechanism to be elaborated in conjunction with, and perhaps in support of, the ongoing reform process in key CPEs. Gaining concurrence on this matter has been very convoluted. Although there has been broad agreement on the need to take another look at key elements of the traditional forms of regional cooperation through planning, to overhaul the passive monetary–financial instruments and institutions at hand, and to introduce innovative institutions and policy instruments, members remain divided on a number of critical economic issues. These include the introduction of a modified form of limited regional convertibility, multilateralism in trade and payments, the determination of unified exchange rates, the revision of the TRP-formation mechanism, the linking of domestic and trade prices, and enhancing the IIB's capital movements. In other words, policy makers emphasize the need to have in place economic instruments, institutions, and macroeconomic policies that foster more intensive forms of economic development and integration. For that, the role of the economic tools of management must be improved, the function of cooperation through the coordination of national plans must be modified, and firms are now to play a much more significant role in the day-to-day pursuit of integration.

Recent Sessions have also emphasized the need to reinvigorate the implementation of *Scientific–technological progress* by measurably improving the organizational prerequisites and indeed the economic conditions for letting firms from different countries interact directly in, for example, the determination of prices and output. This was originally endorsed in 1985 as an important form for implementing *Scientific–technological progress*. But there is an urgent need to invest such relations with economic guidance rules and institutional supports to facilitate effective microeconomic decision making based on real profitability and self-management. The measures envisaged include settlement of accounts for selected transactions, implying in fact some highly limited[15] form of CMEA convertibility, though that is a misnomer as convertibility is not really at stake.[16] In addition, it was envisaged to improve domestic and trade pricing, exchange rates, the IIB's credit mechanism, trade and payments multilateralism through the IBEC, and other aspects pertaining to the indirect coordination of economic decisions. These and other elements of the refurbished mechanism in support of SEI are to be firmly in place in time for the introduction of the next medium-term plans in 1991. An unusual item on the agenda was the creation of socialist multinationals around key national firms, but details are lacking.

Finally, the recent Sessions have paid lip service to the need to improve the traditional forms of plan coordination and indeed to provide support at the regional level for interfirm relations. The GDR and Rumania, in particular, continue to emphasize the paramount role of plan coordination to foster scientific–technological cooperation and to ensure prompt deliveries of adequate volumes of critical fuels and raw materials, respectively. These policy stances contrast sharply with the role accorded to these instruments by other CPEs.

What is the upshot of this soul searching? Expectations regarding the follow-up Council Session, which was repeatedly postponed in 1989 and not convened until 9 January 1990, are very high. Progress on the various components detailed above will have to be recorded without delay if the refurbished SEI mechanism is to be firmly emplaced in time for the new five-year plans. Whether this materializes is a different question. Even if not, the observer of today's CMEA scene has undoubtedly reason for a degree of guarded optimism as concerns the prospects for meaningful change in the SEI mechanisms. This expectation extends well beyond the wildest one that could have been reasonably entertained as recently as two or three years ago. That is not to say that I expect swift movement with SEI. Past experience should be sobering in this regard. At the policy-making level, it will be much more difficult to achieve consensus on the implementation of far-reaching reforms, given that some CPEs remain lukewarm at best toward reform at home, and hence in CMEA relations. From a practical point of view, the present constellation in the CMEA is very far removed from a unified market. Its establishment can be envisaged at best over a protracted adjustment phase. In fact, I do not even subscribe to the notion that all European CPEs can realistically be expected to engage prospectively in genuine wholesale trade on more than a trivial scale. Under the circumstances, it might be useful to rethink the integration mechanism and allow for countries being on different, though synchronized, integration tracks in accordance with agreed-upon modalities, as would now appear to be contemplated. Chapter 5 examines whether this process can be smoothed through greater integration in the world economy and accession to IEOs.

3 International monetary arrangements and Eastern Europe

As explained in chapter 1, World War II and its aftermath ushered in an important watershed in profiling Eastern Europe internationally, including its trading and monetary relations. Soon after the outbreak of the Cold War the socialist countries severed nearly all contacts with IEOs in which MEs also participated and thus isolated themselves within the relatively confined economic format of the CMEA. Inasmuch as the CMEA was conceived as a conduit for serving and propagating the mainstream economic model, the trading and payment systems exhibit a number of peculiar features (see chapter 2).

As explained, the typical CPE economic model and development strategy sought to reduce foreign economic interaction to the bare minimum and to force the geographical distribution of trade in favor of intragroup relations. The domestic insulation has been substantially maintained. The measure of insularity is all but absolute in Albania and North Korea, for example. Others have opened up their economy somewhat, but largely with respect to intragroup trade. Mongolia is a prime example here, but the group also includes CMEA members, such as Bulgaria and Czechoslovakia, which regularly transact about four-fifths of their commerce with the group. Finally, a number of countries have gradually veered away from rigid isolation and some have made hesitant steps toward some *rapprochement* with the international economic regimes in place. Though well aware that more active intermeshing with such interdependent trading, monetary, and financial regimes would not provide a panacea for their economic and other ills, some CPEs hope to derive important gains from membership nonetheless. The degree of interest shown in particular for the financial IEOs took a quantum leap with the recent world economic disturbances. This chapter sketches various tangents of these gradual overtures to the BWS.

Section 1 briefly defines what is meant by the IMS and IFS, the latter seen largely in its original context as its transformation is dealt with in chapter 5.

The next section discusses the genuine systemic obstacles of CPEs to more closely cooperating with the BWS when it was created. Other problems associated with key features of the BWS that clash either with the economic characteristics of the CPEs or, more likely, with their political postures and ideological precepts are investigated in section 4. Before looking at these obstacles, however, I shall briefly explain the four main periods of the relationship between the CPEs and the Bretton Woods institutions, but it would simply breach the boundaries of this book to do so from a strictly historical angle. The official position of the CPEs on an eventual reform of the BWS in the context of the fundamental international policy topics of the NIEO is discussed in section 5. Next I examine a number of aspects related to the participation of CPEs in the IMS. The mainstream perceived strengths and weaknesses of the prevailing monetary order are briefly summarized in section 7. Finally, specific pointers for a reformed IFS and IMS as they emerge from the debate waged until about the mid-1980s are summarized in an attempt to arrive at a more comprehensive picture of the position on the IFS and IMS taken by pre-reform CPEs, and how they then thought to be able to participate more fully in such a modified system. The implications of ongoing reforms for participation in the BWS are taken up in chapter 5.

1 The monetary and financial regimes

Though both the IMS and the IFS have undergone significant change over the past forty years, the former is easier to define as a regime in terms of the definitions specified in the introduction, for reasons to be made clear below.

The monetary regime

The purpose of the IMS conceived at Bretton Woods was to provide external payments financing with a view to ensuring that commitments to the fixed-par system would be maintained to the extent desired through drawings from a common pool of resources and that proper measures would be taken to remedy structural imbalances. This became an international concern if only because "payments financing arises as an issue essentially because of the insistence of national governments on their sovereign rights to create money" (Cohen 1982, 459).

The principles of this regime derived from the basic one that nations should be assured of an adequate but not unlimited supply of supplementary financing for balance-of-payments purposes. These principles are formally articulated in the Fund's Articles of Agreement and backed by explicit organizational arrangements in the Fund. With respect to norms, in the IMS they are essentially standards of behavior defined in terms of formally, that is legally, articulated rights and obligations to which each member subscribes pursuant to its accession. The rights consist essentially of obtaining access to Fund resources within quota limits, upon which various conditionality rules may be imposed. Access to funds over and above the automatic 25 percent limit, particularly in the upper credit tranches, would be subject to explicit conditions specified in stabilization programs and standby arrangements that members in need of loans would have to negotiate with the Fund. The obligations in turn emanate from the general pledges to play by the agreed-upon rules of the game and thus avoid policies that are inconsistent with the provisions of the Fund's Charter. The specific prescriptions or proscriptions for actions that constitute the rules derive from the Fund's prerogative of policy conditionality. Finally, decision-making procedures amount to arrangements for determining the amount of financing to be made available and the policy conditions, if any, to be imposed in individual instances, combined with bargaining in negotiations between the deficit country and the Fund, administrative decision making within the Fund Secretariat, and, if necessary, voting in the Executive Board.

The financial regime

The IFS put in place in the mid-1940s centered on facilitating private investment for reconstruction and development, and supplementing it with Bank-guaranteed loans backed by funds borrowed in private financial markets. The latter would essentially be channeled into projects worthwhile from an economic point of view but for which private capital funds would not be forthcoming for one reason or another. As argued in chapter 1, this was a legitimate concern: without facilitating international capital movements through guarantees or supplementing them through a public goods mechanism, the level of economic activity in the world as a whole and the pace of progress in the borrower in particular would have been lower than justified on technical economic grounds.

The principal purpose of the IFS regime, then, was to enhance economic reconstruction and development by facilitating private capital investment and supplementing it through a recycling mechanism guaranteed by the global community as specified in the Articles of Agreement. This principle is still valid but it has shifted more and more from a single project focus to macroeconomic structural change (see chapter 5). Project financing would be geared by philosophical principles anchored to facilitating private investment activity. The norms of the IFS regime consist of rights and obligations ensuing from membership accession. The former take the form of obtaining access to project financing on conditions that are no worse than what could be obtained by countries in private capital markets. For the least advantaged countries, conditions are actually concessionary in terms of both interest charged and maturity. These subsidies form, of course, part and parcel of multilateral official development assistance (ODA). The obligations consist of pledges to facilitate implementation of the project, to enable Bank staff to investigate the loan application and the implementation process, and to service and repay the loan on time. The decision-making mechanisms are very similar to the Fund's. Obviously with the changeover from project to structural adjustment financing, there have been changes in all aspects of the regime, particularly in the norms and rules as applied in practice, as clarified in chapter 5.

2 The socialist countries and Bretton Woods

For many years the CPEs shunned the Washington organizations and in fact were most critical of a number of their institutional and behavioral features, chiefly for two sets of reasons. One was the Cold War and its adverse impact on international relations (see chapter 1). Much more crucial in explaining the lack of interest in participating in the BWS were certain economic factors. Key features of the traditional CPE (see chapter 2) made these countries ill-suited to a full role in the BWS. From a technical point of view, the Fund, in particular, had little to offer at the time to CPEs adhering to rigid inconvertibility, fiat prices and exchange rates, and strict bilateralism (Holzman 1976, 172).

The Fund's principal purpose initially was to mobilize its resources for the stabilization of agreed-upon exchange rates with the objective of gradually eliminating foreign exchange controls for current-account transactions, promoting multilateralism, liberalizing capital flows, and other such developments that hinge essentially on the existence of real markets. The comparatively small volume of trade of the CPEs and the fact that the bulk of it was conducted under balanced BTPAs left little room indeed for stabilization.

If centrally set plans are implemented on schedule, the CPEs have no reason to subject their exchange regime and broader macroeconomic policies to Fund surveillance. This was all the more so because the particular development strategy chosen by these countries and the supporting planning institutions and associated policy instruments called for deliberately minimizing the role of money and external finance in fostering rapid industrialization. Not only that, these countries severely curtailed their economic interaction with MEs, they deliberately curbed the potential benefit that could be derived from balance-of-payments financing or from financial assistance for structural change, and they chose to veil their national and regional development efforts in great secrecy.

Yet the original features of the BWS, with some exceptions, should have been quite acceptable to the CPEs. Although a different format for practical surveillance of the policies of these countries may have been required, some of the principal objectives of the Fund coincided eerily with those held by the CPEs. Thus, the paramount role of fixed exchange rates in the medium- to long-term whose par value would be changed only upon fundamental disequilibria (Bernstein 1984, 18) blended in rather well with the goals of economic stability sought by these economies. Barring untoward circumstances, fundamental disequilibrium could be avoided through central planning in a comparatively brief period of time, perhaps within the five-year planning compass. The CPEs could, therefore, have been expected to be interested in maintaining a fixed exchange-rate regime. Furthermore, China, Rumania, and especially the USSR are gold producers. The USSR, in particular, decided to cling to the unique mystique of gold for many years. It is in fact not fully obvious that all references to gold have been abandoned in what might be the current Soviet position on IMS reform (see chapter 5). At least some CPEs would therefore have derived direct and indirect gains from having gold as reserve backing in the IMS.

Perhaps the major exception to the Fund's regime would have been the currency inconvertibility that CPEs have maintained, largely as a byproduct of the high policy priority accorded to domestic policy autonomy. Although the CPE system virtually precludes free access to local markets, certainly by nonresidents and in some instances also by residents, unlike other observers (Diebold 1979b, 23; Holzman 1987, 16–18) I do not feel that it is an immanent feature that their currencies need to be absolutely inconvertible (Brabant 1987a, 357–84; Brabant 1989a, 304–5; Brabant 1989f; Brabant 1989g). Even under the strictest of arrangements in the traditional CPE, one can think of potential benefits of financial convertibility for nonresidents and a limited form of commodity convertibility for tourist transactions. Such arrangements might have been quite palatable to the Fund. These would have had to be instituted with some restrictions that could have been designed to avert conflicts with Fund obligations, especially because currency convertibility in its true form was not being enforced upon any other Fund member.[1]

The most important areas in which the CPEs would have encountered vexing dilemmas revolve around the role of the US dollar in the IMS, intrusive surveillance by the Bank and the Fund, stabilization measures prescribed by the Fund, and free external convertibility. But, with some

Table 3.1. *Status of socialist countries in IMF/IBRD*

Country	No relation	Approach	Withdrawal	Application	Membership
Albania	x	1948			
Bulgaria	x	1948		1990	
China		Founder	1950[a]	1980[b]	1980
Cuba		Founder	1964[c]		
Czechoslovakia		Founder	1954/5	1990	
GDR	x	1990			
Hungary		1964		1981	1982
DPR Korea	x				
Laos		Member			1961
Mongolia	x				
Poland		Founder	1950	1981[d]	1986
Rumania		1964			1972
Soviet Union	x	1986			
Vietnam		Member			1976[e]
Yugoslavia		Founder			

Notes:
[a] Did not formally withdraw but its seat was taken by Republic of China.
[b] Request to take over seat held by Republic of China. It had tried in the early 1950s to accomplish the same but was rebuffed.
[c] 1960 in the case of the World Bank.
[d] Approached the Fund in 1956 but did not pursue the matter.
[e] The Socialist Republic of Vietnam became a member in 1976 after the unification of South and North by virtue of the South's membership in the Fund.

good will, even these obstacles could have been circumnavigated. Unfortunately, the DMEs that were instrumental in the creation of the BWS were on the whole patronizing toward the economic problems faced by the CPEs and offered them conditions of membership that were humiliating in a number of respects. At least during the first decade or so, when the BWS was not in fact being applied even among the key members, owing to the still incomplete path toward convertibility in Europe, the CPEs were asked to abide by principles and to commit themselves to policies that the bulk of the actual members did not heed themselves.

There never was a real understanding of the particular and sometimes peculiar problems posed by the economic and institutional characteristics of the CPEs. Four such logical and legitimate constituents of the economic setup of CPEs (see Wilczynski 1978, 246) were then, and still are in most countries, critical in coming to grips with the external economic implications of the CPE: (1) multiple exchange rates, which are the necessary reflection of the tiered domestic price systems; (2) currency and commodity inconvertibility, which derives from the planned allocation of resources; (3) BTPAs, particularly in intragroup relations, to facilitate trade planning; and (4) pervasive exchange controls, which help to insulate domestic from foreign markets and the CMEA region from east–west relations, and thus to protect the considerable amount of policy autonomy sought by decision makers in CPEs.

In what follows, I shall focus chiefly on the Fund. This is not because I think it is more important than the Bank. Rather, Fund membership is a precondition for Bank membership. Moreover, Fund policies have been far more conspicuous than those of the Bank, perhaps because they address macroeconomic issues, that is, items that are inevitably tied in with politics *per se*. Furthermore, the Bank's operations over the last two decades or so have gradually moved away from strictly microeconomic project financing to structural adjustment financing and to extending loans that are in fact in support of balance-of-payments adjustment measures. But, when the role of the Bank in microeconomic affairs of the CPEs might have entailed serious problems, I shall point them out.

3 Evolution of the CPEs and the IMS

As pointed out in chapter 1 in connection with the major milestones that led to the postwar economic order, there are essentially four periods in the relationship between the CPEs and the BWS. The first one centers on the problems encountered in persuading the USSR to become a founder. This unsatisfactory episode gave rise to a protracted hostile state of affairs between key CPEs and the Fund. The second phase encompasses the exit of three CPEs from the Fund and the Bank. Expulsion or voluntary withdrawal is an exceedingly rare event in the Washington institutions. Only one CPE has ever been expelled. Three countries have voluntarily withdrawn – Cuba, Indonesia (which later rejoined), and Poland (Assetto 1988, 12). It is therefore useful to look in some detail at the issues at stake. The third phase comprises the gradual courting of the BWS which resulted in the entry of Rumania into the Fund in 1972. Finally, with the onset of the financial and trading disturbances of the early 1980s and the emerging economic reforms throughout Eastern Europe, a new appreciation for these monetary institutions has come to the fore. This section looks at the latter three phases.

In what follows, I shall refer to the various types of association of the CPEs in the Fund, and by extension the World Bank, detailed in table 3.1.

In addition to membership, this table includes information on withdrawal, seeking readmission, and putting out feelers to these institutions, possibly with a view to exploring informally the chances of becoming a full member.

Overview of the participation of CPEs in IEOs

In reviewing the access sought by CPEs to the Fund and the World Bank later in this chapter, it is important to recall that most present members of that grouping (as clarified in the introduction) had not yet transformed themselves into CPE status when the BWS was germinating. The issues at stake at the time revolved essentially around the role of the USSR in the postwar economic order. Because of historical accident, several of the present-day CPEs were members of the BWS prior to their transition to the CPE system. Some decided to sever relations with these institutions soon after their mutation into the CPE organizational, economic, and political framework. What is of principal interest here is the motivation behind the application for membership after a hiatus of several decades. To understand the explanation offered later, it is useful to bear in mind the chronology of events.

The CPEs in the Bretton Woods institutions

Membership in the Bretton Woods institutions is unambiguous: countries must subscribe to all Articles of Agreement without exception, reservation, or interpretation of any one stipulation. Furthermore, Fund membership is a prerequisite to joining the Bank and its affiliated institutions. As an active participant in the deliberations that led up to the establishment of the Bretton Woods institutions (see chapter 1), the Soviet Union did not object to these features. Yet it never formally refused to join the Fund. For economic and political reasons, however, the USSR did not contact the Fund from 1946 until 1986, when the first informal feelers were extended.

China, Cuba, Czechoslovakia, Laos, Poland, Vietnam, and Yugoslavia joined the BWS from its inception or soon after they gained independence. With the exception of Laos and Vietnam, most were also among the Fund's early members – several were in fact founders, as shown in table 3.1. But a number of them did not remain in these IEOs for very long. In the following two decades, the CPEs stayed away from the BWS for reasons to be examined. Certainly, Albania and Bulgaria made tentative inquiries about Fund membership in 1948, but did not follow them up. Some exploratory talks also took place between the representatives of the Fund and Hungary and Rumania in 1964, on the occasion of the first session of UNCTAD, but there was no follow-up (see Kranz 1984, 32) until Rumania approached the Bretton Woods institutions in the early 1970s and obtained admission in 1972.

Cuba, Czechoslovakia, and Poland leave the Bretton Woods institutions

Poland signed the Articles of Agreement as a founder with the intention of taking advantage of the new institution as a gateway to the World Bank and hence financial assistance for reconstruction, rehabilitation, and economic development more generally. Loans for that purpose were deemed vital to restoring the health of a country characterized by the "appalling conditions caused by warfare and occupation."[2] Poland, like many other countries, including others in Eastern Europe,[3] availed itself of the clauses alleviating the cost of association in the short run for states that had suffered extensive damage from enemy occupation and hostilities during World War II.

Its association with the World Bank, however, was not so auspicious. Poland was one of the first countries to solicit in the autumn of 1946 a reconstruction loan. This request for general reconstruction assistance was rejected implicitly when the Bank proposed a specific loan amounting to only one-fourth of the requested amount for the reconstruction of the coal industry. This would not only benefit Poland, but also expedite recovery elsewhere in Europe, owing to the shortage of coal. Poland submitted a revised second request soon thereafter. But negotiations about the coal loan were stalled, largely for political reasons. Officially, of course, the Bank was delaying the processing of the loan to ensure the application of "sound banking standards" to all applicants. In this, it used a good deal of political content, referring repeatedly to the uncertainties engendered by the transition in political regimes in Eastern Europe in general and Poland in particular, despite the injunction against such in article IV,10 of the Articles of Agreement.

The alleged lack of independence of Poland from Soviet tutelage at the time was the key consideration that delayed further deliberations on the loan request. The invocation of this political factor stemmed from the Bank leadership and the influence of core members, chiefly the United States. The Bank was also worried that its private investors, mainly from the United States, would forgo the purchase of Bank debentures – the principal source of its financing – because the overall political climate regarding Eastern Europe and communist regimes more generally was very adverse and appallingly shortsighted. As the prospects of obtaining recovery finance dwindled and Soviet encroachment on Eastern Europe rose, Poland joined other CPEs in denouncing Bank policies as favoring Western European economic recovery and as supporting the Dutch and French colonial wars.

On 14 March 1950, Poland voluntarily withdrew from the Fund and World Bank, alleging that these institutions had failed in their original purpose because they had become subservient to US interests, as, for example, over the financing of Polish coal production. Its official letter of withdrawal cited three issues, namely the effort of the Fund to force members to devalue their currencies, the subservience of the Fund and the Bank to US interests, and the failure of these institutions to fulfill the spirit of Bretton Woods, that is, to assist Poland in reconstructing its economy. The institutions, of course, rejected this interpretation "summarily" and charged in their turn that Poland had failed to pay in its called-up subscription to the Bank – although many other countries were then in arrears – and to set a par value of its currency.

Poland apparently approached the Fund in October 1956 (see Kranz 1984) with a view to being readmitted, but the Fund made it then politically impossible for that country to contemplate membership in earnest. The events around the Polish October and the subsequent courting of Soviet favors did not make for a positive setting at all. Poland did not reapproach the Bretton Woods institutions until the early 1980s. It lodged a request for accession in November 1981, barely one week after Hungary. It was admitted only in late May 1986, for reasons examined in section 4 below.

Czechoslovakia participated in the Bretton Woods conference and ancillary meetings and negotiations. It did so mainly, as did Poland, to ensure adequate funds for reconstruction and rehabilitation. It benefited at least from two of the concessions granted at Bretton Woods for war-damaged countries, namely the postponement of payment of a portion of their quotas as well as the stipulation on taking into account "exceptional requirements of members" (Proceedings 1948, 555), which had been inserted in lieu of the waiver that Czechoslovakia had agitated for at Bretton Woods.

In August 1946, Czechoslovakia was the second country to request a loan for economic reconstruction. Processing of the application was slowed down, owing to the applicant's failure to supply the requested information but also the unexpectedly strong recovery of the Czechoslovak economy in 1946. Following the February 1948 events, as in the case of Poland, political considerations began to impinge upon the processing of the loan, allegedly because the turn toward the Soviet Union impaired Czechoslovakia's ability to meet Bank obligations. From then on,

Czechoslovakia championed political causes in both the Fund and the Bank, for example with respect to the China seat. But US opposition held firm, and Beijing therefore stayed out of the institutions until 1980.

The unilateral devaluation of the koruna in May 1953, which affected the value of the Fund's local currency holdings, brought matters to a boiling point. This tension was not at all attenuated when Czechoslovakia agreed to restore these funds fully soon after the devaluation. It took the position that the Soviet Union had championed earlier: exchange rates for typical CPEs are meaningless and thus do not affect the competitive position of other Fund members; the Fund should therefore not be consulted about such "internal" price realignments. Furthermore, Czechoslovakia refused to provide the information required for regular membership on security grounds, failed to pay in its full obligation to the Bank, and was incurring default charges on unserviced loans. Because Czechoslovakia had not consulted with the Fund about the June 1953 devaluation of the koruna and the accompanying monetary reform, and had refused to furnish information and cooperate with the Fund, the Executive Directors declared Czechoslovakia ineligible for loans, a position subsequently confirmed by the Board of Governors. As in the Bank, Czechoslovakia was given until the end of 1954 to regularize its status in the Fund; barring that, it would be expelled. This position was maintained and enforced so that, according to the Fund and the Bank, Czechoslovakia was expelled as of end-1954. Czechoslovakia alleged that this turn of events had been politically motivated, and hence submitted a letter of withdrawal in May 1955. This is still Czechoslovakia's position, although the Fund adheres to the former date (Horsefield 1969, 359–64). It did not seek readmission until early 1990, although there were some informal suggestions during the Prague spring that such an overture might soon be made. Czechoslovakia apparently never contacted the Fund or the Bank from early 1955 until late 1988, when an informal delegation of high-level Czechoslovak economists and government officials was received by the Bretton Woods institutions with a view to "exchanging information."

Cuba withdrew from the Fund in 1964, partly because it could not meet its financial obligations and partly because of the far-reaching political changes enacted since the late 1950s. It was, in any case, in a position to be censured, as Czechoslovakia had been earlier, because of noncompliance with the Articles of Agreement (Hamel 1980, 178). Political considerations were probably the major factor in its eschewing accommodation with the Fund on payments due.

Renewal of interest and Rumania's membership

As one manifestation of Rumania's interest in relatively disengaging itself from the CMEA, beginning with the mid-1960s, when it perceived CMEA integration policies as hindering its industrialization ambitions (Brabant 1989a, 68–71), it sought to broaden its foreign economic relations with third markets, including the DEs. On the tail of the reform it instituted half-heartedly in the late 1960s with a view to fostering managerial decentralization and greater enterprise autonomy (see chapter 2), it applied for membership in the Fund and was admitted in December 1972, just when it had decided to abandon the reform through a rapid recentralization of economic decision making. At the same time it embarked on a major import drive that would soon bequeath a sizable foreign debt.

Rumania was the first CPE to join the BWS after the withdrawal or expulsion of China, Cuba, Czechoslovakia, and Poland. The significance of this move lay more in Rumania's aspirations to greater economic and political independence at the time of east–west *détente*, and some western countries' foreign policy ambitions to dismember the eastern alliance, than in terms of a strictly economic confluence of interests. Indeed, Rumania's accession occurred in consequence of its decision in the mid-1960s to disengage itself, relatively speaking, from the particular interpretation of *Basic principles*.[4] It may have been looking for support to expand its relations with the DEs, a policy to which it had been wedded. But the chief motivation of the new policy originated especially in foreign-policy thinking. This shift, which was congenial to western perceptions about "loosening" the Eastern European alliance, found an accommodating resonance in the stance taken by key members on Rumania's application for accession.

It was remarkable that Rumania was admitted to the Fund without having to pass through a special transitory accession arrangement. Certainly, Rumania was not prepared to divulge sensitive information about its domestic economic performance and especially its behavior in external payments and debt, including balance of payments, gold stocks and production, and foreign currency reserves. But it is incorrect to suggest, as does Assetto (1988, 146–7), that Rumania was brought into these financial organizations upon having been granted a formal waiver of the obligation to supply that information or, as does Lavigne (1985b, 232), that the arrangement with Rumania went against international public law. In fact, Rumania succeeded in arranging that sensitive information would be supplied to the Fund and the Bank on a regular basis and during official missions, but that the institutions would refrain from disclosing that information in the regular statistical releases.[5] But that commitment did not, of course, prevent that information from being leaked as soon as it was supplied.

Membership becoming fashionable? – China, Hungary, Poland, and Vietnam

As indicated, the accession of Vietnam to the Bank and the Fund came about because of the reunification of Vietnam under the control of the socialist north. Saigon had been a member of the Fund and, upon the end of the civil war, Hanoi simply took over the south's obligations with respect to the Fund and Bank. Vietnam was not then a very outward-looking country. But it was a formidable foe of the United States, which objected strenuously to it being seated in the Washington organizations. It had just concluded thirty years of war and revolution, was about to sever its relationship with China, and had worked itself into the graces of the WTO members. It therefore had little need for balance-of-payments assistance, provided it could manage its meager foreign exchange reserves. But it found its status in the IEOs congenial enough not to depart from them, perhaps in the hope of eliciting Bank loans.

China finally became a Fund member in 1980, when US policy considerations, in particular, were receptive to the replacement of the Republic of China. After the People's Republic was proclaimed in October 1949, it did not apparently covet its chair, which was held by the Republic of China (Taiwan), until 1978, when Beijing began to explore a more open foreign policy, including participation in international economic affairs. The People's Republic formally took its seat in 1980, after a makeshift solution had been found regarding the outstanding claims on Taiwan.[6] Prior to its resignation in 1955, Czechoslovakia acted on behalf of the People's Republic in seeking the expulsion of the Republic of China but failed in that endeavor for political reasons: the United States as the main supporter of the Republic of China resolutely mustered its clout in support of scuttling any attempt to recognize Beijing in international organizations until the early 1970s, when China entered the United Nations, and later, when it was seated in the IEOs (Cooper 1988b; Kim 1981). China did not attempt to take its seat in the latter until its reemergence in international economic affairs in the late 1970s. With the opening up of the Chinese economy and the drift toward reform, Chinese planners found themselves at that time with a major external payments crisis of their own making. There was therefore a symbiosis of economic and political interest in taking the China seat in the Washington institutions. Nonetheless, considering the virulent opposition expressed previously by the Mao Administration, it was extraordinary that China accepted Fund conditionality at all (Cooper 1988b; Kim 1981, 456–8).

Disregarding the almost accidental accession of Vietnam and the reseating of China, as already noted, the Rumanian example did not elicit any following for about a decade. Then suddenly in November 1981 in a matter of one week both Hungary and Poland requested accession. Both have since been admitted, but on radically different terms. In contrast to the considerable political overtones of Rumania's accession in 1972, Hungary's membership application was logically embedded in the economic decentralization of the NEM pursued with some wavering in the preceding decade and a half and its then sizable convertible currency debt for whose resolution some streamlined, if perhaps unorthodox, adjustment program would have to be formulated, if possible with fresh financial assistance. As János Nyerges (1986b, 342) put it, Hungary was IMF-minded before it joined and so, if it could "get paid for austerity measures, why not?"

The reactivation of the transition toward a comprehensive, if regulated, socialist ME in which trade prices for most goods and services are fed through to a significant extent gave credibility to Hungary's request for admission to the Bretton Woods institutions in 1981. This was further strengthened by Hungary's emphasis on pursuing an outward-looking development strategy and reaching a sustainable competitive position in world markets. It hoped that Fund membership would facilitate access to comparatively inexpensive stabilization funds and provide a powerful psychological fillip to its economic relations with DMEs. The request made in late 1981 was codetermined by the expected further deterioration in the country's terms of trade for several more years; the flagging of its export drive, especially to Western Europe; the then imminent external financial difficulties; and the broader needs to rescale the contemplated adjustments of its economic structure to a dependence on external markets that could not have been accommodated through the traditional instruments of central planning.

The case of Poland is far more complex. Its application in November 1981 can also be placed against the backdrop of the economic devolution sought within its on–off incipient economic reform. From the very first broad-based reform conceptualized in the 1960s, Polish decision makers contemplated a return to the Washington institutions (Toczek 1984). That this step was taken in 1981 was in part because the protracted Polish reform had yet to bear significant fruit in terms of raising the country's capacity to generate convertible currency from exports of manufactures. At the same time, the adaptation of the country's economic mechanism was slated soon to become an essential ingredient of a feasible long-term development strategy. Nevertheless, the immediate reasons for the move stemmed overwhelmingly from the unprecedented slide in Poland's domestic and external economic fortunes. Especially critical was the legacy of the reckless borrowing in world financial markets under the Gierek Administration in the early 1970s as a substitute for obtaining productivity gains from meaningful economic reforms. In spite of the sizable capital inflow, Gierek's advisers failed to boost Poland's export capacity because of ineptness, including the allocation of a substantial portion of the borrowing to current consumption and to projects that were simply not suited to the country.

Around 1980, there was considerable, and growing, concern in world financial markets about the wisdom and procedures of rescheduling Poland's debt, and the form, mode of implementation, and probable payoff of recently inaugurated or contemplated domestic economic policies. Poland therefore needed to reassure official as well as private financial markets abroad that the leadership was committed to steering the economy in a direction that would permit it to service in an orderly fashion the foreign debt in convertible currency, perhaps after some transitory liquidity problems. The application to the Bank and the Fund also provided the cosmetic sheen, at least in the short run, for the promulgation of internal socioeconomic reforms with the active support of all power groups in the protracted societal crisis that erupted in the late 1970s and is only at this juncture finding a satisfactory solution. Furthermore, in the medium to long run the country would have stood to benefit from access to additional financial resources, albeit under mildly disciplinary international scrutiny. Of course, Bank loans and the opportunity to bid on projects sponsored by the Bank were also attractive inducements. As is well known, the political rifts between east and west, owing in particular to the Afghanistan syndrome and the imposition of martial law in Poland in December 1981, stalled the processing of the application until late 1984. Admission was granted only in late May 1986.

Toward generalized membership?

The other European CPEs, including at least Bulgaria, Czechoslovakia, and the Soviet Union, have been carefully monitoring the experiences of the CPEs that are Fund members and may initiate similar, if not as far-reaching, management changes. As noted in the introduction, following the announcement that it would soon undertake a radical reform, Soviet spokespersons in early 1986 launched several trial balloons, including the prospect of the USSR seeking accession to the Bretton Woods institutions or perhaps even simply permission finally to ratify the Articles of Agreement it signed at Bretton Woods in July 1944. This has been denied and confirmed on various occasions since then, with the sense and seriousness of declared interest being directly correlated with the circumstances and spokesperson in question. Also they could benefit in the medium to long run from refocusing the role and place of central planning in economic decision making. Inasmuch as such changes aim at directing economywide planning primarily at desirable structural adaptations and at guiding plan implementation and current managerial decisions by appropriate indirect policy instruments and supporting institutions, membership in the BWS could be most valuable. The situation of these outsiders will be taken up in chapter 5 in conjunction with the current reform ferment.

It may be surmised that other CPEs had been awaiting Soviet moves for some time prior to the revolutions of late 1989. These include in the first instance Bulgaria and Czechoslovakia, both of which applied in early 1990. But in time also the GDR should have an interest in exploring some association. I disagree here strongly with all those who advocate that these other CPEs do not "belong" in the Washington institutions. Thus, Lavigne (1985b, 235) argues that the Soviet Union has no need at all of the Fund for improving its financial credibility or for obtaining additional resources, and thus would not make such a move attractive to other CPEs not in the Fund. Certainly some of the latter could obtain a "seal of approval" for their financial position in western money markets and, especially Bulgaria, could draw resources from the Bank on advantageous terms. But these countries could also play a constructive role in molding thinking about the IFS and IMS, and their possible reforms.

In other words, there is currently the prospect that nearly all CMEA members could in the medium term become members of the IFS and IMS in place. It is, therefore, necessary to scrutinize carefully the systemic and other obstacles to association and how one could best cope with them. This I shall do in chapter 5. Here I shall look at the perceived traditional obstacles to the CPEs playing their proper role in the Bretton Woods institutions.

4 The original critique of the BWS by the CPEs

As emphasized in chapter 1, the CPEs have never had a clear-cut position on an IMS that they could fully support. Yet they have formulated pertinent reform positions that should not be ignored, if only because some are quite sensible. Furthermore, it is always worth the effort to explore ways in which outsiders could be integrated more completely into the global economy. Finally, these reform proposals have been tendered because the CPEs have some interest in joining the IMS, for example, because of the adverse effects of their indebtedness on western private financial institutions. Especially high interest rates, cutbacks in the availability of rollovers and loans, and a very soft foreign market for the products that CPEs can export on a competitive basis have impinged upon the room for policy flexibility.

Although the USSR succeeded in substantially modifying the Fund's draft Articles of Agreement (see chapter 1), the issues then raised have dominated the attitude of most CPEs *vis-à-vis* the Fund and its modifications since the early 1970s. But not all have remained equally important until today. It may nonetheless be useful to look briefly at these items one by one, but without forcibly confining commentary to how matters were viewed in the mid-1940s.

The role of gold in the IMS

The USSR's position at Bretton Woods did not, of course, challenge the unique mystique of gold or its role as a basic monetary reserve or anchor of the IMS. But it objected to the transfer of gold to US territory, the level of the assessed gold quota for some countries, the earmarking of newly mined gold to work off quota drawings, and the disclosure of economic intelligence about gold production and stocks. Mainly because other CPEs are not substantial gold producers (only China and Rumania produce more than trivial amounts), the USSR's attitude toward the role of gold in the IMS until the breakdown of the gold-exchange standard was often mirrored in other CPEs (see Rémy 1981, 1985).

Regardless of the role of ideology in the economic behavior of CPEs, some have traditionally had a doctrinal attachment to gold. The CPEs regard gold fundamentally as a basic reserve instrument, an essential stabilizer in international economic relations, and an instrument of discipline in national monetary affairs. By virtue of gold's rarity, the emission of fiduciary money in strict proportion with gold reserves, in the view of socialist countries, as adherents to metalism before them, provides a strong element of discipline in domestic monetary policies and in balance-of-payments adjustment efforts. Credit money issued in only a loose relationship to its "commodity" or "reserve" backing is wont to entail uncontrollable inflation and monetary chaos with all the attendant adverse consequences for employment, economic stability, and the sustainable pace of growth. Furthermore, of special practical importance is the USSR's position as the world's second largest gold producer. It thus has an obvious stake in the role of gold for monetary purposes and its price. Finally, the ideological underpinnings of the attitude toward gold bear stressing.

Ideology plays a vital role in Marxist economic theory. Its stance on monetary affairs is no exception as it regards money as a special commodity that serves as the universal embodiment of abstract labor and as a bearer of exchange value. As the all-encompassing embodiment of abstract labor, gold is considered to be the crystallization of the exchange value[7] of commodities, and hence the bearer of exchange value. Within that frame of reference, Soviet monetarists in particular argue that the value of money derives essentially from goods. Many goods have been money in the course of history, with precious metals gradually assuming the role of the universal backing of money. Gold is viewed as the culmination of that process, as money in a global sense, and as the quasi-universal backing of national and international liquidity. Of course, gold is an ideological issue also because the main ME producers and reserve holders (including South Africa and the United States) are ideological and political adversaries of the Soviet Union and, by extension, the socialist world.

The role of national and international reserve currencies

The CPEs stress the fundamental contradiction between using national currencies as international reserves and providing adequate liquidity backed by a "basic" international value. This is essentially the old Triffin (1961) dilemma: to provide adequate liquidity for international transactions in an IMS anchored to a national currency that is also a vehicle currency, the latter's supply must steadily increase irrespective of monetary demand in the emitting country. It should, therefore, run a permanent balance-of-payments deficit. But that is bound to outpace the availability of gold backing, and so will in due course erode confidence in the vehicle currency.

As noted, the CPEs emphasize the conflict between the need for monetary stability and the exploration of purely international reserve currencies when their creation is not mainly motivated by the need for adequate liquidity as an essential ingredient of a stable economic environment. That is to say, the creation of international reserves beyond what is required by "commodity backing" should be zero. But such an interpretation of the preceding stance appears to conflict with some of the support that the CPEs routinely provide for the positions on IMS reforms and special drawing right (SDR) allocation taken by DEs, particularly in the context of the Group of Seventy-seven.[8]

As a matter of course, the CPEs have been rather contemptuous of the lack of monetary discipline and responsibility in leading DMEs (Kolloch and Polzin-Walter 1988; Korolëv 1984). The charge of laxity in monetary policy for ulterior capitalist motives (including the unloading of surplus currency, stimulating inflation to erode the real value of debt and external obligations, and facilitating the exportation of capital and thus raising the hegemonic influence of the emitting country) has been especially forceful since the abandonment of the fixed exchange-rate regime in 1973. But this complaint had been levied well before the monetary disturbances of the 1970s, for example at the time of the US's adventurist foreign policy of the 1960s *vis-à-vis* Vietnam. Most commentators argue that the excessive issue of currency and credit, the large and persistent US balance-of-payments deficits to remedy the international liquidity problem and to finance US investment abroad, and the demonetization of gold have all produced uncontrollable inflationary pressures. These have had adverse consequences, for the CPEs as for others, and need to be rectified.

The distribution of voting power

As a matter of principle in international relations, the CPEs object to voting by economic strength. Given the distribution of economic power, they see in this a measure of exercising in particular dollar hegemony and of interfering in the internal economic affairs of sovereign states. Especially since the declaration of the NIEO, they have called for a "democratization" of the official monetary institutions. As a replacement of the present system of weighted voting, these countries have traditionally advocated that the Bretton Woods institutions move closer to the "one country, one vote" system typical of their own intragroup organizations and of most of the UN system.

Surveillance, stabilization policies, and the adjustment process

Together with many MEs, the CPEs have expressed concern over the type of adjustment processes embedded in the philosophy that is at the roots of the BWS and even more so in the guidelines for surveillance and conditionality gradually adopted during the period of flexible exchange rates. The argument is quite general: the CPEs subscribe to the notion, which is incidentally shared by many critics of the BWS, that the adjustment burden has fallen disproportionately on the countries encountering balance-of-payments deficits, although the disequilibrium usually stems from unsynchronized macroeconomic policies in surplus and deficit countries, or perhaps even overwhelmingly on account of mercantilist policies on the part of the surplus countries.

There is little doubt that the CPEs have recently encountered considerable problems with adjustments pursued with the instruments of indirect economic control that are typically among the key targets of Fund recommendations, such as prices, exchange rates, interest rates, the compression of government expenditure, the control of money supply, and credit creation (Brabant 1987a, 87–126). At the same time, it is clear that the CPEs may find it easier than many DEs to pursue absorption-compressing and expenditure-reducing adjustment policies palatable to the Fund within their typical planning and intervention instruments. It is, then, not so much the goals and means of adjustment that are at the roots of the objections to stabilization measures endorsed by the Fund. The prime problem would appear to be the authority of the Fund to prescribe in principle the timing and scope of such policies. The CPEs contest both on the ground that they constitute an inadmissible interference in their own affairs.

Convertibility and exchange rates

The type of central planning typically embraced by CPEs is incompatible with the Fund's prescriptions on commodity and currency convertibility for current account transactions (article VIII). On the other hand, the CPEs have never had conceptual problems with a fixed exchange-rate regime, which they embraced for themselves. But they consider their foreign-exchange regime and changes therein to be intrinsic prerogatives of their economic sovereignty, on which they hold a rather absolute view (see Spiller 1984, 28–31). They maintain that the Fund should not insist on effective convertibility for CPEs because that is incompatible with essential operational features of strict central planning for structural change. Not only that, the CPEs have traditionally refused to consult the Fund about their exchange-rate policies.[9] But the CPEs have found it rather difficult to come to grips with a system of flexible exchange rates in their own exchange rate policies, let alone in properly managing their foreign exchange flows in support of central planning (see Brabant 1985b; Brabant 1987a, 221–35).

Information disclosure

Finally, the disclosure of sensitive economic information has been an important issue from the very start of the debates about the BWS, although a mutually satisfactory solution was then hammered out at Bretton Woods (see chapter 1). But the item of disclosure of sensitive information has been a recurrent component of the CPEs' criticism of the BWS, in spite of significant changes in international affairs since the Cold

War and the relaxation of "state secrets" in CPEs. But some CPEs still do not publish sufficient information to permit a comprehensive independent assessment of their economic situation. In fact, the range and quality of information have markedly deteriorated since the mid-1970s.

5 Official position of the CPEs on monetary reform in the 1970s

The CPEs have usually been quite critical of the IMS and its problems, which they view as but one facet of the more general economic crisis of capitalism. The latter's principal origin they ascribe in particular to the economic policies pursued by large DMEs – the United States in the first instance. Only rarely do political leaders or even informed commentators offer a positive proposal for remedying what they perceive to be the monetary disorder that ensued with the collapse of the fixed exchange-rate regime. Even if aired, such policy positions are rarely adopted explicitly by all CPEs, as underlined in the introduction.

The broadest statements by the CPEs on fundamental principles regarding the IMS have been aired at UNCTAD meetings, especially the Fourth Session in Nairobi in 1976 (UNCTAD 1976, 152–71), the Fifth in Manila in 1979 (UNCTAD 1979, 178–94), and the Sixth in Belgrade (UNCTAD 1983a, 152–3). Without a doubt, the document tabled at Nairobi deserves the most attention since it was issued at the time of the debate on reforming the BWS. The so-called Jamaica agreements (Meier 1982, 227–36) on replacing the fixed-par system with a flexible system anchored to the SDR were then topical; but critical components thereof have in the meantime fallen by the wayside. The substantive points regarding the IFS and IMS in all pronouncements by those who originally endorsed that part of the Nairobi declaration (UNCTAD 1976, 152–4) have not been modified drastically, though several CPEs have rephrased their positions in response to evolving events in the world economy. Moreover, these principles are held so generally that they would appear to be shared by nearly all CPEs, save perhaps Albania and North Korea. That is not to say that they subscribe to each and every element of these pronouncements or that there has not been any evolution at all in the mainstream view. There has, and some countries harbor particular positions on trading and monetary systems. This has come to the fore more and more since the beginning of generalized *perestrojka* (see chapter 5).

Regarding the restructuring of the IMS, the CPEs officially reject the usefulness of measures aimed "at the demonetization of gold, its replacement by [SDRs] and the legalizing of 'floating exchange rates'," which "cannot provide stability and reliability for the international monetary mechanism" or "remove the basic shortcomings of the present [IMS]" (UNCTAD 1976, 153–4). To normalize the international monetary situation, the CPEs in principle advocate measures "to enhance the role of gold in international liquidity and to bring about the gradual abolition and banning of the monopolistic position held by one or several national currencies in the [IMS]." They take a skeptical view of proposals aimed at reforming the Fund from within and contend instead that UNCTAD would constitute "a more suitable forum for taking decisions on international monetary problems" (UNCTAD 1976, 154). It is these positions that have been reiterated numerous times, although since the early 1980s references to a return to gold have become rather rare and muted. But the CPEs have certainly not altogether jettisoned their advocacy of a role for gold in IMS reform (see chapter 5).

Because of important shifts in the global economy since the mid-1970s, one would have expected some transformation in the policy positions of the CPEs on such issues as SDR allocations, the role of gold, Bank lending practices, and Fund surveillance and conditionality. If such fundamental shifts have taken place, they have not been widely publicized to date. I suspect that they did not really begin to crystallize until the penetrating reassessment launched by Soviet *perestrojka*.

In one of the two published documents of the June 1984 CMEA economic summit, the CPEs "advocate the regimenting of monetary–financial relations, stand against the policy of high interest rates, and champion the normalization of terms under which credits are granted and paid back so that those terms, particularly with relation to the indebtedness of the [DEs], should not be used as a means of political pressure and interference in internal affairs" (CMEA 1984, 7). They have declared themselves in favor of convening a new international conference on money and finance, which had been called for to reactivate the stalled NIEO negotiations and to bestow upon the United Nations a different mandate than its eroded one. In a joint statement circulated at UNCTAD VI in Belgrade, Group D outlined seven rules and principles to be observed in order to convene such a meeting. In addition to reiterating the principles touched upon above, some emphasis was placed on viewing monetary affairs in a global economic context, approaching all international economic issues uniformly, and respecting a country's right to maintain an autonomous currency and monetary regime provided it does not disadvantage other countries (UNCTAD 1983b).

The above quotations from and interpretations of the Nairobi declaration suggest that the CPEs did not then make any clear-cut commitment on their preferred IMS. This position, if anything, has been strengthened since then. Nor are they convinced, as many DEs and the more activist members of the Group of Seventy-Seven proclaim, that an acceptable solution could be hammered out at a new monetary conference. In fact, whether Group D or Modified Group D will participate in such a meeting depends critically "on how the specific tasks of the conference are formulated and on the extent to which the legitimate interests of all States are taken into account during the preparatory work" (United Nations 1983, 2).

6 The participation of CPEs in the IMS

In spite of the variety of obstacles that inhibit participation in the BWS, as noted, several CPEs have paradoxically joined the system in recent years; others decided to remain active within the system or have activated their membership; and a growing number of those remaining outside the system have been expressing an active interest in the BWS. In view of the peculiarities of state trading and CMEA bilateralism, not to mention the political and ideological obstacles usually brought to bear in a discussion about the BWS, one would have thought that these countries would seek to make their participation contingent on special waivers and dispensations, especially as concerns: the disclosure of economic information on the balance of payments, currency reserves, and gold stocks and production; Bank and Fund surveillance and the application of conditionality; the path toward convertibility and elimination of exchange restrictions as called for under article VIII, even with the temporary waivers provided by article XIV; and coming to grips with the peculiarities of the CMEA trade and payments regimes. That no such exceptional bargains needed to be struck, particularly on issues involving the financial disclosure and convertibility guidelines of the BWS, is a testimonial to the flexibility with which the financial IEOs have been able over the years to lure countries into their midst in spite of behavior that deviates markedly from that of the core membership of these institutions. The explanation of the paradox, then, requires a balanced evaluation of the advantages and drawbacks of participation, with particular reference to the experience of the CPEs that are in the system and the way in which the BWS has modified its own regulations so as to make the system universally accessible. Before doing that, however, it is useful to take a look at the main functions of the Fund and how the CPEs could possibly fit into that framework.

Fund adjustment policies and the CPEs

At its inception, the Fund's fundamental mission was to assist its members in finding solutions to balance-of-payments problems. Transitory balance-of-payments difficulties would be rectified through relatively short-term borrowing from a common currency pool managed by the Fund. More fundamental external payments problems would need to be corrected through exchange-rate adjustments in combination with a host of domestic policy measures in a comparatively brief period of time. Increasingly, however, the Fund has come to recognize that balance-of-payments problems in many DEs are structural in origin and cannot be eliminated quickly without social and political costs that may be more destabilizing than the balance-of-payments deficit was in the first place. In other words, the Fund has gradually adopted a more structuralist approach to balance-of-payments problems: by encouraging a reallocation of resources toward more productive sectors and a compression of domestic absorption, through its own policy prescriptions and financial assistance packages, the Fund aims at raising economic efficiency and competitiveness.

In formulating its advice and policy prescriptions, the Fund is motivated by its underlying liberal philosophy that seeks to remove as many interferences with the free play of market forces as possible, especially trade and exchange regulations. Considering its short-term policy prescriptions, the Fund undeniably exhibits a monetarist bent. The balance-of-payments deficit is usually attributed to excessive absorption (aggregate demand for domestically produced and imported products), which needs to be compressed in an orderly fashion through deflationary policy measures. The latter are to be implemented typically through a reduction in public expenditures and credit restrictions so as to reduce both investment and consumption levels in some suitable combination. Especially since the early 1970s, the Fund has been elaborating a complement to demand management in the form of purposeful actions on the supply side. These measures are usually formulated in conjunction with new borrowing facilities and loan procedures and, especially in recent years, efforts to capitalize on the Fund's intrinsic role as a guarantor of debt management. Its "seal of approval" on debt-restructuring packages has been perceived as a signal to private commercial banks, official lenders, and other organizations to join in a concerted effort aimed at resolving the structural balance-of-payments problem without compelling any one agent to augment its risk exposure disproportionately. The measures included in a Fund package can be very diverse. They usually entail an exchange-rate devaluation to discourage imports and stimulate exports, and adjustments in interest rates to foster savings and guide investments to the more productive endeavors. At the same time, pricing policies are to be geared increasingly to reflect real scarcity, for instance, by eliminating government retail-price subsidies.

To clarify some of the root causes of the mixed relationship between the financial IEOs and some CPEs and to evaluate the potential that other CPEs may perceive in Fund membership, it is instructive to bear in mind a few stylized aspects of the Fund's policy on surveillance or conditionality. A typical adjustment program consists of a combination of measures aimed at improving the current account through stabilization policies and efficiency through target adjustments in resource allocation. Usually such a program is supported through fresh financing with three conditions: (1) the implementation of the preconditions for adjustment – otherwise financial institutions, private as well as official, could not be expected to be inclined toward marshaling the loans required for smoothing the adjustment process, at least on economic grounds; (2) the fulfillment of quantitative and qualitative policy performance targets upon which further disbursement of the adjustment loans is predicated; and (3) quantitative as well as qualitative policy actions that governments commit themselves to undertake, although these are mostly in the nature of policy intentions and therefore not normally associated with sanctions for noncompliance.

This suggests that there is normally a tie-in between additional loans and the implementation of adjustment measures. Participants in the negotiations as a rule select a quantum target as well as a time sequence for improving the current account. The decision on the amount by which the current account needs to be improved during a given period of time is a function of the volume and timing of the inflow of foreign capital from official and private institutions. Because it is constrained by conditions in international capital markets, the Fund does not, of course, have complete discretion in choosing the depth and speed of a country's adjustment. Nevertheless, it can exert considerable leverage over the concrete terms on which commercial banks may be willing to keep lending.

These areas for policy action are primarily concerned with reducing absorption and switching expenditure epitomized by the slogan "getting prices right." Increasingly, the financial IEOs have been strengthening the supply base directly by focusing policy on the requirements for domestic balance and stabilization. Adjustment policies should be introduced without crippling the ability of the affected country to service its debt in an orderly fashion, that is, without reducing the pace of growth so much that it would in the end undercut the economy's potential to generate export revenues at a faster pace than the rise in import costs. Domestic demand needs to be scaled at a long-term sustainable level without aggravating imbalances and inflation. If prices are not moving flexibly in response to shifts in demand and supply, inflationary pressures tend to be disguised or repressed. But they leave an imprint on the economy just the same. Stabilization usually requires a cut in total absorption so that real expenditure shrinks, which normally also entails a drop in real incomes. The latter alternative is feasible provided there is some room for flexibility in the relatively short run and the policy measures introduced do not get eroded by inertia, real and monetary market segmentation that may be hard to overcome, unexpected setbacks, and sluggish response of microeconomic units to shifts in macroeconomic policies.

Demand management can take on various forms. The primary objective is to reduce expenditures by cutting purchasing power through controlling nominal flows to various actors in the economy. In the household sector, for example, nominal wage levels can be more strictly controlled, thereby possibly reducing household income and expenditure. In the enterprise sector, the reduction in aggregate credit supply from the banking sector curtails investment outlays. Government expenditures need to be compressed while net indirect taxes are normally increased by cutting or eliminating government subsidies. This direct reduction of government demand alleviates pressures on credit and money markets. Furthermore, the government normally curbs the rate of growth of money supply.

Expenditure switching is aimed at bolstering export supply and discouraging import demand. A substantial devaluation raises the price of both imports and exports in domestic currency, and thus can be expected, after dissipation of the factors behind the familiar J-curve effect (by which, upon devaluation, the current account worsens in the short run), to reduce domestic demand and divert it to domestically produced substitutes for imports. Domestic suppliers on balance tend to divert goods from the domestic market to exports.

Supply measures of the adjustment package can take on various forms as well. They mostly consist of enhancing resource allocation by direct and indirect policy means. Direct instruments are in the sphere of tariffs, exchange rates, interest charges, and, in many cases, key product prices. Indirect instruments are contingent on changes in the underlying institutions, such as the liberalization of the trade and payments regimes, or the imposition of controls over nominal variables. Better management of aggregate credit and money supply also improves the setting of financial markets and thus indirectly affects aggregate investment and inflation.

Stabilization and adjustment policies need not depress levels of economic activity, unless the imbalance originated in the first place from output levels that exceed long-run capacity. Nevertheless, recent experience has demonstrated unambiguously, if further proof were required, that a macroeconomic adjustment program usually entails a contraction of economic activity, which may in fact counteract the improvement in economic efficiency that it was designed to elicit. As recent experiences in many DEs and CPEs have so amply demonstrated, austerity usually has a disproportionate impact on investment, which by lowering the growth of capital reduces the capacity to produce over time and thus may entail contraction over a protracted period of time. This conflict between economic efficiency and the need to improve the current account may stem from a variety of sources. The most important are: (1) "overkill" or excessive adjustment measures causing a contraction in economic activity; (2) optimistic assumptions of domestic market flexibility, thus overstating expenditure switching; (3) import cuts affecting not only final consumption but also intermediate and capital goods for which no substitutes from domestic production are available in the short run; and (4) the compression of domestic absorption falling disproportionately on investments, thereby weakening future production capacity.

This rough sketch of recent adjustment programs suggests that the Fund and the Bank's policy instruments are overwhelmingly tailored to a market setting. This may be a proper recipe for economies with fairly mature, integrated markets, where these measures work best and in the least disruptive way as governments should be able to elaborate coherent macroeconomic policies, possibly with the assistance of Fund resources and advice. However, if the environment upon which such measures are imposed, as in traditional CPEs, exhibits serious rigidities in markets by policy design or for other reasons, output losses may far exceed any efficiency gains from better resource allocation (Lavigne 1985a, 35).

Because of the role of planning in traditional CPEs, these economies generate, transform, and finally bring under control their macroeconomic imbalance in relatively distinctive ways. Is the planning mechanism in flagrant contradiction with the Fund's prescriptions? The distinctiveness of CPEs should not be exaggerated, for multiple exchange rates, artificially set administrative prices, multiple domestic and external pricing regimes, trade controls, a sizable state sector, and other nonmarket features are by no means the exclusive preserve of CPEs. What is different between many MEs with less than integrated markets and CPEs is the considerable central control of policy makers over demand and especially supply, so that a question arises as to who really conducts adjustment efforts. This opens up an area for friction between the financial IEOs and the CPEs. But it needs to be made crystal clear at this juncture that the CPEs did not join the Fund only, mainly, or perhaps at all to learn about adjustment policies. So there are at least other rationales to be considered, to which I turn now.

Rationale for CPEs joining the BWS

Because the IMF's prime task is to stabilize international finance by lending from common resources for transitory balance-of-payments reasons, it would have been logical for the smaller CPEs experiencing serious balance-of-payments problems to seek admission. Accession to the BWS would not have helped directly to remedy the TR deficits that emerged after 1974 as the TR not only eludes the Fund's area of authority, but the peculiar institutional and systemic problems of that currency zone, which are largely structural in origin (see chapter 2), transcend the Fund's competence and experience. But access to fresh resources to bridge transitory payments difficulties in east–west relations or to assist in promoting exports to MEs could have directly affected the transactions of these countries with other participants in the TR regime. By reassuring governments, bankers, and traders in MEs that the external financial problems of the CPEs would be managed properly, membership would also have restored confidence in relations with CPEs for at least two reasons.

For one thing, it would have entailed a large-scale disclosure of macroeconomic information, which the CPEs have traditionally guarded rather closely. Such a quantum improvement in the availability of pertinent macroeconomic data of real as well as financial variables would have enabled analysts to construct coherent macroeconometric frameworks for analyzing the behavior and functioning of CPEs. One baffling problem in attaining a mutually acceptable debt-rescheduling agreement, especially for Poland, was precisely the inexperience of governments and private commercial banks of MEs in dealing with a CPE in external payments difficulties; on certain occasions, including the private debt-rescheduling negotiations of September 1981 (Schröder 1982, 89), IMF officials were called in as observers in an effort to help out when Poland could not be admitted to the Bretton Woods institutions for political reasons (Assetto 1988, 176). Certainly, some of the obstacles to working out an orderly debt rescheduling may have been political in nature. Nevertheless the substantive issues that complicated an agreement with the banks and western governments derived largely from a mutual lack of understanding. Western commercial banks (the so-called London Club) and government negotiators (the so-called Paris Club) showed at first only the most rudimentary knowledge of and a stubborn reluctance to learn how the CPEs and the CMEA really function – not unlike the attitude of the Bretton Woods institutions for most of the postwar period. Agents in MEs found it rather cumbersome to negotiate within the framework for fundamental economic decisions that the planners of CPEs normally set for themselves. Both are indeed at odds with free-enterprise objectives or the obligations of democratically elected governments. Similarly, in spite of considerable know-how and sophistication acquired during the burgeoning east–west financial contacts of the 1970s, Eastern European negotiators at times failed to appreciate the ways in which private commercial banks and governments of MEs manage their portfolios.

Though membership in the BWS by itself would not, of course, have altered the intrinsic creditworthiness of the CPEs, it could certainly have imparted a significant psychological crutch in the evolution of events. Joining the BWS would also have enabled these countries to avail themselves of the established mechanisms regarding conditionality, debt management, and macroeconomic adjustment in addition to the self-discipline already presupposed among Fund members. That is not to say that the Fund would have come up quickly with rational policy measures suitable to the specific conditions of CPEs and acceptable to them. In fact, the stabilization measures recommended by the Fund to the two CMEA members that are in the Fund as well as to Yugoslavia (Robinson, Tyson, and Woods 1984) do not appear to have been very well suited to local conditions, except when these packages, as in the case of Hungary, were first put together in the country itself and then endorsed by the Fund (Assetto 1988).

The CPEs generally perceive the economic benefits[10] of membership in the BWS to be: securing access to hard currency credits at moderate interest rates; gaining greater financial respectability in MEs; having the option of availing themselves of the considerable store of expertise in debt management, rescheduling, and the costs and benefits of austerity policies that may offer low-cost assistance for many of the persistent economic problems of many CPEs; being entitled to bid on Bank projects in DEs and thus gaining new export outlets; and for the poorer of the CPEs gaining the status of a DE at the Bank, which enables them to obtain access to convertible currency funds from IDA or similar borrowing windows on particularly advantageous terms. Of course, apart from these immediate benefits, being outside the system inhibits these countries from exerting influence over Bank and Fund policies with respect to other countries. It also weakens the ability of CPEs to influence thinking on international monetary reform and hence the chances of getting positive responses to whatever proposals the CPEs may have (see chapter 5). To the extent that the SDR or a successor may become the world's major reserve asset – a rather remote proposition at this stage – countries that do not take part in the scheme are bound to suffer from a distinct disadvantage in international trade and finance.

The drawbacks consist mostly of the obligation to divulge sensitive economic information and the possibility of having to submit to Fund policy advice that may fail to blend with the CPE's precepts. Aside from alleviating the current external-balance constraints and adding a degree of controlled flexibility in foreign economic policy, thereby facilitating domestic output maintenance, membership as such is likely to affect the domestic economy only marginally. Even if limited external convertibility were to be fostered in the context of ongoing reforms in CPEs (see chapter 5), it would not be of serious consequence as far as the internal and external organization of these economies are concerned, at least in the foreseeable future.

Membership in the BWS would also be most valuable as a further prop to the structural adjustment measures envisaged by the smaller CMEA members. Clearly, the Fund cannot enmesh itself directly in the economic affairs of the CPEs as far as they relate to CMEA membership. However, the Fund can and does intervene in the case of a CPE encountering problems in its convertible currency relationships. By virtue of obtaining several more degrees of external flexibility, membership in the Fund and the Bank could facilitate the transitions in economic policies and institutions that the CPEs deem helpful to cope with both balance-of-payments and structural-adjustment issues. Because the policy measures of the Bretton Woods institutions are normally focused on working off the external deficit, securing competitiveness of the domestic economy, and eliminating market distortions, especially in prices, the Fund's wealth of experience could be brought to bear on shaping similarly flexible policies in Eastern Europe. Loans for structural-adjustment purposes could ease the adaptations required to make the CPEs more competitive in world markets. By this indirect avenue, the policies administered with the guidance and financial assistance of the Bretton Woods institutions could exert, albeit indirectly, a powerful influence on the type of SEI to be pursued with determination.

A surprisingly vexing issue, which has led to considerable political animosity, concerns the terms on which the CPEs are admitted to the BWS, particularly the Bank. The CPEs were not only hoping to be able to bid on Bank-financed projects in the DEs, for which Fund membership is a prerequisite. They were also keen on being admitted at a per capita income level that would entitle them to soft-window loans. This particular criterion presented no big problem when the *de facto* accession of China and the *de jure* one of Rumania were being negotiated. In the case of Hungary, however, the overwhelming majority of outside observers argued that Hungary was a country on a medium level of development with a per capita income level well above the floor established for soft-window loans from IDA. The exchange rate utilized was crucial.[11] Of course, it is not at all straightforward to decide upon a realistic exchange rate for a particular conversion. Should one opt for purchasing-power parity when in fact domestic and external prices are hardly linked? Or should one rather choose a trade-related multiplier? Or a combination of the two? Whichever could have been defended as a suitable converter, Hungary would most likely not have been eligible for DE status. Because it insisted on being treated like any other would-be Bank member, the institution had little choice but to utilize the commercial exchange rate, which deviates markedly from any realistic purchasing-power parity (see Brabant 1985a, 1985b). In the end, this logic prevailed and Hungary is a DE for the Bank's purposes; this label may in the meantime have become more justified in view of the serious absolute as well as relative deterioration in Hungary's standing in the world economy.

Much the same rationale determined the terms of accession for Poland. In view of the successive devaluations of the commercial złoty since it was first introduced in 1982 and the appalling state of its economy, particularly by the time the Bank got around to evaluating the application for accession, Poland could not but have come in under the cutoff point for soft-window loans.

Impact on the CMEA and Fund experience

Because Hungary, Poland, Rumania, and Vietnam are active CMEA members, Yugoslavia is an associated member, and China and Laos are still CPEs for all practical purposes, it is legitimate to ponder the effects of their membership in the BWS on their economic policies, including, for the former group, the effects with respect to the CMEA and SEI. So far, there is no indication at all that the far-reaching economic, financial, or institutional reforms contemplated or put in train in any of these countries have been promulgated simply or mainly to accommodate their participation in the IFS or IMS or as a consequence of their desire to borrow from the Bretton Woods institutions; quite the contrary. The CPEs have not encountered any significant problem in trying to come to grips with the short-term requirements of Fund adjustment programs (Lavigne 1984, 1986). But some, particularly Rumania, have been woefully reluctant, if not altogether truculent, in applying the indirect market-type instruments that the Fund suggested. Because of the enormous powers vested in central decision makers and the significant role of central planning left in virtually all CPEs, the Fund cannot in principle utilize the reasoning that undergirds recommendations in typical DE adjustment programs. Thus, price, interest rate, exchange rate, and other adjustments in market-type instruments do not function well in CPEs when policy makers can still resort to *dirigiste*-type intervention (Gotz-Kozierkiewicz 1988).

Certainly, some erosion of the traditional planning system, the trade and payments mechanisms, the institutional setup of the economic model and strategy, and the forms and goals of SEI held by individual CPEs has taken place over the last decade or so and further changes are likely to be forthcoming. But none can realistically be attributed to Fund membership or surveillance. However, a further autonomous loosening of the discipline presumed in the traditional CMEA trade and payments mechanism could eventually pave the way for more CPEs joining the existing IMS. This might take place in several different ways.

There are perhaps three visible signs that could be imputed to membership in the Bretton Woods institutions, though these events might also have materialized without the countries having joined these organs. These concern information, adjustment, and market-oriented reforms. As noted, the question of information has been satisfactorily resolved for all CPEs in the financial IEOs. Rumania is still a laggard in some respects, but China, Hungary, Poland, and recently Vietnam have been forthcoming. Note that Hungary and Poland had already earlier provided ample macroeconomic information, including information on their external financial transactions, on a voluntary basis or under the prodding of private commercial banks. However, the submissions to the Fund and the Bank by Rumania, in particular, are not only furnished on a confidential basis, but they are also highly incomplete and most of them cannot be reproduced even in regular statistical compilations.

Secondly, inasmuch as the association of these countries was motivated by external payments pressures, their entrance into the BWS has been accompanied by adjustments of various dimensions. Some have worked out fairly well, essentially because the CPE involved had elaborated beforehand its own adjustment program and the Fund simply endorsed these measures. This provided a "seal of approval" not only to the diverse potential constituency but also to the population at large. This is not to deny that the Washington institutions have succeeded in influencing decision making in Hungary and Poland in some respects.

Finally, partly in response to the causes for seeking economic adjustments, the CPEs in the Bretton Woods institutions, excepting Rumania, have recently been exploring wide-ranging economic reforms, in some cases as an intrinsic element of the adjustment efforts. These may lead to measurable shifts in the way in which the CPE is managed. Although this drift toward market-type decision making did not originate with membership in the Bank or the Fund, it certainly received a measurable moral and tactical impetus therefrom (see chapter 5).

7 Weaknesses and strengths of the prevailing BWS

The BWS proved to be of considerable benefit to the DMEs in particular as, for a quarter of a century, it worked reasonably and contributed effectively to the growth of international trade and economic development in general. This success was in spite of the fact that for more than a decade the Fund's mission entailed more measures to sustain growth and help countries to move gradually toward a more liberal trading and financial system than to guarantee maintenance of the key features of the envisaged IMS, including multilateralism, convertibility, fixed exchange rates, and free market access. Yet both the BWS and especially its successor "nonsystem" (Johnson 1975) have given rise to concern about advantages and drawbacks.

There is little doubt that there has been considerable unease about the postwar IMS, especially the floating exchange-rate regime that came about during the early 1970s with few rules on behavior attached to it. But what precisely is wrong and why, and thus what would be a more desirable arrangement, are questions that have eluded even technical analyses by competent economists. When the views of politicians and diplomats are also factored into this complex system of equations, the going gets very rough indeed (Dell 1987; Scammell 1987). Expanding on the admirable survey provided by Andrew Crockett and Morris Goldstein (1987), perceptions of the weaknesses of the prevailing monetary system can be grouped under four headings.

First, there is wide agreement on the volatility of exchange rates since the breakdown of the fixed-par system in the early 1970s. Regardless of how volatility is measured, there is no ambiguity about the fact that the short-run variability of exchange rates during the latter period has been a multiple of what can be measured for the BWS proper; there has not been a sustained tendency for this exchange rate volatility to decline over time; and most exchange rate variations under the floating regime have been unexpected in the sense that prevailing market indicators, such as forward exchange-rate magnitudes, have been poor predictors of short-run variability. Regardless of its etiology, some contend that the latter is costly because the uncertainty associated with it reduces the volume of trade and investment, disproportionately so for countries that do not possess mature financial markets, especially to arrange forward cover.

Volatility is not in dispute. Commentators disagree widely over the proper yardstick to evaluate it and assess its costs. Some argue that all asset prices have been variable during the floating exchange-rate period and that exchange rates have been less variable than many other asset types, such as national stock-market indicators or commodity-price fluctuations. Perhaps the underlying turbulence in the global economic and political environment since the early 1970s has had something to do with it. Also the measurements of real costs have elicited a wide range of responses, with many empirical measurements yielding at best sporadic evidence of a causal link between measures of exchange-rate volatility and the observed volume of international trade.

Secondly, the present system is being indicted on account of perceived large and persistent misalignment of real exchange rates as measured by the deviation of the actual real exchange rate from its "equilibrium" level. Needless to say, economists entertain a wide variety of notions about equilibrium exchange rates and no agreement on that score is in sight. Some see disequilibrium as a sustained, possibly cumulative, departure of the nominal exchange rate from the path implied by purchasing-power parities. Others perceive disequilibrium in exchange rates on the basis of the sheer size of exchange-rate movements themselves on the assumption that, if anything, they should change only gradually in response to structural shifts in competitiveness and comparative advantage. Finally, there is a group that prefers to calculate disequilibrium as the deviation of real exchange rates from the level that would yield "equilibrium" in the balance of payments – itself a disputed notion for it is predicted on current-account imbalances associated with properly specified "normal" capital flows. Regardless of its size and how best to measure it, some commentators argue, misalignments in real exchange rates distort resource allocation because they entail boom-and-bust cycles in tradable goods sectors that leave much higher unemployment levels in their wake than had been anticipated. They also encourage protectionism as firms and governments attempt to overrule the verdict of markets through administrative measures.

That there has been persistent misalignment in real exchange rates is not a contentious issue. Not so clear are the degree of that misalignment and how it compares to the fixed-par regime, the costs generated in the process, and whether alternative exchange-rate systems could have reduced the drawbacks. The costs attributable to exchange-rate misalignment could stem from other factors, including structural weaknesses of manufacturing employment and the more widespread resurgence of protectionist pressures in major industrial countries.

Thirdly, the prevailing system has been reproached for lack of discipline and coordination of macroeconomic policies among the major actors in the global economy. Current exchange rates under a floating regime are influenced by expected future exchange rates, which themselves depend critically on anticipated macroeconomic policies. Because instability of current policies generates uncertainty about future policies, the lack of discipline and inconsistent macroeconomic policies are deemed to be critical factors in exchange-rate instability.

There is little dispute about the lack of discipline and inadequate policy coordination among major actors in the global economy since the mid-1970s and countries suddenly changing monetary or fiscal policies, or both, independently of prevailing policies and intentions of other partners. Neither is it contentious to state that discipline and coordination in macroeconomic policies need to be improved. But whether the exchange rate can contribute to that state is uncertain. Some defend the notion that fiscal reform is a better ingredient for preventing exchange-rate misalignments and alleviating their effects.

The final group of ills of the prevailing system can be discussed under the heading of disintegration of multilateralism. This owes a good deal to the explicit decision made in 1974 to defer the recycling of petrodollars to private financial markets rather than harness these resources from within the multilateral institutions. This decision was due largely to the political clout of the United States in spite of the opposition of members less involved in transnational commercial banking. The abandonment of control over a sizable segment of the financial market, including the burgeoning Eurodollar market, has meant that the role of the Washington institutions in providing financial resources for both balance-of-payments and capital-development purposes has shrunk. By virtue of leaving such important decisions up to the rather narrow interest of commercial banks, a measure of instability was infused into a system in dire need of stability. There is little dispute about the volatility of the changes in the structure of financial markets, the enormously grown role of the commercial banks and their far from constructive behavior in the debt crisis, changes from project to general-purpose financing, and mutations of loans at fixed to floating interest rates and from long to comparatively short maturities.

There are, however, also a number of valuable strengths of the prevailing IMS. Perhaps foremost is the notion that flexible exchange rates promote external payments adjustment, in spite of the absolute size and persistence of current-account imbalances of some large countries. Furthermore, they foster adjustment in both deficit and surplus countries, thereby yielding greater symmetry. This in turn entails a smaller cost of adjustment than under fixed-par regimes because the burden of adjustment falls more on expenditure-switching than on expenditure-reducing, or deflationary, policy measures. But this view is far from uniformly shared in the profession. Critics also argue that exchange-rate variations as a measure to correct payments imbalances depend very much on the economy's size and structural features. Thus, smaller, more open, and more price-insensitive economies suffer proportionately larger domestic price feedbacks and obtain less durable relative price advantages from exchange-rate variations than economies that are larger, less open, and more price-flexible. In other words, the reduction of the cost of adjustment for identical exchange-rate flexibility varies widely among countries.

Secondly, floating exchange rates have always been touted as *the* instrument to insulate an economy against imported inflation and other external disturbances. Floating exchange rates can insulate against the wealth and relative price effects of a general rise in world prices but not against the effects of a shift in relative world prices. As regards other impacts, they cannot be assessed a priori without specifying the nature and origin of the disturbance, what is insulated, and who is to be insulated. But some contend that there has been greater – not less – transmission of disturbances under floating rates.

A related benefit that has wider ramifications, however, is the potential independence and effectiveness of domestic monetary policy. Instead of being targeted at safeguarding or pegging the exchange rate, monetary policy under a floating exchange-rate regime can be utilized for other purposes. Moreover, exchange-rate variability was supposed to strengthen output and employment consequences of an expansionary monetary policy as a result of the beneficial repercussions of induced depreciation of the exchange rate on the trade balance. Although this textbook view is not without a grain of truth, even most supporters of the present IMS acknowledge that the case of independence and effectiveness of monetary policies under floating exchange rates has been exaggerated, perhaps in part because the prevailing floating has been "managed" by countries maintaining exchange rates as both an instrument and objective of economic policy.

Finally, it is argued that a less flexible exchange-rate system could not have survived the strains of, for example, energy shocks, bank failures, differential inflation rates, and variability in national monetary and fiscal policy mixes. The magnitude of the benefits accruing from the resilience of the present system in the presence of such disturbances should not be understated. Although acknowledging this robustness, critics agree that the exchange-rate mechanism is essentially an instrument to facilitate more fundamental economic objectives, such as high employment, sustainable growth, price stability, and buoyant trade. They find the present system wanting on most of these scores.

Proposals for improving the IMS that have been tabled by groups of countries, including the so-called Group of Ten (key DMEs) and Group of Twenty-four (representative DEs), agree that there is room for significant improvement, primarily through better discipline and coordination of macroeconomic policies in the major industrial countries. If so, the core questions revolve around the channels, including Fund surveillance, available to reach this objective. Solutions that have been suggested include various elements of greater automaticity in adjustment and coordination processes: (1) the adoption of "target zones" for the exchange rates of major currencies, (2) the elaboration of some "objective indicators" of macroeconomic policies in major DMEs as a framework for applying Fund surveillance, and (3) policy adjustments and changes in procedure of Fund surveillance that could be accomplished and accommodated within existing exchange-rate arrangements and the existing institutional framework for surveillance in place.

8 Monetary reform and the CMEA prior to the mid-1980s

In spite of the difficulties encountered under the floating regime and the serious delays in replacing the BWS, the IMS has proved to be resilient. Yet the main actors in the world economy cannot forever postpone a restructuring of its key foundations without hampering the smooth functioning of global economic interdependence. It would be unfortunate if such a revamping were to materialize without taking into account the concerns of all participants in the world economy, including CPEs. It is therefore useful to look at the shared interests in fostering greater international cooperation by east and west, the possibility of there being some collusion among MEs and CPEs in hammering out a more satisfactory IMS, and the key characteristics of the ways in which such financial cooperation could be institutionalized.

The overall character of interdependence

In spite of the defects and drawbacks that the CPEs normally attribute to the BWS, they generally acknowledge that the system contributed greatly to the dynamism and stability of economic development and trade in the postwar period, especially of the DMEs. They are, therefore, actively interested in a reform of the IMS. A properly streamlined, smoothly functioning system, even if applicable only to MEs, inhibits trade wars and protectionism, contributes to the stability of international financial relations, and indeed benefits the environment of international relations (Fekete 1972, 154–60).

Common interests in a reformed BWS can emerge only if such a new system reflects the shared economic and monetary goals and prerogatives of most MEs and CPEs. Issues such as influence over policy making, access to liquidity and Fund resources, a reshaped policy on surveillance and stabilization measures administered by the Fund, greater control over exchange-rate movements, dampening exchange-rate volatility and especially reducing misalignment among the major vehicle currencies, and coordination of macroeconomic policies of the key actors in the Bretton Woods institutions are all essential ingredients of the monetary debate. As the frustrating negotiations of the NIEO have so clearly underlined, some of the issues enumerated here cannot be satisfactorily resolved within the existing institutions. A more harmonious, less rancorous north–south relationship may then require a substantial overhaul of the IMS.

Though many of the above-mentioned issues also divide east and west, it would seem easier to formulate for pointed negotiations among policy makers a *rapprochement* on technical grounds anchored to reciprocal economic advantages. The shared economic interests consist of the considerable need of the CPEs for foreign technology and capital resources, and the reported calls by MEs that CPEs should participate more actively in the global division of labor and attendant responsibilities for equity in development, buoyancy of economic expansion, sustainability of the development process, and stability of the global economy. Though an east–west *rapprochement* based on the reciprocity of interests and on respect for the fundamental characteristics of each other's system appears feasible, it does not imply that east and west will eventually be able to join forces in the BWS as it exists today or in any of the tabled reforms. This derives essentially from the key ingredients of any feasible monetary reform.

Toward a new IMS – early positions on issues of critical concern to CPEs

At one of the rare conferences dealing specifically with the role of east and west in monetary reform, Henri Bourguinat (1977, 65ff.) stipulated four pivotal issues of a new IMS: (1) the universality of the reserve unit, (2) the choice of optimum exchange regime, (3) the role of gold and reserve currencies, and (4) the internationalization of the monetary institutions. This conference was attended by two Hungarian and two Polish participants, who apparently went along with most of the arguments. There was no divergence of opinion that the fuller participation of the CPEs, and incidentally a good many DEs, in such a system requires the prior resolution of several other thorny issues. Since then the CPEs have espoused other interests, and I shall therefore detail their position under seven headings.

A universal reserve currency Universality requires that a reformed IMS be anchored to a common *numéraire* as a yardstick for measuring value. There is little doubt that the CPEs are against the central role of the dollar in the IMS. They view this as a form of US hegemony in the world, a source of instability and inflationary pressure because the United States can follow its own precepts, and a sign of inequity in the world economic order (Fárek 1986; Ivanov 1987; Surovceva 1986). They advocate an "ideal" currency constituted independently of any national currency, perhaps along the lines of the bancor, unitas, or TR. The SDR might eventually become a sufficiently habitual transaction medium to be such a unit. For it to be acceptable to the CPEs, however, modifications at least in the rules governing the creation and distribution of SDRs, and probably also in several other of its features, need to be worked out.

Universalism anchored to a common *numéraire* does not forcibly preclude monetary polycentrism for it is difficult to see how the TR – or the Soviet ruble for that matter – could be rendered compatible with a new IMS without entailing important systemic changes that might compromise the expressed interests of some CPEs. Instead of having the IMS anchored solely to one dominant currency, such as the US dollar, or even to a few, greater stability than presently attainable might be reached by harmonizing the global system on the basis of several, largely self-contained monetary regimes, each having a distinct monetary subsystem. Whether such a decomposition should proceed along presently existing political alliances or fairly uniformly pegging monetary systems remains an open question (Matejka 1977, 113; Matjuchin and Smirnov 1984). The former would respect the matrix of current trade flows; it would also allow for a greater diversification of instruments of exchange.

Foreign exchange regime Whether a reformed IMS should encompass fixed or floating exchange rates is a matter yet to be decided (Živkova and Petkova 1988, 72–4). In advocating the "stable but equitable exchange rates" frequently suggested as one important pillar of a reformed IMS, the CPEs undoubtedly accord greater weight to stability than to adjustability (Ačarkan 1984), as emphasized in the second major report of the 1977 conference (see Rączkowski 1977, 94–5). These countries hold indeed that the instability and uncertainty associated with floating rates cannot be outweighed by the internal autonomy afforded by such a regime in principle.

Because the Fund in particular was designed specifically to foster currency convertibility (as required by article VIII), multilateralism in trade, equilibrium exchange rates, and gradually liberalized capital markets, a realistic reform of the IMS in place cannot significantly depart from these fundamental pivots of the international economy. This may pose problems for countries that are not yet "ready" to pursue such goals for systemic or other reasons. But special regimes might be accommodated under either fixed or floating exchange rates, or a combination thereof. They could be similar to the transitional arrangements of the Fund's article XIV, which would, however, have to be spelled out more precisely than the "temporary" clause under which most members of the Fund have spurned convertibility for so many years.

Gold and reserve currencies The actual and potential role of gold in the IMS remains of importance to the CPEs. Until a few years ago, ideology played a central role in buttressing this stance, particularly in the GDR literature (Friedemann 1986; Lemmnitz 1982). Though the Marxian fixation with gold as a "universal currency" has waned considerably, gold remains an ideological concern because the monetary goals that emerged in the 1970s are viewed largely as another manifestation of the more general aims of the capitalist system. Soviet commentators usually explain the global monetary crisis in either of two ways: the root of the monetary problem lies in ending the gold-exchange standard or the decline of the role of gold in international monetary affairs is seen more as a consequence than an independent cause of the monetary crisis, for both economic and political reasons.

The only specific recommendation contained in the Nairobi declaration and subsequent discourses on IMS reform, although with declining frequency, concerned a return to gold as the basic anchor. The Soviet Union would naturally have an interest in anything that affects the price of gold. Indeed when gold was still the official anchor of the BWS, the position of the CPEs in international fora was solidly on recommending a rise in the price of gold (see United Nations 1966, 1970). Any return of gold as an international reserve backing would increase the demand for it and thus its price, to the benefit of gold producers. Whether a return to the gold-exchange standard is desirable from the point of view of the stability and reliability of a reformed IMS and whether such a retrogression is feasible are two different questions, however. Regarding the first, since the breakdown of the gold-exchange standard, Soviet monetary theory, and by extension most of Eastern Europe's, has been divided among two distinct academic groups with connections to different government decision makers (see Lavigne 1978, 373–6; Rémy 1981, 1985). For brevity's sake, I shall borrow Marie Lavigne's apt designations of "traditionalists" and "modernists" (Lavigne 1978, 373).

Commentators and observers, frequently associated with the Ministry of

Finance and its affiliated organizations, cluster their views around the traditional anchoring role of gold. They see the collapse of the gold standard as having provoked the chronic chaos of the capitalist economy. They regard the BWS as having been far from satisfactory, especially because it fostered the worldwide domination of the US dollar. Nonetheless, it admittedly had the merit of having based the monetary system on the dollar, itself convertible into gold and linked with all currencies through fixed parities expressed in terms of gold. Gold is viewed as a key "disciplining tool" (Bogdanov 1976, 116). As the priority of monetary discipline waned, gold had to be allocated a less central role because of the "debt money" increasingly being created to finance budgetary expenditures and balance-of-payments deficits, and to buttress the internationalization of industrial and financial capital. There has been growing recognition, however, that the "function of gold as a universal equivalent is changing" (Krasavina 1978, 145).

The modernist group is usually associated with the more research-orientated institutions of the USSR. Rather than treating gold as the alpha and omega of the monetary crisis, they argue (see Matjuchin 1978) that it had already lost its most important historical attributes as a universal commodity and world money first within individual countries and then between them since the gold-exchange standard came into existence – well before the onset of the global monetary crisis. The demonetization of gold, first after World War II and finally with the breakdown of the BWS, is seen as harmful to the stability of the IMS (Bácskai 1975, 22). Gold no longer retains its function as a means of payment and of circulation inside DMEs, and it is no longer even a measure of value. Various explanations are invoked including the ascent of Europe and Japan, relative to the United States, and hence the rise in international tensions stemming from economic conflicts; resentment of the exclusive role of the dollar and the policy freedom it purportedly affords the United States; and the conflict between monetary nationalism and the supranational tendencies built into the Fund's surveillance mechanisms (Atlas and Matjuchin 1971). The energy crisis and stagflation accelerated this demise of gold as universal money.

Monetary traditionalists see the solution to the current quagmire in the return to the gold standard or at least to the restoration of some form of gold convertibility. The modernists rarely paint a coherent position on how to surmount the contemporary monetary problems. Because they do not consider gold as the main explanatory variable underlying the volatility of the capitalist economic, trading, monetary, and financial systems, changes in socioeconomic conditions rather than in a technical tool such as gold are advocated. But they feel that the crisis of the IMS can be put to rest only by devising a way out in which the role of gold must necessarily be taken into account. But in what precise form remains fundamentally unclear (Djakin 1982).

There has not been any official policy statement on the gold issue since 1976, except in marginal references such as those quoted above. One may therefore question whether, after the experiences and fruitless debates of the past decade, the CPEs still advocate a return to gold. In the absence of official pronouncements, no categorical answer can be provided. But there are three indirect indicators that a return to gold is no longer being propounded, for either doctrinal or practical reasons. First, though the debate between the traditionalists and the modernists has by no means been fully settled, by the late 1970s, a noticeable shift in position had taken place against those advocating a return to gold or the gold-exchange standard. The strengthening of international liquidity is seen chiefly in the form of relatively stable units of account, including the European currency unit or ECU and the SDR, and also the yen and the dollar (see Krasavina and Baranova 1984, 72ff.). But they remain skeptical as to the role of national currencies as international reserves.

Secondly, the emphasis placed on the traditional recommendations regarding IMS reform in key fora such as UNCTAD has sharply eased over the years. The central monetary issues are touched upon at best indirectly, by reaffirming the Soviet stance on UNCTAD's being, as a "universal international organization" (Manžulo 1983, 17), also called upon to devote due attention to monetary problems. If the issue of gold is touched upon at all, it is largely a defensive posture (Mironov and Epanesnikov 1985), such as that the CPEs do "not consider the attempts to restrict artificially the role of gold in the international liquid resources as substantiated especially under the persistent inflationary devaluation of paper money" (Samorodov 1983, 39). At the most recent UNCTAD session in New Delhi in 1987, the CPEs produced virtually nothing of substance on the issue.

The third indirect piece of evidence is a categorical statement by Stanislav M. Borisov, then Deputy Minister of Finance of the USSR, in his in-depth analysis of the role of gold in the world economy: it is "absolutely beyond dispute" that the discussions of a return to an official conversion of paper money into gold are utopian and unrealistic. He considers gold for monetary purposes "a dead weight" (Borisov 1984, 153), although such statements on gold are contested in the Soviet media (Majorov 1985, 37). Borisov concludes that "The gold-standard mechanism is definitely something of the past, none of the objective economic conditions for its restoration prevails, and any attempt to agitate in that direction is in advance condemned to failure" (Borisov 1984, 449).

The role of gold in the future IMS will certainly be of considerable concern to a number of CPEs for the reasons examined above (Majorov 1985). But there are highly likely to be other reserve instruments too. What will be the role of the SDR and the attitude of CPEs toward that reserve unit? One fundamental question is whether countries will be able to participate in the SDR mechanism without becoming full members of the Fund and associated institutions. It is true that the Fund's revised Articles of Agreement provide for such an eventuality, but it is unclear whether this can be interpreted sufficiently flexibly to extend it to the case of CPEs. Even if they were to embrace this option, the CPEs would not obtain SDR allocations (Rączkowski 1977, p. 96). Before the gradual rise in interest rates on SDR loans to market levels around 1982, the CPEs were at a comparative borrowing disadvantage as they had to pay market rates on commercial borrowing (Hamel 1980, 184). Even with interest-rate equalization, having access to funds *per se* to finance convertible currency payments imbalances would be beneficial, particularly when they are managed multilaterally rather than by national political considerations or peculiar commercial decision making.

Many Eastern European monetary specialists view the SDR as an embryonic form of debt money that cannot in itself solve the prevailing monetary problems for as long as its creation is not placed under strict discipline and in line with the requirements of a stable trading and economic environment for the world as a whole (Friedemann 1986). But the SDR is regarded (Matjuchin 1977, 162) as having an "important place" in the evolution of international currency reserves just the same. The CPEs have other, more fundamental problems with the SDR as a basic reserve currency, however (Lemmnitz 1982). Though the SDR has made it possible to gain some distance from the IMS based solely on national currencies, it still exhibits many problems: it is not yet sufficiently acceptable worldwide to replace national currencies, it does not yet circulate widely and therefore it will take a long time for it to replace national currencies, its creation is regulated by political means, and no guarantees are as yet in place to prevent the SDR from being subjected to inflationary reserve creation (see Matjuchin 1977, 46–7; Matjuchin and Šenaev 1978, 51–2). Strict Marxist interpretation argues that the SDR does not have "value" because it has no "backing" at all, in contrast to the ECU (Friedemann 1986, 1183), and can therefore be at best "pseudo money" (Helísek 1986). Because they offer no alternative to the "inappropriateness of the SDR as an international currency unit," they fall back on the "necessity to strengthen the role of gold" (UNCTAD 1980, 3) by default. The ECU in contrast is much more warmly applauded (Majorov 1985, 38–9) because at its creation it was "backed" by 20 percent of the member countries' gold and foreign-exchange reserves pooled in the European Monetary Cooperation Fund. The ECU's attractiveness also stems from this financial innovation's success in commercial and financial settlements as well as east–west financing.[12]

In recent years, the CPEs have been advocating the development of stable units of account for international economic agreements. For example, they have taken a very active part in the study group on universal constant accounting units of the United Nations Commission for International Trade Law (UNCITRAL). In fact, in January 1982 the USSR declared in Vienna that an indexed SDR could be acceptable as such a unit (Spiller 1984, 43), particularly for measuring national contributions to international organizations or international insurance conventions. In recent loan agreements, some CPEs have resorted to clauses that base the loans on a basket of currencies similar to the composition of the currencies that serve as the SDR's measurement base (Konstantinov 1982, 60). Furthermore, the USSR has in recent years signed agreements on the financing of exports of capital goods from DMEs, borrowed funds, and ventured to settle its accounts with France and Italy in ECUs. Moreover, recent commentary has generally applauded the contribution of the ECU to monetary stability and rationality (Šmelëv 1988).

Internationalization of the monetary institutions The BWS's universality aim was in fact an attempt to embrace uniform conditions throughout the world based largely on the policy preferences, economic institutions, and behavior of DMEs. It is quite true, formally, that the countries with the largest voting power can decide autonomously what borrowing can occur, the particular type of adjustment policies chosen by the Fund, and the conditionality conditions associated with either. Certainly, the Fund's article IV,3b states that the principles adopted by the Fund for purposes of surveillance "shall respect the domestic, social, and political policies of members, and in applying these principles the Fund shall pay due regard to the circumstances of members," a rephrased version of a statement that Czechoslovakia and the Soviet Union had insisted upon at Bretton Woods (see chapter 1). In practice, more and more use has recently been made of the stipulation that the Fund pay fuller regard to domestic social and political objectives, and the particular causes of balance-of-payments problems, with room for *ad hoc* accommodation. This more flexible approach could be suitably adapted to CPEs.

Anchoring the IMS to greater symmetry in surveillance and adjustment prescriptions is an issue that has been on the agenda of the DEs for many years and one about which the Fund has been seriously concerned. Also the

CPEs advocate greater surveillance by the multilateral institutions. But they would not necessarily endorse such public monitoring for themselves, of course. The latter role of the Fund is advocated for MEs because their economic policy in general and monetary policy in particular have been poorly controlled. They certainly have not been up to par with the requirements for stable and sustainable economic expansion for all participants in the world economy. In fact, dollar hegemony has allowed the United States to finance its domestically oriented needs with impunity (Konstantinov 1986). On the other hand, the CPEs are not likely to be agreeable to this surveillance being exercised with a high degree of autonomy, policy recommendations essentially being foisted upon members. This they oppose as unwarranted interference in their internal affairs.

At times, the criticism of CPEs is also directed at the asymmetry that disadvantages the development effort of the DEs (Fárek 1986). The asymmetry in resource distribution and the application of rules of the game formulated for developed countries, hence hardly applicable to DEs, fail to contribute to buoyant and equitable growth in the world economy.

The CPEs cannot be treated in the same way and with the same evaluation criteria as an ME experiencing financial difficulties (Lavigne 1985a, 39–40). Such attempts should be avoided at all costs in designing an alternative IMS. As the past has amply demonstrated, countries seek to defend their autonomy and have remained remarkably jealous of their economic sovereignty. A globalization of the institutions of the BWS could proceed with a reasonable chance of success only if the members' interest in maintaining some degree of autonomy and economic sovereignty is explicitly recognized.

Voting power The arduous discussions about global negotiations and the implementation of the NIEO have demonstrated that Fund members basically fall into two categories. Those with a large weight in management are unlikely to yield voluntarily substantial components of their power. On the other hand, the large majority of DEs and CPEs appear to be bent on acquiring a greater stake in the policy making of these institutions without necessarily being committed to absolute equality among unequals. Officially, the conflict between these two groups continues to be as rigorous as in the past. In practice, however, the voting rules have been considerably relaxed, for instance, as a result of *ad hoc* borrowing facilities with various kinds of majorities; on key questions, including the creation of liquidity and the resetting of quotas, the majority required is as high as 85 percent and, for example, 70 percent is required for changing the conditions of a loan program; the CPEs as a group would have more than 15 percent of the voting power,[13] thus giving them collective veto power; and most operational questions within the Bretton Woods institutions are settled by broad consensus rather than through formal voting. Because voting is a matter to which the CPEs attach paramount importance, the USSR has always found it politically unacceptable that only the United States possesses the veto.

Nevertheless, the CPEs' insistence on voting equality would appear to refer chiefly to the bases of the system as a starting position that can be considerably modified through negotiations. Thus, there is in principle nothing to prevent the present members from agreeing to a variable voting allocation on issues of particular concern to the CPEs. They could in effect be provided with a veto, for example, when it comes to Fund adjustment policies for themselves. At the same time, the group of MEs might well be entitled to safeguard their basic interests on matters that are not of vital importance to the CPEs by keeping their present voting power, perhaps after allowing for some of the concerns of the DEs. Such could be the case, for instance, in the establishment of guidelines for exchange-rate parities and fluctuations, and perhaps even in foreign-exchange policies in general.

Especially if a reformed IMS were to be polycentric, it needs to be held together by a truly international monetary unit and by adequate global institutions. A particularly important issue in this connection, as in any alternative aspiring toward universality, is the apportionment of voting power among the various blocs. Should each group obtain sufficient votes to veto decisions, particularly with regard to liquidity creation, or should the voting power be divided equally among the blocs? The CPEs would appear to favor the latter alternative (Matejka 1977, 111).

Convertibility Because convertibility is a critical issue in any IMS, would the CPE currencies have to be made convertible? Would they have to be traded in world markets and their prices determined by the market mechanism? Would it imply that these currencies would be exchangeable into domestic commodities or services, at least in principle? On a number of occasions, actual and aspiring members of the Fund among CPEs have touted the "imminence" of their currency becoming convertible. By now, it is clear that long, arduous work rather than public-relations rhetoric is required to move toward genuine convertibility.

Whether or not the CPEs should be held to a firmer commitment to move toward convertibility than the DEs is a critical matter to which no rough-and-ready answer can be provided. It must be formulated, first, with regard to a process and timetable for moving toward some minimum acceptable form of convertibility and, secondly, with sufficient flexibility so that modifications can be undertaken in light of emerging internal and external development conditions, including those of the CPEs. The likelihood of convertibility emerging autonomously in Eastern Europe, and in what form, will be examined in chapter 5 in conjunction with the advocated transition regime for CPEs.

Information There are several reasons that can be adduced to declare the question of information at this juncture largely a nonissue for most CPEs, excepting perhaps the USSR. First, information can be provided to the Bretton Woods institutions on a confidential basis so that it will not be disseminated by the Fund and the Bank in their regular statistical or other publications. This procedure has worked reasonably well up to now, for Rumania in particular, but sensitive material for the USSR could probably not be contained within the Fund. Secondly, much has changed since the CPEs elevated nearly all economic information to the status of "state secret." But some still do not publish sufficient details to permit a comprehensive assessment of their economic situation. However, it must be recognized, thirdly, that the profession has progressed sufficiently and that one can now construct a fairly reliable picture of macroeconomic trends in CPEs with the quantitative and qualitative information on hand. This admittedly does not yet yield fully accurate estimates, for example, of gold stocks, foreign-exchange reserves, balance-of-payments statistics, and related data. Such information could enhance the confidence in CPE policy makers, although it is not essential to adequate macroeconomic evaluation at this stage.

Participation in the existing system

Most of the CPEs' objections to the past and present IMS concern basic principles or general guidelines of policy making in the member countries or in the monetary institutions themselves. For a long time, their tenor has been on the negative side, meaning that the CPEs would have several fundamental as well as operational objections to participating in the world's monetary institutions. But that has been perhaps more ideological and political posturing than a concern motivated by pragmatic economic and financial considerations, given that several CPEs have for some time now been actively participating in both multilateral financial institutions under regular terms of agreement. In addition to the issues already dealt with, some commentary on voting, surveillance, stabilization measures, and information may be in order.

Certainly, in the cases of China, Hungary, Laos, Poland, Rumania, Vietnam, and, to a lesser extent, Yugoslavia, the Fund has had to come to grips with the special circumstances of CPEs (Pissulla 1983, 1984a, 1984b; Schüller and Hamel 1985). As the adjustment efforts of the early 1980s have amply demonstrated, the CPEs can accomplish the standard expenditure-reducing and expenditure-switching measures recommended by the Fund through the key *modi operandi* of a traditional CPE: investment reduction, a freezing or even a compression of private consumption, import cutbacks, if necessary by strict denial, export promotion, if necessary by baring domestic shelves, and other such measures. Given this, there should formally not be great incompatibility between the Fund and a CPE as far as stabilization is concerned. For the CPEs with the political will to participate in the Fund an appropriate adjustment regime can be worked out. But there may be political opposition from existing members, including foremost the United States (see chapter 5). A different set of knotty issues derives, of course, from the formulation of policy goals acceptable to both the Fund and the CPE.

Regarding the usual objections to the past and present IMS, they appear to refer chiefly to the interpretation of the Articles of Agreement and the way in which the Fund applies them. As explained, modifications of the regime over the years have changed the equation for evaluating the possibility of CPEs joining the Fund. Critical obstacles to joining the BWS are the obligation to furnish information, the commitment to pursue convertibility, and the weighted voting system. The first two issues have been resolved satisfactorily. The weighted voting system is a touchier issue. Minor modifications of the voting structure to accommodate the special features of CPEs could perhaps meet these countries' objections on economic and technical grounds (see chapter 5). But the present Fund members with voting clout are unlikely to yield substantially on their acquired prerogatives.

From the point of view of international economics, then, there are not that many arguments that can be brought to bear against the CPEs joining the IMS. As explained above, the major objections levied against the gold subscription, the central role of a national currency, the voting allocation, the adjustment programs, the determination of exchange rates, the disclosure of information, and others that dominated the debates after World War II have nearly all been sufficiently watered down by past Fund practices. Outright membership in the Bank and the Fund through such compromises has brought the participants measurable benefits in terms of access to World Bank loans at low interest rates and drawings from the IMF. These may become increasingly attractive benefits for other CPEs in the years ahead, but they provide only one reason for membership.

Objections to joining the Fund are likely to emerge from two sides. On the one hand, some CPEs will find the price to be paid far too high relative to the direct benefits to be derived. Neither substantial quote drawings nor credits on soft terms would be a realistic prospect for the USSR, because its quota would inevitably be quite substantial and it could not possibly be treated as a DE. It could in time, however, become a major participant in the execution of World Bank projects. It should therefore carefully weigh the costs associated with Fund obligations and responsibilities against the benefits of a quota. On the other hand, it may prove to be politically undesirable to join outright IEOs that are capitalist *par excellence*. If either of these conditions were to inhibit the implementation of meaningful monetary reform, one should look for a solution that makes the CPEs still part of the new IMS system without compelling them to join in a system that is politically unacceptable.

Attitudes of the CPEs on monetary reform through the mid-1980s

Because the CPEs have made no clear-cut commitment to date, it might be worthwhile to look into the possibilities of their participation in a reformed IMS. This could take on several forms, including a reshaping of the presently existing system from within, a newly created global monetary system, or a multilayered system that is universal only by virtue of all parts being radially centered on the global institution.

A reform of the Fund from within Given the basic objections to key aspects of the BWS, one way in which the CPEs could become associated with it, without compromising their principles, would be through a reform of the Fund from within. The existing system would essentially be retained in name, but some of the fundamental Articles of Agreement could be modified and some new paragraphs added to accommodate the special features and needs of the CPEs. Note, however, that this option is not available if the Nairobi declaration (UNCTAD 1976, 154) still holds:

> The proposals made within the framework of IMF to modify the basis of the existing [IMS] will neither ensure normal currency dealings nor establish conditions to provide stability and the necessary confidence in such an [IMS]. The [Jamaica] modification of the Articles of Agreement of IMF would serve to entrench the privileged position of several Western countries in that organization.

In theory it would be possible to establish the TR monetary region as a subsystem linked technically to the IMF. This could take several forms. One would be the creation of a set of rules for nonmarket economies

(Holzman 1978, 126–7) similar to those that permitted Poland and Rumania to accede to the GATT (see chapter 4). But it is doubtful whether the CPEs in the Fund would be willing to replace their present direct relationship with a "special" one. Another would be to weld the TR and the SDR directly through an agreement between the IBEC and the IMF that offers the CPEs access to SDRs. For example, an interested CPE would borrow SDRs from the IMF and contract then for a loan in TRs that would be convertible. The CMEA as a whole would be held responsible for the repayment of the SDR loan. The interested CMEA countries could as a result have access to a new source of finance without joining the Fund. This might be an interesting option for some CPEs not in the Fund. But it would be unacceptable to others called upon to shoulder this service – the Soviet Union in the first place. It is also doubtful whether the IMF, and the actual and potential member CPEs, would prefer such a link over direct membership. Perhaps a more feasible policy might be to have a dual status: a special technical link between the IBEC and IMF for the CPEs that do not wish to join the IMF now or in the foreseeable future, and full membership for those that prefer to do so.

A new world monetary system Another important issue that has received explicit emphasis in suggestions of how the IMS could be modified is the call of the CPEs to restructure international economic relations on a just, equitable, and democratic basis. In fact, the CPEs have stressed that another international conference on money and finance, as discussed, be convened "with a view to democratizing the current international monetary and financial system on a just and equal basis" (United Nations 1983, 2). This would entail such a change in the Articles of Agreement that the Fund as constituted would not survive.

Exceedingly few CPE policy makers have commented on desirable or mandatory conditions for monetary reform. For example, J. Fekete (1978, 27ff.; 1981, 34ff.; 1986, 59–60), former Deputy Chairman of the Hungarian National Bank, stipulated the following as prerequisites for a workable IMS. He perceived a clear need for a universal monetary institution under the aegis of the United Nations. It should be empowered, under rules to be laid down, to issue new international money as the anchor of the new IMS. The convertibility of that new currency unit should be guaranteed not by one country, as under the gold-exchange standard, or by each country, as under the gold standard, but by all participants in the system. Secondly, the role of gold is to be regularized by using the metal's value as the *numéraire* for establishing the exchange rate of the new world currency. Thirdly, realistic convertible currency parities for the new world currency need to be set and should be stable yet far more flexible than those of the BWS. Finally, within this framework modalities for eliminating bottlenecks in international credit, for making available economically warranted long-term loan capital, or for meeting other capital requirements in an organized way remain to be worked out.

When Soviet commentators enter into positive statements they (see Fomin 1978, 108–9) frequently stress the following conditions for the emergence of a new IMS that takes into account and meets the interests of states with different socioeconomic systems and are at different levels of development: (1) a healthy international political climate; (2) the prior removal of chronic payments imbalances in DMEs and observing symmetry in adjustment by surplus and deficit countries; (3) limit the practice of floating exchange rates and provide for compensation for losses sustained as a result of sharp exchange-rate changes of main currencies; and (4) better ways and methods of ensuring economic cooperation through more perfect forms of international liquidity. Regarding the latter, the reserve instrument must be acceptable to all participants in international exchange, neutral, sufficiently stable, and protected from the influence of exchange-rate fluctuations of all national currencies. It is uncertain whether this must necessarily be based on gold.

A multitier world monetary system Another form of participation would be the explicit recognition of the *de facto* existence of several currency zones, each with its own special needs and characteristics. The European monetary system (EMS), the dollar zone, the yen area, the Arab group, and the nonoil DEs have their own peculiarities. Another one could emerge as a result of the establishment of an effective TR monetary region. Thus Matjuchin and Šenaev (1978, 50) note with some interest that the present IMS "does not preclude regional agreements on fixed [exchange rates]." The interaction among the various regions, however, would be subject to common principles and a universal currency unit (Cooper 1984) to be regulated through rules acceptable to all participants. Surveillance and adjustment requirements would be confined to the interaction among currency zones. Whether this is a realistic option depends importantly on the particular feature of the TR monetary system, which is currently in flux as summarized in chapter 5.

4 The international trading system and the CPEs

This chapter addresses some of the many problems that arise when CPEs seek to integrate themselves into the global trade framework. I shall investigate this issue from four angles: the economic systems of CPEs and their compatibility with the organized trading framework, the ITS as it has evolved since 1947, the actually existing CPEs as they have been transforming themselves from the traditional system, and the potential for revamping the trading framework along principles yet to be formulated and agreed upon, as examined in chapter 5. The conditions that determine the search for such an alternative ITS emerge, of course, from the deficiencies of the one that we have known since World War II as clarified toward the end of this chapter.

Section 1 recapitulates the basic markers of the aborted ITO insofar as it bears on the ITS that crystallized over the subsequent decades. The next two sections examine how the CPEs would have been able to participate in the ITO and their attitude, particularly the Soviet Union's, toward the ITS in the late 1940s and its subsequent evolution. Section 4 analyzes the provisions of the GATT for dealing with CPEs. Next I summarize the basic economic and technical problems of bringing CPEs under the discipline of the General Agreement. Section 6 looks briefly at the provisions of the patchwork attempts to fuse the CPEs into the GATT as well as the experiences gathered in the process. The benefits and drawbacks of the GATT approach are examined in section 7 together with whether it would be rational for the Contracting Parties to seek an accommodation for the CPEs as a group or, alternatively, for the remaining nonmember CPEs individually within the GATT system. I also evaluate this question from the angle of the CPEs themselves. Because the desirability and feasibility of reforming the ITS emerge against the backdrop of the problems faced by CPEs as well as many MEs, these issues are taken up in chapter 5.

1 Salient features of the ITO

Some of the multiple objectives of the ITO were ambitious and realistic. Others were based on a nonexisting environment or outdistanced the then prevailing political premises on international cooperation. I looked at these issues in conjunction with the salient specifications of the Havana Charter in chapter 1. Here I intend to elaborate on the theory that was apparently at the roots of the ITO and the General Agreement, the evolution of organized trading in the postwar world, and the relationship between trade and economic expansion.

Economic theory and organized trading

The instrumental concerns in laying the foundations of essential parts of the ITO as well as in formulating the General Agreement rested on the underlying orthodox doctrine of comparative advantage (Buzan 1984; Cooper 1975a, 1975b) in its neoclassical economic setting (Diebold 1952, 35). Exploitation of variations in relative costs due to different relative factor endowments, immobility of production factors across national borders, and ability to reallocate such factors relatively painlessly within one national economy were presumed to be the main inducement to raising global prosperity. Impediments, counterproductive commercial policies, and other man-made obstacles to free commerce among nations should, therefore, be avoided at all cost. Furthermore, in a world that by assumption is dominated by merchandise trade, it was deemed critical to facilitate such commerce through positive policy measures that may affect the environment for merchandise commerce, even if only very indirectly.

The basic consensus economic theory at the time, which has since been strongly contested (Krugman 1987), held that international trade raised global economic prosperity by improving the well-being of individual countries. By exploiting their respective comparative advantage, it was tacitly taken for granted that countries raised their own level of welfare and, in the process, offered opportunities for others to reciprocate. In this manner, passive as well as positive policy measures mutually reinforced welfare-promoting repercussions of buoyant international trade. Less restricted international trade raised real income for the world as a whole, and usually for individual countries too, and thus resulted in more efficient global use of human and material resources.

Whether the overwhelming body of belief in neoclassical comparative advantage is still relevant at this stage is a moot question. This follows from a number of observed phenomena that contradict some of the doctrine's fundamental assumptions: (1) substantial capital movements and some labor mobility across frontiers do exist; (2) governments are not constrained to facilitate the rational allocation of resources because they have increasingly fostered dynamic trade advantages through pure target choice, they collude among themselves and sometimes with special interest groups, and they interfere with trade for national purposes; (3) product and factor prices do not behave smoothly; (4) increasing returns do occur more than trivially; and (5) identical production technologies are not available to all and the choice of techniques is not solely determined by factor cost differentials. These and a host of other factors call for a more realistic body of trade theory and positive policy prescriptions (see chapter 5).

The doctrine underlying the ITO's philosophy also focused on the effects of trade barriers. Tariffs and other hindrances to trade represent taxes on domestic consumers or on foreign producers. As a result, they shift income within a country in favor of the protected sectors, away from consumers as well as from nonprotected and export-oriented sectors of production. In addition, the ITS envisaged for the postwar period was concerned chiefly about replacing the interwar network of bilateral trade agreements, reducing high tariffs, prohibiting the numerous NTBs and QRs imposed to protect domestic markets, and easing other obstacles to the free flow of goods and services (including restrictive business practices, government procurement, and state trading). Yet for all its economic plausibility, negotiators paid little attention to the advantages that might accrue from unilateral trade liberalization. Commercial policies in particular were viewed as providing fertile ground for bargaining and trading off "gains" in export markets against "losses" from import incursions made possible by the removal of tariffs, the lowering of NTBs, or the compression of other hindrances to the play of market forces.

Finally, the ITO framework was steeped in the concept that an orderly trading system governed by widely accepted rules for world trade and instruments to defuse trade disputes lessens the risk of conflicts, including those over economic issues, and thereby enhances the ability of national states singly and in concert to maintain the peace. This promotion of global economic security as an essential part of broader efforts to maintain durable world peace and prosperity was uppermost in the minds of key participants in the debates.

Commerce and the ambitions of the ITO

The foregoing should not be construed as implying that the evolvement toward a self-contained ITS concept was dominated by economic determinism. This posits that once countries are tightly interlocked in the economic sphere the potential cost to be borne by a country bent on rupturing those relations for unilateral, short-term gain may be so considerable that it dissuades policy makers from entertaining them as viable policy alternatives. But there are evidently other concerns that motivate the behavior of policy makers, and they surfaced during the debates about the ITO, if only because commerce was not a goal in itself as some observers tend to suggest. By contrast, it was the supreme purpose of the General Agreement.

Regardless of the many shortcomings of the Havana Charter, particularly when contrasted with the high hopes held by the multiple negotiating factions, recognition that it constituted at least a firm foundation for world prosperity and peace would have averted the trajectory subsequently traveled. An institutional framework as free as possible of ambiguous and equivocal provisions would have helped to prevent, or at least to minimize, frictions and to diminish the divisiveness of trade disputes, and thus to facilitate the ITO's tasks, including those in the field of state trading. These and other hopes laid down in the Havana Charter contrasted sharply with the commercial policy practices of the interwar period – perhaps the key motivation behind the charter.

Precisely because of the ambitious nature of the charter, it led to a polarized debate. Idealists kept focusing on the ITO's shortcomings, including exceptions from the philosophy of a free world trading order, which had been its foundation stone, without really suggesting any plausible alternative. The major exceptions that would have remained on the books even after the transitory waivers had been whittled down would have been four, namely national security, economic development, agricultural policy, and regional preferences (Loftus 1949). Of these, the provisions on economic development and regional preferences are perhaps the most critical.

Suffice it to recall that the negotiations about the General Agreement, which ran parallel with those of the ITO in mid-1947, had been instigated by the United States. Its chief motivation was to limit the choice of trade provisions essentially to those that the US Administration felt it could implement under existing trade legislation as embodied in the successive RTAAs and would, therefore, not require further Congressional action. For over a decade Congress had devolved some control over commercial policy to the executive branch. But this fell far short of the claim that the "US Congress legislated itself out of making trade policy" (Culbert 1987a, 383) with the first RTAA of 1934. This instrument was in any case valid only for three years and its continuing renewal would be subject to Congressional scrutiny with no guarantee that it would be forthcoming automatically or easily. President Roosevelt had won another extension of that provision in 1945, moreover with an amendment that entitled him to enter into multilateral rather than bilateral tariff negotiations mandated in earlier versions of the RTAA for tariff cuts of up to 50 percent; that mandate was slated to expire in 1948. That was one of the reasons (Finlayson and Zacher 1981, 562) that made the US Administration anxious to negotiate tariff cuts in an MTN round before its mandate expired or was taken away or severely curtailed by an overanxious Congress bent on restoring constitutional prerogatives in commercial policy matters. But the United States also wanted to impart greater buoyancy to trade to promote economic activity, accelerate economic reconstruction, and alleviate the burden of providing relief and rehabilitation to the war-devastated countries in Europe. If such could not be reached by all participants in the ITO deliberations in unison, it was bent on launching interim negotiations only among those prepared to participate in MTNs.

For internal political purposes, the US Administration of that time deemed it politic to make approval of the ITO Charter subject to Congressional scrutiny. Congress was concerned about transferring trade policy altogether to the Administration – a concession first gained by Roosevelt in 1934 in an effort to repeal the forbidding Hawley–Smoot tariff through reciprocal bilateral tariff concessions. In fact, as illustrated in section 3 in connection with the proposed Organization for Trade Cooperation (OTC), the constitutional issue is double-edged. On some occasions, the US Administration succeeded in interpreting its executive powers on commercial policy matters widely. On others, it was prepared to yield to Congressional interest groups.

But there were other groups in the United States that objected to the ITO Charter. One was the protectionist lobby, which protested that under the charter the United States would lose control over its own trade policies. On the other hand, advocates of a liberal trading system objected that the charter had too many loopholes and exceptions (see chapter 1). Finally, defenders of free enterprise opined that the ITO could lead to state control over the economy, in other words socialism – an ideological taboo in North America. Under these competing pressures, the rapid deterioration in the east–west climate, the fact that the United States had achieved important trading goals and the substance of the Havana Charter in its list of priorities (Condliffe 1950, 667) with the just-completed General Agreement, and the overall aura of traditional US reluctance to let government manage economic affairs, the Administration withdrew the charter from the 1950 legislative agenda (Stone 1984, 21). As a result, the ITO was dead; by default, the General Agreement became the core of the ITS.

The evolution of organized trading

Because the evolution of organized trading in the postwar period is well known, I need not spell it out in detail here. Recall that several attempts were made over the years to establish a more comprehensive organization along the lines originally proposed for the ITO, but with modifications reflecting modesty and experience. They all failed, partly because of persistent US opposition to delivering on its ostensible commitment to multilateralism. Nonetheless, over the years the ITS has been enlarged in less structured ways. The evolution has been conditioned partly by the extension of the GATT framework, for example, through various codes, agreements, and the addition of part IV concerning the general system of preferences (GSP) for DEs in the GATT, and partly by the creation of new trade bodies, including UNCTAD; and through the addition of new committees (such as in OECD) or affiliated UN bodies (such as the Centre on Transnational Corporations [CTC]) assigned to one set of ITO problems or another. In fact, there is presently a panoply of institutions that deal with one aspect or another of trade. In addition to the GATT and UNCTAD, there are multilateral official institutions as well as organs of integration groupings concerned with sectoral and regional trade issues. Among the former, sectoral trade issues are dealt with in a number of organizations. These include the Food and Agriculture Organization (FAO) for agricultural trade, various commodity councils that may in time be replaced by the Integrated Programme of Commodities (IPC) in the UNCTAD framework, ILO concerning labor migration, the World Intellectual Property Organization for trading in patents and other intellectual property, various UN organs (including EcoSoc and the Second Committee of the General Assembly), the United Nations Industrial Development Organization (UNIDO) as far as trade in manufactures is concerned, UNCITRAL, which fosters trade and marketing for the benefit of DEs, the World Food Programme, and many others that are perhaps not quite global in character. Among the regional multilateral institutions concerned with trade, at least the UN's five regional economic commissions need to be mentioned. Of course, all organs through which two or more countries try to enhance their economic integration are involved with trading matters in one way or another.

Certainly, even if the ITO had come into its own, the advent of regional integration (Huber 1981; Lortie 1975) and increased recognition of problems specific to DEs would in an important way have modified the stylized 1948 idea of a single worldwide organ taking care of all emerging trade problems in conjunction with the BWS (Kaufmann and Alting van

Geusau 1969, 99). Nevertheless, this diversification could then have emanated from one source and been coordinated within one overarching organ, namely the ITO, rather than haphazardly and with minimal coordination through a diversity of formal and informal intergovernmental organs as has been the case up to now for most of the organs mentioned above.

Of course, I do not deny that some evolution has taken place since the late 1940s. But the international community has failed altogether to surmount the narrowly defined commercial-policy framework tentatively set up with the conclusion of the negotiations of the General Agreement in October 1947. Certainly, this commercial framework has since been extended in depth and in breadth from its original status as a highly truncated version of one chapter of the Havana Charter. As such, it has come close to some of the ambitions that the ITO was to have served. Nonetheless, the present set of rules, regulations, and institutional provisions that define the ITS fall far short of what the ITO was to have accomplished. Of course, the provision in the General Agreement whereby members obligate themselves to heed "to the fullest extent of their executive authority" the principles of all the substantive provisions of the Havana Charter has rarely been adhered to (Stone 1984, 30). Not only that: as the long and frustrating struggle over the NIEO in the 1970s and the fruitless attempts to start up global economic negotiations in the 1980s have so clearly underlined, the international community remains far removed from some of the configurations envisaged in the second half of the 1940s.

2 Provisions in the Charter for CPEs

Because the ITO Charter failed to be ratified, it is impossible to assess how the organization might have gradually accommodated the special trading requirements of the Soviet Union and the countries that subsequently adopted the CPE model. It is useful, however, to recall the ITO's provisions for such countries so as to contrast them in section 4 with the stipulations on state trading embodied in the General Agreement.

The ITO's *Suggested charter* and subsequent drafts included provisions of direct relevance to countries with an MFT (see chapter 1). Note that economies other than the CPEs, DEs for example, were envisaged as engaging in state trading. It referred in particular to state-owned firms in DMEs (such as tobacco and liquor monopolies, public utility companies, and others depending upon the country in question), state-controlled raw material and agricultural marketing boards, particularly in DEs and the colonial associations fostered by the metropolitan countries, and the socialistic element that was expected to allow for considerable influence of the state in postwar economic management, including pervasive control over some trade segments.

Because the Soviet Union chose not to participate in the London Conference or in subsequent meetings on the preparation of the Havana Charter or in the negotiations of the General Agreement, the paragraphs of *Suggested charter* dealing with STCs were *de facto* segregated into the provisions for countries with "a complete state monopoly of import trade" and countries that maintained vestiges of state trading in one sector or another but whose economy otherwise was steered through market-type instruments and policies. The former provisions were not actively negotiated after the London Conference,[1] although some "bracketed"[2] articles were retained throughout the negotiations that led up to the Havana Charter (see Beneš and Jung 1988; Restoration 1947, 582–6). As noted in chapter 1, negotiators hoped that the charter would be sufficiently flexible to permit eventual Soviet participation in the ITO. Some other stipulations on state trading were embodied in the General Agreement (see pp. 167–77).

As compared with the American hopes placed on elaborating a liberal trading world, the draft provisions that could be invoked for CPEs were exceedingly tolerant of economic centralism. They took the MFT for granted and offered technical arrangements to align that monopoly with the principles of *Suggested charter*, namely on ensuring trade expansion and equal treatment. The key stipulation, on which more in section 4, stated that the relevant STC:

> shall promote the expansion of its foreign trade with the other members in consonance with the purposes of this charter. To this end such member shall negotiate with the other members an arrangement under which, in conjunction with the granting of tariff concessions ... and other benefits ... it shall undertake to import in the aggregate over a period products of the other members valued at not less than an amount to be agreed upon. This purchase arrangement shall be subject to periodic adjustment.

In other words, *Suggested charter* had two principal provisions for a CPE. First, it was required to conduct foreign trade in accordance with commercial, that is, nonpolitical considerations. It also provided techniques by which, in exchange for tariff reductions by MEs, the affected country could undertake commitments similar in effect, but not quite identical, to tariff reductions.

In this connection, it is useful to stress for later reference that a global quota, such as required in the Havana Charter, if set in a transparent manner is not necessarily discriminatory in the habitual sense (Wiles 1968, 224). It would, of course, obfuscate discrimination between products of domestic and foreign origin, but that feature would apply also, although differently, to a tariff-driven environment, especially when markets are not fully integrated or transparent. Furthermore, the quantity commitment was not something completely invented by ITO negotiators. It had earlier been used in Soviet–American trade relations (Fink 1974, 195) and in Soviet agreements with Latvia in 1927 and with Finland during the 1930s (Domke and Hazard 1958, 56).

The original ambitions of the ITS aimed at four features. For one, it sought to devise methods so that STCs do not in effect apply export subsidies or high import tariffs in ways prohibited by the Havana Charter. The second aim was to ensure equal treatment, particularly to eliminate manipulation of trade for political purposes, by requiring state-controlled firms to formulate their decisions on commercial considerations. Thirdly, because of the desired elimination of QRs, the charter sought to enjoin governments from resorting to state trading as a means of circumventing the intended ban on quotas. Finally, it aimed at subjecting state-trading firms also to the charter's provisions on curbing restrictive cartel practices (Bidwell and Diebold 1949, 226). These stipulations were perceived to "provide a sound basis for the future clarification, refinement, and expansion of state trading rules" (Committee 1949, 24). Elaborating codes for integrating countries with an economic organization such as the USSR's and to narrow deviations from the market environment – the underlying logic of the arrangement – was slated to be an important assignment of the ITO. Anyway, because of Soviet reluctance to participate in any of the three pillars of postwar IEOs, whatever may have been the motive force behind the efforts to accommodate CPEs tended to get blurred, or to be fully glossed over, in the General Agreement.

3 Attitude of the CPEs toward the ITS

As noted in chapter 1, the Soviet Union elected not to attend the formal conferences and working sessions convened after those that led up to the Bretton Woods institutions, though it had been invited to do so. Thus it was not present at the London Conference in late 1946, the New York redrafting meeting in early 1947, the Geneva Conference in mid-1947, and the Havana Conference in late 1947 and early 1948, when the Havana Charter was adopted. The ostensible reason for absenting itself from the London Conference was that the USSR had not had sufficient time to study the American proposals (Kostecki 1979a, 2). In this connection, recall from chapter 1 that the US proposal was tabled in November 1945 and distributed to EcoSoc before early February 1946; *Suggested charter* had been discussed on several occasions prior to it being formally released in September 1946; and the London Conference did not open till mid-October 1946 (Gerschenkron 1947, 628). So it was at best a disingenuous excuse.

The USSR was not invited to the Geneva Tariff Conference in 1947 from which the General Agreement and the later GATT emanated. Its particular place in the ITO was to be regulated later if and when the Soviet Union chose to participate. Nonetheless, even after London the drafts of the Havana Charter contained some provisions for state trading. These were included in the hope that the Soviet Union's wartime and postwar involvement in plans for a coherent global economic, financial, and trading framework would not be terminated altogether. In the end, it acknowledged having opted for just that and stayed away from the IEOs.

Soon after the General Agreement was negotiated, the Soviet Union and its then growing number of allies sharply criticized the IEOs, particularly within the UN General Assembly and EcoSoc. From the very beginning, the CPEs made it clear that they would not actively participate in the new economic order. They perceived organized international economic relations as having essentially been established by and for the benefit of a select group of DMEs clustered around the United States as hegemon. From their platform in the IEOs, these countries were accused of seeking to dominate others, particularly the DEs, through economic means, rather than as a result of military and political might, as during the colonial era. It is useful to note, though, that this attitude was reversed for the first time as early as 1955, when the CPEs announced that they would embrace multilateralism and nondiscrimination as guiding principles in international economic relations (Kennedy 1987, 28).

The Soviet views on the GATT, MTNs, and related attempts to come to grips with shared global economic problems have not thus far been stated exhaustively or even coherently in one comprehensive stance on principles, such as that adopted, for instance, with respect to the IMS at Nairobi. By virtue of the fact that the USSR stayed away from the gestation of the stillborn ITO and the General Agreement; looked rather negatively upon the GATT; never participated in tariff negotiations; and did not ever, until recent tentative efforts, especially with the 1986 *note verbale* to the GATT, show an active interest in participating in either, it is not at all clear what the Soviet views on the basic principles of a realistic ITS are. Certainly, the formal commitment to multilateralism and nondiscrimination enunciated in 1955 has never been retracted, but I doubt that this declaration can be read as providing the key precepts of an ITS that the USSR even then would have been prepared to support.

The reasons why the CPEs for the first time aired their views on organized international trading in a positive manner in the mid-1950s are several. First, the post-Stalin quest for better international relations through peaceful coexistence and for stronger east–west commercial ties played a critical role in dampening the political invective characteristic of earlier stances. Also, the rapid emergence of the Third World and the nonaligned movement, as they found their philosophical inspiration in the Bandung Conference, not only challenged countries to devise a new relationship through meaningful development assistance but also opened the door for carrying the ideological struggle between capitalism and socialism, as it has crystallized since World War II, into the newly emerging DEs. Thirdly, it should be recalled that the mid-1950s proved to be a very difficult period for the CPEs, economically as well as politically. Economic problems had arisen partly on account of the so-called New Course, which was then in full bloom and was creating problems in the orderly reallocation of resources in line with the sharp shift in political development preferences.[3] It was also the first time that the pronounced autarkic tendency of the CPEs was renounced, partly because of the prevailing imbalances but also because it was slowly being realized that gains could be reaped from trade that would be rather costly to emulate through forced industrialization (Fink 1974, 207–8). Finally, at that time the GATT had agreed to the creation of the OTC as a new global trading organization. The CPEs did not really wish to support this initiative if only because OTC would have meant the extension of the General Agreement outside the UN framework by different means, maintenance of discrimination against CPEs, and the relative neglect of the issues facing DEs in external commerce.

Having shunned the ITO and denounced the GATT framework, the Soviet Union and its allies unexpectedly launched an initiative from within the United Nations – at first in the form of a proposal tabled in the Economic Commission for Europe (ECE) and later at the EcoSoc session – in support of resurrecting and ratifying the Havana Charter. Failing that, the CPEs argued for the creation of an alternative global trade organization. Neither succeeded.

Establishment of a new and broader world trade organization under the UN's aegis remained a theme that the CPEs emphasized from the mid-1950s through the early 1960s. For years, it met only token interest on the part of MEs. The initial skepticism of the DEs, in particular, may have arisen because the proposal was paired with sharp criticism of the GATT as a club for a few DMEs bent on maintaining colonialism and imperialism by different means. It was evidently an attempt to jump onto the bandwagon of critical appraisals of the General Agreement launched around that time by disenchanted, many newly independent, DEs.

Suggestions for changing the GATT or replacing it by an alternative did not emerge only from the CPEs, however. Although the GATT happened to become the main institutional organ of the ITS, it was ill-equipped to discharge that multisided function. This was generally recognized after a few years of operating within the confines of the General Agreement. GATT representatives therefore worked toward creating favorable conditions for taking a comprehensive look at the GATT with a view to revising the General Agreement. It was hoped that an "embodied" organization could more adequately fulfill the role into which it had reluctantly fallen by default. This general review session was held from October 1954 through March 1955. It endeavored to change various provisions of the GATT, many of which reflected the modifications introduced into the ITO's charter during the Havana deliberations but which had not yet been carried over in one way or another into the General Agreement itself. In addition, a charter was drawn up for the OTC as a new formal IEO; it was signed by the negotiators (GATT 1955).

Though there were some parallels between the ITO and the OTC, the latter was by and large constituted as an institutional infrastructure for the General Agreement, in part to obtain the necessary resources, and the mandate if approved by members, to explore solutions to trading problems by other means than ministerial requests or the need to settle disputes among Contracting Parties. Like the ITO, it foundered on the bedrock of US parliamentary organs, which, being dead set against multilateral institutions, refused to ratify OTC (Lamar 1956).

Given the modest ambitions envisaged[4] for the OTC, this US stance was rather extraordinary. To understand its full dimension, it is necessary to explain briefly the OTC's aims and why the United States once again stymied the ratification proceedings. Let us start first by looking at intentions. For all practical purposes, the OTC was envisaged essentially as a reorganization of the GATT to improve its management, that is, to endow the General Agreement with an organizational infrastructure that would otherwise have been provided by the ITO (Committee 1955) to administer the trade rules of the General Agreement (GATT 1955). In essence, it sought to replace the periodic meeting of Contracting Parties by a more stable organizational infrastructure. The latter would consist of a General Assembly, an Executive Committee of seventeen (which would receive its brief through the General Assembly), and a permanent Secretariat.

In addition to smoothing the administration of the General Agreement, the OTC would: (1) facilitate intergovernmental consultations on questions relating to international trade; (2) sponsor international trade negotiations;

(3) study the questions of international trade and commercial policy, and whenever appropriate make recommendations; and (4) collect, analyze, and publish empirical, qualitative as well as quantitative, information concerning international trade and commercial policies, paying due regard to the functions entrusted at the time to other international organizations (including most notably OEEC, FAO, ILO, and the UN's regional commissions). To assuage fears that the ITO would be revived through a back door, the agreement stipulated explicitly (GATT 1955, 2) that the OTC could not amend provisions of the General Agreement and could not impose upon members obligations other than those they had specifically agreed to.

Inasmuch as bringing order in the global economy through a streamlined trade organization had been essentially a US endeavor from the very inception of plans for postwar economic collaboration, the ratification of the OTC charter, like the Havana Charter, rested importantly with the United States. Given its peculiar parliamentary setup, it very quickly transpired that there was a wide range of proponents as well as opponents to ratifying the OTC in the United States. One set of issues revolved around the constitutionality of an agreement like the OTC's. Many members of the US Congress felt that the OTC amounted to an unwarranted delegation of Congressional authority because the US Constitution provides that Congress has the power – hence obligation – to regulate commerce (Lamar 1956, 4). Whereas the constitutional issue was at the core of the controversy, there were also commercial issues at stake.

The General Agreement was acceded to by the United States within the authority provided by the RTAA. But it has never been formally endorsed by the parliamentary organs – quite the contrary. Ratification of the OTC was seen as implicitly endorsing the General Agreement, something that many US politicians have been reluctant to do for more than forty years! The issue was not only a constitutional one, but also stemmed from a deeply felt controversy between the executive and legislative branches of government. The latter firmly believed – and apparently persists in this attitude to this day – that the President routinely exceeds his authority by entering into multilateral trade agreements without express authorization by the Congress. Seen in a broader perspective, there was, of course, the issue of whether foreign trade policy should be formulated in light of the necessities of overall foreign policy or whether the US Congress should be completely free to legislate on tariff and foreign-trade matters mainly in response to domestic considerations, regardless of foreign-policy implications. Furthermore, the opponents felt that the postwar multilateral approach had yielded little, if any, evidence of tangible benefits. It was argued that the ostensible multilateral approach had, in any case, been accompanied by many QRs and other trade barriers that effectively hampered trade. Finally, the United States had already extended too many concessions in exchange for "little if any benefit" (Lamar 1956, 15) in terms of US exports because of the exceptions granted under the provisions of the General Agreement (US Congress 1956). Under those circumstances, the OTC was dead on arrival.

Meanwhile, though rebuffed on the revival of the ITO, the European CPEs kept trying throughout the 1950s to air their own trade problems, particularly on east–west relations in ECE and EcoSoc fora. These efforts met little success until the May 1963 EcoSoc session, when a renewed CPE initiative elicited the support of MEs, including DEs. The latter evidently felt that the envisaged global conference on trade would lead to the solution of some outstanding problems regarding their place in the global economy and linking other issues with trade. Part of the initial proposal for the creation of a new trade organization, which the socialist countries identified as the ITO, was tabled at the first conference on trade and development, which, however, led to the "creation" of UNCTAD in 1964.

While tendering the proposal, Soviet advocates of the ITO, in particular, advanced some reasons why the ITO had been rejected. The kernel of the objections was twofold. First, rather than "naively thinking that the United States proposed the project ... in the interest of the development of world commerce as a whole ... it was hoping to create such conditions in international trade that would facilitate the opportunities for the penetration of American goods and capital into the markets of other states." Furthermore, under the "pretense of a managing role for the ITO, the United States, in essence, offered to endow this organization with the right to interfere in the commercial policy of its members" (Ognev and Ogarev 1964, 16). These are both rather weak arguments, given the convoluted Havana Charter!

When the European CPEs launched their initiative for the establishment of an ITO in the early 1960s[5] they argued that such a new organ was needed to mitigate the shortcomings of the General Agreement and its application under the aegis of the GATT. They perceived these to be fivefold (see UNCTAD 1964a, 52–3). In addition to its lack of universality, it was argued that the GATT was not suited to dealing with the trade problems of DEs, including their relations with DMEs. Thirdly, it was contended that the GATT lacked a mandate in the General Agreement and its postwar activities in particular to treat the problems of primary commodities in a proper way. Fourthly, the Contracting Parties had been seeking to cope with trading problems in a fragmentary way, not as an integral part of the more general, and thus more fundamental, task of fostering economic development, something that must be tackled simultaneously on various fronts and with clearly defined objectives. Finally, the GATT was alleged to have generally limited its activities to raising the volume of trade through reciprocal tariff reductions, thus ignoring in particular the many other, and most critical, issues involved in regulating trade between governments or their direct agents. This lack of a mandate and interest in the problems of the CPEs for that matter had swayed these countries not to subscribe to the General Agreement. In this connection, part IV of the General Agreement introduced in 1965, but which had been under negotiation for some time, was deemed to be insufficient – a policy of "galvanizing" the issues of development and trade as they affected the DEs in particular (Chvojnik 1965, 24ff.).

To mitigate the shortcomings of the General Agreement and the GATT, the CPEs argued the need to create a new, global trading organization that would surmount the enumerated problems not only by its very constitution and mandate, but also by actively agitating for the exploration of suitable solutions. Its mandate would be determined by UNCTAD I and subsequent conferences on trade and development topics, and particularly the interrelationship of the two. The gradual evolution of such new thinking was emphasized. For that reason, the CPEs stated that it was "only by deciding to agree on this new policy that such an institutional reorganization would make sense" and "the reorganization itself, if properly carried out, would facilitate the formulation of this policy" (UNCTAD 1964a, 53). The new institution would have to be endowed with a long-term mandate to come to grips with many sensitive trade and development problems facing the world. It thus called for an "intellectually independent secretariat with authority and ability to submit proposals to governments" within the UN framework and to ensure that policies, once accepted, would be implemented.

The proposals of the European CPEs[6] amounted in fact to a much weaker form of organized trading than that entailed by either the ITO or, at least in the eyes of Contracting Parties, the OTC (see Ognev and Ogarev 1964, 18–19).[7] First of all, the organization should be set up in such a way that it could accommodate all interested countries without any discrimination, yet be endowed with broad competences in all questions concerning international trade. Secondly, though autonomous, the organization would be under the aegis of the United Nations to ensure close cooperation among the specialized UN organs and other institutions involved with some aspect of international trade. Thirdly, its main task would be to foster international trade expansion as an instrument of economic development in the interest of all countries. Fourthly, its activities should be based on universality, equality, sovereignty, noninterference in the internal affairs of member countries, and mutual advantage in trade. Maximum benefit from trade in terms of its contribution to the pace and depth of economic development would have to be ensured by requiring nondiscrimination and abolition of artificial barriers to trade, tasks that would be among the foremost preoccupations of the ITO. Its assignments would include the elimination of "artificially created restrictions and obstacles to trade" and "the adverse effects of the activities of closed economic groupings on the trade of third countries." More concrete purposes and means were to be negotiated. The CPEs dropped this proposal, however, when it became clear that the Group of Seventy-seven supported a different organ.[8] Nonetheless, the original call for a new organization has been reiterated on several occasions since, particularly in UNCTAD fora. But other details with respect to precisely what the Soviet Union, or the other CPEs for that matter, envisages as the role of such an institution have not so far been clarified.

4 The provisions of the GATT for dealing with CPEs

The philosophy underlying the GATT parallels that on which the negotiations around the ITO Charter revolved. But its focus was more narrowly on commercial policy measures and even more dogmatically on neoclassical comparative advantage. Until the eve of generalized reforms in CPEs, comparative advantage was not really fostered there in theory or otherwise (see chapter 2). Of course, neoclassical economics has never been very popular in the theory or economic policy of CPEs. One may therefore question whether the General Agreement is suitable at all for conditions in CPEs. Apart from fundamental disagreement about trade doctrine, what the GATT can mean to the CPEs depends, among other things, on the contribution that it provides to the ITS, how it discharges these functions institutionally, and the application of its provisions to CPEs.

Functions of the GATT

From its inception the GATT has been considered to discharge essentially five functions (Stone 1984, 23–4). First, it provides a permanent framework, however loose in view of constitutional problems, for international consultations on developments and concerns around global trade policy in general and trading practices of individual Contracting Parties in particular. Secondly, in its original form as well as through supplementary codes and agreements, the General Agreement embodies a set of rules for trade conduct that constrain and discipline the trade policies and practices of individual countries. Thirdly, it sets an environment for the further liberalization of world trade basically through tariff negotiations, commitments not to raise tariffs save in exceptional circumstances, and the application of rules that prohibit or restrain the use of NTBs. Fourthly, the GATT offers facilities and agreed procedures to resolve trade disputes among the countries that abide by the General Agreement. Finally, it provides the infrastructure for collecting and disseminating information about ongoing developments in world trade, trade policies and individual actions of Contracting Parties, and relatively independent research on and analyses of trade-related policy and legal issues.

Because the ITS was severely impaired by the ITO's stillbirth and the failure to act under the umbrella of the Havana Charter, it is a regime that cannot be well specified within the framework set in the introduction. But it may be useful for further reference in chapter 5 to make a stab at it. With reference to the regime's principles, the ITS was based on the belief that reciprocal trade liberalization helps to sustain the level of economic activity and contributes to better relations among countries, not just in economic exchanges. The purpose, then, was to ensure that the basis for export expansion of all countries was provided without unduly impairing the position of one single party. For that, the Contracting Parties adopted a host of substantive and procedural norms (Finlayson and Zacher 1981), of which the most important are nondiscrimination, trade liberalization through tariff reductions and removal of QRs and other NTBs, reciprocity, safeguards, and, since the mid-1960s, special treatment for DEs (Patterson 1966). Rules as prescriptions and proscriptions are anchored to the commitment not to raise the level of protection beyond so-called "bound" margins, that is levels negotiated within the ITS framework or brought into it through provisional accession. Regarding decision-making procedures, the ITS provides for ways to arrange Ministerial Meetings, to lower trade barriers through MTN rounds, and to give Contracting Parties access to dispute settlements machinery (through Working Parties and Panels), and for executive-organ decision making, possibly with voting, although that occurs infrequently.

Even when well disposed to the ITS in place, commentators frequently complain that the rules of the General Agreement are weakly enforced, easily circumvented, and widely abused. Seen in the legal context of the General Agreement, it must be realized that the concept of "illegality" in the GATT is elusive at best and that the process of enforcement is complex. The GATT *per se* is not a policing organization nor does it have enforcement powers of its own. In view of its antecedents in reciprocal tariff and other commercial-policy concessions, the General Agreement is anchored to the precepts of nearly balanced exchange of import concessions and export benefits among the Contracting Parties. Reneging on such an arrangement by one partner is, as a result, an act that can lead to the withdrawal of equivalent concessions, or an offer of acceptable compensation for the injury sustained by other Contracting Parties. Furthermore, this injury must be "declared" by the Contracting Parties, as the GATT itself has no powers to initiate such proceedings.

Alternative forms of membership in the GATT

Because the General Agreement has no institutional and organizational provisions, including those on membership (all of which were to be spelled out in detail in the "real" ITS organization – the ITO), the GATT is not legally a full-fledged IEO. As a result, it cannot have members in the ordinary sense of that term. However, the GATT is *de facto* an IEO, albeit one built on political quicksand, as the Contracting Parties organized themselves as best they could under the limited provisions of the General Agreement.

There are several forms of accession to the General Agreement. Four depict the types of association open to countries before the issue of coopting CPEs arose (Jackson 1969, 87ff.). First, there are countries that accept the General Agreement without reservation, as provided for in article XXVI, paras. 2 and 4. Only Haiti and Liberia have ever accepted this arrangement, and the latter withdrew after a short while (McGovern 1986, para. 1.131). Secondly, there are countries that accede under a "Protocol of Provisional Application." These include North America, Western Europe (but not the Federal Republic of Germany and Italy), and most Commonwealth countries. "Provisional" refers to article XXXV or the so-called grandfather clause with respect to the application of the rules of part II of the General Agreement. This stipulates that the Contracting Party accedes fully to the General Agreement to the extent that there is no inconsistency with existing national legislation, which takes precedence. Thirdly, there are parties to "Protocols of Accession." In this case, in addition to acceding provisionally to the General Agreement, the protocol includes a schedule of tariff and other concessions that reflect prior tariff negotiations among the Contracting Parties. Otherwise, because of MFN a new Contracting Party would benefit unilaterally from prior concessions negotiated under the General Agreement without having to reciprocate. These protocols are as a rule negotiated between the country requesting accession and the existing Contracting Parties in principle on an individual basis. There is a variant to this that takes the form of a provisional protocol of accession, which is officially referred to as a Declaration. This instrument is concluded between the applicant and some Contracting Parties individually; it binds only the protocol's signatories, of course. Japan was the first one to be brought under the discipline of the General Agreement in this manner in 1953. Finally, a special provision applies to erstwhile dependent territories, which can accede, if desired, on the same terms and conditions previously accepted by the metropolitan government on behalf of the territory in question. If such conditions are deemed to be onerous, the formerly dependent territory may prefer to negotiate a new schedule as part of a regular accession protocol under article XXXIII. If it wishes to delay a decision on how to proceed, it is invited to apply the General Agreement on a *de facto* basis. There are presently about thirty such countries.

Reflecting the pragmatism of the General Agreement, there are in addition a number of special statuses to accommodate the CPEs in particular. The latter's participation in the GATT is usually regulated by way of declarations of a hortatory character. This certainly applied, for example, to Poland and Yugoslavia when they acquired observership in 1959. Countries and international organizations may be allowed to participate as observers. This has been granted freely in regard to sessions of the Contracting Parties. No country has ever been denied a request for observership of this nature.[9] But observership may be revoked, as occurred in the case of the Republic of China (Taiwan). In addition, CPEs may acquire provisional or associate status, which differs slightly from that provided for in the General Agreement, if only because the protocols signed with CPEs cannot possibly include the same provisions as were used, for example, in the case of Japan in the early 1950s.

By granting an associate status, the Contracting Parties evidently recognized that a common affirmation of a desire to develop commercial relations with CPEs on the basis of mutual advantage and reciprocity would be useful. Associate status also establishes direct, permanent contacts between the associate and Contracting Parties and provides for the full participation of the associate in "general activities" of the organization. In fact, it implies that commercial relations between Contracting Parties and the CPE can be conducted in conformity with the rules of the GATT to the extent possible under the associate's economic system. It also enables the country to participate in various organizational bodies of the GATT, including MTN rounds (Kostecki 1979a, 25). The provisional status that was accorded to Yugoslavia in 1962 was conformable with the General Agreement, although with a slight twist as there was a clear understanding that full Contracting Party status would be accorded only after Yugoslavia completed the transition to an ME status in the GATT sense. Similarly in the case of Poland, it was provisional because it was subject to a special protocol on import expansion signed in July 1967. Finally, as suggested, observership implies the ability to send representatives to the annual meetings, to request representation at other GATT sessions (though some may be withheld as there is a general presumption that the observer will move on to full Contracting Party status when it participates in the Council of Representatives, on which more in the next subsection), and to utilize the GATT's information services.

Organizational infrastructure

Because the ITO's commercial-policy chapter in the Havana Charter was expected soon to incorporate and to supersede the General Agreement, the negotiations around the latter ignored institutional and organizational matters. On this basis, the original signatories met at the two negotiating sessions in Havana and Geneva later in 1948. A secretariat was provided by the United Nations in the form of the ICITO (see chapter 1). In anticipation of the ratification of the Havana Charter and thus the subsequent establishment of the ITO, the conference moved to entrust the ICITO with all current business and the preparation of the ground for the establishment of the ITO, including its first conference. A secondary task was to coordinate for the time being the work of the Contracting Parties to the General Agreement. Though ICITO fell largely into disuse, its secretariat continues to exist. Its rationale derives from the need of the Contracting Parties for service of an administrative body and the availability of precisely such an organ. The United Nations as a result has continued to place the secretariat at the disposal of the Contracting Parties (Curzon 1965, 48–9). This developed into a *de facto* secretariat.

Attempts were made to streamline the organizational structure, most notably in the 1954–5 negotiating round that emanated in the agreement to create the OTC. Because this endeavor also miscarried, incremental changes have been promulgated and enacted over the years. As a result, the GATT has developed the main features of an intergovernmental organization typical of the UN family of specialized organs, although strictly speaking the GATT is not a UN specialized agency. The former Director General of the GATT, Olivier Long (1985, 45) emphasizes that: "Despite its modest beginnings and the ambiguities surrounding its legal status, GATT now has all the attributes of an international organization. It is treated *de facto* as a specialized agency in its relations with the United

Nations as per an exchange of letters of 1952." As such, it has its headquarters in Geneva; a permanent secretariat, which has, however, no statute and is therefore fully subordinated to the resolutions of sessions of the Ministerial Meeting; a budget with assessed contributions; an elaborate Committee structure, some of which emulates what countries had attempted to introduce under the Havana Charter (see chapter 1); and throughout the year an imposing schedule of meetings and conferences on a variety of trade-related topics. Certainly, one of the major differences between the GATT and more institutionalized IEOs is the degree of involvement of delegates from the Contracting Parties in the day-to-day affairs and well-being of the organization. In addition to benefits, this also has disadvantages, as detailed in section 7.

During the first decade of the GATT, the Contracting Parties met regularly for lengthy sessions structured around the management and administration of the General Agreement. This soon became too burdensome, however, and so from the late 1950s onwards attempts have been made to devolve decision making to more formally recognized organs. But representatives of the Contracting Parties, now organized on a standing basis through permanent offices with high-level staff in Geneva, continue to be intimately involved, often informally, even in managerial and operational tasks that could be discharged by a well-functioning secretariat (Stone 1984, 45).

Organizationally, the GATT framework comprises the annual conference, which is periodically held at the ministerial level, usually when important business on principles or framework negotiations is at hand. Ongoing GATT affairs are steered by a Council of Representatives, set up in 1960, in which all Contracting Parties are entitled to be seated. It meets frequently, possibly monthly. Specific trade measures as well as supplementary agreements and codes are entrusted to Committees. The most important ones are: the Balance-of-Payments Committee, which discusses QRs for balance-of-payments reasons; the Trade and Development Committee, which deliberates over the special trade interests of DEs; the Textile Committee, which supervises the MFA and serves as a forum for negotiations about extensions and modifications of the MFA; the Committee on Safeguards, which pursues proposals to establish a Safeguards Code; and a Consultative Group of Eighteen.

The Consultative Group of Eighteen was created in 1975 and transformed into a permanent organ in 1979. It is composed of senior trade officials from the most important Contracting Parties and meets quarterly. It serves as a forum for regular consultations on broad trade-policy developments and provides general direction to the GATT's work program, reviewing trade-policy developments of special interest to DEs, giving broad direction to the secretariat and management of the GATT, and facilitating the coordination between the GATT and the Fund. That is to say, this organ discusses developments in international trade with a view to forestalling sudden disturbances that could threaten the ITS. It also watches over the international adjustment process and, in this context, ensures coordination with the Fund.

Working Parties and Panels are set up as needed to examine specific issues and to facilitate the settlement of disputes. The difference between the two is subtle, but a Panel is as a rule composed of recognized experts, including independent ones, giving a legal opinion on a particular dispute, which is usually accepted by the Contracting Parties. However, little use has recently been made of this potentially important mechanism to defuse and resolve disputes under the General Agreement. A Working Party is often composed to exercise periodic supervision over special arrangements among Contracting Parties.

Finally, operational matters are entrusted to an international secretariat in Geneva. It has grown from a small group of UN employees, known as ICITO, to about 350 professionals. Its main task is to assist and advise Contracting Parties in regard to the GATT tasks and concerns, to service conferences and meetings, to assemble and present information, to undertake research and analyses of significant developments in world trade, and generally to assist in the operation of the GATT. The chief administrative officer of the GATT until 1965 was called Executive Secretary, a title inherited from the ICITO nomenclature. It has since been changed to Director General, as stipulated in the ITO's as well as the OTC's Charter.

Basic principles of the GATT

The foundations of the General Agreement rest on reciprocity, transparency, nondiscrimination, and safeguards. Trade protection was to be based on tariffs as much as politically feasible with a view to restricting divergences between domestic and foreign prices to normal factors of time and place. QRs and other NTBs would have to be replaced by tariffs and the latter gradually reduced through tariff negotiations. In other words, nondiscrimination among all actors in the global economy was preconditioned on the assumption underlying the GATT approach that trade is conducted primarily by private firms whose actions are guided by commercial, particularly profit, motives. In such an environment, it was taken for granted that prices would result solely from commercial decisions but evidently not necessarily based on purely competitive forces. The latter proviso is important for some of the hard-core problems of the CPEs cooperating with the GATT are sometimes attributed to the monopolistic structure of these countries. It is certainly true that CPEs are monopolistic. But that by itself does not inhibit them from adhering to nondiscrimination, reciprocity, transparency, and safeguards – the key foundations of the GATT.

Although nondiscrimination is the principal creed of the General Agreement, from the very inception of the ITS in the postwar period various kinds of waivers and exceptions to that principle were embodied and several others have been incorporated in one form or another over the past four decades. The most important are: (1) to permit the continuation of the tariff preferences existing before 1939 (especially to accommodate the UK's imperial preference and the French colonial arrangements), but the Contracting Parties committed themselves not to raise the discriminatory duties; (2) customs unions of one kind or another that conform to specified and detailed conditions, including free movement of goods and services and external tariffs not exceeding the average of the pre-union tariff; (3) QRs for balance-of-payments reasons; (4) waivers to permit DMEs to extend nonreciprocal tariff preferences to DEs – hence not subject to MFN – and to enable DEs to grant tariff preferences among themselves that are not subject to MFN treatment; (5) a limited number of waivers to permit individual countries to give preferential tariff treatment to particular target imports from specified countries (especially important in the context of the former European Coal and Steel Community and the automobile trade agreement between the United States and Canada); (6) QRs on imports of textile products on a discriminatory basis under the MFA; and (7) conditional MFN treatment under supplementary codes and arrangements concluded during the Tokyo Round.

These objectives of the General Agreement are, of course, tailored to mature, fully integrated economies managed through market-type coordination mechanisms. But they are ill-suited to be transposed to countries that cling to substantial macroeconomic control through direct commands, including control over international trade. This applies especially when their ambitions are predicated on the CPEs' peculiar development strategy or when two or more CPEs decide to mutually reinforce their perceived desire to remain separate from the rest of the global economy (see chapter 2). The expansion of trade on a nondiscriminatory basis and the reduction of tariffs as the paramount guides to bolstering trade would be impaired, and possibly impeded, if private or state-sponsored monopolistic organizations or state-trading firms were permitted to inhibit trade and to conduct it on a discriminatory basis (Gerschenkron 1947, 624). This follows from the difficulty of ensuring "free" market access and of confining the operations of such firms solely to economic motives, given the potential preponderance of the state in the economy (Hartland-Thunberg 1987).

Because the objectives underlying the GATT were modest and geared to DMEs, no effort was made to foster the steady elaboration of a code for state trading, ensure compliance, and provide for conflict resolution. The exclusion of the USSR from the inception of this process precluded gaining valuable experience in dealing with two sets of problems that remain relevant today (Diebold 1979a, 52–4; Diebold 1979b). First, if universality is to be attained in regulating global trade, ways and means have to be found to connect two quite disparate economic systems. This was not really explored at any length at the ITS's inception or at the time of accession of CPEs. Also, experience with CPEs in the ITS would have provided a test for the degree to which economic cooperation could tolerate politicization, which now materializes outside the system by way of east–west tensions.

Provisions for state trading and the CPEs

The General Agreement does, of course, have provisions (mainly article XVII) that regulate the trading behavior and policies of firms owned or controlled by the state. The main purpose is to restrict, basically to tariffs, the government's influence on the private calculations in trade decisions. These concerns, which reflect only one aspect of the proposed Havana Charter, namely article 31,[10] are hardly germane to the practical, rather technical problems and policy concerns relevant to countries whose economy is organized chiefly along other than market criteria. The other one was originally entitled "Expansion of trade by complete state monopolies of import trade,"[11] which was omitted from the Havana Charter (see Preliminary Draft 1946) by the Preparatory Committee. The reason was simply that the USSR, then the only important country to maintain a complete MFT (Dam 1970, 316), chose not to attend the deliberations. Yet it is this particular feature that will be of some interest later.

Article XVII on state monopolies in the context of MEs provides the only basis in the General Agreement for accommodating CPEs. Its major purpose is to enjoin state monopolies from effectuating their purchases and sales in a discriminatory manner (Dam 1970, 321). To ensure that such firms eschew political favoritism in their decision making, these organs were in fact to behave "solely in accordance with commercial considerations, including price, quality, availability, marketability, transportation, and other conditions of purchase or sale, and shall afford other contracting parties adequate opportunity ... to compete for participation in such purchases or sales" (article XVII,1).

State monopolies are also treated under several other articles, particularly those dealing with tariffs and concessions, the national treatment standard, equitable trade margins, and QRs.[12] Regarding tariffs, the degree of protection enjoyed by a state monopoly cannot exceed the average scheduled "for that sector" to ensure that the monopoly emulates as much as possible the behavior of private firms (Mikesell 1947a, 365). Which particular tariff schedule should apply as reference has given rise to much debate as a strict interpretation of the provision implies very limited freedom to determine domestic prices of state monopolies. This harsh implication was somewhat eased by an interpretative note, on which prices ought to be compared, that Contracting Parties sought to attach to this article in the 1950s. It was suggested that the difference between the landed cost and the internal price net of distribution costs should be made the subject of measuring whether or not a Contracting Party abides by a tariff concession granted on a product subject to an import monopoly.[13] That is to say, the difference between the domestic sale price free of normal profits and domestic markups for distribution, packaging, and so on (denoted p^d) and the landed cost (denoted p^f) converted at the official exchange rate (denoted r) relative to the latter magnitude should not exceed the average rate of protection scheduled (denoted t). In other words, the condition stipulated that the following relationship should hold:

$$p^d/p^f \times r - 1 \leqslant t \tag{4.1}$$

If this rule is to apply, two problems arise: which tariff schedule is to be considered and which particular prices are to be compared? Regarding the first, there is considerable confusion about the particular t to apply. The Geneva draft of the Havana Charter in fact specified that it should be the "negotiated tariff for the product" (Restoration 1947, 585). This can be readily applied in the case of monopolies in MEs because the concept is easily identified with a "product schedule." To transpose these provisions to a CPE, however, the country would have to set forth in its GATT schedule all protection offered to domestic firms. This would, in fact, be tantamount to asking the CPE "to disband its central planning" (Dam 1970, 323) or, at first glance, to impose an identical tariff on all activities for each agreed schedule, for otherwise it would not be possible to abide simultaneously by the agreement and the GATT stipulations. In other words, if t is negotiated with the GATT and p^f and r are given, which is the case for many products of CPEs, p^d is no longer subject to domestic pricing policy precepts. Alternatively, if p^d is set domestically and p^f and r

are given exogenously in trading markets, t is predetermined and can thus not be negotiated *ex ante*.

With respect to CPEs, then, the stipulation would gear the core of tariff negotiations to setting internal wholesale price levels and their structure. It is fundamentally unclear to what extent the CPE would have been allowed to maintain disconnected consumer and wholesale price systems, not to mention the particular variety of TRPs for CMEA trade (see chapter 2). Even if entitled to pursue own-price policies in all but domestic wholesale trade, the latter restriction would still have constituted discriminatory treatment for no domestic pricing regulations as such are explicitly imposed upon other Contracting Parties. Furthermore, such negotiations would be exceedingly complex by virtue of the fact that prices in CPEs do not clear markets. In other words, a "proper" margin may yet constitute discrimination because import quantity is, generally speaking, strictly controlled. Failure to fill the gap between domestic demand and effective domestic supply manifests itself in the form of shortages.[14] A more effective way, incidentally, to deal with a CPE would then be to negotiate over the minimum volume of imports, rather than the maximum price margin, because it can be easily identified and measured.

Regarding QRs, as already noted, an interpretative note allows them for MEs in the case of imports (and sometimes exports) for balance-of-payments, economic-development, and agricultural-support purposes. CPEs could hence not be denied the right to such QRs. Because CPEs are chronically short of convertible currency reserves, the balance-of-payments motive may in principle justify their QRs forever.

Do CPEs fit into the GATT?

In drafting the General Agreement, little thought was given to the specific features of economic policy and management of CPEs for various reasons. Regarding politics, the USSR chose not to participate in the negotiations, and so the critical questions were put aside, perhaps on the assumption that the CPEs in the end only wanted rules for their own trade (Liebich 1971, 29). As a result, when the CPEs first approached the GATT in the 1950s, the only way in which they could be brought under the discipline of the General Agreement was through article XVII and the stipulation on pricing divergences for state monopolies. This provision is, of course, ill-adapted to the case of CPEs. Yet, *faute de mieux*, it has had to serve the double duty of catering to CPEs and state monopolies proper, that is, exceptions from the ME framework.

Among the myriad economic factors, as detailed in the next section, it would seem that no satisfactory solution can be imagined that would provide for reciprocity in applying the MFN principle to participants involving CPEs without serious restrictions, which the General Agreement rejects as a matter of principle, though practice has often deviated therefrom. In view of developments since the ratification of the General Agreement, the existence of a preferential trading area such as the CMEA, where trade is based on different principles than those deriving from market-determined comparative-advantage calculations, further complicates matters. Because prices in CPEs by definition rarely result only or mainly from commercial factors or true economic scarcities, the GATT in principle cannot fundamentally regulate the situation of CPEs.

5 Problems of bringing CPEs into the GATT

Many problems arise in the process of attempting to blend the interests of a diverse group of economies and systemic ambitions into one coherent, fairly definitive legal code. Political issues are pivotal in such an attempt at coordination, and I shall sidestep those for the time being (see chapter 5). Perhaps equally important are purely technical economic problems to be clarified in order to identify common ground among the diverse countries.

Basic assumptions of the GATT framework

As already clarified in chapter 1 with respect to the broad doctrine underlying the stillborn ITO and the less ambitious General Agreement, key negotiators at the time held onto the primacy of creating a relatively free-trading world as a fundamental precondition for economic prosperity and global peace. Basic among the premises and assumptions underlying the ITS was that tariffs affect the price competitiveness of private firms: changes in tariffs are measurable for their economic consequences provided their impact is not blunted by direct administrative controls over entrepreneurial decision making regarding the level, geographical direction, and commodity composition of trade. The outcome generated under administrative controls can only by fluke coincide with that obtained under competitive conditions. Whereas this economic rationale may have been correct, it is odd that the negotiators overlooked the fact that GATT negotiations by definition take place among governments; hence, economics and politics would never be far removed from deliberations about reciprocal trade concessions (Reuland 1975, 319). This is particularly the case for east–west exchanges (see the introduction).

The issue of discrimination has been the central concern in commercial diplomacy and the bedrock of the General Agreement. Because of the role of the state in influencing microeconomic decisions in CPEs, how Contracting Parties can safeguard against discrimination has been a prime consideration. If the state ultimately operates all firms and determines in a central plan the kind of goods to be traded and in what quantities, it is impossible to ensure equal treatment for all trading parties on the basis solely of economic merit. Even when such planning intrinsically favors domestic production behind administrative barriers, it need not be discriminatory. All it need do is to ensure reciprocity within the logic of a fairly self-contained economic model designed to foster certain domestic objectives. True, the "planning, price and financial systems form mutually reinforcing barriers between the domestic economy and the rest of the world economy" (Harding and Hewett 1989, 165), but that is not identical with discrimination. Ensuring reciprocity poses a *sui generis* problem in CPEs.

Perhaps the central, if often only implicit, assumption about discrimination in nonmarket economies derives from the contention that an enterprise cannot simultaneously abide by the principles embodied in the central plan under whose auspices it is being directed and remain at complete liberty to formulate its decisions on strictly economic grounds.[15] Again, this is not discrimination, for firms apply their behavioral rules in principle to all potential suppliers abroad. However, nondiscrimination in the GATT sense may be hard to enforce in relations with CPEs as long as the latter's internal price structures remain substantially insulated from WMPs. This inhibits genuine comparisons of true cost, and thus truncates trade. More important is that there is no rational way in which discrimination between domestic and foreign markets can be made transparent or easily assessed by outsiders. But this is not generally done in the sense of nondiscrimination as specified in the General Agreement. Moreover, quantum commitments themselves may be discriminatory unless they truly result from careful exploration of the best resource allocation on a global basis, possibly subject to external payments constraints (Gerschenkron 1947, 626–7).

Finally, there would appear to have been considerable ideological motivation on the part of negotiators in rationalizing state trading simply as an instrument of trade regulation. This is often found in textbooks and it is something that socialist authors stressed for a number of years (Matejka 1974, 209–10). But it need not be so. State trading could simply be a form of ownership in which property rights are not necessarily utilized for other than economic purposes or exercised by the state itself. Only if central policy makers intervene to tax or subsidize firms or to impose QRs upon them will they be in a position to restrict or expand trade. In other words, one could imagine a competitive state-trading firm that in itself is not an instrument of trade control. The latter would have to be exerted through other means (subsidies, taxes, QRs, targets, and the like) that may make the state-trading firm the *object* of trade control, as with private firms, but not necessarily the *instrument* thereof.

Conflicts of the GATT order with CPEs

There has been a good deal of confusion in the literature about what precisely in CPEs inhibits a more coherent association with the ITS. There would appear to be three broad categories of objections, namely the existence of a trade monopoly, the fusion of plans of firms into one coherent central plan (see the preceding subsection), and the steering and controlling of trade through particular trade and payment mechanisms. Perhaps most often mentioned is the existence of the MFT (Bernier 1982). But that in and of itself should not pose a decisive obstacle to nondiscriminatory trade. As alluded to before, a monopoly exercising its commercial interests in a market environment is in a position to restrict trade to maximize its profits. But it cannot regulate it through the means at its disposal solely as a monopoly (Matejka 1974, 211). Regulation of the monopoly would have to occur through commercial policy measures, as noted. In other words, there is a more than semantic distinction to be made between allocation and ownership (Matejka 1982).

In the traditional CPE, a tariff would have little operational meaning because the state would simply raise a surcharge against itself for the goods it decides to import for whatever reason. Hence, the CPE does not normally have customs duties. If it does, the tariff schedule is as a rule without real operational meaning as far as the determination of the level and commodity composition of trade is concerned; it may, however, codetermine the geographical distribution of that trade on the margin.

6 The experience of the CPEs in the GATT

In consequence of the extremely scanty provisions in the General Agreement for anything that even remotely resembles the economic model of the CPEs, integration into the ITS of countries that have adopted the CPE model has posed a number of fundamental analytical and practical problems. Not only has the GATT been deprived of the universal status that the ITO was to have had, but it has also been unable to perform a significant role in fostering east–west trade (Ławniczak 1985). This potentially highly important field of intersystemic interchange has not so

Table 4.1. *Status of socialist countries in the GATT*

Country	No relation	Interest	Observer	Associate	Contracting Party
Albania	x				
Bulgaria			1967		Applied in 1986
China			1982		Reapplied in 1986
Cuba					Founder
Czechoslovakia					Founder
GDR	x	1990			
Hungary		1958	1966		1973
DPR Korea	x				
Laos	x				
Mongolia	x				
Poland			1957	1959	1967
Rumania			1957		1971
Soviet Union	x	1986			[a]
Vietnam	x	1989			[b]
Yugoslavia			1950	1959	1966[c]

Notes:
[a] Expected to submit application in late 1990 or early 1991.
[b] Expected to apply for full accession sometime in 1990.
[c] Provisional accession in 1962.

far been entrusted to any international organization and it is doubtful that there exists one that could assume effective responsibility (Vernon 1979). This section gives a schematic overview of the association of CPEs with the GATT framework. It also summarizes the various solutions adopted over the years to facilitate this cooption of CPEs.

Overview of the association of CPEs with the GATT

The fundamental problems of integrating CPEs into the ITS were on the agenda of the GATT debates at various times, for example, when a regular Contracting Party moved over to CPE status, upon application for accession by traditional CPEs, and upon the accession of modified or reformed CPEs and other countries. Table 4.1 schematizes pertinent details of the association of CPEs with the GATT.

A first case occurred when Czechoslovakia, a founding member, became a CPE shortly after the GATT's creation. This systemic mutation, like that of Cuba when it went over to the status of a CPE in 1962, was largely ignored at the time because Czechoslovakia did not then insist on reciprocity and the other Contracting Parties chose to control imports from it through quantitative as well as price controls (Liebich 1971, 30), and have continued to do so since. In other words, Cuba and Czechoslovakia have been participating unobtrusively in the GATT; they have not sought to enforce the legal obligations of the Contracting Parties and the latter have not pressed for an overt commitment on reciprocity on the part of these two CPEs.

Secondly, the successive requests for accession first as observer, in some cases as an associate member, and later as full member by Poland (in 1957, 1959, and 1967, respectively), Rumania (in 1957, no association, and 1971, respectively), Bulgaria (an observer since 1967 and applicant for full status in 1986), Hungary (in 1966,[16] no associate status, and 1973, respectively), and China (a founding Contracting Party but the Republic of China voluntarily withdrew in 1950, presumably to stave off any attempt of the People's Republic to be seated in Geneva [Cooper 1988b; Kim 1981; Liser 1982]; the People's Republic has been an observer since 1982 and lodged a request for full accession in 1986) reopened the myriad theoretical and practical questions. Poland became an associate together with Yugoslavia on the basis of a special, limited status by means of Declarations (Dam 1970, 320). Yugoslavia, which acceded provisionally in 1962 and gained full status in 1966, negotiated tortuously with the Contracting Parties because it did not have genuine private firms.

Regarding Bulgaria and China, their requests for full accession and readmission, respectively, to the General Agreement are currently pending. Both requests pose fundamental problems for the GATT because China is potentially a large participant in world trade and Vietnam and the Soviet Union, also potentially large participants in global trade, are about to follow suit. Negotiations on reciprocal concessions do not appear to have progressed to date (late 1989). Working Parties have been constituted for both Bulgaria and China and the round of exchanges of questions and answers has been completed, so that the road is clear to start substantive negotiations over accession conditions.[17] The current MTN round may not leave Contracting Parties sufficient resources – and interest – to tackle the delicate issues that arise in considering the applications of large and developing CPEs in the GATT, especially when they desire to accede essentially under provisions applicable to MEs. Both Bulgaria and China have made it clear that they are not prepared to engage in deliberations about quantitative commitments. They wish to be treated instead as Hungary was in the early 1970s. This involves delicate issues regarding reform intentions in the case of Bulgaria and the reform path trodden during the past decade and the trajectory ahead in the case of China. It is, therefore, unclear whether their application could be handled like Hungary's, that is by invoking some of the intended features of the economic reform.[18] Before entering into details of these actual and potential associations, it may be useful to explain the procedures involved in becoming a full Contracting Party.

Membership and application

The kinds of association provided for in the General Agreement (see section 4) are admittedly of marginal interest to CPEs because for most of them special arrangements have been worked out. But a brief illustration of proceedings for full accession at this point may well help to unravel the at times tortuous discussions on whether or not the CPEs "belong" there. Especially at this stage of controversy over the potential association of the Soviet Union with the GATT, two remarks may be useful. First, gaining observer status has traditionally meant that the country obtains a tacit claim on eventual membership. But the delay between becoming an observer and a full member can be protracted, as suggested by the dates in table 4.1. Secondly, the application for full accession starts off a complicated process of give-and-take between the applicant and the Contracting Parties. When a request for accession is lodged, the following key accession steps are now standard.

A request for accession has to be accompanied by a memorandum in which the applicant clarifies its foreign trade regime; trade data; and related legal, organizational, and economic matters. This submission is passed on to Contracting Parties, which may submit questions pertaining to the applicant's foreign trade and exchange regimes to the GATT secretariat. This process may take six months or more. These queries are systematized by the GATT secretariat and passed on to the applicant for reply within three to six months, but it may take longer if there is dissension on seeking accession within the applicant's own government. A formal Working Party to consider the applicant's request for accession will be nominated and convoked several months later. At first, this will be concerned with procedural and organizational matters. I am not aware that formal substantive negotiations in the Working Parties for Bulgaria and China have been instituted to date; in fact, some of the procedural issues to be settled beforehand are apparently still in limbo.

The process of actual negotiations, once it gets under way, is likely to be protracted. Even under the best of circumstances, it takes several years.

For Bulgaria and China, the process may actually be more complex for they have been building their case on features of their intended reforms. This particular claim to ME status has already given rise to considerable controversy. The probing, especially by the EC, is likely to be even more rigorous than in Hungary's case, given that the negotiations with Bulgaria and China are likely to be followed soon by a formal application for full accession by the Soviet Union and Vietnam. It should be remembered that negotiations with Hungary took four years under very favorable political conditions. In other words, seeking membership in the GATT cannot be a panacea for resolving major problems connected with reforms or avoiding undertaking them.

Accommodation of the CPEs into the GATT

There are basically three broad regimes under which the CPEs have participated in the GATT. But yet another may be applied to CPEs presently in a kind of GATT dormancy and for those bent on some form of accession.

Mutating members in a limbo – Cuba and Czechoslovakia Both countries are GATT founders. Following the February 1948 political events, Czechoslovakia soon transformed itself into a CPE, a situation that was essentially ignored until the United States was compelled to raise the issue. By virtue of the trade-negotiating power vested in the Administration by the Congress in 1951, the United States was no longer entitled to grant MFN treatment to communist countries. As a result, its relations with Czechoslovakia in the GATT needed to be reconfigured (Augenthaler 1969, 75ff.). US authorities contended that article XXV allowed it to waive its GATT obligation because of "exceptional circumstances not elsewhere provided for." Czechoslovakia maintained that the article in question can only be invoked if the exceptional circumstances entail hardship for the Contracting Party, something that could not possibly be at stake, given the very low level of its trade with the United States. Other Contracting Parties viewed this controversy as politically charged and recommended simply recognition of the deterioration in economic and political relations, taking note of the facts as they existed, and drawing the inevitable conclusions that both contestants should be entitled to suspend their obligations without hampering other Contracting Parties (Curzon 1965, 298–300).

Because the GATT decided not to act upon the US request, the United States unilaterally suspended benefits for Czechoslovakia and the latter reciprocated. Though officially Czechoslovakia never lost its full status as a Contracting Party to other participants, its trade in the east–west context has been heavily circumscribed by QRs and trade agreements that are not strictly in conformity with at least the spirit of the GATT. Czechoslovakia has not raised the issue since, with the exception of its efforts during the Kennedy Round when it found itself compelled to offer a similar type of arrangement as made by Polish negotiators (that is, specific import quotas for Contracting Parties), but this was rejected together with the Polish proposal (Fink 1974, 205).

When Cuba adopted the CPE model in 1962 it should have received similar treatment to Czechoslovakia's. In spite of serious political disagreements with the United States, this did not occur, but its official treatment has been subdued. As a result, its status in the GATT is very similar to Czechoslovakia's, and so it participates rather perfunctorily. Certainly, the United States suspended MFN treatment through the full trade embargo.

Accession requests by traditional CPEs – Poland and Rumania

Poland was the first traditional CPE not yet on the road to market-oriented reform to seek association with the GATT. As noted, it became an observer in 1957, gained associate status in 1959, and was granted full Contracting Party status in 1967 (Woźnowski 1974). What happened in between and why it took Poland nearly a decade to obtain this coveted position need not detain us here as there is ample literature on that subject (see Kostecki 1979a; Łączkowski 1969, 1971; Michałek 1984; Rémy 1980). What is important for this study is that the GATT sought to accommodate the central planning realities of Poland. Instead of extending reciprocal tariff concessions, Poland finally obligated itself to raise its imports from Contracting Parties by 7 percent per year as a trade-off for limited MFN treatment by the Contracting Parties. The limitation was a serious one inasmuch as MEs committed themselves only to the eventual abolition of their QRs against Poland; in fact, they reserved the right to enact new discriminatory QRs as safeguards. The timetable for gradually reaching the status regarding QRs required by article XIII was to be worked out after the first three years of experience. Because no time limit was set, repeated attempts to place the steady reduction and eventual elimination of QRs on the policy agenda have thus far failed to be resolved (Woźnowski 1974, 125–36).

It is of more than passing interest to recall that the import commitment assumed by Poland was transitory and *not* strictly speaking a global quota or purchase arrangement. For one thing, the quantum undertaking was assumed to remain in force only for the period 1968–70. On 1 January 1971 and thereafter on dates specified, Poland was entitled to seek a modification of its commitment either through negotiation and agreement, in which case the concessions of Contracting Parties would hold, or through unilateral action, in which case the Contracting Parties would be entitled to modify their concessions on an equivalent basis (Łączkowski 1971, 111–12). Beginning with 1971, the Contracting Parties allowed averaging over two and later three years (Baban 1977, 347). Poland's statistical obligation to increase imports from the Contracting Parties by no less than 7 percent per year during the transition phase differed from a "global quota," or a "purchase agreement" for that matter. The former can be interpreted to mean precise quantities or values of commodities to be imported. A purchase arrangement implies precise commitments to import possibly prespecified goods from designated Contracting Parties. In fact, at one point a Polish spokesperson designated his country's arrangement with the GATT as simply a successful attempt to replace bilateral trade arrangements with a multilateral one (Łączkowski 1971, 112–13). Evidently, obtaining GATT association has had a different aura to it than simply working out a multilateral trade arrangement. Furthermore, there were some side constraints to the effect, in the view of some observers, that the import commitment could only be exercised and enforced if Poland had a satisfactory export performance and thus adequate convertible currency reserves to fund the committed imports (Łączkowski 1969, 92).

Though there was thus a difference in the strict letter of the commitment made by Poland and what had been foreshadowed as one way of accommodating CPEs in the Havana Charter, the spirit was identical, namely to trade off tariff concessions by MEs against import obligations by the CPE. Polish commentators are, of course, correct in emphasizing that the original proposition by Poland in 1959 to commit itself to specific global import quotas of some commodities made in its first bid to move from observer to full accession during the Dillon Round (which Czechoslovakia then also felt compelled to propose) was unambiguously rejected by the Contracting Parties, and Poland could thus not participate in that Round (Woźnowski 1974, 115–17). Its offer to assume looser import commitments was, however, accepted during the Kennedy Round.

In exchange for this import commitment, the Polish side had been looking for gaining concessions, not so much on tariffs, but on QRs maintained by certain Contracting Parties, particularly in Western Europe. In addition to a promise not to increase QRs, barring untoward circumstances, the latter had committed themselves only progressively to relaxing QRs so as to make them consistent with article XIII (Woźnowski 1974, 149–74). For that purpose, but also because of the unconventional conditions of Poland's accession, it was agreed to hold an annual review session during which, upon furnishing satisfactory statistics of Polish imports from Contracting Parties, QRs would gradually be reduced so that in due course the Polish situation in the GATT would conform with article XIII. Instead, the annual reviews disintegrated into a simple examination of Polish trade statistics and airing of recriminations about the sluggish pace of the removal of QRs.

Though the solution adopted for Poland was a pragmatic one, it signaled willingness of the GATT to deviate from a general global solution to trade liberalization in favor of a specific one. Instead of maintaining, as it had earlier insisted, that CPEs adjust to orthodox GATT regulations, the accommodation heralded at least a willingness to consider nontraditional methods of participation (Smith 1969, 274). This change of heart resulted from two circumstances. One was the reluctance on the part of the Contracting Parties to compromise too much on their commitment to the ME environment. This concern revolved in particular around the trade effects of a tariff reduction yielding increased imports for the ME but not necessarily the state-trading country. The other reason was outright refusal on the part of the CPE to adopt possibly far-reaching economic reforms to transform its economy to the conditions prevailing in MEs (Łączkowski 1969, 89).

With the Polish accession, then, the GATT for the first time recognized the validity of alternative solutions to the market environment. The Contracting Parties basically validated four features of trading countries that were rather atypical of ME behavior and that partly met the specific needs of CPEs (Müller 1986, 203–4). First, because Poland did not have any customs duties at that time, the GATT admitted that customs duties were not necessarily the only instrument for the regulation of domestic market access. Secondly, a search was made to identify unconventional equivalence, essentially by considering the foreign trade plan intrinsically equivalent to QRs in MEs. Thirdly, the potential usefulness of the MFT and foreign trade planning were recognized as not necessarily running counter to GATT principles. Access to the Polish market could hence be ensured only through appropriate provisions in the foreign trade plan. Finally, the GATT did not find any forbidding obstacle in the autonomy of domestic pricing that was made explicit by Poland. It thereby acknowledged that the function and mechanism of domestic pricing in CPEs were not identical with their role in the ME context.

Rumania's accession was handled slightly differently from Poland's. For one thing, it stipulated a much weaker quantum commitment. Also, specific allowances were included to come to grips with the country's external debt situation and thus balance-of-payments constraints on feasible import efforts. Rumania at that time did not have a full-fledged customs system, yet it was reluctant to enter into any import commitment similar to Poland's if only because it had earlier unilaterally expanded its imports from the Contracting Parties faster than its exports to the group and had thus measurably raised the trade share of the Contracting Parties. After lengthy procedural meetings, Rumania committed itself to the firm intention to raise its imports from Contracting Parties as a whole at least as fast as the planned growth of total imports specified in the five-year plan. In return, the Contracting Parties, especially the EC, assumed the commitment to reduce QRs with the "intent" of removing them altogether by 1974. As it turned out, this commitment remained essentially just that, to the chagrin of the Rumanians. The best that could be obtained under the circumstance was an enlargement of the Rumanian quota, as for textiles, which was taken to be the equivalent of "QR removal" (Nyerges 1986a, 198). Likewise, inasmuch as Rumania's obligation refers to the plan, it is hard to enforce; it becomes wholly indeterminate when the five-year plan does not contain any import target – something that has been the case for the past three plans! At best, the relevant Working Party can examine statistics on the evolution of trade and assess progress on the issue of curbing QRs by MEs.

Rumania had made the commitment in principle within the context of its plan for 1971–5. It subsequently sought in vain to have this percentage measured over the longer run; the five-year period is apparently still the norm, at least pro forma. Averaging over more than three years has so far been also denied to Poland. Given the current reforms under way and the new external trading and customs system in place, Poland is in any case presently seeking to have its status changed to that of a full Contracting Party on the basis of its intended market-oriented reforms.

In other words, the answers provided to the first requests for accession by CPEs were thoroughly pragmatic, reciprocity being based on the granting of MFN by most MEs, but with restrictions, in exchange for a commitment of the CPE to increase its imports from the signatory countries by a fixed percentage. Note that trade between the CPEs and the United States has always been subject to special restrictions as embodied in the US Trade Expansion Act of 1962, which denied MFN to CPEs, except Poland and Yugoslavia; the Trade Act of 1974, which enabled the US Administration to grant, through bilateral trade agreements, a limited variant of MFN, but not unconditional status; and the Jackson–Vanik amendment, which makes the granting of trade preferences to CPEs contingent upon a more liberal attitude toward emigration.

The reforming CPEs and accession proceedings – Hungary and Yugoslavia As noted, Yugoslavia was the first CPE to covet GATT association. Its motivation was simple: because of the rupture of trading relations with the Eastern European countries upon its expulsion from the Cominform in mid-1948, Yugoslavia was desperate to redirect its trade to MEs at the least cost. Not only could it build its case for GATT association on these useful political transitions, but also on the "need" to raise imports from Contracting Parties. Beginning with 1952, it became involved in successively more ambitious attempts at economic decentralization. Furthermore, it was not subject to the Trade Agreements Extension Act, which had led to the US rupture with Czechoslovakia.

When it first explored GATT affiliation in 1950, Yugoslavia was a full-fledged CPE with all the trimmings and consequent obstacles to full ITS participation. Even after the economic reforms of the early 1950s, it could not live up to all of the obligations under the General Agreement. Because Yugoslavia recognized this state of affairs and for other reasons, it was granted associate status in 1959. This was really an experimental approach to developing trade relations with Yugoslavia on GATT terms and to providing an incentive for progress toward full application of the General Agreement. Its subsequent status as provisional GATT Contracting Party derived from the fact that Yugoslavia did not have customs duties in 1962. However, at the time it was already envisaging further decentralization measures. Yugoslavia gained full accession soon thereafter – nearly two decades after its first approach to the GATT.

Yugoslavia's experience may be useful for other CPEs seeking full GATT status. First, it exposed both applicant and Contracting Parties to each other's facilities and difficulties. Secondly, Yugoslavia's participation demonstrated that a CPE could decentralize sufficiently to permit participation in the GATT under the same conditions as an ME. Finally, Yugoslavia's long road to full status underlined the substantial reforms required to shift from CPE protection, as defined, to the GATT trade model; this evolves over years, even if the political environment and will to do so are present.

The accession of Hungary was handled very differently from that of Poland, Rumania, or Yugoslavia. It first requested observership in 1958, soon after Poland gained that status. Upon being informed that the political climate was not particularly conducive to such a move at the time, Hungary withdrew the request. It did gain observer status in 1966, however. Three years later, following upon the NEM's inception, Hungary lodged a request for full accession. The differences in negotiations from those associated with the entry of other CPEs were palpable. There was undoubtedly great skepticism that the NEM would make multitier tariffs effectively mediate between domestic and trade prices, both of which could fluctuate without state control, and could thus form the object of meaningful tariff concessions. But the political climate favored accommodation rather than confrontation over the knottiest issues.

Though admitted as an ME, Hungary's position in the GATT has been weak because of a number of reservations that transcend the familiar US exceptions under article XXXV or the grandfather clause. First, the Contracting Parties decided to make only a token commitment to the "progressive elimination" of QRs under article XIII. But it was tacitly understood that the EC in particular would make substantial progress with their removal by the mid-1970s. Secondly, several Contracting Parties reserved for themselves the right to impose discriminatory QRs in case exports from Hungary were to harm domestic producers. Finally, there were exceptions included under the safeguards clause that in fact nullified a substantial portion of what Hungary had been hoping to obtain from accession.

Second-wave reforms and GATT accession – Bulgaria, China, and other CPEs As noted, Bulgaria and China submitted their request for full accession and readmission, respectively, in 1986. Both countries have been building their case along the same lines as Hungary. It is not clear, however, whether China can succeed in invoking the intended further decentralization and commercialization of enterprise decision making as justification for being treated as an ME for GATT purposes. Its reform has thus far largely been limited to rural activities, leaving the heartland of China's industry firmly in state hands (Hartland-Thunberg 1987; Herzstein 1986; Li 1987). The June 1989 events and their aftermath may, of course, spell the end of that intended widening of the reform.

As noted, Bulgaria's claim to being in the process of establishing effective markets is even more tenuous. However, its commitments are not negligible. For example, if an international reference price system is workable in the creation of domestic transaction prices, if Bulgarian economic organizations can be made to compete, and if exceptions during the transition phase toward full-fledged reform can be minimized, there would be only one obvious violation of GATT principles in the new Bulgarian economic system (Jackson 1987, 558). This essentially derives from the rather haphazard, certainly far from transparent, multiple exchange-rate system that is associated with the reform. Of course, the core questions concerning commitment to reform, the pace at which it will be pursued, and the determination to stave off reversals on account of short-term obstacles remain unresolved at this stage. I shall return to them in chapter 5.

Toward a systemic solution? So far, the CPEs have invariably been accommodated on a country-by-country basis and with special provisions. These give Contracting Parties the right to protect their economies from any damage that might result from trading with CPEs, chiefly through QRs (Pissulla 1985, 232); they thus yield special, limited arrangements. In addition, some CPEs had to grant a special "entrance fee" by making import commitments a quid pro quo for tariff concessions, as foreseen in the Havana Charter but with some modifications.

There is another way in which the CPEs could have been accommodated, namely through a meaningful comprehensive arrangement. This issue was, of course, on the ITO's negotiating agenda and it has surfaced on several occasions in the context of the GATT. I am aware of only one quasi-formal effort launched by the GATT to come to grips with a systemic solution for countries that are CPEs. This was initiated in 1959–60 by Eric Wyndham-White, then Executive Secretary of the GATT, when there was abundant evidence that more than one CPE would be making a bid for some GATT association.

Wyndham-White proposed the application to CPEs of the recognition that the promotion of mutually advantageous trading relations "depends upon the achievement of an equitable balance of rights and obligations" (GATT 1960, 1). For those provisions of the General Agreement that entail systemic obstacles or practical difficulties, he called upon the CPE to establish conditions for trade with Contracting Parties no less advantageous than those secured in its trade through the application of the General Agreement, hence unrestricted benefit of MFN treatment excepting the grandfather clause. Foremost would be "making effective the provisions of article XVII of the General Agreement" (GATT 1960, 1). This called upon import agencies in CPEs to conduct their purchases solely on the basis of commercial relations; to establish facilities for the Contracting Parties that would measurably improve access to domestic markets by raising opportunities for advertising, trade representation, and other measures in CPEs; and to stress the possibility of negotiating markups over the landed cost of imports from Contracting Parties (Smith 1969, 273–4). This, of course, presumed that the CPE had a firm, mature price system in place that would not be manipulated for ulterior, noneconomic motives. Under the proposal, however, the CPE would be free to raise such margins provided they were published and communicated to Contracting Parties. In the end, this effort foundered for lack of interest. There were political and strategic considerations behind that stance. But also the cumbersomeness of the proposal dissuaded Contracting Parties from further exploring a systematic solution.

Since then, no effort at devising a systematic solution has been launched and I have been told reliably that no such solution is even being entertained at this stage. Kostecki (1979a, 92–3) reports two variants of practices of the 1930s and the ITO formulation proposed from outside the GATT to regulate the participation of CPEs. A Swedish diplomat, C. H. von Platen, suggested in 1958 that CPE products be admitted into MEs under the same rules as those applicable to DMEs. In exchange, the CPEs were to increase their total trade with MEs by a certain average annual percentage. A variant of this formula was proposed by Professor Jacques L'Huillier of the University of Geneva. In this project, better access for CPE products to MEs should be exchanged for a commitment to buy specific categories of products equal in value to their planned or intended exports to MEs.

None of these formal and informal suggestions for bridging the gap between the institutional features of CPEs and the provisions of the GATT strikes me as a serious effort to transpose the concepts of nondiscrimination, reciprocity, and regional integration into the key operational criteria of choice in CPEs. That is, rather than relying on vague and hardly controllable promises, efforts should have been channeled into linking key GATT precepts to the core features of a CPE (Kostecki 1984, 106). Inasmuch as nondiscrimination involves the geographical distribution of trade, not necessarily the level and commodity composition of trade, it might have been useful to attempt to isolate the variables that determine the geographical allocation of imports and to link MFN treatment to this decision-making process as well as to the characteristics of import contracts that the CPEs thus routinely engage in (Hewett 1978, 29ff.).

This deliberate eschewing of a systematic solution needs some explanation. Certainly it stemmed in part from the considerable differences in the foreign trade systems of the countries concerned. But the country-specific approach enabled some Contracting Parties too to introduce double standards during the negotiations for accession; indeed, it was part and parcel of the preference of leading MEs for "handling" the CPEs separately as one further attempt to weaken Eastern Europe's economic and political cohesion.

The experience of CPEs in the GATT As illustrated, bringing the CPEs under the discipline of the General Agreement entails a number of peculiarities that do not arise in the case of other Contracting Parties, even if one abstracts from ideal market-type configurations and allows for how the General Agreement has in fact been applied and abused. Looking for a solution, however pragmatic, to these hindrances would be highly desirable. This affirmation may seem paradoxical if only because more than half of the CPEs "belong" already in the GATT in one way or another. Only the GDR and the USSR among the developed CPEs remain outside that framework altogether, although both, as well as Vietnam, have expressed more than casual interest in eventually acceding in some way.[19]

Because requests for accession by CPEs have all been handled on a case-by-case basis, these countries continue to be treated as "second-class" Contracting Parties. However, even if they had negotiated as a group, their being CPEs would have entailed a number of interrelated problems that could not have been brushed over lightly. First of all, the volume commitments for Poland and Rumania have proved to be unsatisfactory. For one thing, the specific magnitude was chosen on rather impressionistic grounds. Little research went into the choice of the target and its realism, giving the plans of the CPEs. Furthermore, the growth rate as a percentage of imports specified in the case of Poland was ambiguous. It was not clear whether this would be in quantum or in value terms; if in value terms, whether it would be in złotych or dollars, the usual denomination of GATT data; or how to cope with the problem of fluctuations in nominal and real values on account of differential exchange-rate movements. Also, no decision was taken as regards the desirability of making the target more flexible if only to allow for annual variations and making provisions for revising the target if economic circumstances warrant it. In the case of Rumania, of course, the specifications were wholly unoperational. If the Rumanian government chooses not to publish an import target in its five-year plan, its commitment is by necessity indeterminate. Also, "the firm promise" not to erode or make inroads into the share of the Contracting Parties in overall imports was anything but firm and could be manipulated depending upon the price and exchange-rate basis chosen, as mentioned. Also, the Rumanian export and import plan targets, as is true for most CPEs, are calculated on the basis of expected quantum movements, not anticipated current values. Given the problem of price and leu–dollar exchange-rate movements, various alternative commitments could be proved *ex post*. With the inflation of the 1970s, which differed in comparison with price inflation in CMEA relations; the shifts in the composition of commodity trade toward goods that exhibit greater price volatility, including fuels; and the adjustment problems of both CPEs and MEs in the 1980s (Patterson 1986), the quantum commitment lost much of its intended purpose. Of course, both countries had hoped soon to settle the elimination of QRs maintained by the Contracting Parties (Baban 1977, 347). In the absence of such an agreement and in the wake of the imposition of new QRs, in violation of article XIX, which condones safeguard action with respect to products but not countries of origin, for that is discriminatory (Liser 1982, 147), both Poland and Rumania have resisted attempts to raise their import commitments.

From the point of view of CPEs, the Contracting Parties have maintained too many QRs, some discriminatory ones have actually been superimposed, and some important GATT participants – mainly the United States – accord MFN treatment only on a conditional basis, or not at all. Even those CPEs that have been accepted as full Contracting Parties have received at best second-class status in the club, in view of exceptions discussed earlier. In short, CPEs have acceded to the General Agreement through "a pragmatic process of negotiation that did not contribute very much to the development of rules" (Stone 1984, 171) governing the participation of nonmarket economies. They have suffered in the GATT from prejudice concerning their economic system, oftentimes because of objections to the politics and human rights conditions in these countries. Perhaps more prevalent has been ignorance about central planning and the functioning of state trading as well as a certain degree of arrogance on the part of key DMEs over which economic system should ultimately hold sway in global economic affairs. Such an outcome could have been foreseen, however, if only in view of the lack of commensurability between the purpose and the instrument of accession. The purpose certainly was to lead CPEs away from autarky. But it was paradoxical to seek to do so through administrative measures of quote enforcement without developing even a minimal economic rationale.

Some of these QRs have been justified because of fear of dumping, which prevails essentially when a country exports a product at a price that is below its domestic price. In the case of CPEs, a strict comparison of trade with domestic prices is not very meaningful, given the substantial degree of price autonomy that these countries maintain for domestic policy reasons. It would therefore have been useful to address the technical issues involved and dissuade Contracting Parties from invoking political rhetoric under the guise of technical obstacles. The same applies to the MFT being an obstacle to ensuring nondiscrimination and reciprocity. The GATT does not so far appear to have sought to make a distinction between utilizing state-trading firms as an object, like private trading but one that is rooted in social property relations, and state trading as an instrument of commercial policy such as tariffs and QRs. GATT negotiators – and incidentally most academic observers[20] – have always taken the second position. But they could have proceeded on the basis of the first, in which case essential aspects of the association arrangement would have involved notification requirements on the trading activities of the state-trading firms, the institutionalization of a complaints procedure as part of an international convention, and the independent collection of data to monitor the behavior of such firms (Matejka 1982, 155).

In consequence, as Maciej Kostecki (1979a, 134) argued a decade ago, there is prima-facie evidence that the accession of CPEs to GATT rules has paradoxically been more beneficial to MEs than to the CPEs. But that impression derives essentially from the empirical fact that in the 1970s the CPEs rapidly expanded the current value of their imports of goods from Contracting Parties. I find it hard to impute this change in trade policy, particularly for Poland and Rumania, to their import commitment. The import spurt stemmed in large measure from autonomous, domestic policy decisions to "intensify" growth; the availability of comparatively cheap credits from money markets; and the determination and resources of large western firms to broach those CPE markets.

The existence of the CMEA and the considerable commitments to trading with that group through bilateral trade arrangements did not bother too much the negotiations with Poland and Rumania. Inasmuch as an attempt was made to ensure that the import share of Contracting Parties would not contract, at least by some definition of measurement, little attention was paid to the discrimination entailed by the intensive trading links of the CPEs with the CMEA. In fact, the Contracting Parties chose to ignore one of the most disturbing features of Eastern European commercial policy (Kostecki 1979a, 136). In the case of Hungary, this procedure could not be followed. As a result, the protocol of accession permits Hungary to maintain trade relations with other CPEs, including the CMEA, but these must not impair its commitments to, discriminate against, or otherwise operate to the detriment of Contracting Parties (Stone 1984, 172).

7 The benefits and drawbacks of the GATT approach

Although there is a wide range of appraisals about the effectiveness of the GATT and the significance of the General Agreement for the postwar evolution of global trade, there is little dissent about the fact that the GATT and its machinery must be ranked as one of the more successful efforts in postwar near-global economic cooperation. Aside from obtaining MFN status and the less developed benefiting from GSP treatment, the GATT certainly offers a multilateral framework for settling trade disputes. Inasmuch as some of the CPEs have set their sights on measurably expanding their exports of manufactures that have been the subject of special treatment under the General Agreement (including foodstuffs, textiles and apparel [Sampson 1987], chemicals, steel, and automobiles), this may be a nonnegligible gain even to large countries. Adhering to an international code might also strengthen the hands of those within a CPE who are bent on forging ahead with a market-oriented reform (see chapter 5).

The GATT is widely considered to yield unique benefits for middle-sized and small countries (Stone 1984, 26). A multilateral trading system enables such countries to influence policy debates at the global level more effectively than they could within a network of simple BTPAs, not necessarily of the Eastern European variety. Though not without discipline for the larger countries, by their nature they will preserve greater flexibility for as long as the ITS is there to facilitate commerce among sovereign states. Nonetheless, in spite of its constitutional limitations the GATT has gradually developed authority in a fourfold role (Gardner 1969, xxxv), namely as a forum for trade negotiations, as a body of principles governing trade policy, as a center for the settlement of trade disputes, and as a vehicle for the development of trade policy. As such, the General Agreement has exerted a valuable constraint on the trade policies and practices of larger countries and has helped governments to stave off, or to withstand, pressures by domestic producer and labor interests to a larger degree than would probably have been the case without it (Hauser *et al.* 1988, 232ff.; Petersmann 1988). Also, MTNs in an environment where currencies are convertible afford small countries a better chance to capture larger markets than they would have otherwise. Finally, the dispute settlements mechanism within GATT, although it has lost much of its earlier luster as the most important Contracting Parties have resorted to bilateral and minilateral arrangements (Lipson 1982, 436), in principle affords these countries the means to settle trade disputes with larger countries more equitably and more expeditiously than they would have been able to accomplish otherwise.

But there is equally wide concurrence that the General Agreement exhibits serious gaps and weaknesses. These stem in part from the inability of Contracting Parties to shore up and extend the provisions of the General Agreement. It also derives in part from the pursuit of policies and practices by Contracting Parties that are inconsistent with the principles and rules of the General Agreement. Some even violate the letter of that document but all defy its spirit. For example, the GATT has not been used very effectively as a framework for consultation on trade policy among Contracting Parties and for the broad management of the ITS. Certainly, with the establishment of the Consultative Group of Eighteen in the second half of the 1970s, the GATT's role in consultations and management on macroeconomic, especially trade-related, topics has been strengthened somewhat. Yet it remains true that dispute settlement has increasingly been taken out of the GATT framework into the arena of intergovernmental, usually bilateral, discussions. This has given rise to all kinds of commercial policy making, ostensibly on the initiative of the exporter but in fact imposed by the importer, thus circumnavigating perhaps the letter but not the spirit of obligations ensuing from the General Agreement. Furthermore, consultative and management functions have been dispersed in two directions. One has been into less specialized, more highly politicized bodies, usually associated in some form with the United Nations (see section 1). The other has favored more narrowly based formal organs, largely of DMEs, including OECD, meetings of the so-called western economic summit, and even more highly restricted groups such as the dollar–yen–mark trireme and bilateral consultative organs.

Also, though the distribution of international economic exchange has shifted sharply in favor of labor services and, even more, transactions on capital account and intellectual property, the GATT system has thus far remained confined mostly to international merchandise trade proper. The Uruguay Round may successfully tackle these other service areas. Even in trade as narrowly defined, countries have nibbled away at the GATT's role in a number of respects. This has been the case for trade in agricultural products since the GATT's very inception. But, since the late 1960s, special regimes have been adopted for a diverse range of traded products. These include especially trade in textile and clothing coming under the provisions of the MFA. But also special *de facto* discriminatory regimes for trade in steel products, automobiles, and other manufactures have arisen. Furthermore, the adverse global economic situation since the mid-1970s (including the recessions, the financial crunch, and high unemployment) has led Contracting Parties, in spite of the discipline of the General Agreement, to adopt new, severely restrictive trade measures designed to shield domestic producers and labor against international competition and to promote domestic economic policies with little concern for their global implications.

Thirdly, the GATT has remained far from universal. For example, in spite of the adoption of part IV, the DEs have not yet been fully integrated into the ITS. Though their own regimes are subject to somewhat more relaxed rules and disciplines than those adopted by DMEs, it is doubtful whether this two-tier arrangement is desirable at all. Similar observations apply to CPEs, which have essentially remained second-class Contracting Parties. This is not to deny the importance of belonging to the GATT for DEs or CPEs. But the expectation of CPEs that they would succeed in removing the discriminatory QRs maintained, especially, by European DMEs and gain unconditional MFN treatment from the United States, thus enhancing their access to markets, has not so far been fulfilled.

Finally, the GATT's rules for economic unions, customs unions, and free trade areas have not been very effective in preventing or controlling a number of arrangements, most notably in Western Europe but also elsewhere, that are simple extensions of trade preferences. Inasmuch as they violate article XXIV regarding the formation of customs unions or free trade areas, these are discriminatory even in the rather permissive GATT sense.

It would be useful to remedy these and other shortcomings of the ITS. In chapter 5, I shall examine issues that may be critical in extending the GATT framework to CPEs. I for one am convinced that ushering the CPEs into the ITS under appropriate conditions would by itself not further erode the framework of the General Agreement, as Gröner (1980) so passionately maintains, particularly if seen in the light of how this has been applied in the last two decades or so. This depends to a good extent on what the advantages and drawbacks of belonging to the ITS could be for the CPEs.

As argued at length in chapter 5, it is useful to distinguish between the benefits that may eventually be reaped from the given regime by forestalling the emergence of arrangements that prospectively narrow the area of fruitful interaction from the gains and losses that may directly ensue from belonging to the regime. Among the benefits that accrue from the General Agreement in the strict sense, it may be useful to highlight four.[21] First, the CPE obtains MFN treatment on a predictable and multilateral basis as compared with having to negotiate for it periodically on a bilateral basis. All CPEs engaged in active commerce with MEs have bilateral trading arrangements in place that grant them MFN, albeit with some QRs and safeguard clauses. The major exception, of course, is the United States as a result of the 1974 Trading Act and the Jackson–Vanik amendment. Inasmuch as countries that have not so far or only conditionally granted MFN treatment to CPEs are not expected to alter their stance, the direct benefit of tariff reductions from generalized MFN treatment is limited. But it might pave the way for negotiating more favorable treatment.

Secondly, the CPEs would benefit from MTN rounds and indeed help to shape them. The importance of this is likely to rise with the inclusion in MTN rounds of such products as services and agriculture. To the extent that a nonmember holds MFN status, it does, of course, benefit from MTN rounds to which it has not been a party, and hence has not been requested to provide reciprocal concessions. Nonmembers are generally not in the mainstream of the most dynamic sectors of international trade around which the key issues of MTN rounds revolve. Yet, the CPEs may have a legitimate interest in influencing both the size and the distribution of the concessions tabled during the rounds. This applies not only to tariffs. Perhaps more important for the CPEs are negotiations about QRs and other NTBs. Because the latter are in good measure contrary to the General

Agreement, being within the ITS may afford these countries ampler opportunities for eventually whittling down the role of QRs and NTBs more generally.

Thirdly, because CPEs are price takers for most of their exports, the tariff disadvantage they incur, whether on a discriminatory or regular basis, has to be absorbed by them. Lower tariffs on their exports would, therefore, make these countries more competitive. This may be important in gaining a market share in DMEs, especially *vis-à-vis* DEs – including the NICs – benefiting from the GSP. They may gain this through free riding, but that is not at all the same as the ensured advantage of having bilaterally endorsed MFN status.

Finally, particularly small and medium-sized CPEs (all but China and USSR) in the GATT can avail themselves of multilateral dispute-settlement mechanisms. Such negotiations would certainly be lopsided and protracted if conducted bilaterally. They also stand to gain information about trade regimes in the broad sense that might be very costly for any one country to compile in isolation.

The corresponding advantages to Contracting Parties are, of course, less clear. Particularly for small Contracting Parties, gaining access to useful economic intelligence and insights into the workings of the external sector in CPEs is undoubtedly a benefit. Being able to press for more transparent forms of reciprocity is also a useful gain, though that certainly should not be exaggerated. However, agitating for better and wider access to CPE markets may yield positive export increments even for these countries.

Regarding broader aspects of the ledger on benefits and costs, the benefits may be discussed under the heading of those that may eventually be reaped from the General Agreement by forestalling the emergence of arrangements that could in time narrow the arena for the fruitful commerce for which the CPEs may wish and be able to compete prospectively. Helping to shape the future trading environment for manufactures is certainly not an important consideration for a country, such as the USSR, that has traditionally concentrated its exports on goods that in fact fall outside the tariff rules of the GATT (such as agriculture) or for which tariffs are close to zero (such as most raw materials and fuels). However, if a country aspires to gain an export-led pattern of development paced by the dynamism of the manufacturing sector, the sign of the membership equation may well change in favor of accession.

Secondly, the CPEs may wish to shape the debate on international trading issues as a public good in its own right but also as a central component of the international economic order in place more generally. Thus, the CPEs are not yet key players in trade in services but they certainly have a considerable potential stake in regulatory arrangements that the global community may draw up for its own sake based on prevailing circumstances. Also, the major importers of agricultural products, including the Soviet Union, have a legitimate interest in any trade negotiations that may lead up to some code on export subsidies and agricultural support programs, or simply to greater transparency in global agricultural trade. Both agricultural products and services were slated as key negotiating platforms at Punta del Este. They offer some rationale for Soviet interest in the GATT (Lavigne and Szymkiewicz 1987).

On the other hand, there are undoubtedly costs in joining the ITS framework. They consist essentially in the obligation to disclose information on trading arrangements and performance, submitting to negotiations when Contracting Parties request them, and sharing in the comparatively small operating budget of the GATT. But these drawbacks would appear minor if the CPE is really bent on integrating itself into the global economy.

There are, of course, also drawbacks to the Contracting Parties. They arise importantly in the separation of some commercial policy issues from the conduct of foreign policy more generally and having to come to grips with stances of countries that for decades were ideological and strategic adversaries and are now possibly bent on exploiting the GATT for political purposes. Although such an eventuality cannot be excluded altogether, I argue in chapter 5 that the probability of that materializing is rather minimal.

5 The CPEs and reform of the global economic order

As clarified in the introduction, this book aims at elucidating the issues that inhibit fuller participation of CPEs in the established order – not *per se* at discussing reforms of the international economy. In particular, I seek to evaluate whether a feasible mutation of that order in combination with measurable progress toward substantive transformation of the economic model and strategy of the CPEs themselves might alter the prospects for integrating these countries more fully into the world economy. Especially the economic but also the multifarious political, organizational, legal, and strategic issues that have affected the postwar evolution of organized economic relations have been set forth in earlier chapters. None of the envisaged reforms will eventually render the CPE economic management systems all but fully compatible with the basic precepts of an ME. The question regarding realistic adaptations in the international economic order and how they would facilitate or further complicate the association of the CPEs, therefore, needs to be addressed.

Section 1 recapitulates basic issues about the unity of trading, financial, and monetary concerns in the world economy. It also discusses what was lost with the ITO's stillbirth. In addition, it makes the case for recasting the core issues of the international economic debates during and immediately after World War II, but in the context of the 1990s and beyond. The next section clarifies the imperative of regaining multilateralism and its implications for IEOs, and how to rationalize the logical components of desirable international regimes. Section 3 then looks at whether the CPEs could constructively participate in such a recast order. Next I point to the efforts under way to encourage national and regional economic reforms in most CPEs. The next three sections amplify on this by examining the key requirements for refurbishing the economic regimes in place and how the CPEs could fit into this set of equations, if at all. The chapter concludes with a few observations on where to go from here.

1 The unity of money, finance, and trade

The discussion of how to recast the fundamental pillars of the postwar international economic order in a coherent and mutually supportive fashion relies on four basic features. But I harbor no illusion that these reforms, singly or in combination, could be implemented all at once. The hard-core issues are no different now from those of the 1940s: how to reconcile outward-oriented economic policies with domestic stability and growth in such a way that international arrangements benefit not just the world community as a whole but each of its parts (Gardner 1969, xviii). Perceptions of the range and depth of the topics that should be on the present agenda differ, of course. First of all, despite the varied concerns that have been expressed about the perceived drawbacks and advantages of the regimes in place, there is broad agreement on the need to renovate the "order" so as to come to grips with issues that could not have been foreseen when it was first molded. The existing IEOs were predicated on a world economic environment and a proclivity for multilateralism that differed markedly from what prevails today. Not only that, but even the existing regimes have not been fully lived up to through many infractions that need to be rolled back.

Secondly, the three pillars of the postwar economic order were conceived as parts of a coherent whole. Unfortunately, the trade leg of the institutional tripod was never as fully extended as the basic provisions and evolution of the Fund and the World Bank warranted. It is self-evident that monetary regulation can impede or facilitate trading arrangements, and vice versa. For example, restrictions that governments impose upon foreign exchange and external payments transactions would lose much of their effectiveness if they were uncoordinated with applicable trade regulations. This was in fact foreseen.[1] Because of the GATT's infirmities, however, the global economic order has not been undergirded by the required institutions.

Thirdly, although the existing IEOs supported economic expansion during the quarter century after World War II, serious questions have arisen as to the ability of the regimes in place to cope with current and emerging economic problems. The manifold issues at stake revolve around the impacts of low long-term growth in developed countries, with persistently high unemployment levels and periodic bouts of inflation, and unpromising prospects for faster growth in DEs. Financial and monetary problems pose a set of even more pressing concerns. These include, among many others, control of money supply in a world of largely unregulated open capital markets, the channeling of development finance to the south, the chronic debt situation of many of the larger DEs, persistent misalignment of key exchange rates, the adoption of national policies by some critical actors with little regard for their implications for the global economy, the growing threat of protectionism, unstable commodity prices, and deeply rooted structural problems in Africa. To remedy these unsatisfactory developments prospectively, it is widely felt that the time has come to put in gear the pertinent international machinery for the comprehensive examination at a high level of both the philosophy and practices of the key IEOs with a view to devising appropriate modifications.

If the Havana Charter had been ratified and the ITO had steadily evolved by fostering a more multilateral environment for economic relations among countries, the global economic order would have been quite different from what we have known for most of the postwar period. For one thing, it would have been a more uniform evolution. The system would probably have adapted itself more smoothly to newly emerging requirements, including new actors in the global economy. At the very least, it would have been a much more universal organization than GATT. The ITS in place would therefore have been spared the recurrent pressures in favor of establishing a more comprehensive trade organization than the GATT could be by default. UNCTAD would probably not have been "required." The study of the particular socioeconomic problems of the south would gradually have become one critical focus of international analysis. The General Agreement would have had a firmer institutional base, in part owing to more predictable financial and human resources. It would also have been entrusted with secretarial functions now discharged by individuals who, in many cases, remain too close to the national interests of Contracting Parties.

Equally important would have been the ITO's focal role in imbuing US policy makers with a more globalist outlook on monetary, financial, and trading matters than what came to prevail because of its temporary role as the postwar hegemon *par excellence*. For example, the constitutional authority associated with ratification of the Havana Charter would have enabled successive US Administrations to hold at bay rather parochial and short-term domestic pressures. The United States would have been impelled to eliminate trading practices that the General Agreement shields under the grandfather clause. Perhaps more important, the postwar leader would have had several more degrees of freedom to adapt its own behavior in international economic relations in line with, or under the prodding of, predictable transformations and unexpected shocks in the international environment, as detailed in section 2.

Similar observations apply to the IFS and IMS. Although both the Bank and the Fund have from the start enjoyed more solid foundations in terms of their constitution and ability to manage global affairs than the GATT, both have suffered from sluggish adaptation to emerging circumstances and inadequate symmetry in enforcing the agreed-upon rules. For one thing, little thought was given to the problem of DEs in the IMS. A strengthened commitment to currency convertibility, if desirable for development purposes, would have called for a clearer definition of the transition regime condoned under the Fund's article XIV. Also, little attention was paid at the time to the transition phase that most countries would have to pass through before they could discharge themselves of even the core obligations ensuing from the Fund's Articles of Agreement.

Perhaps even more critical has been the place of DEs in the World Bank. Most are members but their role is not well defined. Neither is the World Bank's mission as a transmission belt for capital flows for development purposes. Of course, even more cursory attention has been devoted to the position of the CPEs. Earnest efforts were made in the mid-1940s to accommodate the USSR, but essentially through minor variations from the mainstream market approach. The somewhat peculiar institutional, policy-making, and behavioral features endemic to CPEs have received casual attention at best.

There are at least two critical questions concerning east–west aspects of this *anti-monde*. One relates to whether global organizations, particularly the ITO, would have become polarized under the political disputes that have tangled the behavior of the "big powers" in international organizations, including the United Nations, of which the ITO would have been a specialized agency. The other problem revolved around the emergence of the Cold War in the mid-1940s and the subsequent polarization of the east–west conflict. These are not necessarily unrelated. Even prior to the Cold War, the big powers had expressed markedly different precepts about global economic organization, international relations, economic development, and a host of other topics at the core of the UN's role as a world forum for harmonizing the behavior of sovereign states.

It is hazardous to engage in counterfactual historiography if only because, in Ruggie's (1982, 391) felicitous phrase, "it is little better than a parlor game under ideal circumstances." Even though there is no rough-and-ready answer to counterfactual questions, my inclination is in the direction of hazarding a negative one. In the first instance, in a world made up of nation states, even the more technical IEO cannot altogether forgo political considerations and compromises. This follows from the absence of firm and enforceable international law to bind sovereign governments.

Secondly, in modern parliamentary democracies it is necessary for national administrations to enter into international obligations that can pass muster in parliament. Similarly in highly centralized societies where a measure of consensus is required, international obligations can be discharged properly only if the various interest groups, such as those in the Communist Party, concur in the leadership's actions. Though international regimes strengthen the hands of an imaginative leadership to stave off domestic pressures (Bergsten 1976; Bergsten, Keohane, and Nye 1975; Petersmann 1988), by necessity they involve yielding some measure of sovereignty or the right of its members to act entirely in their own interest (Mikesell 1951, 109). This may be difficult to push through in a parliamentary environment. Furthermore, democratically elected officials as a rule have a fairly short time horizon for choice if they want to be reelected. Similarly in highly centralized governments, self-appointed officials are unlikely to act from the perspective of the enlightened global autocrat, although they may have a longer-term outlook. Even if political obstacles can be overcome, multiple technical issues need to be resolved pragmatically before one can realistically contemplate a fuller association of the CPEs in organized international economic relations.

Even so, I would still argue that the ITO as the centerpiece of postwar economic relations under the UN aegis could have, if not averted, at least alleviated in a more than trivial sense some of the worst excesses of the politicization of international relations, including many irrational ambiguities of the east–west conflict. This interpretation derives in part from second guessing and my personal preferences. It is also based on a sobering reminder of what can realistically be accomplished in international organizations in a world of nation states that seek to protect their own, sometimes myopic, interests. One element of this position owes a good deal to what well-managed secretariats of essentially intergovernmental organizations can accomplish in such a world.

When nations jealously guard their sovereignty, international organizations cannot function as a global government. To aspire to it without first tackling the vexing constitutional issues involved is not useful. As matters stand, IEOs belong at best in the category of intergovernmental secretariats that do not owe allegiance to any one government, yet can justify their neutrality and authority only in an advisory capacity. If properly understood, their power is not quite as limited as may be suggested by a narrow interpretation of their constitution and in some cases from their actual behavior in the postwar period. Strong leadership in international organizations endowed with a professionally competent staff can make a big difference in brokering and implementing international arrangements

(Bergsten 1976, 363). Thus, international organizations have at times succeeded in encouraging governments to opt for the international approach, thereby strengthening the hands of outward-looking leaders in dealing with domestic opposition and encouraging them to adopt better economic policies than they might have done otherwise.

Let us take the GATT as an example (Curzon 1965, 49) if only because of its constitutional weaknesses. Its director general is there to be consulted by a Contracting Party regarding the best course of action to be taken in a particular situation. Aside from this passive role, the top executive can make his influence felt by acting as a concerned, yet neutral, mediator brokering innovative solutions. Often his good offices can be used for meetings at an early stage in a conflict and solutions are arrived at that obviate the invocation of the GATT machinery. Also, when opposing interests lead to deadlocked meetings, the GATT's administrative head can use his personal initiative to explore with the disputants acceptable solutions or compromises. In a way, he has won rights that entitle him to be far more than a mere catalyst. Indeed, if the top manager has the necessary professional and diplomatic skills to engage in an activist, if not necessarily obtrusive, course of action, a wide range of alternative positions can be initiated. In this way, he or she can command productive negotiations, including those on substantive policy issues, all of which contribute to the establishment of the integrated world economy for which the GATT's leadership and supporting staff ideally strive.

As Curzon (1965, 335) argued, IEOs that do not have a basic philosophy and therefore function essentially on the foundation of pragmatism, moving from one expedient to another, are likely to codify economic nationalism rather than interpret, enforce, and elaborate an international code of conduct. This applies not only to the GATT and a number of similarly specialized agencies. It prevails equally in global institutions like the United Nations or even in special organs whose existence does not essentially depend on a volatile commitment to the organization's long-term survival by an intrusive membership. Thus, the secretarial operations of the Fund and the World Bank are largely self-financed. Yet basic activities of these organizations are scrutinized by member governments. When the latter are displeased, they will not fail to interfere with operational activities.

Seen against this backdrop, what originally motivated the search for an ITO is still very much valid today and will be so tomorrow. As Knorr (1947, 543) put it at the time with reference to international commerce: "In a world divided into numerous sovereignties, the widespread practice of national intervention makes highly organized forms of international economic cooperation imperative if trade is to expand and maximize mutual economic advantage." This observation applies *pari passu* to other forms of international economic interaction. The highly organized form referred to by Knorr called for governments to be unwavering in their commitment to multilateralism either by delegating part of their sovereignty to international agencies or, at least, by imbuing their own national agencies and representatives with a firm commitment to multilateral action. To this I now turn.

2 Regaining multilateralism and international regimes

There are many reasons that argue for drawing all major actors of the world economy into a coherent, common framework for examining and devising acceptable solutions for problem areas that inhibit the smooth conduct of international economic interdependence. One, certainly, is that international economic relations are not a zero-sum game; that is, international behavior cannot be steered by a single country only. Another derives from the proposition that a well-organized international system is likely to curb the power of big members by transferring some decision making to fora governed not by the will and in the interest of one state, but rather by a multilateral complex of interests, checks, and balances (Sakbani 1985, 173).

As the past has amply demonstrated, the greatest danger to international stability often arises from those actors whose real power is inadequately reflected in both the relevant parts of international arrangements and the symbols of status therein (Bergsten 1976, 364). That is not to say that stability is predicated on universal organizations with equal or even proportional representation in all cases adjudicated within a given regime. Yet imaginative mechanisms for balancing universalism with the need for operationality of the regimes need to be devised. Universal participation could be accomplished by modifying the rules and regulations of the IEOs in place. It could also emerge by providing for the greater participation of, among others, the CPEs in the context of renovated institutional arrangements. However, this does not mean that *all* forms of international interaction need to be entrusted to universal institutions as this would paralyze some regimes or render them dysfunctional. The system would be aided if areas of joint interest or mutual concern for the system as a whole could be delineated separately from those of group reliance. There is, then, a need to think about the appropriateness of institutional channels for cooperation among subsystems. This needs to be understood as the ability to reach a stable equilibrium, which is more readily feasible for some multipolar regimes than an equivalent global one (Guerrieri and Padoan

1986, 39). To clarify this more fully, some further amplification of the international economic order and its accompanying regimes (see the introduction) is warranted.

An international regime's usefulness can be seen from the perspective of self-interest, that is, a country's élite trying to improve upon what it believes it can achieve in isolation by sharing at a comparatively small cost in the benefits of an international regime. But national élites may also have motives underlying their behavior, including expectations of the behavior of others, that transcend their own identifiable interest within a single-country setting. Thus, they may be moved by concerns about international stability, predictability, reliability, and other aspects of international economic relations that do not necessarily directly improve their own well-being.

Projected against this backdrop, the declining commitment to multilateralism in the world economy since the early 1970s can be rationalized as stemming from four factors. One derives from the rise in global interdependence without eliciting a commensurate purposeful modification in the economic regimes in place. Obstacles to greater international cooperation derive in part from disagreement on how economies function (Grauwe 1988, 68ff.) and what the outlook for economic growth and cooperation is. Furthermore, we are nowhere near a consensus on the objectives of international cooperation or on the relationship between the means and ends of cooperation, both how it should be conceived and how it actually works; and there is no workable guideline on how to distribute the costs and gains of cooperation (Cooper 1988a, 98–9). There is, in fact, even serious disagreement about the wisdom of maintaining the IEOs in place (Keohane 1984, 246–7), if only for want of enforcement mechanisms in international economic relations (Yarbrough and Yarbrough 1987, 2ff.). Furthermore, professional economists have demonstrated that some of the assumptions on which the regimes were erected (for example, that national intervention cannot improve on market outcomes in trade) are not likely to hold now, if they ever did (Krugman 1987, 134).

Secondly, negotiating new international economic regimes and setting up commensurate institutions would require horrendous work. For one thing, many more central actors than the pivotal UK–US alliance during World War II are presently in the system. In addition, there is at this juncture little political magnetism for initiating negotiations about advancing cooperation, even on issues on which there has been considerable agreement, such as the debt and the plight of sub-Saharan Africa. The absence of effective and imaginative international leadership has been very pronounced (Bergsten 1976).

The third factor focuses on the array of global economic problems that came to the fore at about the time of the collapse of the fixed-par system. Since then countries have been preoccupied with their own chronic economic problems, and have formulated policies for coming to grips with them that have had severe effects on other countries and the world economy as a whole. The economic recessions of the 1970s and early 1980s led to increased resort to nationalism and defensive trade strategies, although the formal consensus has continued to oppose unilateralism (Helleiner *et al.* 1983).

Finally, there has been a palpable decline in the degree of unselfish multilateral commitment among major élites in the world. This erosion can be attributed in part to disappointment of existing élites and the increased complexity of coming to grips with what should be in their best national interest. This is especially so because of a number of asymmetries. Thus an international economic regime is likely to curb more the unilateral power of big countries through transferring some decision making to fora governed by multilateral interests and checks. The resultant accrual of power stands on the legitimacy granted by the weak in return for established system checks (Sakbani 1985).

The national interest is, at best, an elusive concept. Adherence to a particular regime may yield benefits and costs that are quite visible. There may also be costs that materialize with considerable time lags; these, I submit, are rather small. Much more significant are the benefits that accrue only indirectly and are, therefore, not readily identified as such, or that materialize only through a roundabout evolution over time. In either case, national policy makers may lack the time, imagination, or understanding of how regimes operate to view such demonstrable benefits as gains to the nation to be factored into the balance sheet. It is now rather intuitive that with rapidly rising global interdependence, including that through commercial and financial links, the time lags and complexity involved in reaping all but the direct benefits of a regime escalate, possibly very steeply. Inasmuch as there is little symmetry on the cost side, short-term, perhaps myopic, policy making tends to disregard or underplay precisely those benefits that may accrue very rapidly when international economic interdependence is inexorably expanding. The result is shrinking interest in multilateral solutions, which themselves may be more difficult to formulate. Hence the perennial problem of how to "maintain" regimes and adjust them to newly emerging issues.

Perhaps more important is the ascent of new élites, a shift of generations if you wish, who hold different views on how the world functions and can be managed. This has not been a sudden rupture in regimes but rather a gradual evolution marked by some shocks around the trend. In that sense, one can agree with Ruggie's (1982, 398) notion of embedded liberalism having evolved from within, yet continuing to determine the postwar economic order as originally conceived. Though it certainly aims in essence at devising "a form of multilateralism that is compatible with the requirements of domestic stability" in part "to accommodate and even facilitate the externalizing of adjustment costs" (Ruggie 1982, 399, 413), the economic order, should, and I feel does, exhibit a richer content. With some good will and farsightedness, it could be improved upon. It is the weak response of international regimes from within as well as in the form made possible by their key governing actors that has made them less effective, more nationally oriented than they had originally been envisaged. To cite but one example, the Fund continues as the center for consultation and cooperation in international monetary problems and it has been very helpful in dealing with the payments difficulties of some countries. But it has not found the right role to carry out its responsibilities of surveillance and management in the present system of managed floating (Bernstein 1984).

In seeking to restore a greater sense of purpose in international regimes and their institutions, it is instructive to strive, as R. Gardner (1988) phrased it, for practical, functional multilateralism or, in Jan Tumlir's framework (Hauser *et al.* 1988, 231), for effective multilateralism as an antidote to both dogmatic unilateralism and utopian multilateralism. Pragmatism may be a useful guide. But the core of multilateralism must revolve around the recognition that international economic relations are not normally a zero-sum game, that there are "global problems that can only be dealt with effectively through multilateral agencies" (Gardner 1988, 834).

Can international economic regimes be built around trade-offs between the priorities of different countries that yield nearly equal net benefits to all participants? Both the practicality and the moral justification of such arrangements appear questionable. If only for those reasons, it may be useful to "go back to first principles" (Gardner 1988, 841). But there are other reasons for taking stock in the hope of formulating useful alternatives. The prevailing concern about insecurity in trading, monetary, and financial affairs serves to remind us that "when things get out of hand... it is necessary to go back to fundamentals" rather than "persist in the search for quick fixes" (Culbert 1987a, 382). At the same time, it may be instructive to draw lessons from the experience gained in attempts to establish a coherent international economic order after World War II. Two would seem to stand out. First, although national interests or élite precepts cannot be ignored, constructive thinking about the international economic order could usefully be entrusted to technical specialists. They would be called upon to ensure operational stability and durability of regimes that can suitably cater to well-specified objectives. It would also be instructive to rationalize, and where possible quantify, the palpable noneconomic benefits of a stable, predictable, and reliable international economic environment.

Finally, the case for universal representation on a nearly equal basis could usefully be reexamined.[2] Some regimes as constituted cannot cater to some groups of countries, such as the discipline of the General Agreement for orthodox CPEs. Others only function with representation reflecting the net cost of adhering to them. Also, in a world of unequal actors that do not wish to act altruistically all the time, it is not very helpful to seek invariably to construct institutions on the "one country, one vote" principle.[3] This may be regrettable to some. But it is nonetheless the reality of life.

In this connection, it is relevant to recognize too that the existing regimes are essentially public goods, thus by definition indivisible. Yet one critical aspect of maintaining a regime is to ensure the fair distribution of costs and gains in the presence of considerable potential for free riding. This means that the benefits cannot be apportioned to members that contribute to maintaining the public good; it may even be impossible to limit them to the group (Keohane 1986, 12). As a result, a regime bestows gains upon numerous countries that do not necessarily share in the costs of setting up and maintaining it and the benefits are generally not equally available to all countries. Thus, countries that do not wish to participate, for instance, in the GATT can still benefit from the majority of participants adhering to certain regulations for themselves that can be applied to other countries – hence the potential of free riding. Major actors in the world economy need to accept the inevitability of a certain amount of such free riding. It can only be avoided altogether if the institutions and the regimes they support are universal. There is, therefore, a trade-off between the benefits that a regime bestows upon those that share the maintenance burden and the inefficiency that accrues from making every effort to ensure universality.

There cannot be perfect symmetry in sharing costs and gains, let alone in tying the latter to the former. Medium-sized and smaller countries benefit proportionately more from a public good, such as that provided by the Fund, the GATT, and the World Bank, than large countries. Yet the effective operation of these institutions and their ability to function properly can be ensured only if major trading partners – the United States, Japan, and the EC – provide continued support and positive participation. The dispersal of leadership in multilateral trade policy and commitment among these three, since the late 1960s in particular, and the emergence of the Group of Seventy-Seven as a well-organized mouthpiece for the DEs have altered the makeup and advantages of the regimes in place.

The inevitable conflict between universalism and efficiency in managing the regime may be one proper consideration when a major power desires to explore accession. Rather than outrightly shunning such an overture, it behooves insiders to be prepared for meaningful, intelligent explorations. The argument can be phrased in two different ways. One depends essentially on the pros of multilateralism. A firm commitment to multilateralism is an essential ingredient in maintaining peace, stability, predictability, security, and reliability in international affairs. Participation in one or more mutual-security organs ought to be fostered to the extent that it does not compromise either the basic principles upon which these institutions act or the functional degree of cooperation that can be ensured by expanding membership. In addition to the adjustments that potential applicants may have to engage in, universalization may require some modification on the part of the present membership and perhaps even in the particular focus of the activities of these organizations. The latter could usefully be explored in the context of the long-standing, but stalled, debates about reforming the global trading, financial, and monetary systems. This does not mean, however, that there would be no room for smaller steering groups when it proves to be too unwieldy to manage decisions through universal organs. I shall return to this topic in the discussion of individual regimes and their desirable transformations.

The other set of issues revolves around the fact that economic reforms in core CPEs, including China and, especially, the Soviet Union, are changing fundamental elements in their behavior and management that have in the past inhibited or impaired the participation of these countries in organized international economic relations. This applies not only to the political obstacles to global cooperation within the context of the postwar trading, financial, and monetary systems. It is even more true with respect to a whole sequence of technical–economic aspects of the economic model and development strategy of key CPEs. Because of the overwhelming importance of the USSR in CMEA affairs, a major transition in the Soviet economy is bound to affect the nature of CMEA cooperation and, by extension, the model and strategy of economic development of all participants (see chapter 2).

3 The CPEs and the international economic order

This section recapitulates the CPEs' stances on the postwar economic order; points out key objections to current trading, financial, and monetary regimes; discusses the advantages and drawbacks of joining the regimes; and elaborates on the potential loss in their policy autonomy and the concerns this may raise.

Major stance on the international economic order

With the Soviet Union and at one point China as their mentors, the CPEs have as a matter of course usually looked rather negatively upon the existing IEOs. Lenin's theory of imperialism assumes that the IEOs of mature capitalism are inherently exploitative, conceived to favor the interests of powerful monopolies in the larger DMEs at the expense of the interests not only of workers but also of smaller and less mature countries (Harding and Hewett 1989, 164). For a long time after the withdrawal from postwar multilateral talks, Soviet leaders tended to emphasize in addition that the multilateral organizations are dominated by a few capitalist countries that are mainly seeking to avert an internal collapse through the expansion of international trade and greater capital mobility, if necessary at the expense of other countries, including CPEs (Čeklin 1987, 38). But increasingly more nuanced pronouncements have come to the fore not only from within the various CPEs, but also from within the regimes subjected to criticism. In this connection, it is worth recalling that a rather comprehensive survey by Maciej Kostecki (1979a, 14) of the European CPEs' objections to the ITS anchored to the GATT found that the last open criticism of the GATT – a rather mild one at that[4] – by a leading Soviet official dates back to 1960.[5] Since then, Soviet commentators have admitted that the GATT may yield benefits even to CPEs, emphasized the mutual advantage of trade based on *détente,* and stressed the basic principles of international relations upon which a new ITS could be erected.

Nonetheless, the USSR and its allies have continued to pinpoint a number of shortcomings in the GATT, including the "clublike" character of the organization and the rather casual regard of the institution for the problems of countries that do not form the core of the global economy (see chapter 4). From time to time, the CPEs have shown more than casual interest in the establishment of a new world trade organization, usually in the context of UNCTAD deliberations.[6] But these proposals have never been very explicit on how precisely such an institution was to function.

Criticism of the Bretton Woods institutions and the associated regimes has been more strident and longer-lasting (see chapter 3). These institutions have been viewed as dominated by the United States, as designed to foster dollar hegemony, and as functioning chiefly for the benefit of a few DMEs. More specifically, they have not created conditions conducive to monetary stability, adequate international liquidity, averting monetary policies in one part of the system detrimental to another part and thus giving rise to wild gyrations in exchange rates, a solution of the international debt problem, adequate transfer of resources from north to south, and other issues. These topics do not really differ from those viewed by MEs on a number of occasions in a variety of national and international fora. What could be done to improve upon the situation is something else, of course.

Advantages and drawbacks

The general drawbacks and advantages of belonging to an IEO have been detailed in the introduction and the key advantages and drawbacks of the three regimes discussed in chapters 3 and 4. As indicated earlier, it is useful to distinguish conceptually between two discourses. One is the present and future gains and losses that may directly ensue from belonging to a specific regime in the strict sense. The other is the recognition that there are corresponding, if asymmetric, advantages and drawbacks to profiling a country's position on issues, irrespective of its specific place in the regime under review, thus forestalling the emergence of arrangements that narrow the arena for fruitful interaction.

For the larger CPEs that are seeking greater participation in the international economy, the more general advantages of being within the system, rather than outside it, probably outweigh the specific gains that they can reap from joining. This is particularly so for the USSR and in the short to medium term, given Soviet reluctance to become too dependent on outside "advice," the overwhelming importance of primary goods in its convertible currency exports, and the low probability of it being accepted as a DE in the IFS. Once within the system, the larger CPEs, in particular, could help shape the global institutions and their policies, including those with respect to DEs. Because of the position of some CPEs as world powers or their aspirations to obtain such a status in due course, being absent from the near-global institutions prevents them from discharging their responsibilities as sovereign states in an interdependent world. This has also fostered a gradual reconsideration of their ideologically motivated attitudes, especially *vis-à-vis* the monetary institutions.

Regarding the political problems of IEOs potentially meddling in the internal affairs of CPEs, I recognize the negotiating posture it affords and the dangers that may conceivably materialize under its guise. This is likely to be especially touchy, as at this juncture, during debates on the depth, breadth, and pace of economic reforms. As explained in chapter 2, even highly technical reform proposals have political and social overtones and implications that will probably be contested, as a reform cannot simply be a zero-sum game. Political tangles are also felt once the reform enjoys firm consensus and is being put in place. Because some IEOs, especially the Fund, deal essentially with government bureaucracies, they cannot avoid having to walk a highly sensitive tightrope. But, with a bit of good will and recognition of realities, these obstacles should not be blown out of proportion.

Certainly, the imposition of some external discipline on countries with a substantial degree of policy autonomy, such as China or the Soviet Union, might be perceived as meddling in internal affairs. At first sight, this would be inconsistent with their aspiration to command their own destiny. However, exploration and negotiation could be viewed, quite properly, as a joint effort to permit greatly expanded economic interaction among previously divergent sectors of the world economy. A commitment to search for mutually acceptable adjustments of institutions, to build new trade and financial patterns, and to enhance confidence would go a long way toward allaying fears of unwarranted outside interference in the domestic affairs of even the most powerful CPE.

Necessity of reform

The CPEs individually and as a group could seek to counteract the negative effects of the external pressures that they have recently been exposed to through broad import substitution, vigorous export promotion, or raising their external debt. Growth intensification could conceivably be pursued in isolation.[7] A conscious turning inward by means of magnifying the import curbs enacted since the late 1970s could help to ease the constraints emanating from the payments deficit and the debt. But such a policy shift cannot yield sustainable results because national markets in Eastern Europe are too small; even the USSR needs to procure foodstuffs and technology from abroad. In other words, it is hard to envision how a strong and sustainable impetus to factor productivity might be engineered under an autarkic regime.

Owing to their size and resource endowment, most of the smaller CPEs in the years ahead need to diversify their procurements of fuels and raw materials for two reasons. The region's output of such key products is likely to show modest gains at best, even if present output constraints can be eased. Also, output levels can be sustained only at sharply rising costs. To diversify sources of imports, the only viable strategy is all-around export promotion. This requires that structural adjustments enable the CPEs to exploit trade advantages not only by marshaling opportunities in the CMEA, but also by seeking a suitable global trade profile. It is true that prevailing circumstances confine to a varying degree the room for maneuver as regards the enactment of remedial policies. There is little doubt that, at least conceptually, reformers are of one mind that the growth strategy needs to be geared toward actively exploring markets abroad and strengthening the competitive position of their economies. The CPE leadership may not yet be willing to adjust to global competition. Yet it cannot afford to muddle through for a long time or simply to bulge the external debt. The range of alternatives is, therefore, largely set by the need to restructure gradually the traditional intra-CMEA trade pattern as the foundation of genuine SEI. One critical building block of such a scenario is the revamping of the effective TRP terms of trade, making due allowance for regional preferences regarding the promotion of SEI.

Maintaining in the short run the traditional CMEA trade pattern rests on the conjecture that the foundations of a more buoyant growth trajectory must be solidified through a multipronged approach.[8] Ways and means must be found to sustain the exchange of the bulk of primary goods and fuels needed by most CPEs against manufactures that they can produce with some degree of comparative advantage. Short-term diversion of this trade to third markets can be entertained only at great cost in terms of ballooning foreign debt or sizable cuts in levels of living of the population – both ill-affordable at this stage. At the same time, real cost structures need to be enhanced to regulate demand and supply, and especially to foster the modernization of manufacturing sectors. Although initially focused on intragroup trade and the coordination of investments among the CPEs, this strategy also recognizes the need to encourage the gradual substitution of imports from DEs for domestic and regional production processes intensive in labor and primary goods and to supply local markets with sophisticated manufactures from DMEs without greatly straining external payments. As such, east–west interaction and east–south commerce constitute two pivots of the above scenario. To modernize manufacturing branches, among other things to meet Soviet demands, Eastern Europe cannot forgo imports, especially of selective noncompeting technology. This hardening of the product mix offered may require even more convertible currency procurements than already embodied in present CMEA exports. Any misalignment in relative TRPs should be rectified by modifying policy instruments rather than through administrative intervention.

The aforementioned strategy sets a demanding policy agenda. No easy solution of the implied dilemmas is at hand. Two critical considerations may provide the needed link, however. Countries appear to realize that a resumption of faster growth depends on the enactment of domestic and regional structural adjustment policies. In this strategy, forging a much greater degree of regional economic cohesion is critical in order to counteract constraints on more buoyant growth policies over the next decade or so. I realize that this argument runs counter to the current political rhetoric of the most reform-minded western-orientated policy makers in Eastern Europe. It is nonetheless one that economic reason will inevitably lead back to. The same circumstance will in due course support the proposition that it would be a serious mistake to assume that the preference for CMEA cooperation, over and above the possibilities of domestic expansion and of economic relations with third partners, is without bounds. There is undoubtedly a strong preference for CMEA collaboration in certain areas. But other endeavors exist for which absolute regional sovereignty would impose too high a price. In other words, there must be a turning point among the range of preferences for SEI arrangements that separates those regional endeavors that the CPEs are prepared to finance from others from which they may prefer to pay at best partially. That is to say, the CPEs cannot be expected to ignore their dynamic comparative advantages, given their national and regional preferences (Fröhlich 1987; Grote and Kühn 1986).

Membership in the Bretton Woods institutions and CPE reform

The approximate confluence of requests for accession to the IEOs and embarking on reforms in CPEs raises the issue of whether there is a causal relationship. If so, what impacts can affiliation with the monetary and trading systems exert on the pace, depth, and character of the reform? Or is the relationship between reforms in CPEs and seeking closer association with IEOs more complex? In particular, do the reforms change the conditions for participation of these countries in IEOs singly or as a group?

First of all, the relationship between reform and exploring membership in IEOs is not necessarily a causal one. Thus reforms were tried throughout the European CPEs in the 1960s, when some of them had already extended initial feelers toward the GATT but well before any positive step was taken toward membership in the financial organizations. Some coveted affiliation well before reforms were even seriously contemplated. The Eastern European requests of 1981 to join the Fund and the Bank probably found their origin not in reform considerations but in the external financial difficulties of the early 1980s.

In short, seeking accession to the IEOs is an eminently political act, and it is politics, not economic factors, that decides whether the request succeeds or is rebuffed. For one thing, accession to the GATT is a very complex and protracted affair (see chapter 4). Unlike the GATT, however, accession to the Bretton Woods institutions can be handled more expeditiously as the key decisions revolve around setting the subscription and signing the Articles of Agreement, which usually follow upon an in-depth exploration of the applicant's monetary and financial systems.[9] But, even if membership is attained quickly, arranging for the first standby loan from the Fund or for financial support from the Bank may require another six to twelve months. Political factors may shorten or lengthen these deadlines, as the Polish case illustrates.[10] This simply demonstrates that seeking membership in the IEOs cannot be a panacea for resolving major problems connected with reforms or for avoiding undertaking them.

Countries do not, of course, seek accession to IEOs solely for political prestige. There are usually good economic reasons to explore membership or spurn it at certain points of time. These include debates around reforms, particularly when the latter are to a significant extent predicated on bolstering export performance in world markets. Perhaps the most convincing nexus is provided by the logic of seeking to "normalize" relations with other countries. This could widen the maneuvering room for economic agents that, with the maturation of reform, are or will soon be entrusted with a significant degree of autonomy, including autonomy in foreign trade matters. But the eventual impact could be much more profound, if only because participation in IEOs tends to foster economic reform, but not necessarily, as Rumania's case illustrates without a doubt.

The potential contribution of the Fund and Bank to changing the environment within which reform can be pursued depends on the access that the CPEs obtain to loans, possibly at favorable interest rates, and the stamp of approval, which elicits a favorable psychological response from private and official financial institutions. It can also provide access to a considerable store of expertise in debt management and rescheduling, and in evaluating the costs and benefits of various economic austerity policies. Inasmuch as an economic reform is by definition an attempt to come to grips with some imbalances, it involves a process of adjustment. This may focus in its most benign form on the transition from administrative control to more indirect steering of the economy through macroeconomic policies that mark the arena within which economic agents can operate at their own risk and on their own responsibility. This involves overhauling virtually the entire spectrum of monetary and financial policies and institutions. The Fund in particular is well placed to provide advice on how best to proceed. The Bretton Woods institutions may exert a salutary influence on the reemergence of monetary and financial policies in managing the CPE that has volunteered to undergo economic reform and ensuring a smooth transition to a decentralized economic mechanism.

But there need not necessarily be a nexus with reform. The CPEs first hesitantly explored association with global institutions as early as the second half of the 1950s, when the gradual easing of tensions between east and west led to greater dynamism in interregional trade and finance. Such an opening of markets became all the more necessary when, for their own reasons, these CPEs sought to improve their external economic performance as one means of buttressing domestic growth efforts without necessarily undertaking broad-based organizational or managerial reforms.

Having access to a wealth of adjustment experience may be even more useful when the reform is imposed upon a situation that is in fundamental disequilibrium and the traditional instruments of central control are no longer available or decision makers are reluctant to revert back to them for fear of hollowing out the reform from within. For the smaller CPEs, such imbalances are unavoidably connected with external payments problems, if the latter were not the root cause of the search for reform to begin with. If the CPE obtains an adjustment loan from the Fund (now possibly also from the Bank), the conditionality requirements may well be utilized as a convenient cloak to enact painful changes in the domestic economy and to make them socially and politically acceptable. There is little evidence that conditionality imposed by the Fund has entailed unacceptable conditions for the CPEs or even that it has engendered movements toward greater economic and societal reform than the CPE in question had been contemplating in the first place. Fund and World Bank resources have rather been obtained in support of such reforms and even after reversal of the reform measures, perhaps in an effort to stem the ever-present lobby that takes advantage of temporary disillusion with economic reform to retrogress through recentralization.

4 Economic reforms in CPEs and the international economic order

Country-specific economic and related reforms as well as shifts in the SEI mechanism have been under serious review, most recently since about the mid-1980s (see chapter 2). National policy makers, including those in the USSR, have exhibited more than casual concern about adopting more effective ways to pursue SEI, both through their own policies and in CMEA deliberations about the knottiest issues. The ongoing debate is far from over and ample room for serious reflection remains in any case. Against this backdrop, it might be useful to discuss briefly a realistic alternative mode of CMEA cooperation anchored to the drawing up of what I have elsewhere (Brabant 1987e; Brabant 1987f; Brabant 1989a, 411–17; Brabant 1989e) called a constitutional framework for SEI. My view owes much to the lessons that can be drawn from the sorry history of national reform experiments (Kowalik 1986). It is also imbued with the current ferment about changing economic mechanisms, the shifting stances on the most desirable policy measures to foster national and regional economic "intensification," and how to proceed from the current situation to a more desirable alternative. This requires the implementation of a positive structural adjustment program tailored to the evolving institutional and other requirements of the region; to the aspirations of policy makers, particularly with respect to the preferred extent of interaction with global trade and financial networks; and to the preferred degree of combining relative domestic policy autonomy with CMEA-wide "security of supply" considerations.

On present knowledge of what may be in the offing, three key characteristics need to be borne in mind. First, even the most important goals of the contemplated changes in national economic mechanisms are unlikely to coincide throughout the region in spite of these economies being fairly tightly intermeshed. Secondly, the process of moving toward new policies and institutions is likely to be protracted and painful. Decision makers cannot expect a decisive lift in economic performance as a result of system tinkering, say, within the next three to five years. Instead, they should be prepared to steer and nurse along the transformation of their prevailing economic mechanisms toward a reformed economy over a period of at least a decade, even if no further changes in the envisaged target model were to become necessary – an improbable event.

Finally, the CMEA is unlikely in the near future to become a homogeneous region in which members voluntarily redistribute value added to the degree they tolerate it domestically. This stems in part from the fact that at the CMEA level there is no parallel for the latent power of central decision makers in any individual CPE, in spite of the paramount role of the *primus inter pares*. In other words, on present expectations regarding policy commitments and realistic chances of reforms being implemented, there is likely to be considerable discordance among the CPEs at any one point as well as over time.

These features impose formidable requirements not only on the design and intentions of the reform, but more importantly on how to bring about the processes that may solidify, perhaps after some hesitation and further tinkering, into new institutions and mechanisms better suited to dovetailing economic decisions than those now in place. The lack of parallelism in national and regional policy formulation and enforcement argues even more strongly than in the case of national reforms for the establishment of a proper integration framework. Because of weak internationalism and the near absence of "democratic centralism" at the CMEA level, regional economic cohesion needs to be solidified chiefly on the basis of economic reckoning. Even if countries choose to grant development assistance or to promote factor transfers for reasons other than strict material gain, economic implications need to be examined much more vigorously so that the direct and indirect costs of political decisions can be placed in their proper perspective. This is especially critical for the self-accounting of economic units. At the very least, economic computation needs to be refined as a technical tool to distinguish more clearly between resource appropriations and performance, to weed out what is not up to par, and to foster profitable processes as measured either by economic yardsticks or, given the political preference for self-sufficiency, by the CMEA's ultimate *raison d'être*.

This assessment suggests that the debate on CMEA reform should focus not on whether to change the direction and methods of SEI, but rather on providing answers to the following two central questions of economic policy. First, to what extent do the CPEs consciously opt to safeguard their regional economic organization and their national independence in economic affairs? Secondly, because this preference entails a cost in terms of economic efficiency forgone, as measured by the world standards that some CPEs seek to emulate, who will be asked to shoulder this cost and how will it be apportioned? As in the case of the domestic economic mechanisms (see chapter 2), once an acceptable answer to these questions is negotiated, the work ahead should be of a dual, but complementary, nature and proceed in parallel with the domestic economic reforms under way in some CPEs. One strand of adaptations involves the institutional setup and management of the regional organs, including the way in which they interact with the member countries. Another set of shifts would be geared to economic policies and policy instruments with their related institutions. At any rate, realistic CMEA reform should reflect the pivotal features, the commonality as well as the differences, in the ongoing changes in the CPEs. The positive structural adjustment policy to be embraced could usefully be anchored to a redesigned regional framework. It is here that my suggestion for working out a constitutional framework finds its justification.

I envisage such a compact as a firm agreement encompassing the goals of SEI, the mechanisms to foster progress, the institutions to ensure the smooth functioning of the policy instruments, and the transition mechanism to assist countries that are not yet ready to proceed full steam with domestic economic reform. In other words, a constitutional framework embodies commitments about basic objectives, institutions, instruments, rules, and regulations to be respected by all signatories until revised at infrequent intervals. It sets the boundaries of the arena within which economic agents can pursue their own interests subject to society's. Agreement is desirable, among other things, on the ultimate purposes of integration, the distribution of the gains and benefits, and the basic policy instruments to be placed at the disposal of macroeconomic managers. Against that backdrop, the purposes of SEI can be kept rather vague. It might extend to areas in which regional demand and supply should be geared to the needs of the region as a whole rather than to the simple sum of the national demands. Agreement is also required on the degree of "separateness" from the world economy that the CPEs want to maintain and support jointly according to some distributive rules.

Perhaps more important than the goals is the specification of the means to enhance SEI, to assess its costs and benefits, and to agree upon rules to distribute these results. Certainly these aspects of the SEI mechanism should at the same time be autonomous and, at least for some CPEs, intimately related to domestic policy processes to forestall the typical wavering of past national reforms. Members that do not wish to intermesh their economies at this stage either drop out or seek the right to impose temporarily their own national preferences to enable them to separate regional cooperation from the domestic mechanism. In the other CPEs, the mechanism should dovetail very closely indeed.

Regarding policy instruments and institutions, it is important to emphasize that the SEI economic mechanism in place is exceedingly primitive, geared more to the reciprocal exchange of physical goods and tangible services than to the enhancement of genuine integration through indirect coordination, including integration in the context of national, coordinated, or joint planning within the CMEA (Brabant 1989a, 207–338). Adaptations of SEI mechanisms that have no direct counterpart in any of the participating CPEs are clearly meaningless. As argued elsewhere (Brabant 1987c, 1987g), the CMEA reform could usefully be synchronized with the most ambitious national reform, but no CPE should be compelled to emulate that in the short run.

Among the instruments and institutions that could benefit from a new approach to SEI, the respective roles of planning and market-type instruments need to be sharply distinguished. There is room at the CMEA level for the planning of structural decisions and the preparation of key policy alternatives when it comes to ensuring preference for the region in any further attempt to raise export dependence. Whether this harmonization takes the form of formalized plans is a matter yet to be resolved.

The compact should lay down, however, the core instruments and supporting institutions for coordinating possibly decentralized economic decisions. This is particularly critical to infusing realism into the envisaged project on bolstering interfirm relations. The critical areas involved have been tabled in the meantime (see chapter 2), but decisive action, particularly on regional pricing, exchange rates, multilateralism, and movement toward real convertibility, is long overdue. In this regard, the formulation of a variant of the mechanism used in the 1950s in the context of the European Payments Union (EPU) with a revitalized TR (see Brabant 1989f, 1989g) could be extremely useful, even if only to support interfirm relations. I see little room for progress with interfirm integration in manufacturing sectors without allowing a more flexible pricing mechanism to emerge. Such genuine wholesale trade should preferably emanate directly into the domestic pricing regimes of the participating members.

Finally, it is necessary to come to some agreement on the room for policy maneuver within the region for the most open economy, through which policy institutions and mechanisms that can be exploited, the degree of protection against regional competition that members will be allowed to embrace, and the transitory insulation deemed necessary to buffer the impact of effective integration and smooth the adjustment process within a mutually agreed time frame. The CPEs that are ready to introduce broad-based economic reforms attuned to the revamped SEI mechanism should be in a position to progress without being stymied by others, who per agreement postpone such transitions.

Perhaps the most critical element in the above reform agenda focuses on the TRP regime. I am not advocating that it be abolished but it should not be further refined into the nearly completely independent price system (IPS) that was first on the agenda in the early 1960s and again a decade later. After all, why should the CMEA not have its own preferences on regional protection? These may stem from myopic, second-best choices. They may also be inspired by macroeconomic constraints as perceived by policy makers. But an own-price regime would be desirable, notwithstanding the sharp criticism levied at earlier IPS attempts (see Brabant 1987b, 250–65). In my view, such an autonomous price regime makes a lot of sense for economies that emphatically do not wish to integrate themselves fully into the world economy because they put a premium on warding off perturbations from world markets, on setting domestic prices relatively autonomously, and on funneling possibly narrowly held preferences with a heavy weight into decision making. This could usefully take the form of "virtual prices,"[11] essentially the creation of flexible trade prices that reflect regional supply and demand of preset trade flows and, in some respect, also impact upon domestic prices of at least one CPE. Such virtual prices could promote more efficient trade or, at any rate, facilitate the selection of trade processes that shore up the domestic and external requirements for fostering swift productivity growth. In that respect, it would be exceedingly helpful if the CPEs were to link flexible TRP pricing with domestic wholesale prices.

There is ample evidence of ongoing changes and more to come. One direction is unambiguously in favor of opening up these economies to greater international competition, without this being necessarily channeled through formally liberalized market access. Could membership in IEOs be of assistance in formulating and adhering to the transition phase or would it be more advisable technically to postpone accession until after completion of the transition, perhaps in one or two decades? When exploring the potential for associating CPEs with IEOs, it is useful to clarify first what precisely is meant, in which way this cooperation is to proceed, and what kind of CPE one is referring to. These questions are perhaps easier to answer – they are certainly more important – in the case of the GATT than for the Bretton Woods institutions, if only because GATT relations have been considerably more strained.

5 Do CPEs belong in the ITS?

It would be technically meaningless to associate the traditional CPE with the ITS on the basis of orthodox tariffs and NTB trade-offs. There is simply no justifiable way in which CPEs can be brought into a regime based on reciprocity designed only for mature MEs. At the other extreme, if one is seeking to make the ITS as universal as circumstances "permit" and to distinguish among various types of CPEs, it is not immediately evident where a CPE belongs in a universal ITS, ignoring the semantic problem for now. By "permit" I take it for granted that compromises on principles can be entertained, but they cannot be allowed to hollow out the core foundation of the IEO.

These are not just rhetorical questions, for two reasons. If accession of reforming CPEs can help these countries to strengthen the foundation of the transition mechanism toward decentralization and the determination of policy makers to pursue this goal, ways of facilitating this process need to be explored. This is all the more so when reforms can be expected in time to lead to new export markets for Contracting Parties. Secondly, whatever solution one is willing to ponder in earnest, it needs to be recognized that the CPEs cannot in the short run be expected fully to multilateralize their trade, to eschew their habitual BTPAs, or to enact drastic shifts in their trade patterns. An acceptable proposal for meaningful association needs to be tailored to present needs of the CPEs without overly infringing on the legitimate interests of Contracting Parties.

Reciprocity, MFN, and the ITS

As emphasized in chapter 4, one basic constant in postwar trade negotiations has been their mercantilist bent (Curzon and Curzon 1976). In spite of ambiguities about how reciprocity should be interpreted (Keohane 1986), countries have continued to emphasize gaining export markets while losing less in domestic production as a result of the strengthened import competition resulting from reciprocal tariff and related concessions. This is nothing new for, as Keohane (1986, 3) stresses, it has been a constant of US commercial policy since it signed its first treaty in 1778 with France! If these are to be the principal instruments to erect and maintain a universal ITS, it will be very difficult to accommodate any but the most market-oriented CPE. The reason is simple: even CPEs with an operative customs tariff keep domestic and foreign prices apart through various means. How can one determine nearly balanced concessions through reciprocal tariff reductions when tariffs as such do not play an active role in setting domestic prices of imports and hence in competing for demand with domestic products? Putting it differently, when domestic prices are not really the terms at which alternatives are offered because of persistent micro- and macroeconomic imbalances, how can one ascertain the impact of a reduced import tariff on consumption and substitution for domestic production?

The issue of reciprocity has been a conundrum to which countless hours of negotiations within the GATT and numerous international conferences have been devoted with the predictable negative result. To fix attention, it might be instructive to distinguish between specific and diffuse reciprocity (Keohane 1986, 4). If construed too narrowly, reciprocity will give rise to bilateralism and discrimination (Camps and Diebold 1986, 16). If interpreted too broadly, it leads directly to free riding. There is simply no adequate basis for determining full or specific reciprocity other than by estimating the export effect for the traditional CPE of a tariff reduction by Contracting Parties and enforcing a compensatory incremental import effect through the central planning machinery. The issue of whether the increment would otherwise have materialized is one of those insoluble counterfactual queries. From a practical point of view, it is of less importance than accepting the principle and enforcing it, for here one treads on issues of national sovereignty, the inadequacies of international law, and the great obstacles to enforcing international rulings even when sufficient precedent is at hand. Agreeing on computational methodology and accepting the results obtained in the process of such technically complex estimates are bound to be no mean feat. Finally, the agreement would have to be reexamined in line with shifts in the global economy, the buoyancy of development, and indeed the CPE's own plans. Perhaps more useful for negotiations, including those eventually with the Soviet Union, would be acceptance of the notion of diffuse reciprocity, or an ongoing series of sequential actions that may continue indefinitely without ever balancing mutual concessions within the context of shared commitments and values. This, of course, can work best when international regimes are strong (Keohane 1986, 4), something that does not quite apply to the ITS in place.

Various less complex proposals to improve the participation arrangements in the GATT framework have been tabled on one occasion or another. As a nexus between the two systems many commentators continue to recommend a formula based on market access commitments by the CPEs and on conditional or restricted undertakings of equal treatment by the Contracting Parties. Such a special trade-off could easily be elaborated as a more general, multilateral bridge between the two systems. It would essentially reflect the interest of countries in trade expansion, whenever possible by removing QRs inherited from past inaction as well as those superimposed under the escape clauses, thereby protecting the GATT's inherent mercantilist bent (Wolf 1987). There is nothing inherently difficult in modifying the GATT rules or their interpretation that would inhibit the inclusion of intersystemic trade on an *ad hoc* basis in the present GATT framework. I do not, of course, pretend that negotiation of such an amendment would be straightforward at all. But makeshift adjustments have been enacted in diverse trade-related areas, and one more explicitly to accommodate "state trading" is not out of the realm of the possible.

Although a further amendment of the General Agreement is entirely possible, a codification of a framework for participation of CPEs in the GATT would not provide an arrangement for all or even the most critical east–west commercial-policy issues (Vernon 1979). Some, including policies governing the transfer of technology, the imposition of extraneous conditions on trade liberalization, and the competitive financing of trade, have proved to be very hard to come to grips with and could be handled better in a new framework. Other tasks could not possibly be firmly addressed in terms of the existing rules and regulations if the challenge is to devise a set of institutions and procedures compatible with the growing volume of east–west trade, yet responding adequately to the interests of both sides. This problem area could more usefully be examined in as comprehensive a fashion as politically feasible.

One may well ask whether a general arrangement for CPEs could be grafted onto the recent approaches to international trade policy. These have fallen into two rather distinct processes. One has been concerned with refining rules to make the market-based ITS fairer and freer. This approach is indeed part and parcel of the new MTN round. Participation in such attempts to modernize the General Agreement is apparently less easy for CPEs than for many DEs. The other process is concerned with seeing that state interventions do not shift the burden of adjustment onto others, thus introducing new problems in the course of solving old ones. Systemic differences in this approach tend to become far less important as hindrances to collective action than in other avenues to multilateral trading. For that reason, from a technical and economic point of view, CPE participation in such an approach appears perfectly possible.

The need to reconsider the role of CPEs

There are at least seven reasons that together justify a reconsideration of the traditional trading arrangements and taking into account the potential needs of CPEs. First, the sheer economic importance of east–west economic relations should not be underestimated for either side. Certainly, there are very marked asymmetries in the sense that this largely intra-European trade is comparatively much less important for the west than for the east. But it is not really irrelevant on the margin.[12] Furthermore, effective reciprocity arrangements could help to foster exports by ME firms that cannot afford the resources to "warm up the market," as the transnationals succeeded in doing so well during the 1960s and 1970s. The fact that in the past decade or so some small- to medium-sized enterprises have succeeded in becoming close trade partners of CPEs simply underlines the considerable unexplored potential.

Secondly, the acrimony over east–west trade and finance within the Atlantic Alliance and in other fora suggests that taking some aspects of those relations out of the purely national political realm and placing them under rather more international surveillance would be advisable in any case. It would be most constructive to do so while providing maneuvering room for multilateral discussions of the manifold problems posed by differences in economic systems, particularly their external institutional and political implications.

Thirdly, in areas in which participation in substantive rules or in code making is likely to be useful to all participants, there is every reason to facilitate its emergence. This is especially the case for CPEs that are prepared to make state trading much more a function of ownership and organizational accommodation than an instrument of commercial policy (Matejka 1974, 1982). Major DMEs could usefully reciprocate such a shift in emphasis by CPEs.

Fourthly, to the extent that one grants credibility to the economic reforms under way in CPEs, particularly when placed in their proper sociopolitical context, it would be constructive to seek ways and means of buttressing this process. One should at least do everything possible to avoid deliberately impeding the societal transformation process, whose intentions are unprecedented in several of the reforming CPEs.

Fifthly, there would appear to be sufficient reason today to reiterate Gerschenkron's (1947, 624) evaluation of the USSR's role in world economic affairs forty years ago: "Russia's reintegration into the world economy is of such a stupendous moment" that a careful examination of how it could join the ITS would be worthwhile, even if the USSR were not reforming and there were no major structural problems with the ITS in place. The reform under way and the search for constructive solutions for the multiple problems that beset the ITS argue even more strongly for Gerschenkron's position, even if in the end the Soviet Union, as in 1947, were to decide against joining.

Sixthly, excepting some favored partners, east–south economic interaction has not so far been very extensive or sufficiently dynamic over a sustained period of time to make the CPEs count in the aggregate trade of the south. This has been unfortunate for both sides. DEs have complained, on occasion bitterly, about the paltry financial and trade support, let alone development assistance, provided by the CPEs. This stance has been aired especially in numerous NIEO debates (see chapter 3). An institutional framework for reconciling the differences that inhibit smooth east–south economic intercourse within an agreed-upon global trade compact (Brabant 1989d) might go a long way to solidifying meaningful change.

Finally, a radical change in the Soviet approach to economic decision making is bound to leave an imprint on its major trading partners in Eastern Europe, hence on the CMEA as a whole.[13] It is exceedingly important to bear in mind that the Soviet Union is *the* key CMEA member. Its joining the global trade framework would elicit bandwagon effects throughout the CMEA, including an effect on the functioning of the SEI mechanism (see Brabant 1989a), thereby reinforcing the major changes under way (see chapter 2). To the extent that the latter crystallize in support of domestic reforms,[14] a new set of principles for joining an MFN-based trading system for the CPEs might be conceptualized.

If the Soviet Union were to succeed in its aim to link domestic wholesale and foreign trade prices in a manner that is even moderately acceptable to those championing "free markets," a very significant milestone would have been set toward putting in place the necessary elements to reappraise how STCs can exchange preferences for ME tariff concessions. Upon completion of the first stage of the envisaged reform it would in any case be a misnomer of sorts to apply the old STC designation[15] or to let decisions at this juncture be guided by the old maxim that in an ME "trade can take place unless a government prevents it," whereas in a CPE "no trade takes place unless the state initiates it" (Vernon 1979, 1038). Lloyd (1982, 119) defines state trading as applying to an organization for which the prices and/or quantities of international transactions in commodities are determined as an instrument in the pursuit of the objectives of government policies. Because all organs, even in the modified CPE, by definition further societal objectives, state trading cannot be dissociated from perceived community interests as such. But Lloyd (1982, 120) would exclude from this definition "organizations which are autonomous in terms of deciding themselves the quantities and prices of commodities traded, even though they may be owned wholly by governments and subject to government regulation in other respects." There is bound to be gradual movement away from state trading, though CPEs will continue to conduct trade through firms that enjoy a considerable monopoly over certain tradables. I envision this mutation as evolving for some time. But state trading is likely to remain very important even for the most modified CPE, owing to the nature of its property relations and social organization.

Mutations in the ITS

There is wide consensus in the profession that the ITS has become less and less universal and multilateral. There are many reasons for this situation. To some degree, it stems from the failure to transform the "wayward station" of the GATT into the third pillar of the world economic system on an equal footing with the IMF and the World Bank. This would have yielded the necessary institutional tools to anticipate, identify, and address problems, and to lay the groundwork for systematic negotiations of the many issues at stake.

Since the Tokyo Round, the GATT has as it were been victimized by what Gadbaw calls the "balkanization of international trade policy" (Gadbaw 1984, 38), or derogations from the General Agreement. These "mini-GATTs" emerged because some Contracting Parties failed to settle their differences under the General Agreement, and so resolved to write nearly independent agreements, each of which has somewhat different decision-making and enforcement mechanisms. In fact, this proliferation of pragmatic ways of settling contentious issues is not necessarily a bad way of reaching agreement on specific issues when it is truly impossible for major partners to overcome their differences on trading practices. But it is a mistake to seek to settle trading problems chiefly through the legal approach on separate issues, if only because there are many problems that cannot be handled in this way.

Associating orthodox or reforming CPEs poses one bundle of issues. Others derive essentially from the ITS's nature as a public good, hence the need to come to grips with free riding (Artis and Ostry 1986, 75). Furthermore, the ITS needs to adapt to changes in the global economic and political environment, something that can best be done in a permanent international forum for trade-policy topics. These include the problems of the NICs; the role of DEs in the ITS more generally (Djumilen 1984; Koekkoek 1988); how best to foster structural change throughout the global economy with a minimum of adverse, even if localized, dislocations; graduation rules for countries that presently enjoy preferences stemming from the inability of the DMEs to address development issues head-on in the context of the GATT;[16] the competitive export of unemployment; agricultural protectionism and the role of national security therein (Runge 1988); the proliferation of discriminatory NTBs beyond those condoned by the General Agreement; and east–west economic issues (Paszyński 1988). These multiple problems can be adequately addressed, not through provocation and retaliation, but through persuasion and mutual accommodation that in time may lead to proper codification. Finally, there is room to establish a framework for examining emerging issues, whose scope may be hard to conceive of now.

The many derogations of the General Agreement justify a comprehensive reassessment of the functions of the GATT in the ITS. A concerted effort to improve the institutional mechanism for decision making, rule development, dispute settlement, enforcement, and the coordination of national policies affecting trade might ultimately prove to be a prerequisite to regaining full multilateralism at as global a level as feasible. At the same time, one should harbor no illusion that the immense impediments to such multilateral collaboration could be easily overcome. It is all the more urgent, then, at least to those who believe that foreign trade enhances welfare and fosters international security, that countries jointly attempt to prevent world trade from regressing to a situation where it might become still more precarious and restricted than in the 1930s.

It is doubtful that such a transformation is feasible within the present ITS. It would strain credulity for the GATT to undertake such guidance, foster steady innovation as further progress is made, and ensure adherence to agreed-upon rules. Its frame of reference has proved to be rather restrictive, thus preventing it from coming to grips in an all-around satisfactory way with any of the multitude of emanations of the so-called new protectionism, notwithstanding official statements to the contrary. The GATT rules would appear to be far too compromised by the gap between reality and legal provisions for them to be rescued. Furthermore, the GATT was set up for, and has indeed remained basically geared to, the needs of DMEs.[17] This is not to denigrate the earnest attempt, particularly since the mid-1960s, to include provisions specifically designed to enhance the access of DEs to world markets of some goods. Nor do I deny that, in particular, the NICs among the DEs have derived spectacular benefits from their association with the GATT, from the special niches created for DMEs in that framework, or even simply from the DMEs maintaining the rump ITS. Nonetheless, neither most DEs nor the CPEs fit comfortably into the legalistic framework of the General Agreement. The same applies even more to east–west and north–south relations. Perhaps most in need of streamlining are the relations between east and south. What is required by way of international machinery is a proper combination of the GATT, UNCTAD, and Working Party Three of the OECD's Economic Policy Committee. Regrettably, these organizations in their present cloaks carry too much "institutional history" and "emotional freight" (Camps 1981, 147) to become the nucleus of the new, credible global trading organization that seems to be called for.

Even if it were possible to rewrite the General Agreement, would the outcome resemble what is required at this juncture? Diebold (1972, 348) argues quite cogently that "nothing as liberal as GATT could be negotiated today"; reforms should therefore be sought with considerable circumspection. Yet, given the sharp deterioration in the multilateral trading climate since the early 1970s and the lack of agreement on how to handle a wide range of new problems, I wonder whether it is not now the proper time to reassess the GATT in as comprehensive a framework as consensus among the major trade participants – not just the Contracting Parties – permits. The liberal framework of the original General Agreement, although still on the books, is certainly no longer a universal inspiration for actual trade policy. In other words, the world needs an institution that can reflect and cater to the interests of all participants in a multilateral trading system. For want of a better name, I christen such an institution the "Reconceived International Trade Organization" (RITO). The purpose of such an organ derives from the fact that the world as a whole stands to benefit from an improved institutional mechanism within which trade issues can be addressed systematically and comprehensively. Without this, the General Agreement should be recognized as an exclusive club of like-minded traders – largely the wealthy DMEs.

Reconstituting the ITS could usefully be entertained if major trading partners were favorably inclined to do so comprehensively. But this is far from being the case. Precisely because there are presently such widely diverging views on what should be fair trading practices, it might be the proper time to do what was not feasible in the late 1940s: to invest an international organization with the task of coming to grips with the fundamental requirements of a fair-trading world. This presupposes, as noted, that countries are in principle willing to negotiate in good faith over what constitutes an acceptable ITS. Its institutional and organizational requirements are certainly not insuperable. In spite of improvements in the international climate in recent years, the prevailing political will to engage in such deliberations falls short of the minimum required to commence meaningful negotiations.

Rather than focus the attention of the international community immediately on the elaboration of rules and regulations for such an international organization, prior agreement on key guidelines for the transition phase is critical. Some guidelines might in the end even prove to be more important than a political recommitment to a world dominated by tariffs and MFN treatment. This applies not only to the reforming CPEs. It is even more important to resolve such issues as preferences for and graduation of DEs, transition phases in regional integration schemes, the role of the NICs, and the regulation of the trade of the transnationals. But this is not the proper place to elaborate a full-fledged RITO, if only because I am not sufficiently competent to do so.[18] In the next subsection, I detail some aspects pertaining to CPEs, however.

Before embarking on building such an organ, as noted, it might be advisable first to explore to what extent participants are willing to endorse basic commitments. In this connection, Miriam Camps (Camps 1981, 153–8) has suggested three governing principles to be recognized by all participants prior to initiating negotiations about a RITO. First, it must be recognized that national action in fields to be entrusted to the ITS may have damaging external consequences. A state that considers itself adversely affected by another's action has the right to have the situation reviewed according to agreed procedures.

Secondly, participants need to accept that "like situation should receive like treatment" (Camps 1981, 154). This is a reformulation of the nondiscrimination principle, one of the ITO's foundation stones. Because nondiscrimination has not been adhered to under the General Agreement, the principle deliberately aims at making it workable "among fully participating members of particular codes" (Camps 1981, 156). Although this would technically be out of harmony with an overriding commitment to nondiscrimination, which remains the guiding beacon for the universal body in future rule making, it would facilitate special treatment for certain groups of countries, such as the poorest DEs and rather orthodox CPEs. This runs parallel with the so-called GATT-plus proposal (Advisory 1976).

Thirdly, by accepting these rules and procedural arrangements of the regime, and hence committing itself to abide by them, a member is entitled to the benefits of the regime. This principle is a variant of orthodox reciprocity, with the goal gradually to bring larger and larger areas of interstate conduct under international surveillance. It aims at the elaboration of a set of rules and regulations, if necessary in a formal code with enforcement rules, that may be acceptable only to a subset of participants keenly interested in forging ahead with trade liberalization among themselves. Other members of the ITS may seek to accede at a later stage, when they can fully comply with the existing code.

Before examining more closely the situation of the CPEs, a few other principles could usefully be recognized from the outset. Although it is commendable to seek recognition of uniform rules for all (Camps [1981] second principle), it would not be useful to work toward a new ITS without recognizing from the start major differences in the situation of nation states. Some of these are systemic in nature and cannot be eschewed altogether without altering the system. Others might be temporary and thus require one or more parallel transition phases. With that in mind another explicit principle might be that special rules can be enacted, for example, to accelerate the pace of development in some countries or to accommodate the inherently different status of regional integration schemes in the General Agreement.

It has also been a fiction that all members of the GATT benefit symmetrically from any set of conditions. Given the plight of the vast majority of DEs, it would be highly useful to agree upon the responsibility of the global community for ensuring maximum contribution of commerce to the economic development of the poorest DEs. That is not to say that such advantage should invariably be in the form of infant-industry protection; in most cases, DEs would be better off obtaining more favorable access to markets of developed countries (GATT 1985; Helleiner *et al.* 1983; Wolf 1987). If special preferences are granted, the DEs so identified should recognize that there are issues of graduation involved in moving toward a world with nearly full reciprocity. Geographical or systemic differentiation needs to be explicitly recognized to accommodate integration schemes of CPEs and DEs on an equal footing with those of DMEs. More multilateral surveillance and sharpening of article XXIV are desirable.

Thirdly, it has long been hypocritical to maintain that all traded goods, not to mention services, are dealt with evenly in the ostensibly multilateral trade world. In view of the flagrant violation of GATT rules in the trade of goods such as agricultural products, textiles, automobiles, and steel, participants may decide from the outset to recognize the maximum degree of "natural" protection and in which form it might be acceptable to all major actors (Paarlberg 1988). The precise extent and type of the protection, of course, should be the subject of research and negotiation. But endorsing the principle might well avoid the kind of exceptional law making and outright violation of the unrealistic ideals adopted in the negotiations about the ITO.

Finally, the international economic scene since the 1970s offers hardly any persuasive evidence for the notion that domestic prices of imported goods even in the most liberal ME are almost instantaneously set equal to the landed import price converted at the official exchange rate plus the tariff and domestic distribution and profit margins – the key principle underlying the liberal trade order. As the recent rise and fall of the dollar have so amply demonstrated, domestic prices of importables are frequently "managed" by exporters or importers in the short to medium run in part to protect market share.

The CPEs and the ITS

Would these or similar principles present insurmountable obstacles for CPEs? Would they suffice to permit the CPEs to participate fully in a RITO? The situation is far from hopeless even when discourse is restricted to the prevailing ITS, provided some of its key assumptions are relaxed to reflect three realities of organized trading. One is that the principles underlying the General Agreement have not been fully adhered to, and it would clearly be impossible to enforce them at this stage. This may be regrettable to champions of an untrammeled liberal economic order, but it is a reality to be heeded. Secondly, no single proposed solution by itself is guaranteed to work. Short of falling back upon free-market autonomy, few organizational factors that one could formulate have the simplicity of rules about tariffs and quotas in the postwar ITS (Diebold 1969, 138). Finally, it must be recognized that there are parallels – not exact equivalences or matchups – between the cornerstone of the ITS as it has evolved and the aims of some reforming CPEs.

Commercial commitments made in the context of a free-enterprise system parallel those in which a CPE based on commercial decision making of firms can engage. In the latter case, the state as the ultimate entrepreneur needs to guarantee through practical steps that import decisions under planning will be entirely commercial; but this may require partial devolution of decision making. In an ME, it is presumed that a system based on free-enterprise decisions guarantees a relatively stable and mutually beneficial flow of world trade. Both characterizations share the underlying assumption that political expediency in trading matters is relegated to the background and that economic efficiency is hauled to front stage.

The USSR has left no doubt in recent months that it has been preparing its memorandum and request for full accession to the GATT on the basis of its claim to eventual market-type reforms. Prior to the December 1989 US–USSR "working summit" in Malta, Soviet policy makers stressed that the instruments accompanying the official accession request to the GATT would be transmitted toward the end of 1990 or soon thereafter. This target date was maintained in spite of the fact that the wholesale price reform, originally slated for introduction in 1991, had already been deferred indefinitely. The submission would reportedly have been based on arguments that invoke the decentralization and pricing features of the intended *perestrojka*. Whether this move is still being contemplated now that the Soviet Union has been invited to become an observer after the conclusion of the Uruguay Round, I do not know. Given this and the fact that similarly based accession applications from Bulgaria and China are pending and also Vietnam is seriously contemplating such a request, it is vital to recognize that all three have enunciated far-reaching reforms, some (especially China) have been engaged in reform for a decade or more, at least two (China and the Soviet Union) are politically committed to pursuing their enunciated societal reforms, and the potential applicant for better or worse is *the* key CMEA player and thus affects the role of CMEA Contracting Parties.

It requires, of course, an act of faith to take political commitment to reform as a firm assurance that, barring untoward developments, such societal mutation will be assiduously pursued. But it would be equally unkind to argue that accession proceedings could be entertained only if anchored to some variant of the orthodoxy on import commitments maintained *vis-à-vis* Poland and Rumania. Neither solution will help to ensure greater universalism without seriously compromising on already shaky principles or full reciprocity in conformity with the fundamental GATT rule.

A more constructive contribution could be formulated by recognizing two facts. First, special arrangements, such as for Poland and Rumania, have a certain advantage in their simplicity. By setting up trading arrangements that are not wholly satisfactory, however, they fall well short of the ideal or even the desirable if the ITS is to buttress market-oriented reform. There is value, though, in bringing the CPEs into the GATT if only to provide a forum for the discussion of common trading problems. In pursuing this, it is necessary to understand that membership does not solve these problems (Diebold 1969, 138). Instead, if both sides are willing to act in good faith, membership opens up opportunities to work effectively toward devising solutions to the problems. Safeguards against serious risk should not be too hard to formulate.

Secondly, one cannot possibly ignore the potential for ongoing or contemplated domestic economic reforms in the applicant and would-be applicant. This offers opportunities for shepherding more CPEs into the GATT on a conditional basis by formulating a transition phase that seeks to enhance the realization of these intentions. This transition phase should in any case be experimental and be modified as progress is recorded or setbacks are incurred. Similar proceedings could be entertained for CMEA Contracting Parties (including Czechoslovakia and Poland) that have embarked on or are contemplating far-reaching economic reforms and are prepared to regularize their status in the GATT. It would similarly be instructive to widen this horizon to the remaining CMEA Contracting Parties (Cuba, Hungary, and Rumania) and to elaborate a systemic solution that sets the framework within which future accessions of CPEs (Albania, GDR, Mongolia, and North Korea) can be negotiated.

This suggestion begs two questions. One is a political one: the CPEs would be brought into the GATT on a discriminatory basis on at least two counts. First, the accession agreement would by necessity hold the CPE applicant to a certain time frame for introducing contemplated economic reforms. It might thus be perceived as meddling in the internal affairs of CPEs. The agreement could be considered discriminatory also because other countries with an economic system in flux have been admitted into the GATT without being held to a strict liberalization schedule. The second question, of course, concerns the shape of commitments, concessions, time frames, safeguards, and enforcement guidelines of such a transition mechanism. If the basic decision on whether nondiscrimination and reciprocity can be adhered to hinges on prices and price flexibility, could one not admit that the real world has been confronted more and more with managed prices? The simile of managed trade for CPEs would presumably have to be found in the growing autonomy of firms in reforming CPEs and their entitlement to "manage" their own profits.

There are four pillars of a transition phase that can be distinguished. First, the CPE would commit itself to pursuing maximum scope for economic decentralization and to setting clearly delineated functions for central planning. Secondly, the transition program must spell out the necessary instruments to ensure steady progress toward nearly full financial and managerial autonomy of firms. Thirdly, to the extent feasible, governments need to make explicit those of their preferences that affect the setting of domestic retail prices relative to trade prices, through *ad valorem* subsidies and taxes within an agreed time frame. Finally, clear guidelines need to be set on how trading companies are expected to assist with maintaining some desirable degree of domestic price stability through the intertemporal management of profits, yet play a critical role in ensuring a causal relationship between domestic and trade prices, including those involving CMEA relations. The link between domestic and trade prices would therefore emerge only "on average," but on the basis of commercial decision making by the trading companies. Of course, tariffs would play an integral part in these modified economies and could be made the subject of MFN negotiations.

Special regimes would need to be worked out to accommodate the CMEA, particularly if no uniform code for CPEs can be worked out. The CMEA's preferential treatment needs to be recognized without, however, endorsing all its special implicit preferences (Hewett 1978, 33–4). Provided the USSR as a GATT member were to remain in the vanguard of managerial and organizational innovation in the CMEA, there would not be any major hurdle to be taken, as in time all CMEA members would have to streamline their domestic economic mechanisms accordingly. Certainly, the geographic administration of trade in the planning process needs to be curbed, but it cannot be suppressed altogether.

These commitments are not likely to yield an ironclad guarantee, in the sense of being necessary and sufficient conditions, that the peculiar problems of CPEs in the GATT will henceforth fully vanish. It would be a mistake, however, to regard these and other coveted changes as heralding the erosion or abandonment of the MFT of the CPE or the complete suppression of the role of planning in the CMEA regime for that matter. True, the MFT's character has been shifting toward the macroeconomic steering of foreign trade and payments by indirect instruments and control over trade and foreign-exchange strategies. Many observers posit the abolition of the MFT and central planning as preconditions for seriously considering association of the CPEs in the GATT. This is a fundamental misconception that appears to stem from treating the MFT solely as a means as well as from ingrained reluctance to accept any rules that smack of socialist state intervention. But there is certainly room for greater clarity on realistic reform intentions and how "gradualism" may be wedded to debating Soviet accession to the GATT (Patterson 1986, 203).

To the extent that CPEs still plan trade indicators for the next several years, reciprocity might initially be enhanced by the CPEs committing themselves to regional import targets. These would then be binding, provided the assumptions and expectations upon which the targets were constructed indeed materialize. Several commentators (Dirksen 1987, 230; Kostecki 1979a, 140–1) appear to favor such a tie-in. I do not.

Even if one could persuade the CPEs to include import commitments in their transition phase, the prime justification for reciprocity should be ensuring a tight link between domestic and trade prices according to accepted principles. Import commitments are inconsistent with the spirit of major economic and trade reforms presently under way, if only because of the administrative controls that they require; there is furthermore an exceedingly weak precedent for using them; and because they enshrine rigidities and market foreclosures, they are *in se* incompatible with ongoing reforms.

6 The CPEs and remaking the IMS

I have dwelt more on the reform of the ITS as it pertains to eventual CPE participation than I do here for the IMS and in the next section for the IFS for three reasons. One is that the participation of CPEs in the IMS, as argued in chapter 3, is not primarily a technical matter but one rooted in political controversy over policy autonomy. Also, unlike the ITS and in spite of the frequency with which one hears that the BWS has disintegrated and efforts to rebuild it have foundered (Black 1985; Williamson 1983b), the Fund has demonstrated its ability to evolve and provide critical components of global economic management. Furthermore, the problems of the IMS are in essence due to bewildering macroeconomic policies in key participants in the world economy. These need to be addressed through better domestic management by national authorities rather than through an improvement of the international organization or monetary regime.

Policy discordances do, however, suggest that there might be something to be gained from greater coordination, at least among the key members of the IMS (Bourguinat 1988; Cooper 1985). This could be facilitated through proper Fund support. But there is also room for strengthening the Fund's role at the center of the IMS, if only to ensure that national decision makers increasingly anticipate the impact of their policies on other members and the system as a whole with a view to fashioning policy alternatives that maintain a certain balance of interests. Apart from enhancing policy coordination, the IMS could benefit from improvements that would meet the worlds's need for a universal IMS in which all interested countries participate with the same rights and obligations. Even spokesmen for CPEs (Fekete 1972, 1981; Smyslov 1988) deem this to be the most efficient, because the postwar experience has demonstrated that a genuine IMS helps to maintain the pace of economic development. The earliest possible solution of the gravest problems of our times that are within the compass of the IMS (including combatting inflation, averting recession, and alleviating unemployment) is in the interest of the international community and may help to innovate solutions to other global scourges, such as pollution, starvation, and poverty. Some of these issues can be better addressed through a revamped IMS.

The IMS has obviously been passing through a very difficult period since the collapse of the fixed exchange-rate system in the early 1970s (Bird 1983). Though it has proved to be resilient in spite of serious delays in renovation, the main actors in the world economy cannot forever postpone a restructuring of the key foundations of the postwar economic order without hampering the smooth functioning of global economic interdependence. It would be unfortunate if such a restructuring were to materialize without taking fully into account the concerns of all participants in the world economy, including the relative weight of the CPEs in the world. It is therefore useful to explore the shared interests in fostering greater east–west monetary cooperation, the possibility of there being some collusion among countries in designing a more satisfactory IMS, and the key characteristics of how best to institutionalize financial cooperation.

The overall character of interdependence

In spite of the defects and drawbacks that the CPEs normally attribute to the BWS, they generally acknowledge that the system contributed greatly to the dynamism and stability of economic development and trade in the postwar period, especially of the DMEs. They are therefore actively interested in a reform of the IMS, even if, in the end, they were to decide not to join. A properly streamlined, smoothly functioning system, even if applicable only to DMEs, is believed to inhibit trade wars and protectionism, to enhance the stability of international financial relations, and indeed to benefit the environment of international relations. But these virtues of the BWS have been seriously impaired by developments since the late 1960s, including the *ad hoc* ways in which issues have been addressed.

Long-term institutional reform is desirable. Before an attempt can be made to tackle the issues several preliminaries need to be factored into the equation, however. First, greater awareness of the need to look at a broad array of domestic policies is required. Secondly, it needs to be recognized that the issues involved are politically sensitive and cannot just be dealt with as in any other international conference. Finally, the world today is characterized by an exceptionally dense interconnectedness. But that is not yet fully reflected in the behavior of all but a handful of politically and economically important countries. This has made limited-membership economic summits and organs almost inevitable in a period in which these selected countries were experiencing some combination of inflation, slow growth, and high unemployment.

Common interest in a revamped BWS can emerge only if such a new system reflects the shared economic and monetary goals and prerogatives of countries with different economic and political systems. Issues such as influence over policy making, access to liquidity and Fund resources, a reshaped policy on surveillance and stabilization measures administered by the Fund, greater control over exchange-rate movements, dampening exchange-rate volatility, and coordinating monetary and other macroeconomic policies of the key actors in the BWS are all essential ingredients of the monetary debate. As the frustrating negotiations in the 1970s on the establishment of the NIEO have so clearly demonstrated, some of the issues enumerated here cannot be satisfactorily resolved within the existing institutions. A more harmonious, less rancorous north–south relationship may then require a substantial overhaul of the BWS or the creation *ab ovo* of a new IMS.

Though many of the above-mentioned issues also divide east and west, a *rapprochement* on technical grounds would be easier to conceptualize, if not necessarily to implement, on the strength of reciprocal advantages. The shared economic interests consist of the CPEs' need for technology, managerial skills, and capital resources from abroad, and the repeated calls by MEs that CPEs participate more actively in the global division of labor and attendant responsibilities for equity in development, buoyancy of economic expansion, sustainability of the development process, and stability of the global economy. Though an east–west *rapprochement* based on reciprocity of interests and on respect for the fundamental characteristics of each other's system appears feasible, it does not imply that east and west will eventually be able to join forces in the BWS as it exists today or in any of the tabled reforms (Meier 1982). This derives from the key ingredients of any feasible monetary reform.

Elements in need of improvement

Many items could be checked off under the reform label. In what follows, I focus on monetary control at the global level, symmetry of adjustment, surveillance, and liquidity. Given the inexorable integration of financial markets during the last two decades or so, the IMS has been characterized by a constrained official multilateral lender of last resort and a large number of commercial banks and related financial institutions engaged in lending for all kinds of purposes without them having developed a coherent philosophy on the public-good aspects of the private cost–benefit analysis. Indeed private commercial banks would probably disclaim, and rightly so (Helleiner 1983, 47ff.), responsibility for ensuring that the public good remains accessible, even though their own private benefits depend on it.

The ideal solution would be to have a global central bank (Cooper 1984). Though that may be utopian at this juncture, there is certainly room for improving the IMF in such a way that it could better meet the world's needs with respect to the issuance and management of global reserves, possibly through an improved SDR; regulating the practices of both official and commercial financial institutions with a view to controlling money supply and reserve creation at the global level; promoting the harmonization of macroeconomic policies, at least of the most important actors in the world economy; providing balance-of-payments financing, though it might need to take on more and more the character of countercyclical or structural adjustment financing (McCleary 1989); and having one organization to perform the multiple tasks of acting as the IMS's lender of last resort. These are all very complex topics to be studied and reviewed in the light of recent developments in the global economy. Also the substantial veering away from collective action in favor of greater freedom for national policy flexibility must be taken into account.

Such a decisive movement in favor of internationalization would not only help to redress the setbacks sustained in the past two decades. It would contribute to updating the IMS to the present environment, in which money markets are far more internationalized than other markets or actors, whether official or private. As a result, the IMS could usefully explore forms of management that correspond to the conditions prevailing for what needs to be managed. Though exchange rates are by their very nature a shared policy instrument that cannot be effectively managed by a single country, this imposes more complex problems of coordination in a system with flexible exchange rates. Without some harmonization and understanding of the proper exchange rate to be sought, countries may intervene in currency markets at cross-purposes.

For reasons advanced in the next section, the IMS in its prevailing incarnation or its reformed mode should not itself be responsible for formulating, managing, and modifying the global resource-transfer mechanism. This issue belongs properly in the IFS and the role of the World Bank therein. However, the IMS has a vital function to play in seeing to it that the IFS can function smoothly. For example, without proper authority to control reserve creation and regulate financial institutions, the IMS can ensure neither that adequate resources will be available for the IFS nor that these resources will be distributed in the most effective – efficient as well as equitable – way possible, given overall preferences. This recalls, of course, the old conflict between the center of the IMS acting as a strict disciplinarian and a bulwark against inflation, and it being entrusted with tasks related to maintaining growth and full employment in the global economy. The Fund needs to expand its appreciation of the economic, institutional, political, and social constraints under which policy is pursued in individual countries (Bird 1983).

This raises the lid of Pandora's box regarding collective management. It is certainly wishful thinking to proceed on the assumption that the IMS can be rolled back to the 1950s. There has in the meantime been too much politicization of the monetary issues and too great a diffusion of economic power to make this a feasible proposition. Nonetheless, the IMS would undoubtedly profit from a strengthening of collective management of the Fund or successor institution, rather than proceeding with solutions that result from *ad hoc* crisis management.

A reconstitution of collective management immediately calls to mind the role of surveillance of the IMS, which under the present circumstances can no longer be confined solely to exchange rate or balance-of-payments regulations; as recently documented by Edmund Dell (1987, 11ff.), some even claim that it is futile to strive for collective management at all. I disagree with this position. Collective management needs to be increasingly directed at the coordination of macroeconomic policies. Because this cannot be done without the cooperation of the large DMEs, it might now be proper to innovate in the Fund an organ with limited membership of national policy makers who organize themselves within the general framework of the IMS. Though biased in composition, in terms of equal or weighted country representation, only in this way could one reasonably hope to attain greater symmetry between debtors and creditors as well as between reserve-currency countries and other, and to bring about this degree of harmony without protracted tug-of-war bouts among an unwieldy universal membership. Furthermore, only through such a confined membership would the IMS be able to avoid major conflicts in macroeconomic policy stances of its principal participants and to reinforce one another's stance with a view to contributing positively to a global economic system that is open, orderly, and conducive to noninflationary growth. Finally, only through this medium would it be thinkable to move away from national currencies as basic reserves to a collective one such as the SDR or any other asset that with time gains the wide confidence of users (see Padoa-Schioppa 1988).

Through its participation in the limited membership body, the IMS could discharge its obligations as the "keeper of the global conscience" (Camps 1981, 232). One might think that it would also further raise the already existing degree of asymmetry in the surveillance mechanism. This may well be so at first glance. It certainly deserves to be recognized that key DMEs, which would form the core of the limited-membership body, have proved to be peculiarly sensitive to the criticism that a review procedure by the Fund or another IEO could bring to bear. This derives in part from the fact that the main findings of such bodies inevitably leak and markets can be counted on to bring the desired pressures to bear; hence the restraint on pursuing policy autonomy at any cost.

The issuance of the SDR touches, of course, upon the ever-present topic of liquidity and its adequacy in the IMS. The guideline should be two-pronged: an efficient IMS needs enough liquidity but not too much and reserves are distributed so as to facilitate noninflationary growth and orderly trade expansion. Above all, the IMS needs a lender of last resort. More can be done to strengthen the capacity of the organization entrusted with safeguarding the IMS in all three respects. But for many years to come, the role of steerer, manager, and underwriter of the system will continue to be one that is shared between the Fund and governments of key members. This would not be a forbidding impediment if a revitalized Fund could participate fully in a limited-membership council for actions to be recommended to the membership at large. The present system of quotas, although ensuring broad political support for proposed measures, also embodies the danger that it is easier to block meaningful action, perhaps for frivolous reasons.

The USSR under Gorbachev and the BWS

In this synopsis of the range of desirable reforms that have been debated at length in international fora and in the professional literature of the past twenty years, I have made little reference to what the Soviet position might be as regards such a proposed change. My reason for this was that, as noted, there is currently great ambiguity on the preconditions that the USSR might impose to accede to the IMS or IFS.

Whereas there has as yet not been any authoritative statement on behalf of the Soviet Administration under Gorbachev and indeed his top advisers are far from unanimous on what needs to be done (Corbi 1988; Pissulla 1988), there is sufficient evidence to extract a skeleton position from the literature (Šenaev 1988; Smyslov 1988) and informal interviews on the subject at hand that I have had the privilege to conduct with well-placed Soviet officials. On several occasions during the last two years, authoritative Soviet decision makers, including Ivan D. Ivanov, have categorically denied that the Soviet Union has any interest in joining the BWS because of three perceived shortcomings: (1) too flexible exchange rates, (2) absence of a reserve currency as anchor, and (3) US veto power.

Though not even a quasi-official decision has been made to explore membership in the BWS, there is no doubt that such a move could eventually be entertained. Whether it will be made conditional upon the enactment of a number of advocated changes in the BWS or real modifications emerging mainly from within the Fund, perhaps as outlined in the preceding section, is as yet unclear. My own sense is that the rebuff of the overture to the GATT in August 1986 has acted as a powerful psychological disincentive to exploring other avenues to closer involvement in the international economy without there being a prior diplomatic welcoming signal, even if only conditionally.

If the Soviet Union were to receive such a green light, however dim, what could be its position? Clearly, the USSR is too special an actor in the global economy and the family of nations to seek Fund membership simply to obtain new credits. At least in the view of some Soviet observers, the USSR would strengthen the IMS on the basis of its currency and gold reserves and its desire to become a net lender in the IMS. For that to materialize, the USSR government should obtain some assurances that meaningful restructuring of the BWS will be pursued in the near future. None of the Soviet indicative demands, if handled flexibly, would appear to be onerous (see Solomon 1988).

The USSR does not support the Fund's role mainly as policeman for debt servicing and as a consulting organ of the Group of Seven. Instead, it advocates that the Fund should be mainly entrusted with the management of the IMS and the sharp curtailment of exchange-rate variations in line with its original purposes. For that to be feasible, the USSR deems it necessary that the international community pursue a radical currency reform and restructure the Fund. Both would have to be based on three fundamental principles. First, there is a need to adopt a truly international reserve currency, not one of the national currencies or a straightforward combination thereof. The argument is essentially that as an instrument of monetary policy of the emitting country, a national currency cannot be a suitable instrument to manage the IMS. This, of course, hinges on what precisely is meant by an international currency. There is, unfortunately, no clarity on this issue. But at least one weighty commentator has stressed that the Soviet Union approaches the issue with an open mind and considers the SDR an appropriate, if embryonic, form of such an international currency.

Secondly, one major primary task of the Fund would be to stabilize exchange rates by reducing short-term fluctuations and adopting rules and regulations regarding the dynamic adaptation of exchange rates. How this is to be accomplished is a different matter, of course. Better-informed Soviet commentators recognize that a return to a quasi-fixed exchange-rate regime is meaningless without there being clear understanding on the harmonization of macroeconomic policies. Whether it would be prepared to join the Group of Seven and the latter would be willing to entertain such an enlargement are issues that can be speculated on but for which there is as yet not even a modicum of political consensus. But steady progress with *perestrojka* and more responsible international behavior on the part of the USSR may well entail such a shift.

Finally, it is argued that the decision-making procedures in the Fund, as in other IEOs with weighted majority voting, should be rendered "more democratic." But there is no longer any serious advocacy of the "one country, one vote" rule made, for example, in the Nairobi declaration (Kodinov 1988, 47). There are several ways in which the veto power of the United States could be eroded without invoking a political clash. A redistribution of Fund quotas or new SDR allocations in other ways than the inherited quota proportions and the upgrading of the quotas for other countries, including Japan and some Arab countries, offer face-saving possibilities. There might even be room to divorce quotas from weights in voting, particularly if a limited-membership executive body of national political leaders were to become influential in the Fund.

7 The CPEs and remaking the IFS

Thus far, I have treated the monetary and financial systems along uniform lines. Below I amplify on why I have proceeded in this way and then discuss desirable reforms in the IFS, the position of the CPEs in the IFS, and whether the CPEs would fit into a reconceived IFS.

Relationship between the monetary and financial spheres

For most of this volume I have discussed the twin pillars of the IMS in one breath mainly for three reasons. As related in chapter 1, the separate missions of the Bank and the Fund were not quite clear at the BWS's outset (Ascher 1983). A number of countries, including most notably the Soviet Union and future CPEs involved in the deliberations, were primarily looking for reconversion, relief, reconstruction, and rehabilitation assistance rather than the balance-of-payments support that was to guide the Fund's activities. The Bank's mission was eventually to assist in the reconstruction of war-damaged Europe and aid for development through the rechanneling of private finance.

Secondly, the clearly drawn lines of division between the Bank and the

Fund have become blurred over the years (Feinberg 1988). The Fund has increasingly extended balance-of-payments support to DEs in need of structural finance and hence adjustment policies that could not be addressed through the fairly simple demand-management paradigm (David 1985) that became the hallmark of Fund policies from the late 1950s to the late 1970s. The Bank in turn has increasingly moved away from project financing in favor of explicit structural-adjustment lending. Both have emerged in recognition of the fact that one cannot adjust if in the process the ability to grow is undermined (Helleiner 1983, 46).

Finally, the IFS has gradually become a regime that forms an integral part of the transfer to DEs of financial resources for development purposes. These issues have not really been of focal concern to the CPEs. But they have been gradually emerging with the joining of China and several Eastern European CPEs that can benefit from low-cost financing under the auspices of the World Bank.

In this connection, the brief description of the IFS given in chapter 3 needs to be slightly amended, especially to take into account the drifting away from project financing to the support of structural-adjustment programs. With it, a particular development philosophy has been crystallizing around the Bank's propagation of lending in DEs (Sengupta 1987). Instead of supplementing private-project finance as its main *raison d'être*, the Bank has come to view its mission more and more as stimulating structural change in DEs through loans, perhaps on concessional terms, in the hope of alleviating eventually the severity of external constraints on sustainable development. Not only have these principles been modified. More important have been the shifts in the norms, which have become increasingly motivated by a pronounced advocacy of private-enterprise, market-type economic activity. This has affected in particular the obligations of loan recipients. These have become heavily tilted in favor of dismantling institutions, policy instruments, macroeconomic policies, and behavioral guidelines that appear to hinder entrepreneurial activity, whether of domestic or foreign origin. These shifts in the norms have also affected the rules and the way in which decision-making mechanisms in the Bank function.

Desirable reforms in the IFS

Although the relationship between the Bank and the Fund has become blurred over the years, I can see much value in keeping the two largely apart if only because they serve separate tasks. As a cautious banker and lender of last resort, the Fund has a mission that is distinguishable from the imaginative expansionism that should motivate the Bank. That is to say, the Fund should continue to serve primarily as the overseer of the monetary system, provide short-term balance-of-payments financing, and become effective lender of last resort. The Bank in turn should be geared toward providing and facilitating long-term resource transfers to DEs and its capacity to do so needs to be expanded. But there are obvious areas of overlapping or shared responsibilities (Feinberg 1988, 548ff.). These include, for example, the structure and functioning of financial institutions, the adequacy of money and capital markets, the actual and potential capacity of countries to generate domestic savings, the financial exploration of development programs in the context of the country's current external financial and external debt positions, more general foreign-debt problems, and related matters.

Unlike the ITS or IMS, reform of the IFS has a dominant institutional character for it is primarily propelled by private actors and institutions. Officially, the reform agenda should be concerned with the relationship between the IFS and IMS, the surveillance of international financial activities and exchanges, providing institutional means and arrangements to promote financial cooperation at an operational level, and a common understanding on the question of a pragmatic division of labor (Sakbani 1985, 189ff.).

Given the sorry state of the development process, particularly in the debt-ridden DEs and much of sub-Saharan Africa, I see no need to detail a rationale for the propositions that considerable international resource transfers are required in the years ahead and that, for them to emerge, radical new approaches are called for. The issues range from management of the resource-transfer system, given the unequal access to financial markets; to responsibility of the global system as such for equitable and sustainable growth throughout the world, and thus the need to heed differential requirements for external finance; and sectoral management of resource needs, for example, to raise food and energy output. These and many related features of the IFS are well known (Camps 1981, 255ff.) and have been dealt with at great length by scholars more versed in such matters than I am.

The resource-transfer mechanism is not wholly a matter about which there exists disagreement along north–south lines or about the "public good" an adequate IFS should provide in this respect in conjunction with the IMS (Camps 1981, 202–3). There are different views about *how* the necessary functions should be performed. These fall essentially into three categories: (1) the amounts, terms, and productivity of ODA; (2) the criteria for making choices about the countries and activities to be given priority in resource allocation; and (3) coordination among today's varied bi- and multilateral assistance programs. The prevailing divergent views owe much to political issues such as questions regarding how much autonomy is to be permitted, who decides, who manages, who pays, and who benefits. But there is also genuine intellectual disagreement about how economies really work in today's highly interdependent world, as pointed out in section 2.

The increased capacity of the Bank to channel development funds to DEs would accrue largely from multilateralizing ODA to ensure that more of the available resources for development go to countries that need them most. Furthermore, multilateralizing concessional assistance and consolidating some of the related multilateral funds and programs would reduce the burden of DEs having to comply with a myriad of policies propagated by different agencies.

Regaining control over the global management of the IFS is perhaps most critical. The Bank and the Fund have become increasingly marginalized into policemen and the Fund in addition as lender of last resort, oftentimes giving rise to the bailing out of private commercial banks although minimizing the credit available on low conditionality terms for the poorest DEs (Helleiner 1983, 153). That is not to deny that commercial sources of finance, such as in Euromarkets, have not been important in lending for development purposes (Klausová 1985a, 1985b). But private banks seek profits and thus have an incentive to lend when prospects look favorable and to pull out when they look bad (Bird 1983, 13). The concern of private bankers pure and simple is to generate revenues that yield profit in the interest of protecting stockholders and depositors. In other words, their activities exacerbate cyclicality. This entails economic inefficiencies and inequities from the point of view of desirable global economic performance. A greater degree of central management should therefore be restored under the auspices of the reformed IMS.

Socially responsible behavior in the IMS and IFS needs to be complemented elsewhere in the system. The ability of the IFS to mobilize global excess savings that would otherwise not be channeled from the primary savers to the potential user of funds for lack of a proper transmission mechanism and to offer the financial services needed in an interdependent global economy is in large measure conditioned by the existence of a "safe framework based on the respect of contracts of individual participants as well as the safety of the entire system" (Sakbani 1985, 190). Likewise, too much effort appears to have been channeled into scattered institutions. Certainly, not every issue of development finance could or should be entrusted to one organization, such as the World Bank. Nevertheless, a solid argument against further proliferation of resource-transfer institutions at the global level can be justified. This is not to deny that several of the regional development banks and special funds (such as for food) have been valuable in coping with special problems. But there is a need for clearer coordination and management at the global level to provide for steady and reliable transfer of resources, thus moving away from today's rather discretionary system of disbursements.

The attitude of the CPEs on the IFS

Perhaps the most important consideration has been the lingering ambivalence in the attitude of CPEs toward development finance and especially extending development assistance on concessionary terms from the north to the south (Brabant 1989d). For the CPEs this has always meant from west to south on the ground that the principal blame for development problems of the DEs should be laid at the doorstep of the colonial and postcolonial policies of key powers of the nineteenth and twentieth centuries, including the commercial and other institutions that they "protected." Because the CPEs never had colonies and claim to have engaged in mutually beneficial trade relations from their inception, they cannot possibly be held responsible for the so-called plunder of resources that has made it so very difficult for the DEs to make the transition to sustainable growth at a steady pace. They argue also that, through their trade policies based on mutual advantage, the DEs can avoid getting entangled in the exploitive postcolonial policies embraced by transnationals, big actors in the global economy, and the trade and financial regimes kept in place by key DMEs.

That is not to say that the CPEs have shunned all responsibility for according development assistance. But in their choice they have been guided by a number of principles, some of which are rather difficult to reconcile with the habitual development policies of bi- and multilateral institutions dominated by key DMEs. For one thing, the CPEs have always advocated that development should be anchored to a strong state sector with assistance being channeled on a priority basis to public enterprises. In this respect, they were translating their own development precepts, particularly on forced industrialization in breadth, to the situation of the DEs. Furthermore, the CPEs have traditionally shunned many multilateral development-assistance agencies on the ground that they are simply masks for the neocolonial policies that big contributors are bent on prolonging.

By far the major consideration on development assistance has been that it is a form of foreign economic relations and can thus be utilized to influence donor countries. Development assistance became very much more a battleground for gaining political and strategic ascendency in recipient countries than an emanation of a shared concern for steady growth and stability in the world economy. As such, the CPEs have traditionally concentrated their ODA efforts in a few countries, especially developing CPEs that are members of the CMEA and the more state-oriented among the nonaligned. Furthermore, this aid flow has exhibited a pronounced bias for industrialization and primary-materials sectors. Moreover, the amounts transferred in real terms have not been spectacular by any count, especially when the special relationship with the developing CPEs is considered separately from development assistance more generally. True enough, the CPEs have participated in some multilateral assistance efforts, and the CMEA itself has some programs running, but these have been marginal at best. Furthermore, much of the assistance provided is in tied form. That is to say, aid is transferred as earmarked goods and services. The nongrant portion is repatriated through exports from the donor country, oftentimes from the project thus financed. Yet it needs to be recognized that relative to economic capacity, the ODA inclusive of "peculiar forms" provided by CPEs has not at all been negligible or paltry by international comparison (see Brabant 1989d).

As far as the IFS is concerned, then, the CPEs have considered that to be largely an issue between west and south, with the latter being given moral and verbal support on a number of issues but not anywhere near everything the DEs have wanted to table for negotiations. That stance has not always washed well with the DEs. Particularly during the heyday of the debates about the NIEO in the first half of the 1970s, the DEs expressed their dismay at the comparatively minor access they were getting to markets of the CPEs, the rather skewed distribution of resources, the small value of assets made available for such development assistance, and the tied nature of assistance.

Reform and CPE participation in the IFS

With *perestrojka*, a marked shift in position on development issues appears to be slowly emerging. This is not just a tactical move connected with the Soviet Union's desire to be recognized as a weighty partner in international relations beyond what it can claim through the volume of its own trade and financial flows. This has become evident in the reexamination of the traditional relationship of the developing country CPEs in the CMEA (see chapter 2). It has also been the subject of protracted debates on the diplomatic, political, and commercial relations of the USSR with various DEs. Finally, it has slowly been generating a new position toward the Fund and development finance more generally.

According to a recent, if unofficial, clarification of the Soviet position made by Ivan D. Ivanov,[19] any Soviet participation in the Bank would be based on a careful examination of the balance of merits and drawbacks. Soviet Fund membership would be sought, if at all, as a prelude to accession to the World Bank. Among the latter's merits, he counted the potential advantages that Soviet exporters could derive from the ability to bid singly or in tripartite arrangements with DMEs and DEs on Bank-financed projects. Gathering new experience in markets that will be vital to the envisaged expansion of Soviet exports of manufactures in the years to come was deemed exceedingly important. In other words, by this route the Soviet economy could explore new export avenues and gain a firm position in world markets for manufactures (Hough 1986, 493). Another benefit Ivanov considered to consist in the human capital stock of the Bank, particularly the professionalism of its staff in evaluating the technical and economic merits of development projects. He also deemed the Bank staff to embody a unique repository of knowledge on the global investment climate, from which the USSR through its participation could learn about long-term financial markets.

As to the disadvantages, the Soviet Union would, of course, have to contribute to the Bank's budget, proceed through the gauntlet of the Fund before it could be admitted into the Bank, multilateralize some of its development assistance, and provide that in convertible currency. Ivanov saw no great obstacle in allocating part of the financial resources earmarked for development purposes through multilateral agencies. As an illustration he cited Soviet observership in the Asian Development Bank since April 1987 (Åslund 1988, 29) as an expression of the leadership's desire to learn about and apply more multilateral financial-development policies.

Where precisely the CPEs stand at this juncture on the debt crisis is not clear. Of course, if I am reading current commentary correctly, commercial banks continue to be blamed for short-term predatory practices that exacerbate the exploitation of DEs by transnational corporations. What could and should be done about this situation is a different matter, however. In a number of fora, the USSR has advocated debt forgiveness for the most disadvantaged DEs (something to which it has resorted on occasion and in which it would be prepared to join if key DMEs were willing to enact debt write-offs), a reduction in interest rates, extending the maturity of loans and other such measures that mostly DMEs could take to alleviate the external financial pressures that bear down on a number of DEs. I have the impression from a number of commentaries that the Soviet Union would be in favor of entrusting greater responsibilities for development finance to multilateral agencies, not just the World Bank and its affiliates or regional counterparts. These include UN specialized agencies as well as the Secretariat's role in technical cooperation for development.

It is clear that key Soviet reform participants subscribe to the notion that the needs of the low-income countries can be met only through large transfers on concessionary terms, including program lending (Osipov 1983). The needs of the more advanced DEs would appear to call for different responses that are rooted more in long-term development finance primarily on commercial terms. But there evidently remains ample room for clarifying current and prospective positions on the IFS, as there is without a doubt scope for making stances with respect to the IMS and ITS more transparent.

Conclusions

An international economic order by its very nature borders on both economics and politics, and it may well have a heavier touch of the latter than of the former. If so, before compressing the changes that I have advocated in chapter 5 to their bare essentials, I wish to emphasize that my observations are essentially those of an armchair economist, observer, commentator, and critic of the prevailing global order, not just its economic tangents. I see the role of such an individual partly in concluding, rather plaintively, as Phil Hanson (1988, 75) so pointedly observed, "that politicians should behave like rational people for a change." This is a rather unrealistic hope. But, in the case of global economic policies among groups of countries and widely diverging philosophical outlooks, there has been so much muddle, and so little evidence of careful thought, that even a realist might hope for some improvement.

As discussed in chapters 3 to 5, the various conflicts that erupt when CPEs seek to participate at all or more completely in IEOs can be grouped essentially under two headings: political factors and economic considerations; among the latter I include organizational, institutional, and related facets of steering an economy. At this juncture, the major stumbling block for CPEs would appear to lie primarily in the political domain. A further relaxation of tensions between east and west could measurably help to identify the variety of political obstacles to participation of CPEs individually and as an integrated category, and to what degree they might be relaxed through the formulation and implementation of remedial or corrective measures.

But there is also an entire array of technical economic issues that deserve to be clarified in their own right. At the very least, these issues will need to be tackled head-on once ideological beachheads between east and west are washed away and the political dust settles. The knotty divergences between MEs and CPEs range from organizational features to policy precepts. They include importantly a range of items that impinge upon micro- and macroeconomic decision making. Even if CPEs are willing and able to revise certain aspects of these features of their economic management and organization with a view to participating more fully in IEOs, some of the enumerated items will keep impinging on their ability to do so flexibly and fully in the international economic regimes in place. These differences, I feel, are bound to prevail regardless of the concessions and accommodations that may be crystallizing on the political front.

The technical problems that arise in ensuring full participation of the CPEs in the ITS would appear to be far more complex than the political ones. Among the key requirements of the ITS, in particular the issues that determine how countries can ensure reciprocity in relations between CPEs and ME Contracting Parties, stand out. To integrate the CPEs more fully into that framework, it is useful to distinguish among at least three groups of CPEs. Ensuring reciprocity by orthodox CPEs, as defined in chapter 2, is possible only if recommendations for negotiating the accession instruments recognize the procedures by which such economies arrive at their import decisions and some compensatory import commitments are made by the CPEs that roughly equal the export gains that can reasonably be anticipated from a reduction of the tariffs on their exports to most existing Contracting Parties. This could be estimated according to agreed criteria and built into the planning process. The procedure is admittedly likely to fall well short of the ideal. Yet considerable progress can pragmatically be attained with some political good will. Because of the tediousness of estimating reciprocal concessions and the time required for negotiations, it might simply be too costly to engage in this exercise, say, on an annual basis. But it would not appear to be out of the realm of the possible – and feasible and desirable – to ensure such equivalence over time, perhaps within the five-year planning compass.

The second group refers to countries that have moved away from strict orthodoxy but whose resources continue to be allocated with a great deal of nonmarket discretion. If the acceding CPE has introduced key aspects of administrative decentralization but most resources continue to be allocated overwhelmingly through central controls just the same, the accession negotiations could allot some recognition of decentralized decision making to the CPE in question. An elaborate quid pro quo on permanent safeguards and tariff concessions would probably have to be negotiated.

Finally, there are countries that can be considered reformed toward the market-type model, or can reasonably be expected to make steady progress with such reforms, which in time will allot a major role to decentralized economic decision making by agents whose actions will need to be coordinated through indirect policy instruments, economywide institutions, and coherent macroeconomic policies. Such a reforming CPE should become more closely associated with the ITS by recognizing each step forward and seeking a reinforcement of – certainly not a hindrance to – the process of market-oriented reform. Once the process is reasonably completed, the CPE in question would be enabled to participate in the ITS on a full and equal basis within the GATT statute or its successor regime. During the transition phase toward this coveted state, however, Contracting Parties may well be advised to foster the reform process without completely giving way on the "entry fees" before the accession negotiations can properly get under way. Such entry fees should be determined as part and parcel of the negotiation and monitoring processes. There is no magic formula for ensuring full and equivalent accession. But there is plenty of room for imaginative suggestions and constructive deliberations by all sides involved.

Strong evidence has been emerging that the CPEs, most notably the USSR, are becoming more and more interested in reassessing their eventual or actual participation in the IMS and IFS. To expedite eventual accession, the USSR has already introduced a number of concessions. Key Soviet government and party advisers stress that there is room for further flexibility as regards the principles of the IFS and IMS themselves and how and when they could best be implemented. The economic obstacles to fuller participation in the BWS would appear to have been significantly reduced. A transition mechanism that would foster steady progress toward ruble convertibility as the outcome of economic and trade reforms currently under way would appear to be entirely negotiable at this stage. Given the contemplated CMEA reforms, especially as concerns the mechanism of integration and the future role of the TR and the TR regime more generally, it might now be possible for the Fund to acknowledge the existence of the TR regime and that it might be worthwhile to link it with the IMS through some mechanism that would expedite movement toward TR convertibility. Such a regime would not completely negate the valuable technical advantages of the TR (Brabant 1987a, 299–300). At the same time, it would slowly bring the members of the TR regime into the mainstream of international monetary relations (Kodinov 1988, 44).

In bringing the CPEs more fully under the discipline of the Articles of Agreement of the Fund and the Bank, the most pivotal obstacles to association at this stage would seem to revolve more around politics than technical economic details. On the one hand, there are powerful forces among DMEs bent on keeping the USSR out. The extraordinary changes in the east–west economic and political environment that have been crystallizing these past few months may soon erode this uncooperative attitude too. Certainly, the Bank and Fund bureaucracy and management are looking with trepidation toward Soviet accession, if only because the entrance of Soviet staff might disturb the perceived equilibrium in professional staffing policies and understanding reached there. On the other hand, the Soviet government is still smarting psychologically from the rather callous treatment it received when it requested some form of association with the new MTN round in 1986. The recent commitment to belatedly honor this request, after the conclusion of that round in 1990, may well soon erase this psychological obstacle too. The real heart of the matter, to my mind, is the question whether the USSR as a Fund member would seek to infringe upon the critical role and policy precepts of the United States. Especially important, at least in the eyes of the current membership and key high-level personnel of the organizations, is the degree to which some CPEs may potentially be bent on exploiting the Fund or Bank's forum for politicization. This could place a considerable constraint on the operational abilities of these institutions, thereby inhibiting them from discharging their perceived duties as in the past. It could also alter and interfere with business as usual in these organizations.

Certainly, there is always the possibility that the USSR could opt for an obstructionist position. Postwar behavior in that respect has not been exemplary, at least until the "New Thinking" under Gorbachev. There is little doubt that the USSR would have taken an independent stance on international monetary policy as compared with that of the United States, the EC, the Group of Seven, or the Group of Twenty-four. But that is already the case by virtue of its absence. It would probably seek to muster support for its views among other CPEs and perhaps key DEs. But coalition building of this sort should not come as a surprise in the IMS and IFS in place. Soviet participation would definitely extend the range of alternative arguments. But cogent deliberation and exploration, although perhaps time consuming, may in time yield their own rewards. Given the many grave technical obstacles that hinder economic modernization in the USSR and complicate the process by which the country can hope to find its proper place in a more secure international economy, however, I fail to see the benefits that the USSR could derive in the foreseeable future from politicizing the BWS. This hunch could hopefully be confirmed by a more positive attitude toward Soviet participation on the part of weighty DMEs in the BWS and willingness in principle to negotiate an acceptable transition regime with safeguards. That in itself would bestow positive signals that might influence the question as to whether the USSR is bent on exploiting the BWS for its own narrow political interests.

There are, of course, also multiple technical problems in ensuring that

CPEs share fully in the burden and benefits of the IMS and IFS. Their scope should not be underestimated. However, most of these technical and economic tangles could have been resolved in the past. They were not, largely for lack of political will. The critical element that deserves to be tackled at this stage, especially if the Soviet Union were to apply for accession, revolves around currency convertibility. It would probably be inadvisable to bring the Soviet Union into the Fund under the exceptional statute of article XIV without specifying more concretely the key features of the, in principle temporary, transition mechanism toward the regular status of current-account convertibility specified in article VIII. At the very least, a fairly firm target date by which some prespecified form of currency convertibility should be in place needs to be agreed upon. It would be helpful if in addition the movement toward such convertibility could be monitored and smoothed. Once again, this is a proposal that does not seem to have been investigated in the degree of detail and comprehensiveness warranted by circumstances prevailing during most of the postwar period. This is particularly the case if political good will to work toward accommodation is translated into desired mutually beneficial arrangements. Imaginative and constructive approaches to the various tangents of the issue could only facilitate the process of east–west *rapprochement* on these scores.

In the years that I have observed the various stances assumed and postures taken by those inside as well as those outside the regimes, two developments have distressed me most. One derives from the apparent reluctance – or perhaps inability – of the IEOs in place to innovate and defend constructive proposals for negotiating how best to come to grips with the special features of CPEs in the established international economic regimes. The other set of issues revolves around the reluctance on the part of MEs to admit CPEs and the latter's refusal to accept any temporary arrangement on the ground that it might be tantamount to discriminatory treatment. Little attention appears to have been given to the fact that it might be a vehicle that enables these outsiders to accommodate gradually to the fundamental features of the regimes in place. There is, of course, a risk: the transitional regime could be perpetuated under force of circumstances not fully foreseen when the conditions were first hammered out. One can sympathize to some degree with this stance of the CPEs. But that calls for careful negotiation, monitoring, and adaptation rather than a simple trade-off.

I do not, however, find it helpful that the countries that have remained outside the regimes, especially the CPEs, do not even appear to have given thought as to how best they could come to grips with the differences between their own economic, organizational, and management systems and the features of regimes that were basically set up for comparatively mature MEs. Still less comprehensible is the fact that the CPEs bent on obtaining accession to the regimes in place refuse even to formulate in a coherent manner their own perceptions of how they could gradually assume full responsibilities as stipulated in the regimes in question.

These peculiar features of postwar international economic relations have lingered on, even though the signs that major changes are under way in key CPEs are unmistakable. The wait-and-see attitude on the part of western policy makers may be a constructive tactic, even at the present juncture. Being unprepared for the inevitable, such as a Soviet request for full accession to the discipline of the General Agreement, in my view, is clearly not. Such a request may well have been staved off for now. But the critical issues of bringing a country such as the Soviet Union under the discipline of the General Agreement are bound to resurface in the near future. The comprehensive evaluation of the advantages and drawbacks of such a move, therefore, still need to be addressed, preferably now. At the very least, technicians both from the potential candidate and within the organizations ought to look at the multiple, at times very complex, technical issues involved. It would be useful too if member countries could prepare their own national position, in both technical and political terms. But these matters could legitimately be deferred, at least openly, until an accession request materializes.

In other words, bringing CPEs fully or at all under the discipline of the international monetary, financial, and trading regimes in place, thus enabling them to participate in the formulation of feasible alternatives to the present international economic arrangements, calls for carefully exploring the advantages and drawbacks of providing for some deviation from the habitual accession arrangements typical in the case of MEs. Under some circumstances, this might legitimately be perceived as tantamount to discrimination and infringement upon the economic sovereignty of the applicant. These are certainly real concerns to be addressed and mitigated through proper diplomacy. A key issue would be the desire of the would-be applicant to submit itself to the discipline of the international regime according to criteria that it might find most productive and that can be reconciled with the standard prescriptions without hollowing out all meaning of the regimes.

To render these attitudes into a feasible negotiating strategy, it would be very constructive if the candidate could undergird a position that is more nuanced than the undifferentiated – in some cases quite naïve – stance of simply requesting forthwith unconditional accession. This, in my view, is a nonstarter. A constructive stance has to be built around equivalences and similarities – not exact matchups or identities, for they do not presently exist and are not likely to emerge in the foreseeable future – between the accession requirements negotiated for MEs and concessions that PECs may be able to agree upon without losing political face.

Of course, even after successfully completing their envisaged reforms the CPEs are likely to differ substantively from MEs. In that vein, it might be instructive not only to investigate how these countries could be brought under the existing international disciplines, but also to explore their willingness to look into the preconditions for working toward a RITO. For that reason, it would be a highly useful strategy to ascertain in the first instance to what degree the USSR would be prepared to join in the elaboration of principles, including those concerning entrance fees, that might make it accept accession to a new international order, for that would mitigate the need to negotiate "exceptional" arrangements.

Seen in that perspective, the Soviet overture of mid-1986 should have been seized upon as a unique opportunity to provide well-balanced, if perhaps tentative, answers to the desirability of working toward a RITO as viewed by governments of MEs as well as CPEs. At the very least, had the GATT been a more institutionalized framework, such as the envisaged ITO, it could have fostered a useful exchange of information, identified problems, suggested solutions, and explored feasible policy options. The latter observation pertains in particular to the "market-access issue." This presents complex, if perhaps not insurmountable, problems not only for an association of the USSR with the GATT, but also for China (Herzstein 1986, 374) and other CPEs – and indeed many MEs. If especially the larger of the CPEs and DEs are to play a major, constructive role in world trade, they should have an interest in helping to shape the rules under which other nations will expect them to operate. In other words, the chances for realistically reconceiving an ITO could have become a lot clearer than they have been over the past decades.

Whether it would be advisable to work toward international economic reform with the full participation of the CPEs or whether one should first try to fuse the interests of the CPEs with the existing institutions is a matter that depends very much on the prevailing degree of consensus on what is to be accomplished through international economic regimes. If they are to be more than a technical device to galvanize the interests of sovereign countries organized on the basis of compatible economic principles, it would seem inappropriate to strive for universality and to include countries that fit properly only on the margin or not at all into the basic premises of the regime. If policy makers feel, however, that international organization, in economic affairs as elsewhere, is a goal worth pursuing to ensure prosperity, reliability, stability, and buoyant growth in an environment with minimal conflicts and with predictable rules and regulations, then it would be worthwhile to sit back and explore the more complete integration of groups of countries that behave according to different precepts than the mainstream roots of the organization.

The occasion of the launching of a new MTN round was perhaps not the most opportune moment for the full consideration of such a momentous request. But why could the two not have been tackled separately but simultaneously? That is to say, efforts to restore a greater degree of credibility to the GATT framework in the MTN round initiated at Punta del Este could have proceeded unhindered, while at the same time the ways and means of associating the "outsiders" with the multilateral trading world could have been explored more thoroughly in parallel negotiations. It is regrettable that the opportunity offered by the Soviet request was not utilized to ascertain the feasibility of crafting a meaningful relationship of the USSR with a multilateral trading world built on market-type instruments and institutions. Would the latter have remained supportive of effective interaction in a compatible international environment with the USSR as full constituent without encroaching upon the manifold benefits of expanding trade from the participants? It is to be hoped that the emerging partnership between the United States and the Soviet Union will soon provide an answer to that question.

Certainly, the imposition of some type of external discipline on a country such as the USSR might have been perceived as meddling in internal affairs. This would hence have been inconsistent with the USSR's aspiration to command its own destiny. However, exploration and negotiation could have been viewed, quite properly, as a joint effort to permit greatly expanded economic interaction among previously diverging sectors of the world economy. A commitment to search for mutually acceptable adaptations of institutions, building new trade patterns, and enhancing confidence would have gone a long way to allay fears of outside interference in Soviet affairs.

I hope to have sorted out in this volume some of the central issues in the debate that will eventually have to be waged. These deliberations would be most fruitful if these manifold issues, some of which are doubtlessly very complex, if perhaps not altogether intractable, could be studied in depth. Only in this way could the international community hope to come to grips in an intelligent, professional, and responsible manner with the peculiarities of "outsiders" to international regimes – not only the CPEs that have so far chosen to keep to themselves. Only by exploring the room for maneuver and political will to compromise without jettisoning key ingredients of the regimes in place will it be possible at all to come to a constructive dialogue that in time may yield greater international economic security. Attaining such greater reliability, predictability, and stability in international economic relations and ensuring in the process a greater degree of equity in economic development would be as desirable at this juncture as they were in the 1940s: they constitute one key platform for maintaining global peace and defusing areas of conflict.

Notes

Introduction

1 In what follows, I refer to it as the General Agreement, when I have the document and its underlying doctrine in mind. For other purposes, including institutional aspects of organized trade, I invoke the acronym GATT.

2 There was even speculation that, from a strictly legal point of view, all the USSR need do is ratify the Articles of Agreement it endorsed in 1946 (see chapter 3). Dell (1988) denies this, perhaps because changes have been introduced in the Articles of Agreement since 1946, which would have to be approved retroactively. Though the finer legal ramifications and intricacies of Dell's bland statement elude me, these amendments do not legally inhibit the USSR from ratifying the original Agreement since that procedure has never been closed off by a terminal date. Only ratification as a founder member was time-bound, ultimately to end-1946 (Assetto 1988, 63–4).

3 Because the GATT really does not have "members," acceding countries are referred to generally as contracting party, without capitals, and collectively as CONTRACTING PARTIES because that is the designation enshrined in the General Agreement; colloquially, "members" are referred to as Contracting Parties (Long 1985, 6) – a convention that I adopt here too.

4 It is, of course, perfectly possible that the rebuff provided an indication that the western community – or perhaps mainly the United States? – is not at all prepared to entertain any change in the ITS. I am not yet sufficiently cynical to subscribe to this reading of events, however.

5 These have found some reflection in Brabant (1987d, 1988a, 1989b, 1989c).

6 Such as the commitment sought under the Jackson–Vanik amendment to the 1974 Trade Act of the United States, which calls for liberalizing emigration policies as a partial trade-off for MFN treatment.

7 Economic statecraft usually also includes foreign aid as a pivotal ingredient of foreign economic policy. This has not so far been a crucial element in western policy toward the CPEs. But it might well emerge in the near future if efforts to redraw the division of Europe succeed, perhaps through a latter-day Marshall Plan that may be hammered out at the forthcoming international conference on providing economic assistance to Hungary and Poland.

8 I have kept the old designation of system in the acronyms because it is

enshrined in some IEOs, such as the Fund (Gold 1987, 15/3ff.) and the mnemonic value of IFS, IMS, and ITS exceeds that of IFR, IMR, and ITR. But the term is increasingly jettisoned by specialists (see Cooper 1975a).

9 For useful views on where China stands, see Cooper (1988b), Liser (1982), and Mu (1987).

10 Only CPEs are full members. In addition to the associate, there are nine cooperants and a number of observers (see Brabant 1989a, xvii–xix).

11 By virtue of Mongolia's tight economic relations with the USSR and its highly monopolized state-controlled trade sector, which interacted nearly exclusively with the USSR, Mongolia was *de facto* a CPE for the purposes of this study. Because the latter had voluntarily chosen not to seek closer interaction with countries outside the Soviet orbit, the core questions concerning the place and role of CPEs in the global economic environment revolved in the 1940s around the position of the Soviet Union.

12 Conventionally the designation World Bank refers to the IBRD plus the International Development Association (IDA). The World Bank Group includes in addition the International Finance Corporation (IFC), the Multilateral Investment Guarantee Agency, and the International Center for Settlement of Investment Disputes. For simplicity's sake, I shall use the designation World Bank or Bank.

1 Wartime planning for a new economic order

1 For a useful review of the major factors impinging upon the decision making of the time, see Gerschenkron (1947).

2 For details and quotations, see Dormael (1978), Kennan (1969), Mikesell (1951), and Proceedings (1948).

3 The seminal contribution to this part of international economic diplomacy is still Gardner (1969). Useful documents are in United Nations (1946).

4 Soon after the endorsement of the Agreements, White was publicly accused of having passed on information about the US Treasury to the "enemy" – the Soviet Union – without authorization (see Oliver 1975, xvi). But there never was solid evidence. White died in August 1948 before he could clear his name. Judging from Acheson's evaluation (1970, 31), as a person White was not liked because of his abrasiveness, his lack of courtesy, and his "restless spirit," to which Acheson wanted to pay tribute with "kindliness," but evidently a strained one.

5 He may have been inspired in these endeavors through his interest in the contribution of "planning" to maintaining stable and high growth rates. At one point, he applied for a stipend to study for a year at the Moscow Planning Institute.

6 For future reference, the Soviet Union voted for the resolution.

7 There is actually some confusion in the literature, which often refers to the Committee of Eighteen as called for in the Resolution. Part of this mix-up may stem from the fact that both Belgium and Luxemburg were invited, although in trading matters the two had earlier (already in July 1921) formed an economic union – the Belgian–Luxemburg Economic Union or BLEU.

8 The often bewildering policy stances of the Soviets are documented in Dormael (1978, 191–7), Mikesell (1951), and Proceedings (1948, 1187ff.).

9 For a wide-ranging documentation of this early history, see Horsefield (1969, 77–117), Lavigne (1978, 367–72), and Mikesell (1951, 101–16).

10 The evolution of the USSR's stance on gold is documented in Rémy (1981, 1985).

11 For details, see Horsefield (1969, 98–9). Some of the exchanges between the US and Soviet negotiators, particularly during the meetings of April and May 1944, make it clear that the USSR was primarily bent on obtaining sizable loans for rehabilitation, reconstruction, and bolstering economic activity (see Dormael 1978; Mikesell 1951; Oliver 1957, 1975; Proceedings 1948).

12 But recent commentary singles out politics and the Cold War as the overwhelming deterrents to active participation (Blusztajn 1982, 109).

13 These elements are succinctly recalled in Dam (1970, 10–11). Other views on what transpired during this period are in Diebold (1952) and Wilcox (1949).

14 These are the chapter headings of the drafts of the Havana Charter.

15 For later reference, it is important to recall that article XI of the General Agreement, which provides the overall framework of QRs, explicitly singles out agriculture and fishery as two sectors for special treatment. This was embedded on the urging of the United States (Paarlberg 1988, 45–7).

16 With hindsight, EcoSoc has not been very effective (Bertrand 1986, 92ff.) because membership has elected to bypass it in the formulation and coordination of economic policies, to the extent that there has indeed been more than national policy formulation in recent years. However, at their inception, the work of these Councils was slated to be critical in promoting consultative cooperation between sovereign states. Because conflict is easily dramatized and the issues of political conflict lend themselves to it in exemplary fashion, the proceedings of the Security Council received most publicity in the first years.

17 This task was eventually assumed by the Centre on Transnational Corporations (CTC) of the United Nations.

18 For some of the more virulent objections from the left as well as from the right, see Brown (1950), Cortney (1949), and Wilgress (1949).

2 Basic features of CPEs

1 Recall that the very definition of this concept in Marxist theory implies that marginal producers vacate the sector and others expand their scale of operations until in equilibrium the averaging rule leaves nobody at a big loss or extraordinary gain. For details, see Brabant (1987b, 18–22).

2 For a summary of the relationship between internal and external prices in various CPEs at the height of these reforms, see Mitrofanova (1973, 90ff.; 1974, 41ff.) and United Nations (1968, 43ff.; 1973, 36ff.).

3 An exception might be in the case of external financial difficulties, when the CPE also needs to target explicit import restrictions for lack of suitable exportables, and will thus "protect" domestic absorption and output levels.

4 The Keynes plan is compared with the IBEC in Zwass (1974, 128–9).

5 This is known as *Basic principles of the international socialist division of labor* (henceforth *Basic principles*). For details, see Brabant (1989a, 64–71).
6 Its full title reads *Comprehensive program for the further extension and improvement of cooperation and the development of socialist economic integration by the CMEA member countries*. For details, see Brabant (1989a, 85–9).
7 This effect could be offset by compensating households through income transfers from, say, income taxes. This presupposes a well-developed fiscal policy, which is not typically a feature of the CPEs, even in Hungary.
8 The full title reads *Comprehensive program to promote the scientific and technological progress of the member countries of the Council for Mutual Economic Assistance up to the year 2000*. It was endorsed in December 1985 (for details, see Brabant 1989a, 117–21).
9 This has the working title of *Collective concept of the international socialist division of labor for the period 1991–2005*.
10 This is the highest official organ of the CMEA. Above it are informal organs, including the economic summit and meetings of Central Committee Secretaries in charge of economic affairs (see Brabant 1989a, 131–5).
11 As noted, the summit of Party and government leaders of the CMEA members is the highest, if unofficial, CMEA organ. For details about this organ and its role in molding SEI, see Brabant (1989a, 132–4).
12 Carlos Rafael Rodriguez mentioned (*Rudé Právo*, 6 July 1988, 2) "the reduction of the number of permanent bodies from 107 to 34, the establishment of new committees, and the merging of activities [that] will result in greater flexibility in the CMEA mechanism." But the precise context is unclear.
13 The Bulgarian Prime Minister, Georgi Atanasov, reported that Bulgaria would be prepared to participate in "71 of the total of 178 actions envisaged in the specific comprehensive programs" (*Rabotničesko delo*, 6 July 1988, 6). But the donor countries have already made it clear, in Ryzhkov's words, that most "require clarification as regards construction deadlines, assessments of the economic expediency of individual projects, and measures to ensure that they produce returns as soon as possible" (*Pravda*, 6 July 1988, 4). Recent indicators are that only half a dozen or so of these projects are actively being considered.
14 Interview with the CMEA Secretary reported in *Rudé Právo* (8 July 1988, 2).
15 For details in the case of Czechoslovakia and the Soviet Union, see Větrovský and Hrinda (1988, 3); for Czechoslovakia and Bulgaria, see *Svět Hospodářství* (1988:88, 2).
16 Instead, seven CPEs (all but the GDR, Rumania, and Vietnam) envisage offsetting imbalances incurred on account of settlements at special exchange rates for selected interfirm transactions via the IBEC's TR accounts for regular transactions. For details, see Brabant (1989f, 1989g).

3 International monetary arrangements and Eastern Europe

1 At the end of the war, Sweden, Switzerland, and the United States were the sole Fund members with a truly convertible currency for current-account transactions.
2 Quoted in Assetto (1988, 69–70) from the report prepared by Dr. Ludwik

Grosfield to Commission II (on IBRD) at Bretton Woods. Dr. Grosfield represented the Polish noncommunist government in exile.

3 Recall that the Bretton Woods conference took place during World War II, so the "enemy" countries of Eastern Europe (Albania, Bulgaria, Hungary, and Rumania) as well as the GDR, which did not then exist, were not invited to participate.

4 I am referring here to *Basic principles*, a document endorsed in 1962 but that soon thereafter ignited a submerged feud, which led to a major rift in CMEA affairs (see Brabant 1989a, 63ff.).

5 Combined with Rumanian reluctance to be forthcoming with information, this understanding explains why the Rumanian "sheets," for example, in *International financial statistics* are so uninformative. To Rumania's credit, the Bank and Fund for a long time did not press for the information and, in a number of instances, did not known what to insist upon as they had only a rudimentary understanding of Rumania's statistical practices.

6 China's gold was sold on the open market but the assets were valued at the official price. The difference was used to amortize Taiwan's Bank and Fund liabilities, leaving a handsome net profit for Taiwan (Feeney 1984, 271–2)!

7 Value and price concepts play a critical role in Marxian and Marxist philosophy, economic theory, and ideology (see Brabant 1987b, 13–33).

8 Called this because it was the mouthpiece of seventy-seven DEs at UNCTAD I, held in 1964 in Geneva. The historical backdrop is detailed in Sauvant (1981). The present membership is much larger, of course, and includes several CPEs, as noted in the introduction.

9 Illustrations are Czechoslovakia in 1953, and Rumania in October 1984 when it abruptly revalued the leu in defiance of Fund recommendations to pursue steady devaluation toward a rate that could support greater economic decentralization and an effective link between domestic and external markets.

10 For a Polish perspective on the benefits and drawbacks of Bank and Fund membership, see Głuchowski (1981, 62–4) and Kranz (1984, 38–40).

11 At the time, a broad-based search for converters and comparability of the national account statistics of CPEs was sponsored by the World Bank. The latter appointed an expert group, which, after lengthy deliberations, recommended unanimously the rejection of the official commercial exchange rate for both Hungary and Poland, the official ones for other CPEs, and the calculation of implicit converters that the Bank had utilized earlier for its *World atlas* series. The work then undertaken is brought together in Marer (1985). In my contributions (Brabant 1985a, 1985b), I recommended that for the Bank's purposes it would be most useful to adopt some rate derived from purchasing-power parity comparisons.

12 For a fascinating Hungarian statement on the ECU's potential role in east–west relations, see the address by Ferenc Bartha to "Intergroup European Currency" of the European Parliament, Strasbourg on 18 January 1989 as reported in *BIS Press Reports* (BIS – Bank for International Settlements). On the role of the ECU in recent French–Soviet relations, see Nême and Nême (1986).

13 The CPEs in the Fund presently have over 5 percent of the voting power. An eventual Soviet quota would probably be between 10 and 14 percent.

4 The international trading system and the CPEs

1 The provisions regarding STCs agreed upon in London, particularly as they apply to the Soviet Union, are examined with a critical eye in Gerschenkron (1947).

2 In diplomatic parlance, a "bracketed" item signals that some negotiators have doubts about its formulation, but that it has not yet been rejected. Further negotiations on the issue in question are therefore deferred, pending the resolution of more urgent, less contentious issues.

3 Unfortunately, I cannot go into this important historical backdrop in this volume. My views on the issue are in Brabant (1989a, 25–62).

4 Some writers (including Kostecki 1979b) exaggerate the ambitions of the OTC. One need only look at the provisions in GATT (1955) to buttress this position.

5 The draft resolution tabled at UNCTAD I and the principles of the new ITO are reproduced in UNCTAD (1964b, 424–7, 428–9).

6 Excepting Albania, the GDR, which was not then a UN member, and Rumania, which at the time was at loggerheads with the USSR.

7 Cutler (1983, 123) resorts to some hyperbole when he alleges that the CPEs then sought to establish the ITO "to coordinate and oversee the activities of the United Nations, of its organs and of any other international organization concerned with trade."

8 UNCTAD continues legally as the conference on trade and development, financed through the regular UN budget, which should lead up to a more formal organization – an ITO – with its own budget. However, *de facto* it is treated as a "special" – not specialized – organ within the UN family, essentially a debating venue for DEs that is shunned by many DMEs and at times treated skeptically even by CPEs.

9 As explained in the introduction, the Soviet request did not strictly fall in that category because it was asking for observership in the Uruguay Round.

10 The particular numbering of articles through successive drafts is bewildering. The one referred to here was article 27 of *Suggested charter*, 32 of *Preliminary charter*, and 30 of the Geneva draft.

11 It was article 28 of *Suggested charter*, 33 of *Preliminary charter*, and 31 of the Geneva draft. This formulation was kept in square brackets from the London Conference through the final draft. The quote is from Preliminary Draft (1946).

12 These include article II, 4 on tariffs and other concessions; article III, 4 on the national treatment standard; article XXXVII, 3 on the use of equitable trade margins in the case of governments directly or indirectly determining the sale or resale price of some products; and an interpretative note on QRs.

13 It came about as a reinterpretation of this stipulation for MEs. Because of Uruguay's opposition, however, it has never been approved. Though not official, it would appear to be invoked in disputes, which tend to be rather rare. The precise meaning of this interpretation has remained rather murky, however.

14 Article 31 of the Havana Charter required that countries import "such quantities of the product as will be sufficient to satisfy the full domestic demand," a provision that was not carried over into the General Agreement.

15 There is only one, rather trivial exception, namely when the central plan is in fact the simple aggregate of all enterprise plans. The central plan is then not a rigid instrument of policy making and control, but by and large simply a source of information and bookkeeping.

16 Hungary first applied for observer status in 1958 but it had to withdraw its request under political pressure from key MEs, notably the United States.

17 In the case of China, these were to have started in June 1989, but China asked for a deferral, owing to the backlash of the suppression of the student democracy movement. Bulgaria does not seem to have pushed hard, probably in view of the lackluster progress being made with its reform.

18 For interesting reviews of the issues facing China, but with a bearing on other CPEs too, see Hartland-Thunberg (1987), Herzstein (1986), and Li (1987).

19 For example, during the Tokyo Round the USSR was invited to join but refused to consider this proposal. It approached the GATT for the first time in 1982, with a view to obtaining observer status in the Ministerial Meeting. It did so again in 1984 in an effort to take part in the deliberations of the GATT Council and MTN Code Committees, which would yield a somewhat lesser status than full observership (Patterson 1986, 185).

20 Bernier (1982, 245) states categorically that "state enterprises ... are created precisely to fulfill roles not normally assumed by private enterprises." It is paradoxical that this paper appears in the same volume in which Matejka (1982) stresses the importance of this distinction!

21 Some are usefully detailed in Baumer and Jacobsen (1976, 34–5). Others are examined, particularly with reference to Poland and state trading in Michałek (1984, 63–72), Woźnowski (1974, 136–49), and Wrębiak (1986).

5 The CPEs and reform of the global economic order

1 Article XV of the General Agreement, which provides for relations between the Fund and the GATT, aims at policy coordination by accepting the Fund's findings on foreign exchange, monetary reserves, and balance of payments, and whether action in exchange matters is in accordance with the Fund's Articles of Agreement. The former Executive Secretary of GATT (Wyndham-White 1975, 325–7) stressed that this nexus has not been very useful. In his view, the Fund and GATT should, in fact, have been merged into a single institution.

2 Gardner (1969) still constitutes a very fine inquiry into "universalism" and "economism" as *in se* irreconcilable objectives of the postwar global negotiations.

3 For a useful, cogently argued discussion of alternatives pertaining to the most egalitarian organizations, namely the United Nations, see Bertrand (1986).

4 Dirksen's contention (1987, 228) that the USSR until very recently referred to the GATT as an "instrument of imperialist oppression" rests on a questionable reading of the pertinent literature. But Kostecki's (1979a) survey is not quite exhaustive either, as suggested in chapter 4 with reference to the revival of the ITO in the early 1960s.

5 Reportedly Anastas Mikoyan, then the USSR's Deputy Minister of Foreign Trade, in *Handelsblatt* (20 May 1960).

6 The USSR's support for UNCTAD is on the whole "simply a part of the general Russian preference for UN organizations, where the one-nation, one-vote principle is strongly entrenched" (Camps 1981, 193).
7 For a thoughtful evaluation of the inward-turning and outward-looking policy options available to CPEs, see Köves (1981, 1985).
8 I have elaborated such a program elsewhere (Brabant 1987a, 399–401; Brabant 1987c, 97–9; Brabant 1989a, 402–4). Here I recapitulate only the major pillars.
9 For example, Hungary applied in November 1981 and was admitted in May 1982; Rumania did so in September 1972 and was admitted in December the same year.
10 Although a full member since May 1986, by late 1989 Poland had not yet received a loan from the Bank or the Fund, owing to disagreement over the length of the first Fund loan; the Bank has essentially been awaiting a resolution of this political dispute between the Fund and Polish authorities.
11 This was first used in connection with CMEA price reforms in Neustadt (1968, 223).
12 As in the mid-1970s, when CPE demand propped up economic activity in DMEs.
13 Shifts in SEI mechanisms will only marginally affect the non-European CPEs (see Abolichina, Bakoveckij, and Medvedev 1987, 139). But, as part of the ongoing CMEA reform (Brabant 1988b, 1989a, 1989e, 1989h), the European CPEs are hoping to enact major changes here too (see chapter 2 and Brabant 1989d).
14 I have worked out some conditions for the CMEA to become more supportive of domestic economic reform ambitions in Brabant (1989a, 404–17; 1989e).
15 But state trading in agricultural products by DMEs generates a much larger volume of trade than total CMEA trade (Kostecki 1982, 26)!
16 But this is often seen as a device utilized by the DMEs to assuage DE claims, and therefore frowned upon by CPEs (see Constantinescu 1987, 93).
17 Recall that in 1947 there were only twenty Contracting Parties. Their number in late 1989 stood at ninety-seven. Another thirty apply the GATT rules on a *de facto* basis (GATT 1989, inside front cover). With Namibia's impending accession, the United Nations will soon have 160 members.
18 I can only repeat what Frank Holzman (1974, 219) has said so eloquently: Because "I am an economist rather than a lawyer, political scientist, or politician, my proposals are very general and should be viewed as judgments and sentiments based on economic analysis."
19 From an oral statement by Ivan D. Ivanov to the workshop on "The future of the United Nations in an interdependent world" on 8 September 1988 in Moscow.

Bibliography

Abolichina, Galina A., Oleg Bakoveckij, and Boris I. Medvedev (1987) "Suščnost' i novye formy socialistčeskoj integracii," *Voprosy ėkonomi*, 1, 129–40.

Ačarkan, V. (1984) "Valjutnye kursy – mechanizm formirovanija i mežimperialističeskie protivorečija," *Mirovaja ėkonomika i meždunarodnye otnošenija*, 9, 72–82.

Acheson, Dean (1970) *Present at the creation – my years in the State Department* (New York: New American Library).

Advisory (1976) *Gatt plus – a proposal for trade reform – with the text of the General Agreement* (New York: Praeger, for the Atlantic Council).

Ansari, Javed A. (1986) *The political economy of international economic organization* (Boulder, CO: Rienner).

Artis, Michael and Sylvia Ostry (1986) *International economic policy coordination* (London: Routledge & Kegan Paul, for the Royal Institute of International Affairs).

Ascher, William (1983) "New development approaches and the adaptability of international agencies: the case of the World Bank," *International Organization*, 3, 415–39.

Åslund, Anders (1988) "The new Soviet policy towards international economic organisations," *World Today*, 2, 27–30.

Assetto, Valerie J. (1988) *The Soviet bloc in the IMF and the IBRD* (Boulder, CO and London: Westview Press).

Atlas, Z. and Gerogij Matjuchin (1971) "Vsemirnye den'gi: zoloto ili dollar?" *Mirovaja ėkonomika i meždunarodyne otnošenija*, 8, 96–108.

Augenthaler, Zdenek (1969) "The socialist countries and GATT," in *Economic relations after the Kennedy round*, edited by Frans A. Alting van Geusau (Leyden: Sijthoff), 75–82.

Baban, Roy (1977) "State trading and the GATT," *Journal of World Trade Law*, 4, 334–53.

Bácskai, Tamás (1975) "Währungspolitische Diskussionen in den sozialistischen Ländern," *Europäische Rundschau*, 4, 21–6.

Baldwin, David A. (1985) *Economic statecraft* (Princeton, NJ: Princeton University Press).

Baran, Paul (1947) "Discussion," *American Economic Review*, 2, 646–8.

Baumer, Max and Hans-Dieter Jacobsen (1976) "Integration of Comecon into the world economy?" *Aussenpolitik*, 1, 31–45.

Bautina, Ninel' V. (1968a) "O meždunarodnych socialistčeskich proizvodstvennych otnošenijach," *Mirovaja ėkonomika i meždunarodyne otnošenija*, 4, 64–71.

(1968b) "Nekotorye osobennosti formirovanija internacional'noj stoimosti," in *Cenoobrazovanie na mirovom socialističeskom rynke*, edited by V. P. D'jačenko (Moscow: Ėkonomika), 38–51.

Beneš, Otto and Zdeňek Jung (1988) "GATT – postavení státního podniku," *Zahraniční Obchod*, 11, 10–13.

Bergsten, C. Fred (1976) "Interdependence and the reform of international institutions," *International Organization*, 2, 361–72.

Bergsten, C. Fred, Robert, O. Keohane, and Joseph S. Nye (1975) "International economics and international politics: a framework for analysis," *International Organization*, 1, 3–36.

Bernier, Ivan (1982) "State trading and the GATT," in *State trading in international markets – theory and practice of industrialized and developing countries*, edited by Maciej M. Kostecki (London: Macmillan), 245–60.

Bernstein, Edward M. (1984) "Reflections on Bretton Woods," in *The international monetary system: forty years after Bretton Woods* (Boston, MA: Federal Reserve Bank of Boston), 15–20.

Bertrand, Maurice (1986) *Refaire l'ONU – un programme pour la paix* (Geneva: Zoé).

Bidwell, Percy W. and William Diebold, Jr. (1949) "The United States and the International Trade Organization," *International Conciliation*, 449, 185–239.

Bird, Graham (1983) "Reforming the Fund: the future role of the International Monetary Fund in the international financial systems," *Three Banks Review*, 4, 3–21.

Black, Stanley W. (1985) "International money and international monetary arrangements," in *Handbook of international economics*, vol. 2, edited by Ronald W. Jones and Peter B. Kenen (Amsterdam: Elsevier Science Publishers), 1153–93.

Blusztajn, Mięczyslaw (1982) "Polska a Międzynarodowy Fundusz Walutowy," *Bank i Kredyt*, 4/5, 105–10.

Bogdanov, Oleg S. (1976) *Valjutnaja sistema sovremennaja kapitalizma (osnovnye tendencii i protivorečij* (Moscow: Mysl').

Borisov, Stanislav M. (1984) *Zoloto v ėkonomiki sovremennogo kapitalizma*, 2nd ed. (Moscow: Finansy i statistika).

Bourguinat, Henri (1977) "The international payments crisis and the foundation of east–west cooperation," in *The international payments crisis and the development of east–west trade* (Brussels: Etablissements Emile Bruylants), 17–70.

(1988) "The European monetary system (EMS): first lessons and new challenges," in *Macroeconomic management and the enterprise in east and west*, edited by Christopher T. Saunders (London: Macmillan in association with the Vienna Institute for Comparative Economic Studies), 133–53.

Brabant, Jozef M. van (1980) *Socialist economic integration – aspects of contemporary economic problems in Eastern Europe* (New York: Cambridge University Press).

(1985a) "Eastern European exchange rates and exchange policies," *Jahrbuch der Wirtschaft Osteuropas – Yearbook of East-European Economics*, 11/1, 123–72.

(1985b) *Exchange rates in Eastern Europe – types, derivation, application* (Washington, DC: World Bank Staff Working Papers, No. 778).

(1987a) *Adjustment, structural change, and economic efficiency – aspects of monetary cooperation in Eastern Europe* (New York: Cambridge University Press).

(1987b) *Regional price formation in Eastern Europe – on the theory and practice of trade pricing* (Dordrecht: Kluwer Academic Publishers).

(1987c) "A constitutional framework for economic integration in Eastern Europe?" (New York: paper presented on 27 April at Columbia University).

(1987d) "The GATT and the Soviet Union – a plea for reform," *DIESA Working Paper Series*, 6.

(1987e) "Economic adjustment and the future of socialist economic integration," *Eastern European Politics and Society*, 1, 75–112.

(1987f) "Monetarism and the future of integration in Eastern Europe" (New York: paper presented at the University of Minnesota, 24 November, manuscript).

(1987g) "Recent growth performance, economic reform, and the future of integration in Eastern Europe," *DIESA Working Paper Series*, 5.

(1988a) "Planned economies in the GATT framework – the Soviet case," *Soviet Economy*, 1, 3–35.

(1988b) "Whither the CMEA? – reconstructing socialist economic integration" (Honolulu, HA: paper presented at the AAASS convention, 18–21 November).

(1989a) *Economic integration in Eastern Europe – a reference book* (Hemel Hempstead: Harvester Wheatsheaf and New York: Routledge).

(1989b) "The Soviet Union in the GATT? – a plea for reform," *International Spectator*, 4, 72–93.

(1989c) "Requirements for full and equal participation of planned economies in the global trade framework" (New York: paper prepared for symposium on "Economic reforms and the role of Asian centrally planned economies, China, Eastern Europe, and the Soviet Union in global economic relations," Helsinki, 12–16 June).

(1989d) "Socialist countries and development assistance" (New York: paper prepared for conference on "Alternatives to superpower competition in the third world: Latin America and beyond," Vienna, 29 May – 2 June).

(1989e) "Economic reform and monetary cooperation in the CMEA," in *Financial reform in Eastern Europe*, edited by Christine Kessides, Timothy King, Mario Nuti, and Catherine Sokil (Washington, DC: World Bank) 170–95.

(1989f) "Economic reforms and convertibility in Eastern Europe," in *Le economia socialiste*, edited by Claudio de Vincenti and Marcello Mulino (Naples: Liguori), forthcoming.

(1989g) "Regional integration, economic reforms, and convertibility," *Jahrbuch der Wirtschaft Osteuropas – Yearbook of East-European Economics*, 13 (1), 44–81.

(1989h) "Integration reform – new horizons for the CMEA and east–west economic relations?" in *The political economy of greater east–west economic cooperation*, edited by Michael Kraus and Ron Liebowitz (Boston, MA: Ballinger), forthcoming.

Brada, Josef C. (1988) "Interpreting the Soviet subsidization of Eastern Europe," *International Organization*, 4, 639–58.

Brown, W. A. (1950) *The United States and the restoration of world trade* (Washington, DC: The Brookings Institution).

Buzan, Barry (1984) "Economic structure and international security: the limits of the liberal case," *International Organization*, 4, 597–624.

Byrnes, James F. (1947) *Speaking frankly* (New York and London: Harper & Brothers).

Caffet, Jean-Pierre and Marie Lavigne (1985) "Les pays à économie centralement planifiée sont-ils protectionnistes?" in *Le protectionnisme – croissance–limites–voies alternatives*, edited by Bernard Lassudrie-Duchêne and Jean-Louis Reiffus (Paris: Economica), 283–92.

Camps, Miriam (1981) (with the collaboration of Catherine Gwin) *Collective management – the reform of global economic organizations* (New York: McGraw-Hill, for the Council on Foreign Relations/1980s Project).

Camps, Miriam and William Diebold, Jr. (1986) *The new multilateralism – can the world trading system be saved?* (New York: Council on Foreign Relations, reissued with a new introduction).

Čeklin, Vladimir N. (1987) "SSSR i GATT," *Vnešnjaja torgovlja*, 7, 37–9.

Chvojnik, P. (1965) "Diktat ili ravnopravie – posle ženevskoj konferencii po torgovle i ravitiju," *Mirovaja ėkonomika i meždunarodyne otnošenija*, 12, 15–27.

CMEA (1984) "Deklaracija stran-členov Soveta ėkonomičeskoj vzaimopomošči 'sokraneni mira i meždunarodnoe ėkonomičeskoe sotrudničestvo'," *Ėkonomičeskaja gazeta*, 26, 6–7.

Cohen, Benjamin J. (1982) "Balance-of-payments financing: evolution of a regime," *International Organization*, 2, 457–8.

Committee (1949) Committee for Economic Development, *The International Trade Organization and the reconstruction of world trade* (New York: Committee for Economic Development).

(1955) Committee on Commercial Policy, *The Organization of Trade Cooperation and the new G.A.T.T.* (New York: Council of the International Chamber of Commerce).

Condliffe, John B. (1950) *The commerce of nations* (New York: Norton).

Constantinescu, Adrian (1987) "Tendances dans l'activité des organisations et organismes économiques internationaux pendant les années '80," *Revue Roumaine des Sciences Sociales – Série Sciences Economiques*, 1, 87–101.

Cooper, Richard N. (1975a) "Prolegomena to the choice of an international monetary system," *International Organization*, 1, 63–97.

(1975b) "Economic assumptions of the case for liberal trade," in *Toward a new world trade policy: the Maidenhead papers*, edited by C. Fred Bergsten (Lexington, MA: Lexington Books), 19–31.

(1984) "A monetary system of the future," *Foreign Affairs*, 1, 166–84.

(1985) "Economic interdependence and coordination of economic policies," in *Handbook of international economics*, vol. 2, edited by Ronald W. Jones and Peter B. Kenen (Amsterdam: Elsevier Science Publishers), 1195–234.

(1988a) "International economic cooperation: is it desirable? Is it likely?" *Washington Quarterly*, 2, 89–101.

(1988b) "China and international economic organizations" (Cambridge, MA: Harvard University, January, mimeographed).

Corbi, Gianni (1988) "Un impero che bussa alle porte del capitale – Mosca si prepara allo choc del mercato," *La Repubblica*, 16 April, 13.

Cortney, Philip (1949) *The economic Munich* (New York: Philosophical Library).

Crockett, Andrew and Morris Goldstein (1987) *Strengthening the international monetary system: exchange rates, surveillance, and objective indicators* (Washington, DC: International Monetary Fund).

Culbert, Jay (1987a) "War-time Anglo-American talks and the making of the GATT," *The World Economy*, 4, 381–99.

(1987b) "James Meade's war-time proposal for a liberal trade regime," *The World Economy*, 4, 399–407.

Curzon, Gerard (1965) *Multilateral commercial diplomacy – the General Agreement on Tariffs and Trade and its impact on national commercial policies and techniques* (London: Michael Joseph).

Curzon, Gerard and Victoria Curzon (1976) "The management of trade relations in the GATT," in *International economic relations of the western world, 1959–1971* vol. 1, edited by Andrew Shonfield assisted by Hermia Oliver (London: Oxford University Press, for the Royal Institute of International Affairs), 143–283.

Cutler, Robert M. (1983) "East–south relations at UNCTAD: global political economy and the CMEA," *International Organization*, 1, 121–42.

Dam, Kenneth W. (1970) *The GATT – law and international economic organization* (Chicago, IL: University of Chicago Press).

David, Wilfred L. (1985) *The IMF policy paradigm – the macroeconomics of stabilization, structural adjustment and economic development* (New York: Praeger).

Dell, Edmund (1987) *The politics of economic interdependence* (New York: St. Martin's Press).

Dell, Sidney S. (1988) "The future of the international monetary system" (Paper prepared for the UNITAR/USSR Association of the United Nations Roundtable on the "Future of the United Nations in an interdependent world," Moscow, 5–9 September).

Dell, Sidney S. *et al.* (1987) *The international monetary system and its reform – papers prepared for the Group of Twenty-Four* (Amsterdam: North-Holland, for the United Nations, 3 vols.).

Diebold, William, Jr. (1952) *The end of the I.T.O* [*sic!*] (Princeton, NJ: Princeton University – International Finance Section).

(1969) "Future negotiating issues and policies in foreign trade," in *Economic relations after the Kennedy round*, edited by Frans A. Alting van Geusau (Leyden: Sijthoff), 123–45.

(1972) *The United States and the industrial world – American foreign economic policy in the 1970s* (New York: Praeger).

(1979a) "The Soviet Union in the world economy," in *Soviet economy in a time of change*, vol. 1, edited by Joint Economic Committee, Congress of the United States (Washington, DC: Government Printing Office), 51–70.

(1979b) "Rethinking the problem of trade and payments: the Soviet Union and the process of reforming relations among industrialized market economies," in *The Soviet Union and the world economy* (New York: Council on Foreign Relations), 17–29.

(1988) "The USSR and the world trading system" (New York: paper prepared for the Council on Foreign Relations Study Group on the Soviet Union in the International Economy, January).

Dirksen, Erik (1987) "What if the Soviet Union applies to join the GATT?" *The World Economy*, 2, 228–30.

Djakin, V. (1982) "Sredstva meždunarodnych rasčëtov v mirovom kapitalističeskom chozjajstve," *Mirovaja ėkonomika i meždunarodnye otnošenija*, 7, 61–70.

Djumilen, I. (1984) "Sostojanie mirovoj torgovli i problemy razvitija," *Mirovaja ėkonomika i meždunarodnye otnošenija*, 8, 94–6.

Domke, Martin and John N. Hazard (1958) "State trading and the most-favored-nation clause," *American Journal of International Law*, 1, 55–69.

Dormael, Armand van (1978) *Bretton Woods – birth of a monetary system* (London: Macmillan).

Ellsworth, P. T. (1949) "The Havana charter: comment," *American Economic Review*, 3, 1268–73.

Evans, John W. (1971) *The Kennedy round in American trade policy – the twilight of the GATT?* (Cambridge, MA: Harvard University Press).

Fárek, Jiří, (1986) "Soudobé problémy měnové finančního systému kapitalismu," *Politická Ekonomie*, 12, 1267–79.

Feeney, William (1984) "Chinese policy in multilateral financial institutions," in *China and the world – Chinese foreign policy in the post-Mao era*, edited by Samuel S. Kim (Boulder, CO: Westview Press), 266–92.

Feinberg, Richard E. (1988) "The changing relationship between the World Bank and the International Monetary Fund," *International Organization*, 3, 545–60.

Fekete, János (1972) "Some connection between the international monetary system and east–west economic relations," *Acta Oeconomica*, 2, 153–65.

(1978) "Monetary and financial problems in east and west," in *Money and finance in east and west*, edited by Christopher T. Saunders (Vienna and New York: Springer-Verlag), 15–29.

(1981) "Reflections on international monetary policy," *New Hungarian Quarterly*, 84, 33–44.

(1986) "The crisis of the monetary system," *New Hungarian Quarterly*, 102, 56–61.

Fink, Karl-Hermann (1974) *Sozialistiches internationales Wirtschaftsrecht* (Berlin: Berlin-Verlag).

Finlayson, Jock A. and Mark W. Zacher (1981) "The GATT and the regulation of trade barriers: regime dynamics and functions," *International Organization*, 4, 561–602.

Fomin, Boris S. (1978) "Monetary and financial aspects of east–west economic cooperation," in *Money and finance in east and west*, edited by Christopher T. Saunders (Vienna and New York: Springer-Verlag), 99–110.

Friedemann, Erich (1986) "Zur Rolle des Goldes und anderer Währungsreserven im gegenwärtigen Kapitalismus," *Wirtschaftswissenschaft*, 8, 1171–89.

Fröhlich, Gerhard (1987) "Zum Artikel 'Komparative Vorteile und ihre Ausnutzung im Außenhandel sozialistischer Länder'," *Wirtschaftswissenschaft*, 3, 415–20.

Furth, J. Herbert (1949) "Short-run escape clauses of the Havana charter," *American Economic Review – Papers and Proceedings*, 3, 252–60.

Gadbaw, R. Michael (1984) "The outlook for GATT as an institution," in *Managing trade relations in the 1980s – issues involved in the GATT ministerial meeting – 1982*, edited by Seymour J. Rubin and Thomas R. Graham (Totowa, NJ: Rowland and Allenheld), 33–49.

Gardner, Richard N. (1969) *Sterling–dollar diplomacy – the origins and the prospects of our international economic order* (New York: McGraw-Hill, new expanded edition).

(1988) "The case for practical internationalism," *Foreign Affairs*, 4, 826–45.

GATT (1955) *The Organization for Trade Cooperation* (Geneva: GATT).

(1960) *Terms of accession for a country with a centrally-planned economy* (Geneva: GATT, document no. INT(60)20, mimeographed).

(1985) *Trade policies for a better future – proposals for action* (Geneva: GATT).

(1989) *International trade 88–89* (Geneva: GATT).

Gerschenkron, Alexander (1947) "Russia and the International Trade Organization," *American Economic Review*, 2, 624–42.

Gilpin, Robert (1987) (with the assistance of Jean M. Gilpin) *The political economy of international relations* (Princeton, NJ: Princeton University Press).

Głuchowski, Jan (1981). "Miėdzynarodowy Fundusz Walutowy a członkostwo Polski," *Sprawy Miėdynarodowe*, 12, 55–64.

Gold, Joseph (1987) "Public international law in the international monetary system," in *Public international law and the future world order*, edited by Joseph J. Norton (Littleton, CO: Rothman), 15/1–15/82.

Gordon, Margaret S. (1949) "The character and significance of the general commitments that nations will make under the ITO charter," *American Economic Review – Papers and Proceedings*, 3, 241–51.

Gotz-Kozierkiewicz, Danuta (1988) "Dewaluacja jako środek polityki w sietle programów stabilizacyjnych MFW," *Finanse*, 6, 10–22.

Gräbig, Gertrud, Gerhard Brendel and Hans-Joachim Dubrowsky (1975) *Ware-Geld-Beziehungen in der sozialistischen Integration* (Berlin: Die Wirtschaft).

Grauwe, Paul de (1988) "Le système monétaire international – problèmes et perspective," *Cahiers Economiques de Bruxelles*, 3, 267–83.

Gröner, Helmut (1980) "Zur Meistbegünstigungsgewährung durch Staatshandelsländer – die Frage der GATT-Mitgliedschaft von RGW-Ländern," in *Außenwirtschaftspolitik und Stabilisierung von Wirtschaftssystemen*, edited by Alfred Schüller and Ulrich Wagner (Stuttgart: Gustav Fischer Verlag), 233–48.

Grote, Gerhard (1981) "Einige theoretische und praktische Fragen des staatlichen Monopols auf dem Gebiet der Außenwirtschaft," *Wirtschaftswissenschaft*, 2, 143–52.

Grote, Gerhard and Horst Kühn (1986) "Komparative Vorteile und ihre Ausnutzung im Außenhandel sozialistischer Länder," *Wirtschaftswissenschaft*, 8, 1138–56.

Guerrieri, Paolo and Pier Carlo Padoan (1986) "Neomercantilism and international economic stability," *International Organization*, 1, 29–42.

Hamel, Hannelore (1980) "Zur Frage der Mitgliedschaft der RGW-Länder im Internationalen Währungsfonds," in *Außenwirtschaftspolitik und Stabilisierung von Wirtschaftssystemen*, edited by Alfred Schüller and Ulrich Wagner (Stuttgart: Gustav Fischer Verlag), 177–94.

Hanson, Philip (1986) "East–west trade and technology transfer," in *The Soviet*

Union and Eastern Europe, edited by George Schöpflin (New York: Facts on File Publications), 404–14.

(1988) *Western economic statecraft in east–west relations – embargoes, sanctions, linkage, economic warfare, and detente* (London: Routledge & Kegan Paul, for the Royal Institute of International Affairs).

Harding, Harry and Ed A. Hewett (1989) "Socialist reforms and the world economy," in *Restructuring American foreign policy*, edited by John D. Steinbruner (Washington, DC: The Brookings Institution), 158–84.

Hartland-Thunberg, Penelope (1987) "China's modernization: a challenge for the GATT," *Washington Quarterly*, 1, 81–97.

Haus, Leah A. (1989) "The western politics of east–west trade negotiations: East European countries and the GATT" (Athens, GA: paper prepared for the 12th workshop on "East–west economic interaction," 1–5 April, mimeographed).

Hauser, Heinz, Peter Moser, Renaud Planta, and Ruedi Schmid (1988) "Der Beitrag von Jan Tumlir zur Entwicklung einer ökonomischen Verfassungstheorie internationaler Handelsregeln," *Ordo*, 39, 219–37.

Havana Charter, United Nations Conference on Trade and Employment (1948) *Havana charter for an International Trade Organization including guide to the study of the charter* (Washington, DC: Government Printing Office).

Helísek, Mojmír (1986) "Stále neuzavřená diskuse o demonetizaci zlata v kapitalistické ekonomice," *Politická Ekonomie*, 6, 641–7.

Helleiner, Gerald K. (1983) "The rise and decline of the IMF," in *Banking on poverty – the global impact of the IMF and World Bank*, edited by Jill Torrie (Toronto: Between the Lines), 42–54.

Helleiner, Gerald K. *et al.* (1983) *Towards a new Bretton Woods – challenges for the world financial and trading system* (London: Commonwealth Secretariat).

Henderson, Hubert (1949) "A criticism of the Havana charter," *American Economic Review*, 3, 605–17.

Herzstein, Robert E. (1986) "China and the GATT: legal and policy issues raised by China's participation in the General Agreement on Tariffs and Trade," *Law and Policy in International Business*, 2, 371–415.

Hewett, Edward A. (1978) "Most-favored nation treatment in trade under central planning," *Slavic Review*, 1, 25–39.

Holzman, Franklyn D. (1974) "East–west trade and investment: past and future policy issues," in *Foreign trade under central planning*, edited by Franklyn D. Holzman (Cambridge, MA: Harvard University Press), 192–239.

(1976) *International trade under communism – politics and economics* (New York: Basic Books).

(1978) "Comments," in *Money and finance in east and west*, edited by Christopher T. Saunders (Vienna and New York: Springer-Verlag), 126–7.

(1987) *The economics of Soviet bloc trade and finance* (Boulder, CO and London: Westview Press).

Hoover, Calvin B. (1949) "Discussion," *American Economic Review – Papers and Proceedings*, 3, 276–9.

Horsefield, Keith J. (1969) *The International Monetary Fund 1945–1965 – twenty years of international monetary cooperation*, vol. 1, *Chronicle* (Washington, DC: International Monetary Fund).

Hough, Jerry F. (1986) "Attack on protectionism in the Soviet Union? a comment," *International Organization*, 2, 489–503.

Huber, Jürgen (1981) "The practice of GATT in examining regional arrangements under article XXIV," *Journal of Common Market Studies*, 3, 281–98.

Ikonnikov, Igor' (1988) "Soveršentsvovanie struktury SĖV," *Ėkonomičeskoe sotrudničestvo stran-členov SĖV*, 2, 20–1.

Ivanov, Jurij A. (1987) "Čem vyzvana 'valjutnaja lichoradka'," *Pravda*, 21 January, 5.

Jackson, John H. (1969) *World trade and the law of GATT* (Indianapolis, IN: Bobbs-Merrill).

Jackson, Marvin R. (1987) "Bulgarian economic reform and the GATT," *Süosteuropa*, 9, 544–59.

Johnson, Harry G. (1975) "On living without an international monetary system," *Euromoney*, 4, 34–5.

Kaufmann, Johan and Frans A. Alting van Geusau (1969) "The institutional framework for international trade relations," in *Economic relations after the Kennedy round*, edited by Frans A. Alting van Geusau (Leyden: Sijthoff), 94–112.

Kennan, George F. (1969) *Memoirs (1925–1950)* (New York: Bantam).

Kennedy, Kevin C. (1987) "The accession of the Soviet Union to GATT," *Journal of World Trade Law*, 2, 23–39.

Keohane, Robert O. (1984) *After hegemony – cooperation and discord in the world political economy* (Princeton, NJ: Princeton University Press).

(1986) "Reciprocity in international relations," *International Organization*, 1, 1–27.

Kim, Samuel S. (1981) "Whither post-Mao Chinese global policy?" *International Organization*, 3, 433–65.

Klausová, (1985a) "K některým otázkám mezinárodnich měnových vztahů po rozpadu Brettonwoodského systému," *Politická Ekonomie*, 3, 285–94.

(1985b) "SDR – zvláštní práva čerpání po patnácti lětech existence," *Finance a Úvěr*, 6, 404–17.

Knorr, Klaus E. (1947) "The functions of an international trade organization: possibilities and limitations," *American Economic Review*, 2, 542–4.

Kock, Karin (1969) *International trade policy and the Gatt 1947–1967* (Stockholm: Almqvist & Wiksell).

Kodinov, Stoil (1988) "Meždunarodnata finansova sistema na kapitalizma i razvitieto na vrŭzkite meždu socialističeskite i kapitalističeskite strani," *Ikonomičeska misŭl*, 9, 35–47.

Koekkoek, K. A. (1988) "The integration of developing countries in the GATT system," *World Development*, 8, 947–57.

Kohlmey, Gunther (1955) *Der demokratische Weltmarkt – Entstehung, Merkmale und Bedeutung für den sozialistischen Aufbau* (Berlin: Die Wirtschaft).

Kolloch, Eveline and Jutta Polzin-Walter (1988) "Interdependenz und Rivalität in den imperialistischen Währungsbeziehungen," *IPW-Berichte*, 7, 23–9.

Konstantinov, Jurij A. (1982) "Valjutno-kreditnye osnošenija stran-členov SĖV s razvivajuščimisja stranami," *Finansy SSSR*, 3, 53–60.

(1984) "Valjutnaja sistema socialističeskogo gosudarstva," *Finansy SSSR*, 3, 28–35.

(1986) "Gegemonija dollara v valjutnoj sisteme kapitalizma," *Finansy SSSR*, 1, 29–37.

Korolëv, I. (1984) "Mirovoj kreditnyj krisis," *Mirovaja ėkonomika i meždunarodnye otnošenija*, 9, 36–47.

Kostecki, Maciej M. (1979a) *East–west trade and the GATT system* (London: Macmillan, for the Trade Policy Research Centre).

(1979b) "L'U.R.S.S. face au système de commerce multilatéral," *Revue d'Etudes Comparatives Est-Ouest*, 3, 75–90.

(1982) "State trading in agricultural products by the advanced countries," in *State trading in international markets – theory and practice of industrialized and developing countries*, edited by Maciej M. Kostecki, (London: Macmillan), 22–54.

(1984) "Can tariff be effective under central planning?' *Economia Internazionale*, 1/2, 94–107.

Köves, András (1981) "Befelé vagy kifelé fordulás – gondolatok a KGST-országok külgazdaság stratégiájáról," *Közgazdasági Szemle*, 7/8, 878–95.

(1985) *The CMEA countries in the world economy: turning inwards or turning outwards* (Budapest: Akadémiai Kiadó).

Kowalik, Tadeusz (1986) *On crucial reform of real socialism* (Vienna: Forschungsberichte des Wiener Instituts für Internationale Wirtschaftsvergleiche, no. 122, October).

Kranz, Jerzy (1984) "Państwa socjalistyczne w MFW i Banku Światowym," *Sprawy Międzynarodowy*, 11, 27–44.

Krappel, Franz (1975) *Die Havanna Charta und die Entwicklung des Weltrohstoffhandels* (Berlin: Duncker & Humblot, 1975).

Krasavina, Lidija N. (1978) "Diskussija o roli zolota v meždunarodnych ėkonomičeskich otnošenijach," *Voprosy ėkonomiki*, 2, 145–9.

Krasavina, Lidija N. and E. Baranova (1984) "Aktual'nye problemy meždunarodnych valjutno-kreditnych otnošenija," *Den'gi i kredit*, 6, 72–8.

Krasner, Stephen D. (1982) "Structural causes and regime consequences: regimes as intervening variables," *International Organization*, 2, 185–205.

Krugman, Paul R. (1987) "Is free trade passé?" *Journal of Economic Perspectives*, 2, 131–44.

Łączkowski, Bohdan (1969) "Poland's participation in the Kennedy Round," in *Economic relations after the Kennedy round*, edited by Frans A. Alting van Geusau (Leyden: Sijthoff), 83–93.

(1971) "Poland's accession to GATT," *Journal of World Trade Law*, 1, 110–19.

Lamar, Harold T. (1956) *Organization for Trade Cooperation – selected pros and cons* (Washington, DC: Library of Congress, mimeographed).

Lavigne, Marie (1978) "The International Monetary Fund and the Soviet Union," in *International economics – comparisons and interdependencies*, edited by Friedrich Levcik (Vienna and New York: Springer Verlag), 367–82.

(1979) *Les relations économiques est-ouest* (Paris: Presses Universitaires de France).

(1984) "Eastern European countries and the IMF" (Paris: Université de Paris I, paper presented at the "Conference on east–west economic relations in the changing global environment," Budapest and Vienna, 8–12 October; published in shortened version as Lavigne 1986).

(1985a) "Les pays socialistes européens et le Fonds Monétaire International," *Courrier des Pays de l'Est* 291, 29–42.

(1985b) *Economie internationale des pays socialistes* (Paris: A. Colin).

(1986) "Eastern European countries and the IMF," in *East–west economic relations in the changing global environment,* edited by Béla Csikós-Nagy and David G. Young (New York: St. Martin's Press), 298–311.

Lavigne, Marie and Krystyna Szymkiewicz (1987) "Les pays à commerce d'état et le GATT" (Toulouse: Université de Sciences Sociales, paper presented at the colloquium organized by GRECO on "Economie et finance internationale quantitatives," 29–39 June, revised version September).

Ławniczak, Ryszard (1985) "Multilaterale handelspolitische Rahmenbedingungen der Ost-West-Wirtschaftsbeziehungen," *Osteuropa-Wirtschaft,* 3, 189–200.

Lawson, Colin (1988) "Exchange rates, tax-subsidy schemes, and the revenue from foreign trade in a centrally planned economy," *Economics of Planning,* 1/2, 72–7.

Lemmnitz, Alfred (1982) "Inflation und Geld im heutigen Kapitalismus," *IPW Berichte,* 3, 36–43.

Lenin, Vladimir, I. (1964) "O monopoli vnešnej torgovli," *Polnoe sobranie sočinenij,* 5th ed. (Moscow: Izdatel'stvo političeskoj literatury), 333–7.

Li, Chung-chou (1987) "Resumption of China's GATT membership," *Journal of World Trade Law,* 4, 25–48.

Liebich, Ferdinand, K. (1971) *Das GATT als Zentrum der internationalen Handelspolitik* (Baden-Baden: Nomos).

Lipson, Charles (1982) "The transformation of trade: the sources and effects of regime change," *International Organization,* 2, 417–55.

Liser, Frorizelle B. (1982) "China and the General Agreement on Tariffs and Trade (GATT)," in *China under the four modernizations,* part 2, edited by Joint Economic Committee, Congress of the United States (Washington, DC: Superintendent of Documents), 137–49.

Lloyd, P. J. (1982) "State trading and the theory of international trade," *State trading in international markets – theory and practice of industrialized and developing countries,* edited by Maciej M. Kostecki (London: Macmillan), 117–41.

Loftus, John A. (1949) "Permanent exceptions to the commercial policy provisions of the ITO charter," *American Economic Review – Papers and Proceedings,* 3, 261–8.

Long, Olivier (1985) *Law and its limitations in the GATT multilateral trade system* (Dordrecht: Martinus Nijhoff).

Lortie, Pierre (1975) *Economic integration and the law of GATT* (New York: Praeger).

McCleary, William A. (1989) "Policy implementation under adjustment lending," *Finance and Development,* 2, 32–4.

McGovern, Edmond (1986) *International trade regulation – GATT, the United States and the European Community* (Globefield, Exeter: Globefield Press).

Majorov, Boris (1985) "Slovo učënomy-ėkonomistu," *Vnešnjaja torgovlja,* 10, 35–40.

Manžulo, Aleksej (1983) "Šestaja sessija JUNKTAD: celi i zadači," *Vnešnjaja torgovlja,* 4, 15–20.

Marer, Paul (1985) *Dollar GNPS of the U.S.S.R. and Eastern Europe* (Baltimore, MA: Johns Hopkins University Press, for the World Bank).

Mason, Edward S. and Robert E. Asher (1973) *The World Bank since Bretton Woods* (Washington, DC; The Brookings Institution).
Matejka, Harriet (1974) "State trading: instrument or object of trade control?" *Journal of World Trade Law*, 1, 209–14.
(1977) "Conclusions of the colloquium," in *The international payments crisis and the development of east–west trade* (Brussels: Etablissements Emile Bruylants), 107–19.
(1982) "Trade-policy instruments, state trading and the first-best trade intervention," in *State trading in international markets – theory and practice of industrialized and developing countries*, edited by Maciej M. Kostecki (London: Macmillan), 142–60.
Matjuchin, Georgij G. (1977) "Novaja forma mirovych deneg," *Mirovaja ėkonomika i meždunarodnye otnošenija*, 4, 38–47.
(1978) "The role of gold in the future monetary system," in *Money and finance in east and west*, edited by Christopher T. Saunders (Vienna and New York: Springer-Verlag), 243–9.
Matjuchin, Georgij G. and Vladimir Šenaev (1978) "Novaja valjutnaja sistema i uroki Bretton-Vudsa," *Mirovaja ėkonomika i meždunarodnye otnošenija*, 6, 43–52.
Matjuchin, Georgij G. and Evgenij Smirnov (1984) "Nužny li poiski novogo Bretton-Vudsa?" *Vnešnjaja torgovlja*, 7, 43–9.
Mee, Charles L., Jr. (1984) *The Marshall Plan – the launching of the pax americana* (New York: Simon and Schuster).
Meier, Gerald M. (1982) *Problems of a world monetary order*, 2nd ed. (New York and Oxford: Oxford University Press).
Miastkowski, Lech (1980) "Zmiany struktury i poziomu cen detalicznych w gospodarce socjalistycznej," *Ekonomista*, 4, 893–915.
Michałek, Jan Jakub (1984) "Sytuacja Polski i innych krajów socjalistycznych w GATT," *Sprawy Międzynarodowe*, 12, 57–72.
Mikesell, Raymond F. (1947a) "Quantitative and exchange restrictions under the ITO Charter," *American Economic Review*, 3, 351–68.
(1947b) "The role of the international monetary agreements in a world of planned economies," *Journal of Political Economy*, 4, 497–512, reprinted in *Readings in the theory of international trade*, edited by Howard S. Ellis and Lloyd A. Metzler (Philadelphia, PA: Bakiston Company, 1949), 56–80.
(1951) "Negotiating at Bretton Woods," in *Negotiating with the Russians*, edited by Raymond Dennett and Joseph E. Johnson (Boston, MA: World Peace Foundation), 101–16.
Mironov, M. P. and V. K. Epanesnikov (1985) "Konferencija 'kruglogo stola' po meždunarodnym valjutno-finansovym problemami v Deli," *Bjulleten' inostrannoj kommerčeskoj informacii*, 23, 2, 8.
Mitrofanova, Nina M. (1973) "O vzaimosvjazi vnutrennich i vnešnetorgovych cen v evropejskich socialističeskich stranach," *Planovoe chozjajstvo*, 9, 90–7.
(1974) "Perspektivy dal'nejšego soveršenstvovanija vnešnetorgovych cen socialistčeskich stran," *Planovoe chozjajstvo*, 4, 41–9.
Mu, Rui (1987) "Chinese view on the future possibilities of international law and the world economic order," in *Public international law and the future world order*, edited by Joseph J. Norton (Littleton, CO: Rothman), 3/1–3/8.

Müller, Hans-Jürgen (1986) *GATT – Rechssystem nach der Tokio-Runde* (Berlin: Staatsverlag der Deutschen Demokratischen Republik).

Myrdal, Gunnar (1963) *Challenge to affluence* (New York: Random House).

Nême, Jacques and Colette Nême (1986) "L'avenir de l'ECU dans les relations CEE-pays de l'est," *Courrier des Pays de l'Est*, 2, 28–36.

Neustadt, Alojz (1968) "External economic relations and the system of management in Czechoslovakia," *Bulletin of the Research Institute for Economic Planning*, 2, 215–34.

Nuti, D. Mario (1987) *Financial innovation under market socialism* (Florence: Istituto Universitario Europeo, working paper 87/285).

Nyerges, János (1986a) "Hungary's experiences in GATT," in *East–west economic relations in the changing global environment*, edited by Béla Csikós-Nagy and David G. Young (New York: St Martin's Press), 196–204.

(1986b) "Comment," in *East–west economic relations in the changing global environment*, edited by Béla Csikós-Nagy and David G. Young (New York: St. Martin's Press), 341–2.

Ognev, A. and Ju. Ogarev (1964) "Sozdanie meždunarodnoj torgovoj organizacil – važnejsaja zadača konferencii," *Vnešnjaja torgovlja*, 2, 16–19.

Oliver, Robert W. (1957) *The origins of the International Bank for Reconstruction and Development* (Princeton, NJ: Department of Economics, unpublished Ph.D. dissertation).

(1975) *International economic co-operation and the World Bank* (London: Macmillan).

Osipov, Ju. (1983) "Problemy perestrojki meždunarodnoj valjutnoj sistemy i razvivajuščiesja strany," *Mirovaja ėkonomika i meždunarodnye otnošenija*, 11, 57–72.

Paarlberg, Robert L. (1988) *Fixing farm trade – policy options for the United States* (Cambridge, MA: Ballinger).

Padoa-Schioppa, Tommaso (1988) "The ECU's coming of age," in *The quest for national and global economic stability*, edited by Wietze Eizenga *et al.* (Dordrecht: Kluwer Academic Publishers), 159–73.

Pankin, M. (1986) "SSSR i GATT: perspektivy vzaimodejstvija," *Ėkonomičeskaja gazeta*, 49, 23.

Paszyński, Marian (1988) "International organizations, economic security and normalization of east–west economic relations," *Development and Peace*, 1, 39–51.

Patterson, Eliza R. (1986) "Improving GATT rules for nonmarket economies," *Journal of World Trade Law*, 2, 185–205.

Patterson, Gardner (1966) *Discrimination in international trade – the policy issues, 1945–1965* (Princeton, NJ: Princeton University Press).

Petersmann, Ernst-Ulrich (1988) "Handelspolitik als Verfassungsproblem," *Ordo*, 39, 239–54.

Petrakov, Nikolaj Ja. (1986) "Cena – ryčag upravlenija," *Ėkonomičeskaja gazeta*, 16, 10.

(1987) "Planovaja cena v sisteme upravlenija narodnym chozjajstvom," *Voprosy ėkonomiki*, 1, 44–55.

Pissulla, Petra (1983) *Der Internationale Währungsfonds und seine Bedeutung für die osteuropäischen Länder – Rumänien, Ungarn, Polen* (Hamburg: Verlag Weltarchiv).

(1984a) "Der Internationale Währungsfonds und seine Bedeutung für die osteuropäischen Länder – Rumänien, Ungarn und Polen," *Osteuropa-Wirtschaft*, 2, 97–107.

(1984b) "The IMF and the countries of Eastern Europe," *Intereconomics*, 2, 65–70.

(1985) "International organizations," in *Economic warfare or detente – an assessment of east–west economic relations in the 1980s*, edited by Reinhard Rode and Hans-Dieter Jacobsen (Boulder, CO: Westview Press), 226–42.

(1988) "das Verhältnis der Sowjetunion zum GATT und zum Internationalen Währungsfonds," *Osteuropa-Wirtschaft*, 4, 319–26.

Popov, Konstantin I. (1968) "Ob obëktivnych osnovach postroenija sistemy cen v torgovle meždu socialističeskimi stranami," *Voprosy ėkonomiki*, 8, 67–75.

Preliminary Draft (1946) *Preliminary draft: Charter for the International Trade Organization of the United Nations* (Washington, DC: US Superintendent of Documents).

Proceedings (1948) *Proceedings and documents of the United Nations Monetary and Financial Conference*, Department of State Publication 2866 (Washington, DC: United States Government Printing Office, 2 vols.).

Rączkowski, Stanisław (1977) "The international monetary crisis and the socialist countries," in *The international payments crisis and the development of east–west trade* (Brussels: Establissements Emile Bruylants), 71–105.

Rémy, Alain (1980) "Commerce d'état et mécanisme de marché – les pays socialistes et le GATT," in *Stratégies des pays socialistes dans l'échange international*, edited by Marie Lavigne (Paris: Economica), 185–207.

(1981) *Le rôle de l'or dans l'économie monétaire occidentale: analyses soviétiques* (Paris: Université de Paris I – Panthéon-Sorbonne, thèse de 3ème cycle, mimeographed).

(1985) *Un retour à l'or? Analyses soviétiques sur le système monétaire international* (Paris: Economica).

Restoration (1947) "The restoration of international trade – development and proposals before the United Nations – text of Geneva draft charter for an international trade organization," *International Conciliation*, 434, 524–690.

Reuland, James M. (1975) "GATT and state-trading countries," *Journal of World Trade Law*, 3, 318–39.

Richter, William L. (1988) "Soviet 'participation' in GATT: a case for accession," *New York University Journal of International Law and Politics*, 2, 477–523.

Robinson, Sherman, Laura d'Andrea Tyson, and Leyla Woods (1984) "Conditionality and adjustment in socialist economies: Hungary and Yugoslavia" (paper presented at the "Conference on the Soviet Union and Eastern Europe in the world economy," Washington, DC, 18–19 October).

Ruggie, John G. (1982) "International regimes, transactions, and change: embedded liberalism in the postwar economic order," *International Organization*, 2, 379–415.

Runge, Carlisle F. (1988) "The assault on agricultural protectionism," *Foreign Affairs*, 1, 133–50.

Sakbani, M. Michael (1985) "The crisis of the international economic system: proposals for monetary and financial reforms," *Trade and Development*, 6, 149–93.

Samorodov, Aleksandr (1983) "JUNCTAD-VI i valjutno-finansovye problemy," *Vnešnjaja torgovlja*, 5, 37–44.

Sampson, Gary P. (1987) "Pseudo-economics of the MFA – a proposal for reform," *World Economy*, 4, 455–68.

Sauvant, Karl P. (1981) *The Group of 77 – evolution, structure, organization* (New York: Oceana Publications).

Scammell, W. M. (1987) *The stability of the international monetary system* (London: Macmillan).

Schröder, Klaus (1982) "The IMF and the countries of the Council for Mutual Economic Assistance," *Intereconomics*, 2, 87–90.

Schüller, Alfred and Hannelore Hamel (1985) "On the membership of socialist countries in the International Monetary Fund," *Acta Oeconomica*, 1/2, 113–30.

Šenaev, Vladimir (1988) "Die Sowjetunion und der Internationale Währungsfonds – Gespräch mit Klaus Fritsche," *Osteuropa-Wirtschaft*, 4, 335–41.

Sengupta, Arjun (1987) "The role of the IMF in the international monetary system and the developing countries," *Journal of Development Planning*, 17, 167–82.

Širjaev, Jurij S. (1988) "SĖV: sovremennaja strategija ėkonomičeskogo i naučno-techničeskogo sotrudničestva," *Izvestija akademii nauk – serija ėkonomičeskaja*, 1, 3–17.

Šmelëv, V. (1988) "EKJU – kollektivnaja valjutnaja edinica Obščego rynka," *Vnešnjaja torgovlja*, 3, 43–7.

Smith, Asa P. (1969) "Eastern Europe and GATT: a case study of accommodation in economic relations between east and west," *Columbia Essays in International Affairs*, 4, 263–91.

Smyslov, D. (1988) "V poiskach putej soveršentsvovanija meždunarodnoj valjutnoj sistemy," *Mirovaja ėkonomika i meždunarodnye otnošenija*, 3, 81–8.

Solomon, Robert E. (1982) *The international monetary system, 1945–1981* (New York: Harper & Row, expanded and updated edition).

(1988) "Impressions of the Soviet Union," *International Economic Letter*.

Spiller, Hans (1984) *Finanz- und Währungsbeziehungen zu nichtsozialistischen Ländern* (Berlin: Staatsverlag der Deutschen Demokratischen Republik).

Spröte, Wolfgang (1983) "The socialist countries' position on international economic relations," in *The Transformation of the International Economic Order*, special issue of *Asia, Africa, Latin America*, 2, 19–32.

Stone, Frank (1984) *Canada, the GATT and the international trade system* (Ottawa: Institute for Research on Public Policy/L'Institut de Recherches Politiques).

Surocceva, V. (1986) "Rol' reservnych valjut v obostrenii problemy meždunarodnoj valjutnoj likvidnosti kapitalističeskogo mira," *Ekonomičeskie nauki*, 8, 57–63.

Syčëv, Vjačeslav V. (1988) "SĖV: korennoe preobrazovanie mechanizma vzaimodejstvija," *Vnešnjaja torgovlja*, 2, 2–6.

Tew, Brian (1967) *International monetary cooperation, 1945–67* (London: Hutchinson University Library).

Toczek, Józef (1984) "Polska a MFW i Bank Światowy," *Rynki Zagraniczne*, 69/70, 8.

Triffin, Robert (1957) *Europe and the money muddle – from bilateralism to near-convertibility, 1947–1956* (New Haven, CT and London: Yale University Press).

(1961) *Gold and the dollar crisis – the future of convertibility* (New Haven, CT and London: Yale University Press, revised edition).

Tussie, Diana (1987) *The less developed countries and the world trading system – a challenge to the GATT* (New York: St. Martin's Press).

UNCTAD (1964a) *Proceedings of the United Nations Conference on Trade and Development, Policy statements,* vol. II (United Nations publication, sales no. E.64.II.B.12).

(1964b) *Proceedings of the United Nations Conference on Trade and Development, Financing and institutions,* vol. V (United Nations publication, sales no. E.64.II.B.15).

(1976) *Proceedings of the United Nations Conference on Trade and Development, Fourth Session,* vol. I, *Reports and annexes* (United Nations publication, sales no. E.76.II.D.10).

(1979) *Proceedings of the United Nations Conference on Trade and Development, Fifth Session,* vol. I, *Reports and annexes* (United Nations publication, sales no. E.79.II.D.14).

(1980) *Consideration of requirements of the international monetary system which would foster world trade and development* (Geneva: UNCTAD, document no. TD/B/AC.CRP.1).

(1983a) *Proceedings of the United Nations Conference on Trade and Development, Sixth Session,* vol. I, *Reports and annexes* (United Nations publication, sales no. E.83.II.D.6).

(1983b) *The world economic situation with special emphasis on development: proposal submitted by the German Democratic Republic on behalf of Group D,* document TD/L.230 of 18 June, reproduced in German in *Gemeinsame Erklärungen sozialistischer Staaten zu Fragen der Umgestaltung der internationalen Wirtschaftsbeziehungen auf demokratischer Basis* (Berlin: Ministerium fur Auswärtige Angelegenheiten), 1–16.

United Nations (1946) *United Nations documents, 1941–1945* (London: Royal Institute of International Affairs).

(1966) *International monetary issues and the developing countries – report of the group of experts* (United Nations publication, sales no. E.66.II.D.2).

(1968) "Note on the institutional developments in the foreign trade of the Soviet Union and Eastern European countries," *Economic Bulletin for Europe,* 1, 43–52.

(1970) *International monetary reforms and co-operation for development – report of the expert group on international monetary issues* (United Nations publication, sales no. E.70.II.D.2).

(1973) "Recent changes in the organization of foreign trade in the centrally planned economies," *Economic Bulletin for Europe,* 1, 36–49.

(1983) *Joint statement of Group D and Mongolia regarding the launching of global negotiations* (New York: United Nations, document A/38/479).

US Congress, House, Committee of Ways and Means (1956) *The agreement on the OTC* (Washington, DC: Government Printing Office, document 5550).

Varga, Evgenij S. (1947a) "Ženevskaja konferencija po voprosam mirovoj torgovli," *Novoe vremja* 20, 3–10.

(1947b) '"Plan Maršalla' i nadvigajuščijsja ėkonomičeskij krizis v SŠA," *Novoe vremja,* 39, 4–7.

(1947c) "Amerikanskij plan zakabelenija Evropy," *Novoe vremja*, 48, 4–9.

Vernon, Raymond (1979) "The fragile foundations of east–west trade," *Foreign Affairs*, 5, 1035–51.

Větrovský, Jiří and Vasil Hrinda (1988) "Zúčtování přimých vztahův národních měnách ČSSR a SSSR – rubl a koruna," *Hospodářské Noviny*, 15, 3.

Voznesenskij, Nikolaj A. (1948). *War economy of the U.S.S.R. in the period of the patriotic war* (Moscow: Foreign Languages Publishing House).

Wilcox, Clair (1947) "The London draft of a charter for an international trade organization," *American Economic Review*, 2, 529–41.

(1949) *A charter for world trade* (New York: Macmillan).

Wilczynski, Jozef (1969) *The economics and politics of east–west trade – a study of trade between developed market economies and centrally planned economies in a changing world* (London: Macmillan).

(1978) *Comparative monetary economics – capitalist and socialist monetary systems and their interrelations in the changing international scene* (New York: Oxford University Press).

Wiles, Peter J. D. (1968) *Communist international economics* (Oxford: Basil Blackwell).

Wilgress, Edward D. (1949) *A new attempt at internationalism – the international trade conferences and the charter: a charter study of ends and means* (Paris: Société d'Editions d'Enseignement Supérieur).

Williamson, John (1983a) "Keynes and the international economic order," in *Keynes and the modern world*, edited by G. D. Worswick and J. S. Trevithick (Cambridge: Cambridge University Press, reprinted in *Political economy and international money – selected essays of John Williamson*, edited by Chris Milder (New York: New York University Press, 1987), 37–59.

(1983b) "International monetary reform: an agenda for the 1980s," in *Towards a new Bretton Woods* (London: Commonwealth Secretariat), reprinted in *Political economy and international money – selected essays of John Williamson*, edited by Chris Milder (New York: New York University Press, 1987), 212–27.

Wolf, Martin (1987) "Differential and more favorable treatment of developing countries and the international trading system," *World Bank Economic Review*, 4, 647–68.

Wolf, Thomas A. (1988) *Foreign trade in the centrally planned economy* (Chur: Harwood Academic Publishers).

Woźnowski, Jan (1974) *Polska w GATT* (Warsaw: PWE).

Wrębiak, Andrzej (1986) "Handel państowowy w przepisach GATT," *Handel Zagraniczny*, 9/10, 29–31.

Wyndham-White, Eric (1975) "Negotiations in retrospect," in *Toward a new world trade policy: the Maidenhead papers*, edited by C. Fred Bergsten (Lexington, MA: Lexington Books), 321–40.

Yarbrough, Beth V. and Robert M. Yarbrough (1987) "Cooperation in the liberalization of international trade: after hegemony, what?" *International Organization*, 1, 1–26.

Živkova, Snežana and Ivanka Petkova (1988) "Plavastite valutni kursove i proekti za tjachnata reforma," *Ikonomičeska misŭl*, 7, 67–77.

Zwass, Adam (1974) *Zur Problematik der Währungsbeziehungen zwischen Ost und West* (Vienna: Springer-Verlag).

Index

Soviet and East European Studies

61 FRANCESCO BENVENUTI
The Bolsheviks and the Red Army, 1918–1922

60 HIROAKI KUROMIYA
Stalin's industrial revolution
Politics and workers, 1928–1932

59 LEWIS SIEGELBAUM
Stakhanovism and the politics of productivity in the USSR, 1935–1941

58 JOZEF, M. VAN BRABANT
Adjustment, structural change and economic efficiency
Aspects of monetary cooperation in Eastern Europe

57 ILIANA ZLOCH-CHRISTY
Debt problems of Eastern Europe

56 SUSAN BRIDGER
Women in the Soviet countryside
Women's roles in rural development in the Soviet Union

55 ALLEN LYNCH
The Soviet study of international relations

54 DAVID GRANICK
Job rights in the Soviet Union: their consequences

53 ANITA PRAŻMOWSKA
Britain, Poland and the Eastern Front, 1939

52 ELLEN JONES AND FRED GRUPP
Modernization, value change and fertility in the Soviet Union

51 CATHERINE ANDREYEV
Vlasov and the Russian liberation movement
Soviet reality and émigré theories

50 STEPHEN WHITE
The origins of détente
The Genoa Conference and Soviet–Western relations 1921–1922

49 JAMES MCADAMS
East Germany and détente
Building authority after the Wall

48 S. G. WHEATCROFT AND R. W. DAVIES (EDS.)
Materials for a balance of the Soviet national economy 1928–1930

47 SYLVANA MALLE
The economic organization of war communism, 1918–1921

46 DAVID S. MASON
Public opinion and political change in Poland, 1980–1982

45 MARK HARRISON
Soviet planning in peace and war 1938–1945

44 NIGEL SWAIN
Collective farms which work?

43 J. ARCH GETTY
Origins of the great purges
The Soviet Communist Party reconsidered, 1933–1938

42 TADEUSZ SWIETOCHOWSKI
Russian Azerbaijan 1905–1920
The shaping of national identity in a muslim community

41 RAY TARAS
Ideology in a socialist state
Poland 1956–1983

40 SAUL ESTRIN
Self-management: economic theory and Yugoslav practice

39 S. A. SMITH
Red Petrograd
Revolution in the factories 1917–1918

38 DAVID A. DYKER
The process of investment in the Soviet Union

36 JEAN WOODALL
The socialist corporation and technocratic power
The Polish United Workers Party, industrial organisation and workforce control 1958–1980

35 WILLIAM J. CONYNGHAM
The modernization of Soviet industrial management

34 ANGELA STENT
From embargo to Ostpolitik
The political economy of West German–Soviet relations 1955–1980

32 BLAIR A. RUBLE
Soviet trade unions
Their development in the 1970s

31 R. F. LESLIE (ED.)
The history of Poland since 1863

30 JOZEF M. VAN BRABANT
Socialist economic integration
Aspects of contemporary economic problems in Eastern Europe

28 STELLA ALEXANDER
Church and state in Yugoslavia since 1945

27 SHEILA FITZPATRICK
Education and social mobility in the Soviet Union 1921–1934

23 PAUL VYSNÝ
Neo-Slavism and the Czechs 1898–1914

22 JAMES RIORDAN
Sport in Soviet society
Development of sport and physical education in Russia and the USSR

14 RUDOLF BIĆANIĆ
Economic policy in socialist Yugoslavia

The following series titles are now out of print:

1 ANDREA BOLTO
Foreign trade criteria in socialist economies

2 SHEILA FITZPATRICK
The commissariat of enlightenment
Soviet organization of education and the arts under Lunacharsky, October 1917–1921

3 DONALD J. MALE
Russian peasant organisation before collectivisation
A Study of commune and gathering 1925–1930

4 P. WILES (ED.)
The prediction of communist economic performance

5 VLADIMIR V. KUSIN
The intellectual origins of the Prague Spring
The development of reformist ideas in Czechoslovakia 1956–1967

6 GALIA GOLAN
The Czechoslovak reform movement

7 NAUN JASNY
Soviet economists of the twenties
Names to be remembered

8 ASHA L. DATAR
India's economic relations with the USSR and Eastern Europe, 1953–1969

9 T. M. PODOLSKI
Socialist banking and monetary control
The experience of Poland

10 SHMUEL GALAI
The liberation movement in Russia 1900–1905

11 GALIA GOLAN
Reform rule in Czechoslovakia
The Dubcek era 1968–1969

12 GEOFFREY A. HOSKING
The Russian constitutional experiment
Government and Duma 1907–1914

13 RICHARD B. DAY
Leon Trotsky and the politics of economic isolation

15 JAN M. CIECHANOWSKI
The Warsaw rising of 1944

16 EDWARD A. HEWITT
Foreign trade prices in the Council for Mutual Economic Assistance

17 ALICE TEICHOVA
An economic background to Munich
International business and Czechoslovakia 1918–1938

18 DANIEL F. CALHOUN
The united front: the TUC and the Russians 1923–1928

19 GALIA GOLAN
Yom Kippur and after
The Soviet Union and the Middle East crisis

20 MAUREEN PERRIE
The agrarian policy of the Russian Socialist-Revolutionary Party
From its origins through the revolution of 1905–1907

21 GABRIEL GORODETSKY
The precarious truce: Anglo-Soviet relations 1924–1927

24 GREGORY WALKER
Soviet book publishing policy

25 FELICITY ANN O'DELL
Socialisation through children's literature
The Soviet example

26 T. H. RIGBY
Lenin's government: Sovnarkom 1917–1922

29 MARTIN CAVE
Computers and economic planning
The Soviet experience

33 MARTIN MYANT
Socialism and democracy in Czechoslovakia 1944–1948

37 ISRAEL GETZLER
Kronstadt 1917–1921
The fate of a Soviet democracy